Justice is a central concern in everyday life; we are constantly confronted with situations that require us to assess the fairness of individuals' acts and institutional policies. These situations often involve difficult trade-offs between equality and efficiency, self-interest and cooperation, or short-term consumption and long-term savings. *Psychological Perspectives on Justice* explores intuitions about fairness in the distribution of costs and benefits. The mixture of theoretical and applied perspectives provides a balanced look at the psychological underpinnings of justice.

Cambridge Series on Judgment and Decision Making

# Psychological perspectives on justice

Cambridge Series on Judgment and Decision Making

# Psychological perspectives on justice

## Theory and applications

*Edited by*

*Barbara A. Mellers*
University of California, Berkeley

*Jonathan Baron*
University of Pennsylvania

CAMBRIDGE
UNIVERSITY PRESS

CAMBRIDGE UNIVERSITY PRESS
Cambridge, New York, Melbourne, Madrid, Cape Town, Singapore, São Paulo, Delhi

Cambridge University Press
The Edinburgh Building, Cambridge CB2 8RU, UK

Published in the United States of America by Cambridge University Press, New York

www.cambridge.org
Information on this title: www.cambridge.org/9780521431996

First published 1993
This digitally printed version 2008

*A catalogue record for this publication is available from the British Library*

*Library of Congress Cataloguing in Publication data*

Psychological perspectives on justice: theory and applications /
edited by Barbara A. Mellers, Jonathan Baron.

p.   cm. – (Cambridge series on judgment and decision making)

ISBN 0-521-43199-9

1. Social justice – Psychological aspects.   2. Decision-making –
Psychological aspects.   I. Mellers, Barbara A.   II. Baron,
Jonathan, 1944–.   III. Series.
HM216.P79      1993
303.3'72 – dc20                          92-27263   CIP

ISBN 978-0-521-43199-6 hardback
ISBN 978-0-521-08998-2 paperback

# Contents

# Series preface

The Society for Judgment and Decision Making first collaborated with Cambridge University Press in 1986, with the publication of *Judgment and Decision Making: An Interdisciplinary Reader*, edited by Hal R. Arkes and Kenneth R. Hammond. As the editors stated in their introduction, "judgment and decision making are of critical importance, and the fact that it is possible to study them in a scientific, empirical manner is a new and exciting event in the recent history of science" (p. 1).

The decade of the 1980s witnessed the flowering of the intellectual seeds planted by theoretical pioneers and seminal researchers in the area of human judgment and decision making. The founding and expansion of the Society was one feature of this growth. At the same time there has been an explosion of research and teaching in departments of psychology, economics, and schools of business, engineering, public policy, and medicine, with significant practical contributions through applied research and consulting in public and private institutions.

The Arkes and Hammond Reader was successful as an outline of the core ideas and approaches of the field and an illustration of the impressive range of useful applications. The Society, with Ken Hammond's encouragement, recognized the potential for a series of books to provide an educational and intellectual focus for the continued growth and dissemination of judgment and decision making research. Ken became the first Chair of the Publications Committee for the Society, devoting enormous amounts of time, creativity, and charm to this new initiative.

The Publications Committee is pleased to include this volume in the Society's series, because it exemplifies the fresh ideas, multidisciplinary approaches, and attention to theory, empirical research, and application that characterize the field of judgment and decision making. Each subsequent volume in the Series will be devoted to a domain of practical and/or theoretical interest, offering an accessible presentation of the best new ideas and empirical approaches from the field of judgment and decision making.

John S. Carroll, Chair
For the Publications Committee

# Contributors

Maya Bar-Hillel  *Department of Psychology, The Hebrew University, Jerusalem*

Jonathan Baron  *Department of Psychology, University of Pennsylvania, Philadelphia*

Ivy E. Broder  *Department of Economics, The American University, Washington, D.C.*

Colin F. Camerer  *Center for Decision Research, University of Chicago, Chicago*

Robyn M. Dawes  *Department of Social and Decision Sciences, Carnegie Mellon University, Pittsburgh*

Jon Elster  *Department of Political Science, University of Chicago, Chicago*

Robert D. Enright  *Department of Psychology, University of Wisconsin, Madison*

Richard J. Harris  *Department of Psychology, University of New Mexico, Albuquerque*

Sheri E. Hembree  *Department of Psychology, University of Wisconsin, Madison*

L. Robin Keller  *Graduate School of Management, University of California, Irvine*

George Loewenstein  *Department of Social and Decision Sciences, Carnegie Mellon University, Pittsburgh*

Barbara A. Mellers  *Department of Psychology, University of California, Berkeley*

David M. Messick  *Department of Psychology, Northwestern University, Evanston*

Gregory Mitchell  *Department of Psychology, University of California, Berkeley*

Colleen F. Moore  *Department of Psychology, University of Wisconsin, Madison*

Lisa D. Ordóñez  *Department of Psychology, University of California, Berkeley*

Rakesh K. Sarin   *Graduate School of Management, University of California, Los Angeles*

Linda J. Skitka   *Department of Psychology, Southern Illinois University, Edwardsville*

Philip E. Tetlock   *Department of Psychology, University of California, Berkeley*

Tom Tyler   *Department of Psychology, University of California, Berkeley*

Menahem Yaari   *Department of Economics, The Hebrew University, Jerusalem*

# Part I
# Introduction

# 1  Introductory Remarks

*Barbara A. Mellers*

Justice is a central problem in everyday life: We often assess the fairness of individual, interpersonal, and institutional acts. This book explores theoretical and applied questions about judgments of fairness. How do people make trade-offs between equality and efficiency, self-interest and cooperation, or short-term consumption and long-term savings? When are these trade-offs based on assumptions of deservingness? To what extent are they predictable from an observer's political point of view?

The chapters in this book provide a broad overview of current research on justice. Justice research is traditionally divided into three categories: retributive, distributive, and procedural. These categories distinguish among fair punishments and compensations, fair allocations of scarce resources, and fair methods or procedures. An alternative scheme, grounded in the decision making literature, categorizes justice research as normative, descriptive, or prescriptive. Normative research on justice focuses on rational theories for the general welfare of individuals within a society. Normative theories in this category are more diverse and span a broader range of perspectives than normative theories of individual decision making. Descriptive research on justice examines psychological theories of fairness and other measures of morality. Prescriptive research on justice investigates methods and policies for reducing conflict, encouraging cooperation, and resolving differences among individuals or groups. Because most of the chapters address more than one of the above categories, the book is organized around common themes: psychological questions, economic considerations, variations in perspectives on justice, and policy issues.

We would like to thank John Carroll for providing helpful comments and suggestions throughout all phases of preparation of this book.

### Common themes

Part II of the book examines psychological questions. What rules capture how we think about fairness? To what extent do judgments of fairness depend on context? What models account for fair allocations of scarce resources when individuals differ in effort and productivity?

David Messick examines heuristics by which people reason about distributive justice. He argues that people often rely on an equality heuristic. Messick points out that the dimension along which people desire equality might not always be clear; different outcomes can result from the selection of different dimensions. For example, some colleges and universities strive for equality of opportunity in their admissions policies, whereas others strive for equality of result. Messick argues that psychological theories of justice should reflect our egalitarian intuitions, which often serve as a good starting point for fair allocations.

Much of the psychological research on justice examines fair allocations of resources among individuals with legitimate claims. This literature is known as equity theory, with theoretical roots in social exchange theory, social comparison theory, and dissonance theory. In equity theory, fairness is represented using the Aristotelian concept of proportionality, and numerous studies are cited in support of this principle. Nonetheless, some researchers, such as Richard Harris, think that fairness is better described by other rules.

Harris explores how fair allocation judgments depend on the context. He shows that judged allocations can differ when subjects are given the same problem but are instructed to divide profits or divide expenses. Harris identifies factors that lead people to recognize the inconsistencies. Furthermore, he demonstrates that fair reward allocations can be influenced by the "match" between input units and outcome units. Harris summarizes the results by claiming that fair reward allocations are better captured by a linear rule than a proportionality rule.

Maya Bar-Hillel and Menahem Yaari examine limitations of the Aristotelian rule of proportionality when people make fair allocations given information about the needs, beliefs about needs, and tastes of individual claimants. Their experiments show that when individual claimants differ in needs, whoever is needier receives more. When individual claimants differ in their beliefs about needs (i.e., what they think they need), allocations tend to be equal. When claimants differ in their tastes, utilitarian rules emerge; whoever receives more pleasure from a good receives more of that good.

Part III of the book investigates economic questions of justice. In many discussions of welfare economics, justice is viewed as part of a larger problem of maximizing social welfare. One normative solution to this problem is utilitarianism. Utilitarians believe that society should be arranged to maximize the total (or the average) utility of all individuals. Other theories of moral philosophy, such as those proposed by Rawls and Nozick, treat justice as a more central concern. The authors of these chapters investigate deviations between normative theories and human behavior. When does the neoclassical view of people as self-interested, rational agents fail? When do human judgments deviate from utilitarian principles? To what extent are people willing to tolerate inefficiency to achieve fairness?

Tom Tyler and Robyn Dawes challenge the economic view that behavior is described by utility maximization. Tyler and Dawes draw on parallel lines of research on social dilemmas and procedural justice to argue that people are sometimes willing to make substantial sacrifices for the groups to which they belong, even if there is no apparent payoff to them, as individuals, for doing so. Tyler and Dawes develop the idea that cooperative versus selfish behavior is at least partially predictable from the social bond established between the individual and the group.

Jonathan Baron makes a bold claim that utilitarianism is the proper normative theory of justice. He then identifies situations in which human judgments deviate from utilitarian principles. Baron shows that people punish offenders, even when the punishment does not deter potential perpetrators. People also assign greater compensation to victims when harm is caused by humans than when it is caused by nature. Furthermore, people are reluctant to harm someone in order to help someone else. Finally, people are less likely to initiate reforms if the benefits are unequally distributed, even when the reforms are beneficial overall.

A fundamental concept in economics is that of efficiency. Lisa Ordóñez and I explore the extent to which people are willing to make trade-offs between economic efficiency and income inequality in their evaluations of societal fairness. We show that when judging the fairness of hypothetical societies, people accept some income equality at the expense of economic efficiency. But when these factors are manipulated along with others, trade-offs primarily occur on other dimensions. Societal fairness is better captured by trade-offs between the minimum reward and the effort–reward correlation than by equality and efficiency.

Colin Camerer and George Loewenstein also argue that judgments and decisions can deviate from rational economic theory. They discuss the role of fairness in game theoretic models of bargaining. Game theories based solely on assumptions of rationality imply that increasing shared information among bargainers increases efficiency (the tendency to reach agreements that benefit everyone). Camerer and Loewenstein show that increasing shared information can improve efficiency. They also show that shared information can reduce efficiency and interfere with settlements when people feel they are unfairly treated.

Part IV of the book, Variations in perspectives on justice, examines ways in which people differ in their judgments of fairness. Individual differences are studied along dimensions of age, sex, political persuasion, and other factors. Are there developmental trends in people's perspectives on justice? To what extent can a person's judgments of fair resource allocations be predicted from his or her political views?

Colleen Moore, Sheri Hembree, and Robert Enright take a developmental look at reward allocations. If people use decision heuristics, as argued by Baron and Messick, when do they acquire them? What is the origin of a person's repertoire of heuristics? To what degree are they modifiable? Moore et al. examine developmental changes in fair reward allocations and contrast equity theory with the cognitive-developmental or Piagetian approach. Both views look for a fixed set of stages that eventually lead to a single, ultimate developmental stage. Moore et al. argue against the notion that individuals follow a single developmental path and provide empirical evidence for multiple paths and multiple endpoints in reasoning about fairness.

Linda Skitka and Philip Tetlock examine the extent to which existing theories of attribution, distributive justice, and political ideology can describe individual differences in fair resource allocations. They explore judgments of fairness in problems of expensive medical treatments, low-income housing, and vocational training. Conservative allocators tend to deny help to claimants who are personally responsible for their predicaments, even under conditions of no scarcity. Liberal allocators are more variable and context dependent in their responses. Although they deny assistance to irresponsible claimants under conditions of scarcity, help is not denied when resources are available. Results are consistent with a contingency model of distributive justice.

Philip Tetlock and Gregory Mitchell point out how individual differences in the initial assumptions can influence final conclusions in psychological research on justice. They identify eight sets of starting assumptions – flattering and unflattering cognitive and motivational portraits of liberals and conservatives – and argue that these assumptions can have predictable effects on the outcome and interpretation of justice research.

The fifth and final part of the book addresses policy issues. These chapters discuss normative, descriptive, and prescriptive concerns. How should societies allocate scarce resources? What types of incentives follow from different policies? What descriptive measures might policymakers use when fairly allocating health risks or environmental risks?

Jon Elster focuses on problems of "local justice" or institutional procedures for allocating scarce goods and necessary burdens. He discusses the allocation of scarce resources in three arenas: the selection of patients for kidney transplants, the admission of students to colleges and universities, and the selection of workers to be laid off when a firm reduces its work force. In each arena, Elster identifies the procedures used to allocate goods and discusses why that procedure might be used. He also addresses issues such as equity–efficiency trade-offs, discrimination, and incentive effects.

Rakesh Sarin presents measures of risk that policymakers might consider when evaluating the fairness of societal policies. He examines aspects of risk that highlight problems for individuals and groups within a society. Measures of "individual risk equity" and "group risk equity" are proposed when equality of risk is desirable. When one group receives greater benefit from the risk than another, equality of risk may be unfair. Other measures are proposed for these situations.

Ivy Broder and L. Robin Keller use the measures of risk proposed by Sarin to examine fair social policies in Antarctica, an area of international concern. In Antarctica, risks are often indivisible, nontransferable, and irreversible. Broder and Keller discuss issues of fairness in health, safety, and environmental risks and show how policymakers might benefit from considering these measures.

The final chapter, by Jonathan Baron, ties together common themes and ideas. Baron compares and contrasts normative and descriptive views of justice. He discusses implications for public policy and proposes several lines of future research. Baron believes that future research should focus on the rules that people using for distributing rights, resources, rewards, punishments, costs, and so on. When do those rules reflect considerations of fairness, efficiency, or power? Votes are often distributed on the basis of equality, welfare on the basis of need, jobs or fellowships on the basis of ability, income on the basis of productivity, and goods on the basis of supply and demand. Future research should address instances in which these principles come into conflict and the extent to which these rules can be altered by situational variables or restatements of the problem.

The theoretical and applied perspectives presented in this book should introduce the reader to many of the issues and concerns in justice research. By contrasting normative and descriptive theories, by discussing the way in which societies allocate scarce resources, and by considering implications for public policy, the chapters provide a multifaceted view of the psychological underpinnings of justice.

# Part II

# Psychological perspectives

# 2 Equality as a decision heuristic

*David M. Messick*

## Introduction

In this chapter I propose to examine the concept of equality or equal division as a heuristic that is used to facilitate decision making in situations involving the allocation of goods and bads. The kinds of situations that I have in mind involve two or more people who must share resources, responsibilities, or liabilities. This is the same class of situations about which much has been written from the point of view of ethical theories of distributive justice (e.g., Nozick, 1947; Rawls, 1971) and from the psychological perspective of equity theory (Adams, 1965; Messick & Cook, 1983; Walster, Berscheid, & Walster, 1973). This chapter does not deal with ethical issues per se and it pertains to equity theory and related concepts only insofar as equity theory is viewed as the outcome or product of a certain type of social decision making. The focus of the chapter is the individual cognitive processes involved when a person must make a decision about how some resource or cost should be allocated. I propose that the idea of equality has properties that make it a useful guideline or benchmark in making allocation decisions. It will become obvious that the use of equality as a decision heuristic does not imply that such decisions are simpleminded or uninteresting. On the contrary, they can be quite intricate.

## Decision heuristics

To my knowledge, the earliest use of the concept of heuristics in decision making and problem solving was Polya's (1945) advocacy of heuristic prob-

I want to thank Scott Allison, Terry Boles, Richard Harris, Barbara Mellers, and Tom Tyler for their thoughtful suggestions for the improvement of this chapter. This chapter was completed while I was a visitor at the Social Science Information Technology Institute at the University of Groningen, The Netherlands. I am grateful for the support provided me during my visit.

lem solving in the solution of mathematical problems. In his influential book, *How to Solve It*, Polya argues for the value of "heuristic reasoning," reasoning that is "not regarded as final and strict but as provisional and plausible only. . . . We may need the provisional before we attain the final. We need heuristic reasoning when we construct a strict proof as we need scaffolding when we erect a building" (p. 112). Polya clearly sees heuristic reasoning as an augmentation to, not a replacement for, formal mathematical reasoning. Heuristics could lead to hypotheses, hunches, and approaches, but they would have to be validated eventually through rigorous proof. Moreover, he defines *modern heuristic* as the effort "to understand the process of solving problems, especially the *mental operations typically useful* in this process" (p. 130, italics in the original). Polya's definition of modern heuristic sounds almost like a definition of modern cognitive psychology.

The concept of heuristics, or heuristic reasoning, became a central component of the effort to simulate human thinking. In this domain, heuristics represent "rules of thumb" that can be useful in solving problems or in proving theorems. Newell and Simon (1963) put it as follows: "First, the incorporation of 'rules of thumb' in this program is highly typical of programs that have been devised for symbol identification, pattern recognition, learning, and problem-solving tasks. We call processes of this kind, which generally contribute to a result but whose results are not 'guaranteed,' *heuristic processes*" (p. 390). These authors suggest two reasons why heuristic processes are employed: First, there are, in some cases, no ways known to perform the task that do not involve heuristic processes, and, second, it is known that humans use such processes. In problem solving programs of this sort, effective heuristics tend to be reinforced and used more frequently, while ineffective ones tend to be tried less often (Green, 1963).

In the pioneering work of Kahneman and Tversky (1972, 1973; and Tversky and Kahneman, 1971, 1973, 1974), the concept of heuristic use was contrasted with the hypothesis that humans are relatively accurate "intuitive statisticians" (Peterson & Beach, 1967). On the contrary, Tversky and Kahneman argued, the processes that people use in making judgments about probabilities, frequencies, and likelihoods have little resemblance to statistical principles. The use of heuristics like representativeness, availability, and anchoring and adjustment was demonstrated in judgmental contexts that highlighted the difference between heuristic use and normative statistical practice. Heuristics, thus, became associated with inaccuracy, shallowness, and cognitive dimness. While the focus on the error-proneness of heuristic use was important to differentiate such psychological processes from the normative principles, it also made fashionable the search for new and different intellectual foibles, many of which were eloquently described by Nisbett and Ross (1980). Heuristic use became associated with mistakes and errors (Funder, 1987), illusions (Sherman & Corty, 1984), biases (Hogarth, 1981; Tversky & Kahneman, 1974), and inconsistencies (Slovic & Lichtenstein, 1983; Tversky & Kahneman, 1986).

It has been claimed by Hogarth (1981), von Winterfeld and Edwards (1986), Funder (1987), and others that the contemporary focus on the weaknesses of human cognition misrepresents reality and constitutes "a message of despair" (von Winterfeld & Edwards, 1986, p. 531). Christensen-Szalanski and Beach (1984) have argued that scientific papers highlighting cognitive inabilities are more frequently cited than papers highlighting abilities and thus provide more publicity for the weaknesses than for the strengths of human capability. I raise this issue because the sense in which I want to use the concept of a decision heuristic is the original sense in which the concept was used by Green (1963), Newell & Simon (1963), and others. That is to say, I want to argue that equality is often used as a decision heuristic in circumstances when other normative decision procedures are absent or when their application, like theorem proving algorithms, would be inefficient.

In contrast to the view that the use of heuristics leads to poor performance, there is good evidence in some contexts that simple heuristics can produce highly efficient results. I will describe four well-known instances in which simple heuristics do as well or nearly as well as normative procedures. My intent is to illustrate cases in which heuristic decision processes are impressive, not to argue that they are always so. The extent to which simple rules of thumb lead to performance decrements will depend on the context in which they are used. It is unlikely that glib generalizations will be useful.

*Improper linear models.* Dawes (1979) has argued that in fitting linear models to data, some types of nonoptimal linear models make predictions that are nearly as accurate as the normatively optimal model – that is, the model whose weights are selected to optimize the prediction criterion. One type of improper model that does exceedingly well is the so-called equal-weight model – the one that simply weights all predictors equally. Such a model ignores information about which predictor variable is most highly correlated with the criterion and treats all predictors as if they were equally important. Dawes (1979) has shown that there is only a slight drop in predictive accuracy involved with using the simple equal-weighting model in place of the optimal one. For instance, in predicting the grade point average (GPA) of graduate students at the University of Oregon and the University of Illinois, the ideal model correlated .69 with the actual GPA and the equal weight model correlated .60.

*Efficient decision heuristics.* One way to evaluate the efficiency of various decision rules is simply to create environments in which the ideal or optimal decision rule is known and to compare the performance of the alternative rules to that of the best. This is precisely the strategy adopted by Thorngate (1980) and later by Bordley (1985). I will use Thorngate's paper as an illustration of circumstances in which simplified decision rules do nearly as well as optimal ones.

Thorngate used a computer to generate random payoff matrices in which there were either 2, 4, or 8 choices, and in which there were also either 2, 4, or 8 possible states of the world on which the payoff depended, yielding 9 types of payoff structures. For each possible choice, a randomly selected payoff (drawn from a rectangular distribution) was assigned for each state of the world, and for each possible alternative, a randomly generated probability distribution was created. So in the case where there were 2 choices and 4 states of the world, the computer program generated 8 randomly selected payoffs and 1 probability distribution for each of the 2 possible choices. From the payoffs and the probability distributions, the expected payoff for each choice was calculated. Thorngate then applied each of 10 other choice heuristics to the decision problem and recorded which of the alternatives each of these heuristics selected. The 10 heuristics included the following rules: *Equiprobable*, which is to treat all payoffs as if they were equally likely and to select the option with the largest total payoff; *Minimax*, or select the option for which the minimum payoff is the largest; and *Most Likely*, or find the most likely payoff for each option and choose the option for which the most likely payoff is largest. The first two of these rules ignore the probability information completely while the third ignores all but the most likely outcome for each possible choice.

The performance of these and the other choice heuristics was measured in terms of the relative frequency with which they picked the best alternative (in terms of expected payoff), the second best, and so on. Thorngate reports, for instance, that the Equiprobable rule, which is analogous to the equal-weighting model of Dawes (1979), correctly picks the best option 88% of the time when there are 2 options, 80% when there are 4 options, and 73% when there are 8 possible choices. The equivalent figures for the Minimax rule are 76%, 67%, and 62%. For the Most Likely rule the results were 84%, 72%, and 66%. Even when these heuristics pick something other than the best option, they usually pick an option with a high expected payoff. For instance, the Minimax rule picks one of the top 2 options 93% of the time when there are 4 options and 88% of the time when there are 8. Thorngate has thus shown that heuristics that ignore most of the information in a decision situation, like the probability distribution, or all payoffs but the worst, in the case of the Minimax rule, nevertheless do an impressive job in selecting the best or the next best of the alternatives.

*Tit-for-tat.* To move to a somewhat more social domain, Axelrod (1984) reports an ingenious competition in which he invited scientists to submit programmable strategies for playing the notorious Prisoner's Dilemma Game (PDG). He then conducted a round robin tournament in which each program played with each other program. From each of these interactions, the score or total accumulated points of the two programs were recorded. A program's score for the tournament was simply the sum of its scores for all interactions. The surprising result of this tournament was that the simplest strategy submitted, the tit-for-tat strategy submitted by Anatol Rapoport, was the winner. This strategy always makes a cooperative first choice and then simply repeats the others' last choice on each subsequent trial. Tit-for-tat's success is all the more remarkable because it can never win more points than the program it is playing against. Its success is based on the fact that it encourages the other programs to be cooperative and, hence profitable for both. In a follow-up tournament that was held after the outcome of the first competition was publicized, tit-for-tat was again the winner, even though many programs were submitted to this second round that were explicitly designed to defeat tit-for-tat.

In this case, the simplest program of all was the best, a result that was not anticipated by the organizer of the competition. It did better than some very sophisticated programs that were designed to detect and exploit weaknesses in the other player. And it won by cooperating, which in the classical treatment of the PDG, is the irrational choice. So tit-for-tat represents a case in which a simple decision heuristic, "start cooperatively, but then do unto other as other did unto you on the last trial," emerged as the best of a collection of decision procedures.

In the first two examples that I have discussed, improper linear models and efficient decision heuristics, it was possible to compare the success of the heuristics to uncontroversial normative models. It was also possible to specify exactly what information the heuristics was ignoring. In the case of tit-for-tat, there is less clarity about the normative solution. Indeed, no normative solution for the tournament has been offered. Many of the programs would have been normatively correct in some environment, under some assumptions, but in Axelrod's situation, those assumptions were clearly not met. Despite the absence of a clear optimal solution, tit-for-tat is a genuine heuristic in that it used fewer lines of code and less information about the history of the interaction than any of the other programs.

*Win-stay, lose-change.* It should not be surprising that the efficiency of a decision rule might depend on the context in which it is used. In the last example that I want to describe, the win-stay, lose-change rule proves to be an efficient heuristic when used in a two-person social situation in which the other person also uses the same heuristic. In a study by Kelley, Thibaut, Radloff, and Mundy (1962) subjects played a two-person, mutual fate control game in which one person's choices delivered either a reward or a punishment to the other player (Thibaut & Kelley, 1959). Each player has complete control over the payoff to the other. If Column chooses left, Row gets 1 and if Column chooses right, Row gets −1. Likewise, Row completely determines Column's payoff; Upper provides 1 and Lower yields

−1. The question is whether the two subjects, who have no knowledge of the payoff matrix and who only know the outcome (which is determined by the other's choice) will be able to "discover" the mutual reward cell, Upper Left.

Kelley et al. hypothesized that if the subjects used a simple strategy in which they repeated a response that was followed by reward (1) and changed the response that was followed by a punishment (−1), they should "find" the mutually cooperative cell, without even being aware that there was such a thing. Their analysis was as follows: Suppose that the initial joint responses put them in the upper right cell. Row, who is punished, will change and move to lower, but Column, who was rewarded, will stay on right. The next joint choice will then be bottom right. In that cell both subjects will be punished, and both should change, putting them in the upper left cell. In that cell they will be rewarded, so they should stay there forever more or until the experiment ends, whichever comes first. Kelley et al. report convincing data indicating that this process was indeed involved in the emergence of mutual cooperation.

The virtue of the win-stay, lose-change heuristic is that it may produce adaptive behavior in a wide variety of situations (Campbell, 1960). In the current context, it is efficient only if it is used by both of the players. Moreover, if the group is larger than two, and if each player's choices provide payoffs to one player and has his or her payoffs provided by the choices of a different player, then this heuristic will lead to mutual reward only when the number of players is a power of two.

### Equality as a decision heuristic

In situations in which allocations have to be made, equality may be a useful heuristic. First and foremost, it is a simple rule to apply when the goods or bads being distributed are divisible. One needs to know the number of individuals to share whatever is being divided and to perform a division to calculate a per capita share. Problems applying the rule may arise when the number of people involved is either unknown or disputed (as with census figures that will be used to allocate financial and political resources), or when the good being allocated is "lumpy." Giving each of three people one third of a valuable oriental rug is not an intelligent division. In such cases, other allocation strategies, still based on the concept of equality, could be developed. Raiffa (1982, ch. 19) describes several of these.

Equality is symmetric. It is a rule that does not require the identification of the parties (unless, like the pigs in George Orwell's *Animal Farm*, some are more equal than others).

Even in situations in which all agree that equality constitutes an inappropriate allocation, it can nevertheless be a very useful anchor or benchmark from which adjustments can be made. The calculation of equal shares, which are then adjusted in some way, is probably a common strategy both in individual decision situations and in interpersonal bargaining contexts. In dividing a dinner bill, it is not unusual to divide the bill first into equal shares and then to adjust those shares according to who had dessert or wine, for instance, and who did not. Thus, equality can be used as an initial anchor in an anchor and adjustment process that will not necessarily yield equal allocations. Equality would nevertheless be a crucial element of such a process.

From a social perspective, equality might be thought of as an equilibrium outcome. This is to say that if departures from equality evoke objections from those relatively disadvantaged, and if these objections are more strenuous than the defenses of those relatively advantaged, the imbalance will tend to reestablish equality. A slightly different version of this point is to note that if receiving a unit less than an equal share carries a greater disutility than the utility associated with having a unit more than an equal share, then equality will (under some other reasonable assumptions) maximize the total utility of the group. In fact equality as a utilitarian solution follows from the assumption of decreasing marginal utility of outcomes (see Baron, in Part III of this book).

While equality as a heuristic has some very positive features, it also has some potential drawbacks. For one, equal divisions may be inefficient. That is to say, in some contexts, it may be possible for all parties to do better if they accept unequal payoffs. Splitting the difference in bargaining or negotiation sometimes leads to joint payoffs that are lower than those provided by log-rolling (e.g., Pruitt & Rubin, 1986; Thompson, 1990). An experiment of McClelland and Rohrbaugh (1978) has shown that subjects often prefer equal outcomes to those that are larger but unequal. A reliance on equality in such situations may limit the total group assets.

I mentioned earlier that division of lumpy goods is often problematic but solvable (Raiffa, 1982). Allison, McQueen, and Schaerfl (1992) have also shown that the division of nonpartitioned resources may also be difficult. They note that it is easier at dinner for five people to know how to divide five drumsticks among themselves than to divide the bowl of mashed potatoes. They also present experimental evidence that subjects violate equality more when dividing a nonpartitioned resource (24 pounds of sand) than when the resource is partitioned (24 blocks). It is also harder to estimate one twelfth of a resource than one half or one third, and these authors also report more violations of equality with larger groups ($n = 12$) than smaller ($n = 3$). Partitioned or countable resources are more amenable to equal division that unpartitioned or uncountable resources like air, water, or mashed potatoes.

The use of an equality heuristic is not a guarantee that conflict over the allocation of goods or bads will be eliminated. In most complicated social decisions there will be several dimensions on which equality may be established. The agreement that equality is appropriate does not constitute agreement on what it is that should be equal. Thus, saying that equality is a cognitively simple strategy for division is not to imply that there are not problems associated with it. In organizational settings, one could argue that salaries should be flat equal, equal conditional on years of service, equal per some measure of achievement (like commissions on sales), or equal per some measure of effort like number of sales calls made. In most interesting situations, equality can be established with regard to a variety of criteria and this fact may tempt decision makers to favor criteria or dimensions on which equal allocations would yield them better outcomes. So a parent might believe that her son's allowance should be the same as their neighbor's son of the same age, while the son may argue for the same allowance as his older sister. Disputes of this sort are not about equality, they are about the question Equal to what?

It should be noted as a digression that the problem of dimension selection in the use of equality is not restricted to interpersonal applications. Bazerman (1990) describes a prediction problem in which one is to forecast sales for 1991 for each of nine stores in a chain using the stores' 1989 sales figures. The only constraint is that the total sales for the group of nine stores should be 10% above the 1989 total sales figures. Bazerman claims that most people tend to increase each store's budget by 10% (equal proportion) which is proper if one assumes a perfect correlation between 1989 sales and 1991 sales. If there is no correlation, so that differences in sales are due to purely random fluctuations, the proper strategy is to forecast equal sales for all stores and to ignore past sales altogether. A third possibility that Bazerman does not mention is to forecast an equal increase to be added to the past sales for each store. And yet another approach, which reflects one's uncertainty about the correlation between annual sales, might be to take the average of the first two forecasts. This strategy involves three uses of an equality heuristic: taking an equal mixture of two forecasts, each of which is based on the idea of equality.

In the remainder of the chapter I would like to describe four experiments that illustrate four different aspects of decision making using an equality heuristic. It is not my objective in reviewing these studies to suggest that all allocation decision making involves the use of an equality idea. Even though the notion of equality may constitute the foundation for our beliefs about fairness, many allocation practices do not hinge on the idea of dividing resources equally. Efforts to secure procedural justice are frequently independent of distributional concerns altogether (Lind & Tyler, 1988) even though such efforts may ultimately achieve equality of treatment of individuals. Moreover, there are allocation situations in which equal division is completely inappropriate. Competitive tournaments allocate benefits to winners only. Jobs, slots in medical schools, and Nobel prizes are not allocated equally to all applicants. Markets do not allocate goods equally to all potential buyers. From a psychological perspective, it is interesting to question when equality is or is not appropriate, and further, what factors determine what type of equality is deemed reasonable.

In my discussion of the experiments in the next section, I will try to show that the results can be interpreted "as if" subjects were using equality as a decision heuristic. This is not to imply that there are not other ways to interpret the studies as well. In most cases there is not enough experimental data to allow one to select one interpretation in preference to another. In some cases, seemingly different theories may amount to the same underlying processes, making theoretical differentiation futile. For instance, in the sales forecasting example from Bazerman discussed previously, my interpretation in terms of equality is not incompatible with a pure regression approach to the prediction problem. Mathematically, they amount to precisely the same thing. Viewing the problem from the point of view of equality highlights aspects of the problem that may not be otherwise obvious, like the different ways in which equality can be applied, for example, and the way it can be used to generate new forecasts from the basic ones. In some of the studies I will discuss, heuristic decision making will be contrasted to normative alternatives, but I have made no effort to argue that mine is the only possible account of the data. My major goals are (1) to present evidence in support of the idea that equality is used as a decision heuristic and (2) to illustrate the types of ideas that follow from this hypothesis and the range of its potential applications.

The studies I will discuss deal with four broad questions that arise with the assumption that equality is used as a decision heuristic. First, there is the question of how one can tell when people are using a "divide equally" heuristic as opposed to some other decision procedure. This is a complicated issue, but an experiment by Harris and Joyce (1980) illustrates one clever way in which the use of this rule may be detected. A second issue concerns the types of situations that evoke equality as opposed to other allocation principles. Little is understood about this problem, but an experiment by Allison (1987) illustrates one way to approach it. The issue of Equal how? is the focus of the third experiment that I will describe. When there are two or more dimensions along which equality may be established, and when equality on one dimension implies inequality on another, the application of the equality heuristic may be expected to be guided by several factors, an important one of which will be the decision maker's self-interest. The dissertation of van Avermaet (1974) provides an excellent illustration of this type of process. Finally, I want to demonstrate how equality can be used to make social decisions in which the allocations are not equal. A public goods study conducted by Messick and Rutte (1992) exemplifies how equality can be used as an anchor that is later adjusted to determine the magnitude of one's contribution to a public good. In all of these examples, I hope to demonstrate that the use of a simple equality heuristic in social decision making does not imply that such decision processes are simplistic nor that they necessarily result in poor decisions.

### Equality in allocation decisions

*Heuristics or normative rules?* In many social decision making situations normative decision rules do not exist. This is the case in many situations in which resources or obligations must be allocated to members of a group. Raiffa (1982) addresses the problem of fair distribution and illustrates several different ways in which fair distributions or allocations can be made. The different methods have different advantages and drawbacks, but it is not possible to claim that one is preferable to the others. If one cannot contrast heuristic decisions against normative ones, how can one garnish empirical support for the hypothesis of heuristic decision making? One approach is to use the criterion of consistency. The goal is to create situations in which inconsistent judgments can be evoked if subjects are using heuristics, but in which inconsistencies ought not appear if subjects are following some normative procedure. This approach was taken in the experiments reported by Harris & Joyce (1980).

In the experiments Harris and Joyce reported, subjects read about a joint business venture involving five persons. The persons set up a furniture business, in one study, or a plant sales business, in another. Each of the partners had a turn minding the business and they had differing levels of gross sales. There were also joint expenses (e.g., rent and supplies) that had to be paid for the partnership. The difference between the total sales and the total expenses represented the total profit that the partnership earned. Roughly half the subjects in each of the two studies was asked to assign "fair shares of the expenses" to the partners, while the other half was asked to assign profits "to be as fair as possible." If equality of profits was judged to be the fair outcome of the partnership, then expenses could be allocated to achieve this result. If equality of expenses was judged fairest, then profits would have to differ. This is not what happened, however. Of the 142 subjects who allocated profits, 37% assigned them equally whereas only 2 subjects assigned profits so as to equalize expenses. When allocating expenses, 47% of the 141 subjects used equality and none did so to create equal profits. In this study there was a powerful tendency for subjects to apply the equality heuristic to whatever component of the problem they were asked to allocate even though equal profits implied unequal expenses and vice versa. Similar results were reported in a third experiment in which the subject's own outcome was involved.

These results suggest that fairness is rather superficial in this task, in that few subjects tried to use one dimension to establish equality on the other. None of the subjects adjusted expenses to create equal profits and only 2 of 142 subjects adjusted profits to create equal expenses. The appeal of equality was so strong that some subjects asserted that the partners should get equal expenses and profits, failing to see the impossibility of that outcome given the constraints of the problem.

In the Harris and Joyce experiments, there is no normatively correct assignment of expenses and profits to partners. Considerable thought would have been required to allocate one dimension so as to equate outcomes on the other. The use of the equality heuristic in this context has the advantage that it reduces the cognitive work needed to make an allocation although it leads to inconsistencies with regard to the final allocation of profits.

*Equal or all?* The task environment will generally influence what types of psychological processes are appropriate. Payne's (1982) concept of contingent decision behavior supposes that different choice rules will be evoked and used in different decision environments. Similarly, we may ask about situations in which an equality rule will and will not be perceived to be appropriate. The equality heuristic should be evoked in situations in which sharing is considered appropriate or in which one is asked to allocate quantities to others, including, possibly, one's self. However, when one is allocating to a group including the allocator, other impulses may be evoked that may differ from equality. Self-interest is such a motive. Allison and I (1990), for instance, have shown that one factor that determines whether or not subjects will deviate from taking an equal share of a resource in six-person groups is whether or not the amount of the resource is divisible by 6. Divisibility of the resource by 6 tended to make equality more salient and hence acted as a restraint against taking more than an equal share. Other more or less subtle features of the situation should also have an influence.

There are other contexts in which sharing is not considered an appropriate strategy. Competitive situations, in which the winner is entitled to the entire prize, are good examples of such contexts. For the most part, we are familiar with the proper construal of social situations and we know how to behave appropriately. If we are at the head of the line for concert tickets, we do not feel that we should share the good seats with those at the back, but if we are the first to take food from a collective plate, we do not feel entitled to take it all. We may occasionally find ourselves in novel and unfamiliar situations (like psychological experiments) whose construal is ambiguous. In these situations we should be sensitive to cues that would help us to choose from among the conflicting interpretations of the situation. An interesting illustration of this sort is provided by an experiment of Hoffman and Spitzer (1985).

In an earlier study, Hoffman and Spitzer (1982) created a task in which a pair of subjects could share one of three pairs of monetary payoffs. One subject, randomly assigned to the role of controller, could unilaterally select the pair, but the subjects could also bargain over the distribution of total amount involved. The authors predicted that the subjects would select the pair containing the largest sum and that the division would provide the controller with a payoff that was at least as large as the controller could get unilaterally. The first prediction was supported, but the second was not. Instead, Hoffman and Spitzer found a pervasive tendency for subjects to divide the money equally to the relative disadvantage of the controller.

Hoffman and Spitzer (1985) hypothesized that when subjects were randomly assigned to the role of controller, they did not feel that the method of assignment legitimized their right to take more than half of the money. To investigate the hypothesis that the method of assignment determines whether or not subjects take more than half the money, these authors randomly assigned half the subjects to the role of controller and permitted the other half to achieve this role by winning a simple game. For each group, half the subjects were told that they had "earned the right" to be controller, whereas the other half were told that they had "been designated" controller. In the context in which the controllers were determined by the outcome of the game and in which they were told that they had earned the right to be controller, only a third of the decisions involved equal or nearly equal division, and the remainder of the subjects took the maximum. In the other conditions, the frequency of use of equality was twice as great as in the game-entitlement condition and maximizing responses occurred half as often.

The interpretation of these data from the current perspective is that the situation is an ambiguous one and that the two variables that were manipulated change the interpretative texture of the situation. Winning the game and "earning the right" to occupy the advantaged position are both cues that one is entitled to take more than half.

Random devices, like lotteries, as well as competitions may justify a self-serving "Winner take all" construal of an ambiguous situation. What should tend to impede such a construal is the perception that the assignment procedure was unfair. Winning a fair lottery or competition is unlikely to elicit guilt or the perception that the outcome of the procedure is illegitimate. If the procedure is perceived to be tainted, then any advantage afforded by the procedure may be perceived as illegitimate. The fallback option then would be equal division.

Allison (1987) has reported data that support this hypothesis. Allison had subjects report to the laboratory in groups of six. Their task was to share a resource that could be exchanged for money. The rules were that they were going to draw sequentially from the common resource pool and that when one's turn came, that person would have complete knowledge of how much the preceding persons had taken and how much of the resource was left. When the resource level was equal to zero, no one could take any more. The resource pool always began with 45 units. The six subjects had only to be assigned their position in the sequence. In this experiment, a deception was used to be able to assign all subjects to the first position, so that every subject believed that he or she was going to be the first one to make a withdrawal from the pool.

Allison (1987) used four different procedures to assign the subjects to their advantaged role. Some of the subjects were told that they had won a simple lottery (Lottery). Others were given a 12-item quiz and were told that they won the first position because they answered more items correctly than any of the other subjects (Real Quiz). Another group also took a quiz, but one that was patently unfair (Trivial Quiz). These subjects were shown a quiz that was divided into six subsections. The instructions said that each subject was going to be assigned one of the subsections to answer and that the assignment was going to be random. The questions in five of the subsections were very difficult, for example: "What is the diameter of the planet Neptune?," "What is the unit of currency in Pakistan?," "Who is currently Canada's ambassador to the United Nations?." The questions in one of the subsections, however, were very easy: "Who invented the electric light?," "What is the capital of Mexico?," "Who is currently Vice-President of the United States?." It was clear that whoever was assigned this easy subsection was going to win the first position. The procedure was a lottery in an achievement test's clothing.

The major dependent variable was the proportion of the 45-unit common pool that the first subject took. In the Lottery, Real Quiz, and Trivial Quiz conditions, respectively, those proportions were .62, .58, and .40. When the procedure was a lottery disguised as a test, the decision makers took significantly less of the pool than when the procedure was a genuine lottery or a genuine test. The subjects also rated the Trivial Quiz procedure as much less fair than either of the other procedures.

In Allison's (1987) situation, the equality heuristic conflicts with self-interest in the form of a "Winner take much" construal. Allison modified the task slightly to demonstrate that equal division is salient. In the modified version, which Allison called "fate control," the task was such that if the total of the requests of the six subjects exceeded 45, none of the group members would get anything. In this case the first subjects had a clear and simple strategy if they assumed that the other five players preferred more money to less and believed that all other players did so. The strategy was to take all but five units of the resource. The second player would then take one unit, leaving four for the remaining four subjects, and so on. This is not, of course, what the subjects did. The first subjects took very close to one sixth of the pool on the average. Furthermore, the amount they took did not depend on the procedure for allocating sequential position. Since a sixth of the pool (7.5) was not a round number, subjects had to decide whether to deviate by taking more than one sixth, or by taking less. There were systematic individual differences with cooperative subjects (determined by a prior test) taking a little less than a sixth and noncooperative subjects taking a little more.

It is compelling to think about this kind of decision making as an anchoring and adjustment process, in which equality defines the anchor and an adjustment is made whose magnitude and direction depend on other factors. If subsequent group members can deprive one of one's resources, the adjustment is a small one up or down depending on the personality of the subject. If later group members are powerless, the adjustment is much larger and in the direction of self-benefit. Under these circumstances, however, the magnitude of the adjustment also depends on the procedure which advantaged the subject. There is remarkably little known about the perceptions of and responses to such procedures (Lind & Tyler, 1988).

One additional aspect of Allison's (1987) study suggests that perceived fairness may not be the sole criterion influencing the salience of the equality heuristic. There was a fourth group of subjects assigned to the first position for whom the procedure was essentially a lottery, but a lottery that depended on a personal characteristic of the subject, namely the subject's birthdate. These subjects were told that the experimenter had randomly selected a day of the year, and the subject whose birthday came closest to this day would go first. Subjects whose advantage came about through this process took less than subjects in any other condition, on average about one third of the pool. They also rated the procedure as being very fair, almost as fair as the lottery. For reasons that are not yet clear, this procedure suppresses the winner-take-all more than any of the other procedure. Perhaps the reason stems from the obvious fact that people do not choose their birthdates and hence should not be penalized for them. In any case, this experiment along with that of Hoffman and Spitzer, makes it clear that subtle changes in the situational texture can produce dramatic changes in allocation decisions, changes that can be traced to differences in the use of the equality heuristic.

*How equal?* Many authors distinguish between equality and equity as rules of distributive justice (Deutsch, 1985; Hook & Cook, 1979; Leventhal, 1976). Equality is simply the division of a resource into equal parts regardless of considerations of deservingness, whereas equity is the allocation of the resource in proportion to each party's inputs. The implications of these rules are very different. Equality does not require one to specify what constitutes an input, for instance, whereas equity does, making equality a simpler rule than equity. However, it is possible to think of equity as an application of the equality heuristic to a different scaling of the payoff dimension. Equal pay for a job, for instance, can be construed to mean equal absolute payments (equality), equal pay per hour (equity when time worked is the input), or equal pay per unit accomplished (equity when amount completed is the input). These three "rules" are just equality applied to three different scales of payment – money, money per hour, and money per job. Thus conflicts between equality and equity may be viewed as conflicts about appropriate bases of payment.

In situations in which the proper basis of payment is ambiguous, there should be a tendency for people to prefer those that provide higher payoffs. This rather obvious hypothesis assumes that people apply the equality heuristic to the different possible payment scales and to favor the one or ones that are the most beneficial. The equality heuristic is thus able to guide decisions in ambiguous situations in ways that benefit the decision maker.

An experiment by van Avermaet (1974) illustrates the psychological processes involved in these decisions. Van Avermaet had subjects come into a laboratory setting and fill out personality questionnaires. Some of the subjects worked for 45 minutes and some worked for 90 minutes. The questionnaire lengths were constructed so that for each duration, some subjects completed six questionnaires and some completed only three. After the subject had worked for the time and had completed the number of questionnaires designated by his or her experimental condition, the experimenter interrupted the subject and said that he had to leave for an unexpected emergency. Before leaving, the experimenter explained that he had, unbeknownst to the subjects, money to pay them for their participation in the study. For accounting reasons he was paying them in pairs and he could pay each pair $7.00. However, because he was in a hurry, the experimenter asked the subject if he (or she) would divide the $7.00 between himself or herself and the other subject. At this point, the experimenter gave the subject information about how much the other (bogus) subject, as well as the true subject had done. This description consisted of information about (1) how many minutes the subjects worked and (2) how many questionnaires they completed. The true subject was told that he or she worked a longer, the same, or a shorter time than the other, and that he or she completed more, the same, or less than the other. The subject was then given six $1.00 bills and some change together with an addressed and stamped envelope, and was asked to send the appropriate amount of money to the other subject.

The dependent variable was how much money the subject sent to the other person. Unbridled greed would dictate that subjects would keep the $7.00 and the stamp. The other subject, after all, was not expecting to receive any payment, and the experimenter could not know what happened to the money. (There was a slight deception involved here because the address on the envelope was the neighbor of the experimenter and the envelopes were inconspicuously coded to indicate the subject's experimental condition.) The hypothesis was that subjects would favor the pay scale that was most beneficial to them. If they worked less than the other and if they did less, they should favor simple equality. However, if they either worked longer or got more done, they should favor that dimension and keep more than half of the money.

The results were in agreement with the hypothesis. Ninety of the 94 subjects sent some money to the address on the envelope. (One subject refused to take the money, one was suspicious, and no envelope was received from two others.) When the subjects were not favored by either performance dimension, they kept half of the money, on average. When they were favored by one dimension, they kept more than half regardless of how they stood on the other dimension. The pattern of means further revealed that subjects did not take two thirds of the money ($4.67) in every case in which they were favored by one scale. They kept this amount only in the condition in which they both worked longer and did more than the other. In the other conditions, they kept an average amount that fell between two thirds of the money and one half. This result suggests that when the application of the equality rule generates two or more possible divisions, these divisions may operate as benchmarks or anchors such that the final decision is a compromise between, or average of them. An allocation that falls between strict equality and strict equity, the type of allocation that would result from such a compromise, has been called *ordinal equity* by Hook and Cook (1979) and it corresponds to Harris's concept of a weighted-solutions model (in this book).

*How much to donate?* Suppose you were asked to estimate the average daily egg production of the United States. How might you do that? One method that turns up frequently when I have asked people this question is to (1) make an estimate of the number of eggs a typical person might eat in a day, (2) multiply that number by an estimate of the number of people in the United States, and (3) adjust that answer somewhat depending on whether you think the resulting estimate is an overestimate or an underestimate. If you think the typical American eats an average of one egg a day and if you think there are 240 million Americans, the initial estimate is 240 million eggs a day. You may adjust upward, thinking that there are many nondietary uses of eggs, or downward, because some people do not eat eggs. This method of generating an estimate relies on a heuristic that has three components. First is the use of an equality concept – the per capita consumption of eggs. The use of this concept does not imply that every person eats the same number of eggs every day, only that the average can summarize the central tendency. Not all equality concepts are useful in making this estimate, however. The useful ones are those for which one could make a reasonable guess. One could, for instance, use the average number of eggs laid per day per pullet and multiply that estimate by the number of pullets. However, most of us have no idea how many eggs per day an average chicken lays. Worse yet, we have no inkling of how many chickens there are at work laying eggs in the United States.

Second, one must estimate the population size. Most people can come up with a ballpark figure for this. Third, one must adjust the product of the first two estimates to reflect one's belief that the product is too large (some people do not eat eggs) or too small (eggs are used in lots of things other than food). (The actual daily egg production in the United States in 1988, the last year for which data are available as I write this, is about 190 million.)

A similar process to the one described above can be used to calculate one's "fair share" of a resource or obligation. In Messick and Rutte (1992) my coauthor and I have described a public goods experiment that illustrates one way in which this approach might work. In this experiment, I told an audience of 43 people that they were going to be subjects in an experiment. The rules of the experiment were as follows: Everyone in the room received an envelope into which some money could be put, to be collected by the experimenter. If the total amount of money collected was 250 Dutch guilders or more (the experiment was conducted in the Netherlands), about $U.S. 125 at the then rate of exchange, everyone in the room would be given a 10 guilder bill. If the total collected was less than 250 guilders, the experimenters would keep it all and no one would be given anything. The group, by contributing 250 guilders, could earn 430 guilders, a profit of 180 guilders, so the task was a straightforward public goods task. The members of the audience were given some time to think about the decision and to discuss it with their neighbors, after which their envelopes, either empty or containing some money, were collected. The participants were also asked to write the total amount of money that they expected to be collected on the inside of the envelope.

One normative theory of how people make their choices in tasks of this kind (see for instance Rapoport, 1988), assumes that people estimate the amount that will be contributed by others. Based on this estimate, they then determine if their contribution could enhance the probability of winning the good enough to compensate for the loss of the contribution. They contribute, this theory supposes, if the increment in expected payoff brought about by their contribution is greater then the contribution itself. If this were indeed the way people were making their decisions, then we would expect a clear relation between the estimates of the total amount that would be given and the participants' decisions. Specifically, people who estimate that the total will be either quite small or quite large, extreme enough so that the participant's contribution could not influence whether or not the group wins the bonus, will not contribute. This prediction was clearly incorrect. First, there was only one participant who estimated that his or her contribution would be critical in that the group would have failed had the contribution not been given and succeeded if it were given. The prediction was reasonably accurate for the 12 participants who predicted failure (that the total would be less than 250 guilders). They contributed fewer than 2 guilders per person. However, the 27 people who predicted success – that is, optimists who predicted that the amount collected would exceed 250 guilders even without their contribution – contributed an average of 7 guilders each. This behavior contradicts expected value maximization theories.

We hypothesized that the participants engaged in a two-step decision process. First they asked themselves whether or not the group would succeed. If they guessed that it would not succeed, then they gave little if anything to the collective effort. If they believed that the group would succeed, however, they then had to calculate a reasonable contribution to make to participate in the success. At this stage, we proposed, the participants employed the equality heuristic to estimate what an equal (per capita) share of the 250 guilders would be. It comes to about 6 guilders. Contributing 6 guilders might well fail, however, because some of the people in the room might not contribute anything. Therefore, it would be necessary to add a cushion to the equal share to compensate for those not contributing or not calculating correctly. The cushion in this case was about 1 guilder on average. If the estimate of the number not contributing was reasonably accurate, and if the cushion was large enough to compensate for the shortfall, then the group could succeed. In fact, the set of contributions could result in an asymmetric equilibrium in which some contribute and some do not, but in which none would want to change their decisions. Conversations with the participants following the experiment confirmed that many of them used a process of anchoring (with an estimated equal share) and upward adjustment to make their decisions. Collectively, the outcome was very nearly in equilibrium in that the total amount collected was about 246 guilders.

### Conclusions

My goal in this chapter is to explore some implications of the view that social decision making is largely heuristic in nature. That is to say that people use simple rules of thumb to guide their decisions when they are in ambiguous, novel, or complex social situations. The particular rule that I have highlighted is the equality heuristic, the concept of equal division. While the idea of equal division is, superficially, almost trivially simple, I have tried to convey my impression that decision making employing the rule is anything but simple. The notion of equality competes with other rules, like "First come, first served" in some situations, and the question of equality with regard to what is a lingering question of great social and political importance in modern society. Do we want to achieve equality of representation of all social groups in all strata of society (how do we select the social groups to which we apply this rule?) or do we want to create equality of opportunity (which may imply inequality in representation)? The idea that we can have both may be as illusory as that of Harris and Joyce's (1980) subjects who maintained that they could allocate both the expenses and profits of the partners equally. The appeal of equality may stimulate efforts to build an impossible social order, and the frustration flowing from the failure to achieve such a goal may be destructive.

A general point that I hoped to convey in this chapter is that intelligent and reasonable decisions can be heuristic-based. Complex and adaptive choices can be based on simple underlying rules as Campbell (1960) and others have argued. Equality is one of these simple rules. To qualify as a useful social decision heuristic, a rule should have at least three characteristics. First, it should be simple. One should not have to have an advanced degree to use the rule. Certainly, equality qualifies as a simple rule in most cases even if there may be controversy about how it is we are supposed to be equal.

Second, a rule should be effective, which is to say it should yield a choice. A rule like "Ask my accountant" is not an effective everyday rule unless one happens to be continuously in the company of one's accountant. A rule like "Choose the alternative on the right" is effective if options are spatially displayed. It is not effective if options are arrayed in time but not space. In most allocation situations, equal division will generate a decision, an allocation. Contrast equality to the idea that all parties should be given what they "deserve." "Deservingness" tends to be a less effective rule than equality because it is often too vague or subjective to lead to an allocation.

Finally, a social decision heuristic has to be justifiable. Social decisions are consequential in that they influence the well-being of others and those others will generally not be indifferent to the decision. The issue of the justifiability of a decision is a complicated one that involves perceptions of procedural justice (Lind & Tyler, 1988), causal explanations for actions (e.g., Bies & Shapiro, 1987), and the accountability of the decision maker (Tetlock & Kim, 1987). Nevertheless, it is hard to imagine a more pervasively justifiable principle of making allocation decisions than the principle of equality.

### References

Adams, J. S. (1965). Inequity in social exchange. In L. Berkowitz (Ed.), *Advances in experimental social psychology* (Vol. 2). New York: Academic Press.

Allison, S. T. (1987). The use of social decision heuristics in response to uncertainty in social dilemmas. Unpublished doctoral dissertation, University of California, Santa Barbara.

Allison, S. T., & Messick, D. M. (1990). Social decision heuristics and the use of shared resources. *Journal of Behavioral Decision Making, 3,* 195–204.

Allison, S. T., McQueen, L. R., & Schaerfl, L. M. (1992). Social decision making processes and the equal partition of shared resources. *Journal of Experimental Social Psychology, 28,* 23–42.

Axelrod, R. (1984). *The evolution of cooperation.* New York: Basic Books.

Bazerman, M. H. (1990). *Managerial decision making.* New York: Wiley.

Bies, R. J., & Shapiro, D. L. (1987). Interactional fairness judgments: The influence of causal accounts. *Social Justice Research, 1,* 199–218.

Bordley, R. F. (1985). Comparing different decision rules. *Behavioral Science, 30,* 230–239.

Campbell, D. T. (1960). Blind variation and selective retention in creative thought as in other knowledge processes. *Psychological Review, 67,* 380–400.

Christensen-Szalanski, J. J., & Beach, L. R. (1984). The citation bias: Fad and fashion in the judgment and decision literature. *American Psychologist, 39,* 75–78.

Dawes, R. M. (1979). The robust beauty of improper linear models. *American Psychologist, 34,* 571–582.

Deutsch, M. (1985). *Distributive justice*. New Haven, CT: Yale University Press.

Funder, D. C. (1987). Errors and mistakes: Evaluating the accuracy of social judgment. *Psychological Bulletin, 101*, 75–91.

Green, B. F. (1963). *Digital computers in research*. New York: McGraw-Hill.

Harris, R. J., & Joyce, M. A. (1980). What's fair? It depends on how you ask the question. *Journal of Personality and Social Psychology, 38*, 165–170.

Hoffman, E., & Spitzer, M. (1982). The Coase theorem: Some experimental tests. *Journal of Law and Economics, 25*, 73–98.

   (1985). Entitlements, rights, and fairness: An experimental examination of subjects' concepts of distributive justice. *Journal of Legal Studies, 14*, 259–297.

Hogarth, R. M. (1981). Beyond discrete biases: Functional and dysfunctional aspects of judgmental heuristics. *Psychological Bulletin, 90*, 197–217.

Hook, J., & Cook, T. (1979). Equity theory and the cognitive ability of children. *Psychological Bulletin, 86*, 429–445.

Kahneman, D., & Tversky, A. (1972). Subjective probability: A judgment of representativeness. *Cognitive Psychology, 3*, 430–454.

   (1973). On the psychology of prediction. *Psychological Review, 80*, 237–251.

Kelley, H. H., Thibaut, J. W., Radloff, R., & Mundy, D. (1962). The development of cooperation in the "minimal social situation. *Psychological Monographs, 76*, No. 19.

Leventhal, G. S. (1976). The distribution of rewards and resources in groups and organizations. In L. Berkowitz & E. Walster (Eds.), *Advances in experimental social psychology* (Vol. 9). New York: Academic Press.

Lind, E. A. & Tyler, T. R. (1988). *The Social psychology of procedural justice*. New York: Plenum.

McClelland, G., & Rohrbaugh, J. (1978). Who accepts the Pareto axiom? The role of utility and equity in arbitration decisions. *Behavioral Science, 23*, 446–456.

Messick, D. M., & Cook, K. S. (1983) *Equity theory: psychological and sociological perspectives*. New York: Praeger.

Messick, D. M. & Rutte, C. (1992). The provision of public goods by experts: The Groningen study. In W. Liebrand, D. M. Messick, & H. Wilke (Eds.), *Social Dilemmas*. London: Pergamon.

Newell, A. & Simon, H. A. (1963). Computers in psychology. In R. D. Luce, R. R. Bush, & E. Galanter (Eds.), *Handbook of mathematical psychology* (Vol. 1). New York: Wiley. (361–428).

Nisbett, R. E., & Ross, L. (1980). *Human inference: Strategies and shortcomings of social judgment*. Englewood Cliffs, NJ: Prentice-Hall.

Nozick, R. (1974). *Anarchy, state, and utopia*. New York: Basic Books.

Payne, J. W. (1982). Contingent decision behavior. *Psychological Bulletin, 92*, 382–402.

Peterson, C. R., & Beach, L. R. (1967). Man as an intuitive statistician. *Psychological Bulletin, 68*, 29–46.

Polya, G. (1945). *How to solve it*. Princeton, NJ: Princeton University Press.

Pruitt, D. G., & Rubin, J. Z. (1986). *Social conflict: Escalation, stalemate, and settlement*. New York: Random House.

Raiffa, H. (1982). *The art and science of negotiation*. Cambridge, MA: Harvard University Press.

Rapoport, A. (1988). Provision of step-level goods: Effects of inequality in resources. *Journal of Personality and Social Psychology, 54*, 432–440.

Rawls, J. (1971). *A theory of justice*. Cambridge, MA: Harvard University Press.

Sherman, S. J., & Corty, E. (1984). Cognitive heuristics. In R. Wyer & T. Srull (Eds.), *Handbook of social cognition* (Vol. 1). Hillsdale, NJ: Erlbaum.

Slovic, P., & Lichtenstein, S. (1983). Preference reversals: A broader perspective. *American Economic Review, 73*, 596–605.

Tetlock, P. E., & Kim, J. I. (1987). Accountability and judgment in a personality prediction task. *Journal of Personality and Social Psychology, 52*, 700–709.

Thibaut, J. W., & Kelley, H. H. (1959). *The social psychology of groups*. New York: Wiley.

Thompson. L. (1990). The influence of experience on negotiation. *Journal of Experimental Social Psychology, 26*, 528–544.

Thorngate, W. (1980). Efficient decision heuristics. *Behavioral Science, 25*, 219–225.

Tversky, A., & Kahneman, D. (1971). The belief in the "law of small numbers." *Psychological Bulletin, 76*, 105–100.

(1973). Availability: A heuristic for judging frequency and probability. *Cognitive Psychology, 5*, 207–235.

(1974). Judgment under uncertainty: Heuristics and biases. *Science, 185*, 1124–1131.

(1986). Rational choice and the framing of decision. *Journal of Business, 59*, S251–S278.

van Avermaet, E. (1974). Equity: A theoretical and experimental analysis. Unpublished doctoral dissertation. University of California, Santa Barbara.

von Winterfeldt, D., & Edwards, W. (1986). *Decision analysis and behavioral research*. Cambridge: Cambridge University Press.

Walster, E., Berscheid, E., & Walster, G. W. (1973). New directions in equity research. *Journal of Personality and Social Psychology, 25*, 151–176.

# 3  Two insights occasioned by attempts to pin down the equity formula

*Richard J. Harris*

This chapter is a defense (rationalization?) of research on the equity formula – that is, on the nature of the relationship that holds between inputs and fair outcomes. The defense consists primarily of pointing out substantive insights into the processes governing subjects' behavior when asked to allocate group outcomes fairly that have resulted from relatively recent research on what most textbook authors and most equity researchers consider the dry and at best tangential topic of the equity formula. I'll focus on two such insights:

1. The tenuous nature of the "equality norm," as demonstrated by its virtual disappearance when subjects are induced to be consistent in their allocation of outcomes and of outcome–input differences.
2. Dependence of the criteria that subjects use for judging the fairness of an allocation scheme on the match between the units in which inputs and outcomes are measured – this particular insight occasioned by attempts to specify the conditions under which nonlinearity (à la Mellers, 1982) creeps into the equity formula.

### What's an equity formula?

Readers of this book are unlikely to need convincing that equity considerations arise in a very wide range of social settings: education, economics, business, intimate, and so on. You may be less familiar with the notion of an equity *formula*. An *equity formula* is simply an algebraic expression of the functional relationship between outcomes and inputs that holds when observers deem the social exchange among the participants to be (have been) a *fair* one. Almost all such formulas can be expressed as follows (Harris, 1976).

*Generic form of an equity formula*
$$r_i(O_i, I_i) = \text{constant for all participants } i \tag{1}$$

where $I_i$ is a measure of participant $i$'s *input*, $O_i$ is a measure of that participant's *outcome*, and $r_i$ is participant $i$'s *relative outcome* (relative to his inputs). Relative outcome is an important construct in its own right. For instance, Walster, Walster, and Berscheid (1978) define an *exploiter* as one who has caused another's relative outcome to be lower than his or her own (this other person being defined as the *victim* in this exploitive relationship). Note, too, that equity judgments are doubly relative, in that a relative outcome is a measure of one's outcome relative to your input, and one's status as underbenefited, overbenefited, or in an equitable relationship to others in the exchange is determined by the magnitude of your relative outcome *relative to* the relative outcomes of the other participants.

There is a large amount of empirical evidence that no single, parameter-free function can account for the interindividual and cross-situational variability seen in what subjects judge to be fair, but the hope is to find a single functional form that comes close (once a few parameter values unique to the individual or to the situation have been specified) to encompassing all of these various relationships between inputs and fair outcomes. A form that has performed well in this respect is the following formula (Harris, 1976).

*General linear formula*
$$r_i = O_i - aI_i, \text{ whence } O_i = aI_i + r, \tag{2}$$

where $a$ is a parameter representing the rate of exchange between inputs and (fair) outcomes – or, alternatively, the degree of differentiation between low-input and high-input partners' outcomes a given subject in a given situation considers fair; and $r$ is interpretable both as the intercept term in the linear relationship that holds between inputs and fair outcomes when the subject deems equity to hold and as each participant's relative outcome.

Three of the most salient norms about distribution of outcomes are special cases of the general linear formula: The *equality norm* arises when we set $a$ arbitrarily close to zero (and $r$ thus equals $\Sigma O_i/n$ where $n$ is the number of participants in the exchange); the *equal excess norm* follows from $a = 1$ (and $r$ thus equals $(\Sigma O_i - \Sigma I_i)/n$, the average excess of outcomes over inputs for the group); and *Adams's ratio formula* arises when $r = 0$ or, equivalently, $a = \Sigma O_i/\Sigma I_i$. Not surprisingly, then, the linear formula usually fits both individual subjects' allocations and mean allocations for groups of subjects quite well (Harris, 1980; Harris & Joyce, 1980; Harris, 1983).

Many more exotic formulas have been proposed (e.g., those I labeled in Harris, 1976, as the WBW-2 and exponential formulas), but despite whatever normative appeal they may have, their fit to data is quite poor – with the possible exception of Mellers's (1982) psychological relativity model.

### Equality and consistency don't mix

In an attempt to assess the extent to which the often large proportion of subjects who recommend equal final outcomes, regardless of differential inputs (the *equal outcomes* solution, $a = 0$ in the linear equity formula) do so because they truly believe this is the fair thing to do, and to what extent they are motivated instead by the fact that this is a salient, easily applied solution to the allocation problem, Joyce and I (Harris and Joyce, 1980) set up an alternative task for which the equal outcomes solution is no longer a very easy solution. What we uncovered (since replicated in studies reported in Harris, Tuttle, Bochner, & van Zyl, unpublished, and summarized briefly in Harris, 1983) was the *equity phrasing effect*.

Consider, for instance, one of the scenarios to which subjects in a positivity study (Harris, 1981) were asked to respond. Partners A through E contribute to a business partnership net sales (after deduction of cost of materials, travel expenses, etc.) of $200, $280, $400, $440, and $480, respectively, for a total net sales of $1,800 for the partnership. However, $840 in operating expenses not attributable to any one partner (e.g., centralized accounting, answering service, etc.) must be deducted from this $1,800 before distributing the remainder of $960 among the five partners. In the *outcomes-allocation condition* subjects were asked to indicate what they considered the fairest way of distributing this $960 among the partners. One salient approach is the *equal outcomes solution*, which simply assigns to each of the five an equal share ($192), ignoring any differences in inputs. Another possibility is to deduct from each partner's net sales an equal share ($168) of the general operating expenses, thus yielding final outcomes of $32, $112, $232, $272, and $312, respectively; this is the *equal expenses solution*. In the *expenses-allocation condition* the subject's task is to indicate what portion of the general operating expenses each of the five partners should "absorb." Subjects are explicitly told that each partner's final share of the $960 group outcome will be equal to that partner's net sales minus his or her share of the general operating expenses, so that any desired distribution of final outcomes can be achieved through appropriate choice of shares of the expenses. Thus, for instance, an equal expenses solution is obtained by assigning each partner a $168 share of the expenses, while an equal outcomes solution would require asking partners A through E to pay $8, $88, $208, $248, and $288, respectively. (Note that $200 − $8 = $192, as do $280 − $88, $400 − $208, $440 − $248, and $480 − $288.) However, achieving an equal outcomes solution in this expenses allocation condition is not as easy as in the outcomes allocation condition, so the difference between the two conditions in the percentage of subjects recommending an equal outcomes solution should indicate what percentage of the equal outcomes solutions so commonly observed in equity studies were due to the fact that it is an *easy* solution, rather than to the subjects' belief that it is a *fair* solution.

The *equity phrasing effect* uncovered in the various studies (cited earlier) that have contrasted recommendations under outcomes-allocation and expenses-allocation conditions consists of three differences between those two conditions:

(a) A drop (frequently to zero) in the percentage of equal outcomes solutions in the expenses-allocation as compared to the outcomes-allocation condition. For instance, in the positivity study (Harris, 1981) used as an example before, 15 of the 59 subjects recommended equal outcomes in the outcomes-allocation condition, while none recommended shares of expenses that led to equal outcomes in the expenses-allocation condition.

(b) A rise (often from about 5% to about 60%) in the percentage of equal excess solutions in the expenses-allocation as compared to the outcomes-allocation condition. For instance, one of the 59 subjects in the positivity study (Harris, 1981) recommended an equal expenses solution in the outcomes-allocation condition, while 35 of 59 made this recommendation in the expenses-allocation condition.

(c) A much higher mean $a$ parameter (and thus much greater difference between the outcomes assigned the highest- and lowest-input partners) in the expenses-allocation as compared to the outcomes-allocation condition. For instance, the mean allocations to the highest-input and lowest-input partners in the positivity study differed by $2.53 (yielding a mean $a$ parameter of .35) in the outcomes-allocation condition, but by $6.10 (yielding a mean $a$ parameter of .87) in the expenses-allocation condition.

This phrasing effect casts considerable doubt on the existence of an equality norm as that term is usually interpreted, so it is important to try to determine whether the phrasing effect is primarily attributable to decision simplification, scripted behavior (applying the same allocation rule to whatever you're given to divide up, regardless of the implications for final outcomes), or a general "toughening" of one's approach to allocation issues engendered by the discussion of expenses. Within-subject manipulation of allocation task (having the same subject respond under both allocation conditions, so as to be able to examine the relationship between his or her responses to the different tasks) seemed likely to be very useful at distinguishing among these explanations – provided that being asked to perform both tasks didn't engender such strong pressure (experimental demand?) on subjects to appear consistent in their recommendations that we were left with no phrasing effect to be explained. To keep this from happening Tuttle, Bochner, van Zyl, and I (Experiments 1 and 2 of Harris et al., unpublished) had subjects respond to two different scenarios (a Flea Market scenario involving selling plants at a flea market, and an Anagrams scenario involving sharing a group prize earned through performance on a problem solving task), with each subject being asked to allocate outcomes directly for one of the scenarios and to do so indirectly, via allocation of the general operating expenses, in the other. The scenarios were constructed so that the inputs, general operating expenses, and sum of outcomes remaining to be distributed in the Flea Market scenario were each 40 times the corresponding figures in the Anagrams scenario. Further, assignment of scenario to allocation condition and the order in which the two allocation tasks were presented were counterbalanced, and multivariate analyses of variance revealed no statistically significant main effects or interactions attributable to differences between the two scenarios.

With these precautions, the subjects were hardly overwhelmed by pressures for consistency between what they saw as fair under the two logically equivalent allocation procedures. Combining the results from Experiments 1 and 2, 8.6% of the subjects recommended the same distribution of outcomes in the two conditions, and a full-blown phrasing effect was observed. This raised our curiosity about what it would take to get subjects to be consistent in their recommendations under the two conditions. We were also interested in what subjects who *were* induced to make consistent recommendations would see as the fairest allocation rule. Therefore Tuttle and I conducted a study (Experiment 4 of Harris et al., unpublished) that was designed to apply maximum pressure for consistency by

1. Designing all scenarios so that no negative numbers need be used to achieve equal expenses in the outcomes-allocation condition or equal outcomes in the expenses-allocation condition.
2. Having subjects rate the fairness of allocations provided by the experimenter, as well as giving their own recommendation. This should both eliminate the complexity of the equal outcomes solution (since subjects need only rate it as the fairest solution) and provide models for subjects to use in coming up with their own recommendations.
3. Having each subject allocate both expenses and outcomes for the same situation, with both tasks appearing on the same page under a single description of the situation.
4. Explicitly pointing out the relationship between the two allocation tasks. While the expenses-allocation condition instructions for all experiments had heretofore included the statement that each partner's final outcome would be equal to his input minus his share of the expenses, the present study added to this an explicit statement that specifying either expenses or final outcome completely determines the other quantity.
5. Having subjects give their recommendations (and rate the fairness of allocations suggested by the experimenter) in five different scenarios (five years of the same appliance-repair partnership) so as to give each subject a great deal of practice in both allocation tasks.

All five of these manipulations were applied together.

These "heroic" efforts were successful, in that 112/150 (74.7%) of subjects' pairs of fairness ratings and 109/140 (77.9%) of their pairs of recommended outcomes were consistent across the two allocation conditions, and the equity phrasing effect was not statistically significant when all subjects' data (consistent or not) were included. The mean difference in $a$ parameter between the expenses-allocation and outcomes-allocations condition ranged from $-.040$ to $-.144$ across the five scenarios to which subjects responded – all opposite to the direction consistent with the phrasing effect and none statistically significant.

Focusing on the 109 consistent recommendations, 45.8% of these were Adams solutions, 39.4% were equal expenses recommendations, 4.6% were consistent with the equal-weights version of the Weighted Solutions Model (Harris, Messick, & Sentis, 1981), 0.0% were of the equal outcomes solution, and the remaining 11.0% fit none of the above categories. Apparently the equality norm loses its charm when one recognizes that equating final outcomes implies assigning very unequal outcome/input differences. (This is an inference; subjects were not directly asked why they were consistent or inconsistent in their recommendations.)

Weil took on the task of determining which of the various consistency-inducing manipulations Tuttle had employed was most effective in getting subjects to see the connection between the two allocation conditions (Harris & Weil, 1983). Two plant-sales-at-flea-market scenarios were employed in a 3 (Ratings of experimenter-provided allocations vs. Subjects' own recommendations vs. Both) × 2 (Explicit reminder of the outcomes-expenses connection vs. no such reminder) × 4 (Situation 1 employed in the outcomes-allocation condition, Situation 2 in expenses-allocation vs. Situation 2 in outcomes-allocation, Situation 1 in expenses-allocation vs. Situation 1 in both allocation conditions vs. Situation 2 in both) factorial design.

No statistically significant effects of any of these manipulations emerged. The overall level of consistency was much lower than that achieved in Tuttle's study (Experiment 4 of Harris et al., unpublished): 37.3% consistency for ratings of experimenter-provided allocations and 21.5% consistency for subjects' own recommendations, averaged over all other factors. A statistically significant phrasing effect was obtained: The percentage of equal outcome recommendations decreased from 32.9% to 3.8% and the percentage of equal expenses recommendations increased from 13.9% to 49.4% in the expenses-allocation condition relative to the outcomes-allocation condition.

Our current guess is that the larger number of scenarios employed in Tuttle's "heroic" study (Harris et al., unpublished) – the one factor we didn't explore in the Harris and Weil (1983) study – was responsible for his subjects' greater level of consistency. (Of course, Tuttle exposed all subjects to all 5 consistency manipulations, while only 2 of the 24 Harris and

Weil conditions combined 4 of these manipulations.) We did, however, replicate Tuttle's finding of unpopularity of the equality norm among consistent subjects. Among the 17 subjects whose $a$ parameter in the expenses-allocation condition was close to that employed in the outcomes-allocation condition, only 1 (5.9%) had an $a$ parameter of 0 (i.e., adhered to the equality norm in both conditions). In fact, across all studies that have employed a within-subjects manipulation of allocation task, the proportion of inconsistent subjects who recommend equal outcomes in the outcomes-allocation condition was 42.6%, while that same proportion among consistent subjects was only 5.9%. This finding, together with the robustness of the equity phrasing effect, would appear to pose some difficulty for those equity theorists (e.g., Messick, this book) who have suggested that the dominant ethic underlying all conceptualizations of fairness is that of equality. (Messick might alternatively be interpreted as having discovered the generic form of an equity formula – Equation (1) of the present chapter, i.e., that almost all equity heuristics involve equating some function of the outcomes and the inputs across participants.)

The equality norm appears not to be very deeply held, since adherence to this norm virtually disappears either when its application is no longer easy (i.e., when subjects are asked to specify outcome–input differences) or when its inconsistency with the equal excess norm is recognized. Allocations consistent with Adams's ratio formula and the equal excess norm, on the other hand, are recommended by sizable percentages of consistent subjects, though the absolute levels of these percentages can be expected to vary considerably across situations. (Across the five scenarios employed in Tuttle's study, for example, the percentage of equal excess solutions among consistent subjects ranged from 18.2% to 59.1%.) The one "norm" that appears to be robust across individuals and situations is that fair outcomes should be linearly related to inputs – put a bit more heuristically, that individual contributions (inputs) should be converted to deserved outcomes at the same rate (the $a$ parameter of the linear formula) for all participants.

### Conditions under which the equity formula is linear in ranks, rather than linear in inputs

If equity theory is to be successfully applied to explaining what groups will see as fair ways of distributing the results of their joint efforts, it is crucial that we have available an accurate definition of the relationship between outcomes and inputs that will be seen as "fair" (equitable). I have shown (Harris, 1976), for instance, that neither the derogation hypothesis nor the matching hypothesis dear to the hearts of equity theorists actually follows from equity theory if the equity formula employed fails to meet the fundamental criterion that fair outcomes should increase as inputs increase. The derogation hypothesis states that when you have harmed another by causing that other's relative outcome to be lower than your own, you can move closer to equity by lowering your estimate of the victim's inputs. The matching hypothesis states that mating and dating couples tend to be matched in their rank orders on socially valued dimensions. Further, I demonstrated (Harris, 1980) that subjects "care about" the quantitative details of the equity formula, in that they demand more of an outcome–input relationship than that it meet the fundamental criterion, and have strong preferences among alternative equity formulas even when they all satisfy the fundamental criterion. Similarly, different equity formulas rank order dating and mating couples differently in terms of the degree to which they feel inequitably treated (and thus in the predicted longevity of their relationship), even if the alternative formulas all satisfy the fundamental criterion. Finally, if an equity formula that accurately describes what subjects see as a fair relationship between outcomes and inputs could be developed for situations where measurement of the outcomes ($O_i$s) and the inputs ($I_i$s) was relatively nonproblematic, this functional relationship could then be used to assign numerical values to more qualitative inputs or outcomes.

I have summarized (Harris, 1983) a great deal of evidence that the linear equity formula, Equation (1), does an excellent job of accounting both for mean outcomes and for individual subjects' recommendations for fair outcomes. On the other hand, Mellers (1982, 1986) provides clear evidence of *non*linearity in the outcome–input relationship. This nonlinearity is attributed by Mellers to a general tendency for subjects in any experimental situation to behave as if they feel that their responses should be distributed evenly across the full range of the scale provided. I attribute (in Harris, 1983) the nonlinearity instead to a tendency for subjects to simplify a complicated task (that of allocating outcomes fairly) by making their recommended outcomes linearly related to the *rank order* of the inputs, rather than to the actual numerical values of those inputs. These alternative explanations have identical implications for the observed outcome–input functional relationship and thus cannot be decided between on the basis of the obtained functional relationship alone. Regardless of the explanation for the nonlinearity, however, it is important to specify the conditions under which it occurs.

Mellers obtains good fits to her data by assuming that each subject's recommended outcomes are a weighted average of two tendencies:

(a) A tendency to make outcomes a linearly increasing function of subjective inputs (where subjective inputs are a monotonic transformation of the objective inputs). This tendency is, of course, exactly as described by Equation (1), and may be referred to as the linearity-in-inputs, or LII component of Mellers's model.

(b) A tendency to distribute responses evenly across the available response scale. This second component can also be explained as a preference for linearity, rather than as a preference for uniformly distributed responses: If the respondent gave recommendations that were linearly related to the *rank order* of the inputs, rather than to their numerical values, the resulting outcomes would indeed be uniformly distributed and thus systematically *non*linearly related to the unequally spaced inputs. We can thus refer to this second tendency as the linearity-in-ranks, or LIR component, and we can express Mellers's "psychological relativity" model as

$$O_i = (1 - w)\text{LII}_i + w\text{LIR}_i, \tag{3}$$

where

$\text{LII}_i = aI_i + r$ for some positive choice of $a$;
$\text{LIR}_i = bR_i + d$ for some positive choice of $b$;

and

$R_i =$ the rank order of participant $i$'s input within the distribution of all $n$ participants' inputs ($1 =$ rank of the lowest input, $n =$ rank of the highest input).

Mellers actually assumes that the LII component applies to *subjective* inputs that need only be monotonically related to the objective inputs. Ignoring this distinction, as I usually do, may thus underestimate the goodness of fit of Equation (3) to data.

A precondition for discriminating between linearity in ranks (LIR) and linearity in inputs (LII) is that the participants' inputs not be evenly spaced across the range of inputs. (If the inputs are evenly spaced, then both LIR and LII imply equally spaced outcomes.) Given that this precondition is met (e.g., by Mellers's 1982 use of both positively and negatively skewed distributions of inputs, and her 1986 use of bimodal and unimodal distributions), what situational aspects might be conducive to subjects' adopting (or being influenced by) LIR, rather than solely by LII? Two candidates emerge from a comparison of the input distributions typically employed by Harris versus those employed by Mellers: the number of participants (and thus the total number of inputs in the distribution) and the degree of nonuniformity (unequal spacing) of those inputs. I (1980; Harris & Joyce, 1980) usually use four- or five-participant situations, whereas Mellers (1982, 1986) employed 13 participants. And the sets of inputs I employed have generally not departed grossly or systematically from fairly even spacing. Both differences are, moreover, consistent with my preferred explanation of LIR being invoked as a means of simplifying a difficult allocation task, in that both a large number of participants and a highly nonuniform distribution of inputs might be expected to increase the difficulty of applying a linear formula to the actual numerical values of the inputs.

I thus decided to test the possibility that increasing the number and/or the degree of skewness of the inputs would (a) increase the difficulty of the allocation task and thus (b) increase the degree to which subjects' allocations of outcomes are influenced by a tendency to employ a linear relationship between outcomes and the ranks (rather than the actual numerical values) of the inputs.

There are a number of properties of outcomes conforming to Equation (3) that can be used to gauge the degree to which subjects are being influenced by LII versus LIR considerations. These will be introduced as the appropriate measures and significance tests are described in the Results section.

## Method, Experiment 1

### Subjects

Subjects for this study were 74 students in introductory psychology courses who volunteered to participate in exchange for extra-credit points on their final exams. Eight subjects omitted recommendations for one or more of the participants in one or both of the scenarios they were assigned, so that total $N$ for some analyses was as low as 66.

### Design

Four scenarios were employed, each involving the assignment of salaries to the faculty members in a department at a hypothetical university, based on the available salary pool and on the salary that had been recommended for each faculty member by "an objective outside observer (or panel of such observers)" who had "read each member's annual report on his activities and accomplishments for the year" and had then been asked, "Given this faculty member's publications, service, teaching, and years at the University, what salary do you think s/he deserves for the next academic year?" In each case the sum of these objective merit (deserved-salary) ratings exceeded the total money allocated to the department for salaries by about 25%, so that the respondent couldn't simply adopt the committee's recommendations as his or her own, but had to treat the committee recommendations as an overall merit (input) measure.

Each subject made recommendations for two departments: one 5-member department and one with 13 faculty members, with about half of the subjects responding to the 5-member scenario first and about half making their recommendations in the reverse order. About half of the subjects were confronted with merit ratings that were nearly uniformly distributed for both of the departments, and about half made recommendations for two departments whose merit ratings were strongly negatively skewed. The overall design was thus a 2 (nearly uniform vs. skewed distribution) × 2 (5-member department vs. 13-member department first) × 2 (5-member department vs. 13-member department) factorial design, with the third factor manipulated within subjects.

### Questionnaire

Subjects' recommended salaries were gathered via a three-page questionnaire. The first page was headed "Fair Salary Allocation Procedures" and explained to the subject that "We are interested in what people see as the fairest way to determine salaries for the members of an organization" and then gave an overview of the subject's task. The second and third pages were headed by the name of a department, followed by a table whose three columns gave an alphabetic label for each faculty member, that faculty member's "Merit Rating (Deserved Salary)," and blank spaces in which the subject was to fill in the "Recommended Salary" for that faculty member. The sum of the merit ratings appeared at the bottom of that column, and the total to which the recommended salaries were to add (with a footnote designating it as "Total salary pool; your recommended salaries must add to this number") appeared at the bottom of that column. Next, a 5-point scale for the subject's "Rating of difficulty of task" appeared, with "1" labeled as "Very Easy" and "5" as "Very Difficult."

### Input distributions

The two 13-partner sets of inputs were linear transformations of Mellers's (1982, Experiment 3) nearly uniform and negatively skewed input sets. The negatively skewed distribution was chosen because it produced a greater departure from linearity in Mellers's experiment than did the positively skewed distribution. The inputs were transformed from Mellers's merit ratings (which ranged from 0.5 to 3.5 in steps as small as 0.1) to a range that constituted realistically possible annual salaries so as to make the subject's task a bit less abstract. The 5-member set of inputs corresponding to each 13-member set was chosen so as to match it in sum and range and as closely as possible in the squared correlation between inputs and their ranks ($r_{IR}^2$). The resulting four sets of inputs and their essential properties are listed in Table 1.

### Results, Experiment 1

### Task difficulty

An analysis of variance (ANOVA) on the task difficulty ratings yielded a main effect of number of participants, $F(1, 69) = 36.418$, $p < .001$, with the mean difficulty rating being 2.86 for the 5-input tasks and 3.49 for the 13-input tasks. Contrary to prediction, the rated difficulty of the uniform distributions (3.30) was slightly *higher* than for the negatively skewed distri-

Table 1 *Properties of input distributions*

| Condition | Inputs (thousands of $) | Step sizes | Inputs and ranks[a] |
|---|---|---|---|
| u5 | 20, 27, 35, 43, 50 | 7, 8 | .999 |
| u13 | 20, 23, 25, 27, 30 | 2, 3 | .999 |
|  | 33, 35, 37, 40, 43, 45, 47, 50 |  |  |
| n5 | 16, 33, 38, 42, 46 | 17, 5, 4 | .875 |
| n13 | 15, 20, 25, 30, 35, | 5, 2, 1 | .877 |
|  | 37, 38, 40, 41, 42, 43, 44, 45 |  |  |

[a] The higher this figure, the more nearly uniform the distribution.

butions (3.05). The corresponding ANOVA using whether or not the subjects' recommended inputs summed to the correct total as a dichotomous dependent variable again showed the main effect of number of participants (19 of 73 errors when making recommendations for 13 faculty members versus 5 of 73 subjects making the same mistake for a 5-input distribution) as the only statistically significant effect, $F(1,69) = 13.37$, $p < .001$. The uniform and negatively skewed distributions yielded 12 errors each in sum of recommended salaries.

### Outcomes versus inputs and input-ranks

Table 2 reports a number of statistics based on the correlations between outcome (recommended salary) and input (deserved salary) or input-rank.

For describing the relationship between mean outcomes and inputs we need not look beyond the two processes of Mellers's (1982) psychological relativity model, LII (linearity in inputs) and LIR (linearity in ranks). If these two processes perfectly accounted for the $\overline{O}_i$ versus $I_i$ relationship we would obtain a multiple $R^2$ for $\overline{O}$ predicted from the numerical value of the input ($I_i$) and the rank order of that input ($R_i$) of 1.0. The squared multiple correlation was .999 or higher for each of the four number-of-participant/distribution-shape combinations. We can turn, then, to a consideration of the relative magnitudes of the LII and LIR tendencies.

If subjects recommended outcomes that were linearly related to the actual numerical values of the inputs, then the squared correlation between input and outcome ($r_{OI}^2$) for each subject, as well as that between input and mean outcome across all subjects ($r_{\overline{O}I}^2$), would equal 1.0, while the squared correlations with input-rank ($r_{OR}^2$ and $r_{\overline{O}R}^2$) would each equal the squared correlation between input and input-rank ($r_{IR}^2$). The reverse would be true if subjects gave recommendations that were linearly related to input-ranks – that is, if they attended only to the linear-in-ranks (LIR) component of Mellers's (1982) two-component psychological relativity model. As Table 2 shows, the squared correlation between input and mean outcome ($r_{\overline{O}I}^2$) was

Table 2 *Correlations among outcome, input, and input-rank, Experiment 1*

| | Distribution | | | |
|---|---|---|---|---|
| | Nearly uniform | | Negatively skewed | |
| Statistic | 5 Inputs | 13 Inputs | 5 Inputs | 13 Inputs |
| Squared $r$ betw. mean outcome and input | .9997 | .999 | .998 | .997 |
| Squared $r$ betw. mean outcome and rank | .999 | .999 | .90 | .91 |
| Squared multiple $R$ for mean outcome vs. input and rank | .9997 | .999 | .99997 | .999 |
| F for departure of means from linearity in inputs | .80 $w$/3, 30 | 3.01* $w$/11, 19 | .23 $w$/3, 31 | .18 $w$/11, 23 |
| F for departure of means from linearity in ranks | .83 $w$/3, 30 | 2.85* $w$/11, 19 | 1.18 $w$/3, 31 | .91 $w$/11,23 |
| F for departure of means from LII, LIR combined | .78 $w$/2, 30 | 2.80* $w$/10, 19 | .39 $w$/2, 30 | .89 $w$/10, 22 |
| Mean individual $r$ between outcome and input | .99 | .98 | .99 | .96 |
| Mean individual $r$ between outcome and rank | .99 | .98 | .94 | .92 |
| F for difference between mean $r$'s with input, rank | 2.29 $w$/1, 31 | .36 $w$/1, 31 | 54.46** $w$/1, 33 | 60.32** $w$/1, 33 |

*$p < .05$
**$p < .001$

.997 or higher. Furthermore, with one exception it exceeded both $r_{IR}^2$ and $r_{\hat{O}R}^2$, and the F for departure from LII was statistically nonsignificant. Contrary to the prediction that nonlinearity would increase with degree of skewness of the inputs, the exception was the 13-partner, nearly uniform condition (u13), where $r_{\hat{O}R}^2$ exceeded the squared correlation with inputs (.9988 versus .9986) and where there was statistically significant evidence for departure from LII (as well as from LIR), $F(11,19) = 3.01$ and 2.85, respectively, $p < .05$ in each case.[1]

Mean outcomes that are very nearly linearly related to inputs could arise from individual-respondent outcome–input relationships that are quite nonlinear in compensating ways. It is therefore important to consider how well the LII and LIR processes described individual subjects' recommendations. As Table 2 shows, the mean correlation between individual recommendations and inputs varied from .96 to .99 across the four number-of-partners/distribution shape combinations and was greater than the mean correlation with input-ranks in all but the u13 condition, with this evidence of greater reliance on LII than LIR being highly significant in the two negatively skewed conditions ($F(1, 33) = 53.11$ and 60.32, respectively).

## Discussion

The present study failed in its attempt to determine the conditions under which the relationship between inputs and outcomes will be substantially nonlinear. That condition of Mellers's (1982) Experiment 3 that appeared (on the basis of visual inspection of the graphs provided) to show the greatest departure from linearity (the 13-partner, negatively skewed-inputs, or n13, condition) yielded statistically nonsignificant nonlinearity in the present study, and the only condition to yield statistically significant evidence of nonlinearity was instead u13 (the 13-participant, nearly-uniform-inputs condition). By comparison, reading mean salaries from Mellers's graphs and correlating them with the merit ratings yielded squared correlations of from .89 to .97 across the three negatively skewed conditions of her Experiment 3, version 1. It is clear that there is simply a lot less nonlinearity to be explained in the present study than in Mellers's data. Nevertheless such small departures from LII mean that if "real-world" effects are closer to those of the present study than to those of Mellers (1982, 1986), the best answer to the question of when LIR considerations are likely to be of sufficient magnitude to require going beyond the general linear formula, Equation (1), is probably "never."

It is far from clear how to account for this lower magnitude of LIR-based effects in the present study. What *is* clear is that the hypotheses that attention to LIR considerations is triggered primarily by difficulty of the decision making task, and that difficulty is an additive function of number of participants and nonuniformity of the input distribution, receive no support in the present study. First, task difficulty, whether measured by self-report or error rate, appears to be a function solely of number of participants. Second, and more tellingly, the conditions that appear to be most difficult for subjects are not the same as those that yield the greatest evidence for attention to LIR considerations. Indeed, there is logical and anecdotal evidence that calls into question the whole notion that employing LIR is an easier way of allocating outcomes than is employing LII. First, the presumed greater ease of employing LIR vanishes if subjects give it less than 100% weight ($w < 1$), since generating a weighted average of the LII and LIR solutions requires that both sets of recommendations be generated so long as $w$ doesn't equal 0 or 1. In the present study only 13 of 210 individual estimates of $w$ were 1.0. Second, in a pilot study perpetrated upon social psych lab students at the University of Georgia I had each student generate both LII and LIR solutions for four scenarios very similar to those of the present study, recording time-to-solution and providing a rating of the difficulty of the task for each scenario. The results showed significantly more errors, significantly longer times to solution, and mean ratings significantly closer to the "very difficult" end of the scale for the LIR solutions. These findings were confounded somewhat with these students' having had extensive instruction in and practice with Equation (2) before serving as pilot subjects, but they certainly don't suggest that spontaneous resort to LIR is apt to be most subjects' first response to a difficult allocation task.

What, then, does lead to a respondent's recommended salaries' showing evidence of having been influenced by LIR considerations? The only remaining difference between Mellers's scenarios and mine that I was able to think of upon completion of this study was the linear transformation of her 0.5 to 3.5 merit ratings into less abstract deserved salaries covering a $30,000 range, and I was unable to think of a rationale for this difference being an important one. Hindsight stimulated by a reviewer and by subsequent data demonstrating the importance of this variable were about to provide such a rationale.

### Experiment 2: Importance of input scale

An anonymous referee pointed out that range–frequency effects (the tendency to give responses that are evenly distributed across the response scale, regardless of the spacing of stimuli) of the sort from which the nonlinearity of the outcome–input relationship obtained in Mellers's studies can be derived are generally obtained only when the stimulus and response scales are qualitatively different. (Cf., e.g., Tversky, Sattath, & Slovic, 1988.) It is thus possible that what I had thought was an "innocent" transformation from Mellers's abstract merit rating scale to "deserved salaries" that I hoped would make the allocation task a bit more concrete to UNM students was instead a manipulation of a crucial mediating variable. It seemed important to check this possibility, implausible though it seemed to me.

### Method, Experiment 2

#### Subjects

Fifty-nine subjects were recruited as in Experiment 1, with the exception that between the two studies the UNM introductory psych subject pool was switched from a purely voluntary, extra-credit system to a course requirement (with the writing of brief research-article reports as an alternative). Three of the subjects recommended outcomes that were nonmonotonically related to the inputs.[2] These subjects' data were thus dropped from further analyses, leaving 56 subjects.

#### Questionnaires

Each of the four questionnaire types employed in Experiment 1 was used in this study. In addition, a second version of each was created by replacing the "deserved salary" inputs with merit ratings on an abstract, 0.5 to 4.0 scale. In the 13-partner scenarios the merit ratings were those em-

ployed by Mellers (1982, Experiment 3) in her nearly uniform and negatively skewed scenarios. (This was just a matter of reversing the linear
transformation by which these sets of merit ratings had been converted to
deserved salaries in designing Experiment 1.) In each 5-partner scenario
the merit ratings were a linear transformation of the deserved-salary inputs
for the corresponding 5-partner condition. Thus each 5-partner, merit-rating
set of inputs was matched with its corresponding 13-partner, merit-rating
input set in the same way as were the deserved-salary scenarios: in terms
of number of distinct step sizes, range of inputs, and squared correlation
between inputs and rank-ordered inputs.

For the abstract-merit-rating questionnares, the first (cover) page omitted any mention of deserved salary, and the second page's column of inputs was headed "Merit Rating" and did not have the sum of the inputs
listed at the bottom of the column.

## Results, Experiment 2

### Task difficulty

Experiment 1's findings with respect to difficulty ratings were replicated,
in that the only statistically significant effect was the main effect of number
of participants, $F(1,48) = 13.02$, $p < .001$, with mean difficulty ratings being
2.35 for the 5-input tasks and 3.06 for the 13-member departments.

### Outcomes versus inputs and input-ranks

As Figure 1 most clearly demonstrates, the nature of the input scale had a
clear, dramatic effect on the (non-)linearity of the outcome–input relationship when there was enough difference between LIR and LII recommendations (i.e., a sufficiently low $r_{IR}^2$) for any nonlinearity to be visible to the
statistically naked eye.

Table 3 backs up this graphic evidence with quantitative measures of fit.

LII and LIR both provided close fits to subjects' mean recommended
salaries across all nearly uniform conditions ($r_{OI}^2$ and $r_{OR}^2$ both $> .99$ in all
cases), with no appreciable nonlinearity. In the negatively skewed conditions, however, mean outcomes were almost perfectly fit by LII ($r_{OI}^2 = .997$
versus $r_{OR}^2 = .91$) when deserved salaries were employed, but almost perfectly fit by LIR ($r_{OR}^2 = .992$ versus $r_{OI}^2 = .92$) when abstract merit ratings served
as inputs.

## Discussion, Experiment 2

Experiment 2 would appear to have resolved the discrepancy between Mellers's consistent finding of a nonlinear relationship between fair outcomes
and inputs when inputs are nonuniformly distributed and my consistent

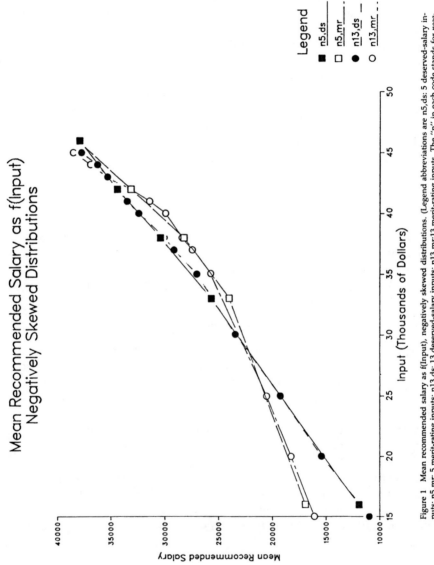

## Mean Recommended Salary as f(Input)
## Negatively Skewed Distributions

**Legend**

- ■ n5,ds
- □ n5,mr
- ● n13,ds
- ○ n13,mr

Figure 1  Mean recommended salary as f(Input), negatively skewed distributions. (Legend abbreviations are n5,ds: 5 deserved-salary inputs; n5,mr: 5 merit-rating inputs; n13,ds: 13 deserved-salary inputs; n13,mr:13 merit-rating inputs. The "n" in each code stands for *negatively skewed*. A number of means for different conditions were so close as to hide one plotting symbol behind another.)

Table 3 *LII vs. LIR, ignoring order, Experiment 2*

| Condition | Squared correlation between mean outcomes and | |
|---|---|---|
| | Actual input | Rank-ordered input |
| u5 | .99 | .998 |
| u13 | .996 | .997 |
| n5, Des Sal | .998 | .90 |
| n5, Abstr | .92 | .99 |
| n13, Des Sal | .996 | .92 |
| n13, Abstr | .93 | .991 |

(until Experiment 2 was completed) finding of a strongly linear input–outcome relationship regardless of input distribution. When we use inputs (in the present case, committee-recommended salaries that are said to summarize a variety of relevant performance dimensions) that are expressed in dollars and cents (such as the net sales – reflecting the time, effort, and ability devoted to the group effort – that had heretofore been used in all of the studies conducted by me and my colleagues), we get no evidence of any but trivial departures from linearity; when we use abstract merit ratings as inputs (as has been the case in all of Mellers's equity studies) we get very clear evidence of a tendency toward a linear relationship between outcomes and rank-ordered inputs – and thus substantial departures from linearity between outcomes and the actual numerical values of the inputs.

What is somewhat more problematic is how to characterize the conceptual dimension underlying the distinction between deserved salaries and abstract merit ratings. Mellers and Birnbaum (1982) and Tversky et al. (1988) identify the crucial distinction as that between *within-modality* versus *cross-modality* judgments, with stimulus-spacing effects coming into play only when the stimulus and response dimensions are qualitatively different (as in the present case of abstract merit ratings versus dollars of salary). This suggestion has a strong claim to our acceptance in that it was used to explain Experiment 1's failure to replicate Mellers's usual finding of an influence of LIR *before* Experiment 2 had been run.

Nonetheless my own post hoc speculation (after having been very skeptical that such a logically irrelevant transformation from deserved salaries to identically spaced merit ratings would affect the linearity of subjects' responses) is that the crucial distinction is instead the extent to which the dimensions along which the inputs and outcomes are stated are taken seriously as, in essence, providing interval-scale (rather than purely ordinal) measurement of those individual contributions and individual outcomes. My preference for this interpretation of the input-scale effects in Experiment 2 stems in part from my continuing skepticism about the suggestion

that subjects have an aesthetic preference for uniformly distributed responses, and my even greater skepticism that such an aesthetic preference
would be operative if and only if those responses lay along a qualitatively
different dimension than did the stimuli. (Mellers, personal communication, emphasizes that the tendency toward uniformly distributed responses is purely an "as-if" device for generating the psychological relativity predictions and that she has no commitment to any particular process
generating that tendency.)

My preference is also driven by the intuitive appeal the *linear increments
model* has as a description of a self-monitoring process that I *can* imagine
subjects following to arrive at outcomes consistent with linearity in ranks.
Once a set of recommended outcomes that satisfy the "fundamental criterion" of a monotonic increasing relationship to inputs has been constructed, subjects faced with very unevenly spaced inputs might also apply
a second, somewhat less fundamental criterion: Do the sizes of the *differences* between pairs of recommended outcomes bear a consistent (e.g., linear) relationship to the corresponding differences in inputs? For instance,
is it fair that Participant C's increment of $5,000 over B's input is being
rewarded with a $4,000 increment in outcome, while I'm recommending
that same $4,000 increment be applied to Partner E's outcome relative to
D's even though the difference in inputs is only $1,000 for those two par-
ticipants? While most subjects will probably not be especially concerned
about the form of the function relating outcome-difference to input-
difference, it will probably be reasonably well approximated by a linear
function. It can be shown[3] that if this relationship *is* linear, that is, if

$$O_{i+1} - O_i = c(I_{i+1} - I_i) + e,$$

then Equation (3) will fit the subject's recommended outcomes perfectly
with

$$w = \frac{1}{1 + x(c/e)}$$

where $x = (I_{max} - I_{min})/(n-1)$. If $c = 0$ (all differences between adjacently ranked
outcomes equal to a constant, $e$), $w = 1$ and LIR fits perfectly. If $e = 0$ (outcome differences directly proportional to input differences), $w = 0$ and LII
fits perfectly. If (as in the example) the input dimension is one for which
relative spacing (comparison of differences) seems meaningful, this second-order comparison will be taken seriously and the spacing of recommended outcomes will be adjusted toward proportionality of outcome and
input increments, and thus toward linearity in inputs. If, however, relative
spacing along either the input or the outcome dimension is not considered
meaningful (e.g., "So what if the B−C difference in merit ratings is 0.5
units while the D−E difference is 0.1 units? All that matters with such a
fuzzy dimension as merit ratings is whether your rating is higher than

someone else's."). This second-order comparison never gets made (or if made is not taken seriously enough to trigger adjustment of the relative spacing of recommended outcomes) and, on average, the differences in adjacent outcomes are left approximately equal and linearity in ranks describes the resulting relationship between subjects' mean recommended outcomes and the inputs quite well.

The crucial test of the two alternative explanations would be to find two qualitatively distinct dimensions that could be used for inputs and outcomes, respectively, and that we're confident subjects would "take seriously" as providing meaningful information about differences, rather than simply providing a rank ordering of relative contributions or of relative outcomes. Alternatively one might attempt through instructions to induce subjects to treat, say, deserved salaries as carrying only ordinal information and see if this leads to the same shift to LIR that use of abstract merit ratings does, despite the within-modality nature of this stimulus–response pairing. Be sure to let me know how these experiments turn out.

### The (fairly) big picture

Let's return to the claim made at the beginning of this chapter: that attempting to pin down the quantitative details of the equity formula leads to substantive insights into the processes governing allocation of outcomes. To what extent were the two insights offered in this chapter dependent on quantitative (algebraic?) examination of the equity formula?

Our insight into the difference in number of processes dictating subjects' equity judgments when input and outcome dimensions match, versus when they don't, can hardly even be summarized except in the context of quantitative models. The linear increments model – which essentially proposes a process by which psychological relativity theory's predictions might come to describe subjects' recommendations – suggests that linearity-in-rank (LIR) considerations arise (and the linear equity formula is thus not fully adequate) when subjects follow a *simpler* process (checking only for the relationship between outcomes and inputs and *not* for the relationship between outcome differences and input differences). On the other hand, the process used (in as-if fashion) to derive psychological relativity theory (subjects' tendency to distribute their responses uniformly across any response scale) implies that LIR considerations arise when subjects follow a *more complex* process (worrying about the distribution of their responses across the outcome scale in addition to the outcome–input relationship). Whether nonlinearity of the outcome vs. input relationship indicates a more or a less complex underlying process thus awaits a test of whether a preference for uniformly distributed responses or concern for the relationship between outcome differences and input differences best accounts for nonlinearity in the outcome–input relationship.

The equity phrasing effect could, admittedly, have been uncovered by any researcher who became suspicious of the depth of commitment to equal final outcomes represented by subjects' choice of the equal outcomes solution in the typical equity experiment. However, the push toward within-subjects manipulation of allocation task and the resultant discovery that "consistency and equality don't mix" came from algebraic manipulations of the linear equity formula that showed that alternative explanations of the phrasing effect implied quite different relationships between the $a$ parameters adopted by a given subject in the two conditions. (See Harris, 1983, and especially Harris et al., unpublished, for details of these differential predictions.)

Finally, a third insight that space precludes treating in any detail here: Anderson (1976) has suggested that situations involving negative inputs are so different from those in which all participants make positive contributions that equity theory must simply be declared inapplicable to negative-input situations. One advantage of such a declaration would be to "rescue" Adams's ratio formula from its violation of the fundamental criterion that outcomes should increase monotonically with inputs. However, this "rescue" is effective only if negative outcomes are also ruled out, since Adams's ratio formula also violates the fundamental criterion when all inputs are positive but some outcomes are negative (Harris, 1976). A number of studies (e.g., Harris, 1980; Harris & Joyce, 1980; Harris, 1981) have established that the version of equity theory embodied in the general linear formula, Equation (2), handles negative-input situations quite well. However, those studies have all involved positive total outcomes ($\Sigma O_i$) for the group as a whole. It remains possible that situations in which the group must share a loss differ in important ways from those in which they must share a gain. However, a meaningful comparison between loss-sharing and gain-sharing situations is only possible if we can distinguish between differences attributable to the difference in the *sign* of $\Sigma O_i$ from those attributable to the fact that $\Sigma O_i$ is algebraically *lower* in the negative-total-outcomes situation. As demonstrated in Harris et al. (1981), the Weighted Solutions Model accounts quite well for the change in the linear formula's $a$ parameter as (positive) $\Sigma O_i$ is varied across situations involving the same set of inputs. In particular, I showed (in Harris, 1991) that the WSM implies that the $a$ parameter should be a positive linear function of $\Sigma O_i$. We can thus employ 3 or more positive-outcome conditions to establish (by linear projection) what $a$ parameter to expect in a negative-outcome situation if the same process (taking a weighted average of the recommendations of the equality norm, the equal excess norm, and Adams's ratio formula) underlies the sharing of losses and the sharing of gains. I conducted such a study (Harris, 1991) and found that, when the lowest-input partner's minimal contribution was due to neglect of responsibilities, rather than to an accident, subjects gave significantly lower weight to Adams's ratio formula in the negative-outcomes situation than they did in the three positive-outcome situations. The $a$ parameter for the negative-outcome condition did not, however, depart significantly from the straight line fitted to the three positive-outcome conditions in the low-fault condition – in part because a substantial proportion of the subjects followed Adams's formula in that situation despite its violation of the fundamental criterion. The main point for present purposes is that the fitting of a quantitative model for the changes in the $a$ parameter with changes in $\Sigma O_i$ (which in turn requires convincing demonstration that the general linear formula fits subjects' recommendations in each of the situations) is a necessary precondition for a meaningful test of differences between loss-sharing and gain-sharing situations.

The attempt to pin down the equity formula thus has the potential to contribute substantive insights into allocation processes, rather than being solely a preoccupation of those few of us who favor formal modeling of social psychological phenomena.

### References

Anderson, N. H. (1976). Equity judgments as information integration. *Journal of Personality and Social Psychology, 33*, 291–299.

Harris, R. J. (1976). Handling negative inputs: On the plausible equity formulae. *Journal of Experimental Social Psychology, 12*, 194–209.

(1980). Equity judgments in hypothetical four-person partnerships. *Journal of Experimental Social Psychology, 16*, 95–115.

(1981). The phrasing effect: Easy way out or aversion to negative shares? *Australian Psychologist, 16*, 304–305.

(1983). Pinning down the equity formula. In D. M. Messick & K. S. Cook (Eds.), *Equity theory: Psychological and sociological approaches.* New York: Praeger.

(1985). *A primer of multivariate statistics* (2d ed.). Orlando, FL: Harcourt Brace Jovanovich.

(1991). What's so special about negative total outcomes? Presented at the meetings of the American Psychological Society, Washington, DC.

Harris, R. J., & Joyce, M. A. (1980). What's fair? It depends on how you phrase the question. *Journal of Personality and Social Psychology, 38*, 165–179.

Harris, R. J., Messick, D. M., & Sentis, K. P. (1981). Proportionality, linearity, and parameter constancy: Messick and Sentis reconsidered. *Journal of Experimental Social Psychology, 17*, 210–225.

Harris, R. J., Tuttle, W. A., Bochner, S., & van Zyl, T. (unpublished). Is there an Equality Norm? Explorations of explanations of the phrasing effect. Unpublished manuscript.

Harris, R. J., & Weil, K. (1983). In fairness judgments, equality and consistency don't mix. Presented at meetings of the American Psychological Association, Anaheim, CA.

Mellers, B. A. (1982). Equity judgment: A revision of Aristotelian views. *Journal of Experimental Psychology: General, 111*, 242–270.

(1986). "Fair" allocations of salaries and taxes. *Journal of Experimental Psychology: Human Perception and Performance, 12*, 80–91.

Mellers, B. A., & Birnbaum, M. H. (1982). Loci of contextual effects in judgment.

*Journal of Experimental Psychology: Human Perception and Performance, 8,* 582–601.

Messick, D. M., & Sentis, K. P. (1979). Fairness and preference. *Journal of Experimental Social Psychology, 15,* 418–434.

Tversky, A., Sattath, S., & Slovic, P. (1988). Contingent weighting in judgment and choice. *Psychological Review, 95,* 371–384.

Walster, E., Walster, G. W., & Berscheid, E. (1978). *Equity theory and research.* Boston: Allyn and Bacon.

### Notes

1 Neither $F$ would have been significant had the univariate approach to testing repeated-measures effects been employed, since the variance across subjects for linear trend was from 13 to 167 times as high as that for the lowest-variance trend component, leading to univariate-approach $F$s for quadratic and higher-degree trend components that were grossly (often more than 50 times) lower than multivariate-approach $F$s, which take into account each trend component's reliability across subjects. (See Harris, 1985, sec. 3.8, for a discussion of this issue.)

2 Further, their response sheets showed evidence of erasures consistent with having generated a monotonic set of outcomes, noticed that their recommended outcomes didn't sum to the total available salary pool, and then modified one or two recommendations so as to add up to the correct figure without considering the overall pattern.

3 Without some additional assumption, estimation of the relative weight given the LIR versus the LII component is confounded with differences in the $a$ and $b$ (degree-of-differentiation) parameters of the two respective components. If we assume that LIR is purely a distributional criterion and thus set $a/b$ to a value that equates $(\text{LIR}_{max} - \text{LIR}_{min})$ to $(\text{LII}_{max} - \text{LII}_{min})$ – that is, we assume that the two sets of recommendations the subject averages together imply the same difference in outcomes between the highest- and lowest-input participants – then the expression for $\hat{w}$ becomes

$$\hat{w} = \frac{(r_p - r_{obs})}{x\left(\dfrac{r_{obs} - 1}{I_{j+1} - I_j}\right) + (r_p - r_{obs})} \qquad (4)$$

where $r_p = (I_{i+1} - I_i)/(I_{j+1} - I_j)$; $r_{obs} = (O_{i+1} - O_i)/(O_{j+1} - O_j)$; and $x = (I_{max} - I_{min})/(R_{max} - R_{min})$ = the ratio between the total range of inputs and the total range of input-ranks (which equals number of participants$-1$). This formula yields a $\hat{w}$ that decreases monotonically from unity to zero as $r_{obs}$ increases from 1.0 to $r_p$, and is negative for all cases where $r_{obs}$ exceeds $r_p$. For outcome-difference ratios where $r_p < \dfrac{x}{I_{j+1} - I_j}$, however, values of $r_{obs}$ below unity yield $\hat{w}$s that first increase to $+\infty$ and then drop to $-\infty$ as a discontinuity is crossed. Of course subunity values of $r_{obs}$ occur only when the larger of two increments in input has yielded the smaller increment in outcome and are thus unlikely.

# 4 Judgments of distributive justice

*Maya Bar-Hillel and Menahem Yaari*

## Background

Consider three formulations of what is often referred to as the basic psychological rule of distributive justice, which were expressed over a time span ranging from antiquity to the present. "Justice involves at least four terms, namely two persons for whom it is just and two shares which are just. And there will be the same equality between the shares as between the persons, since the ratio between the shares will be equal to the ratio between the persons; for if the persons are not equal, they will not have equal shares" (Aristotle, 1967, p. 269). In a more contemporary formulation, Jouvenel (1957, p. 149) stated similarly that what people "find just is to preserve between men as regards whatever is in question the same relative positions as exist between the same men as regards something else." Homans (1961, p. 249) expressed this rule somewhat more formally, as follows: "Distributive justice involves a relationship between . . . two persons, $P_1$ and $P_2$, one of whom can be assessed as higher than, equal to, or lower than, the other; and their two shares, or . . . rewards, $R_1$ and $R_2$. The condition of distributive justice is satisfied when . . . : $P_1/P_2 = R_1/R_2$." Similar models were suggested by Adams (1965), Anderson (1976), and Walster, Berscheid, & Walster (1973).

Although these formulations are in agreement that distributive justice amounts to some sort of proportionality between "investments" and "rewards," they are silent on just what might be the dimensions or attributes that, when individuals are found to differ in them, justify giving these individuals unequal shares. This problem is still largely unresolved. There can be, and are, many standards – and therefore many empirical predic-

In one form or another, this essay has been around for several years, and has been presented in many forums. The list of people from whose comments it has benefited is too long to detail. We wish to thank them all.

tions – as to what constitute investments, or, for that matter, rewards. For some people or historical periods, for example, even "ancient lineage counted as a legitimate investment, . . . , [or] being a man rather than a woman . . . [or] a white rather than a black" (Homans, 1961, p. 245). The main goal of this chapter is to question the feasibility of having a single rule for all distribution-of-goods contexts, combined with an attempt to elucidate the nature of the inputs ("investments") and outputs ("rewards") that do preserve its form.

The characteristics that can provide a possible justification for departure from equality are discussed most extensively in philósophical writings (see, e.g., bibliographical listings in Rescher, 1966). The variables that might entitle different people to justly deserved differences in allocation can be classified in terms of the following six broad categories (Yaari & Bar-Hillel, 1984, p. 7):

  i. differences in rights or in legitimate claims;
  ii. differences in effort, in productivity, or in contribution;
  iii. differences in endowments;
  iv. differences in needs;
  v. differences in tastes, or in the capacity to enjoy various goods;
  vi. differences in beliefs.

Many discussions in social philosophy, political science, and the theory of jurisprudence are concerned with category i. Category ii has been the focus of *equity theory* (e.g., Adams, 1965; Walster et al., 1978). There, the proportionality rule is called "the contributions rule," stressing that justice in equity theory typically emphasizes proportionality to what individuals actually *do* toward deserving the reward (in contrast to the variables in the other categories, which focus on what people *are*). In the prototypical situation that is studied in equity theory, two people jointly perform a task, with one striving or contributing more to the completion of the task than the other, and the dependent variable is the manner in which the reward for successful task completion is divided between them.

Category iii encompasses a body of research regarding bargaining situations that has been conducted by experimental economists. In the simplest paradigm, recipients must bargain their way to a joint agreement on how to divide some reward or good between themselves, else risk losing it altogether (e.g., Camerer & Loewenstein, this volume; Guth, 1988; Selten, 1978). The observed results are then compared with normative predictions based on game theoretical considerations on the one hand, and with predictions derived from notions of justice or fairness, on the other. This tradition fits within category iii insofar as the difference between the bargaining powers and capabilities of the players can be construed as a difference in endowments. The present study addresses categories iv, v, and vi, as will presently be described.

Equity theory and the behavioral theory of distributive justice, as often admitted by their own proponents, are at once too broad and too narrow. On the one hand, their interpretation of the basic rule of distributive justice is not specific enough. An example in equity theory is: Suppose that A and B jointly perform some task, and that A has invested twice as much effort as B, yet A's productivity was three times higher than B's. Should A's reward be three times or twice as high as B's – that is, proportional to effort or to productivity? Both of these possibilities are compatible with the contributions rule. An example in the behavioral theory of distributive justice is: Suppose that A and B, whose investments in some task are equal, are being paid for it in lottery tickets. However, in case of a winning ticket, A's prize is twice as high as B's (Roth & Murnighan, 1982). Would A and B be concerned with how to divide *probabilities to win* (i.e., should they get equal numbers of tickets), or with how to divide *monetary expectations* (i.e., should B get twice as many tickets as A)?

On the other hand, theories that have incorporated the basic rule of distributive justice have disregarded its potential generality. Homans (1976), for example, stated that there are "important cases in which the rule of distributive justice is . . . treated as wholly irrelevant. One of these is the case of need" (p. 237). He seems to have ignored the possibility that the selfsame rule – namely, proportionality – could serve as the appropriate rule of distributive justice just as well in the case of needs, except that the parameters characterizing the "ratio" between $P_1$ and $P_2$ would be parameters of need, rather than of contribution. Indeed, the proportionality rule is flexible enough to subsume even a rule of strict equality. One need only take "personhood" (or what Guth has called "the personal investment standard") to be the sole basis for determining the allocation of some goods – as it is, for example, in the case of certain political or legal rights.

The present study focuses on the last three categories (needs, tastes, and beliefs). What these categories roughly share with each other, and not with the other three categories, is that they characterize the recipients as differing in the value or utility they derive from the things being distributed. In other words, a given good is valued differently by A and by B either because A needs it more (iv), or because he likes it more (v) or because he entertains different beliefs about it (vi), than B. On the other hand, in categories i–iii, the good may have equal value to both recipients, but for various reasons one recipient claims entitlement to more of it than the other.[1]

As far as we know, ours is the first effort of its scale to collect systematic empirical data on the question of what is judged to be a just division of simple bundles of consumer goods between passive recipients who differ only in one variable, taken from categories iv–vi. We will test whether, insofar as variables within these three categories will be judged as justifying deviations from equal distributions, the distributions will be governed by the basic rule of distributive justice – that is, proportionality.

*Methodology*

Most of the empirical studies of distributive justice observe how people in the real world, or subjects in a psychological laboratory, actually divide a given bundle of goods between them. In contrast, this study elicited people's judgments of justice via their answers to a set of hypothetical, schematic questions, of the form: In such and such a situation, how ought a given bundle be divided for the division to be *just?* This approach can be labeled "empirical philosophy."[2] The scholars who proposed normative theories of distributive justice relied, after all, on their personal intuition. What we have done is increase the size of the sample of introspectors.

Besides its obvious pragmatic advantages, is this methodology viable? We believe that "justice" can usefully be studied via "judgments of justice," and that these judgments can justifiedly be elicited to hypothetical questions, for the following reasons.

A research strategy that has often been fruitful in psychology is to study people's subjective or intuitive judgments of variables whose ontological status is independent of such judgments, and which can be defined or measured in some objective fashion that does not rely on judgment. Comparisons of subjective judgments with their objective counterparts has led to interesting psychological insights. A notable example is Weber-Fechner's law, the psychophysical "law of diminishing returns." Other examples from perception are the phenomenon of the color wheel, uncovered by the study of color perceptions against wavelength, and the phenomenon of size constancy, uncovered by the study of color perceptions against wavelength, and the phenomenon of size constancy, uncovered by the study of perceived size of objects against retinal and real world size.

With respect to other constructs, the study of people's judgments can pay off not only by shedding light on the psychology of the judge, but also by modifying the conceptualization of the very construct being judged. Such, to some extent, has been the case of the concept of rationality in choice under uncertainty (see survey in Tversky & Kahneman, 1986).

For yet other constructs, the reliance of theories thereof on intuitive corroboration is even more pronounced. In the philosophy of language, for example, theories of meaning, of reference, or of truth have little hope if they come into serious conflict with people's intuitive judgments of meaning, reference, or truth. In other words, the facts of the matter that such theories need to meet seem to be not out there in the real world, but embedded in people's minds. Thus, in modern linguistics, grammaticality is actually defined via the grammatical intuitions of suitable speakers (Chomsky, 1957).

The successful history of theories of "hard" physical constructs such as mass or space set a model that other areas of inquiry have always hoped to emulate. It is far more likely, however, that "soft" constructs such as morality or beauty will prove ultimately to be in the eyes of the beholder, in the sense that a theory of these constructs will have no independent standing from a theory of judgments thereof. Such also, we believe, is the construct of distributive justice. At the very least, intuitions about specific cases serve alongside theoretical conceptions in a mutual process of self-correction that Rawls (1971) called "reflective equilibrium" (see also Yaari & Bar-Hillel, 1984).

Granting that judgments of justice are a legitimate topic of inquiry, there remains the question of how these judgments are to be elicited. One could ask people directly about various principles (e.g., "A distribution is not just if each of two recipients envies the other's share"), or describe situations and ask for an evaluation of how just the described distribution is (the approach chosen by Kahneman, Knetch, & Thaler, 1986a,b, in their study of fairness; see also Mellers, 1982). In the present study, we elected to give people hypothetical distribution problems, and asked them to solve them justly. We are not necessarily confident that were subjects actually given the goods and instructed to distribute them justly, the same distributions would have emerged (although by the time a real-world situation could be created that is as pure as the hypothetical one, it is hard to see why the actual distributions would differ from the hypothetical ones). Nonetheless, the focus of this research is precisely the ethical notions in people's minds – not their actual behavior. Actual behavior is inevitably contaminated by political, strategic, and other considerations. Likewise, "psychological experiments . . . are interpreted solely in terms of justice concerns, whereas one or more other motives are often involved such as politeness, fear of retaliation, status assertion, and impression management" (Furby, 1986, p. 161). Admittedly, hypothetical judgments are also subject to contamination, by demand characteristics, social desirability, and other factors. Yet hypothetical problems allow more control, and, moreover, it is people's expressed sentiments (namely what they say ought to be done) rather than their revealed ones (namely what they actually do) that primarily guides the search for a *normative* theory of justice, as well as the rhetoric of public debate on issues of distributive justice.

### The problem set

Before we can spell out the rationale and motivation behind our choice of variables and questions, it is necessary to describe these in some detail. The questions used in the present study share some common structure. Each describes a bundle consisting of either one or two goods, and two recipients characterized by a single attribute on which they are said to differ. The respondents were each given a single question, and asked to indicate the way the bundle should be divided between the two recipients in order for the division to be *just*. No explanation was offered (or solicited) for what was meant by "just." An example follows:

A shipment containing 12 grapefruit and 12 avocadoes is to be distributed between Jones and Smith. You, the respondent, are asked to do the dividing. The following information is given:

- Jones's metabolism is such that his body derives 100 milligrams of vitamin F from each grapefruit consumed, while it derives no vitamin F whatsoever from avocado.
- Smith's metabolism is such that his body derives 50 milligrams of vitamin F from each grapefruit consumed, and also 50 milligrams vitamin F from each avocado.
- Both persons, Smith and Jones, are interested in the consumption of the fruits only insofar as they contain vitamin F (and the more the better). All the other traits of the two fruits such as taste, etc., are of no consequence to them.
- After the fruits are divided between them, Jones and Smith will not be able to trade, or to transfer fruits to any third person.
- The fruits are to be divided between Jones and Smith in a manner that is as *just* as possible. How would you do it?

The respondents were then asked to choose one of a number of suggested distributions, or to indicate any other distribution they wished. For the present question, which we denote $N_{2a}$,[3] the response options were as follows:

| | | | |
|---|---|---|---|
| \_\_\_\_a. | *Jones:* | 12 grapefruit and 0 avocado | (yielding 1200 mg vitamin F) |
| | *Smith:* | 0 grapefruit and 12 avocado | (yielding 600 mg vitamin F) |
| \_\_\_\_b. | *Jones:* | 9 grapefruit and 0 avocado | (yielding 900 mg vitamin F) |
| | *Smith:* | 3 grapefruit and 12 avocado | (yielding 750 mg vitamin F) |
| \_\_\_\_c. | *Jones:* | 8 grapefruit and 0 avocado | (yielding 800 mg vitamin F) |
| | *Smith:* | 4 grapefruit and 12 avocado | (yielding 800 mg vitamin F) |
| \_\_\_\_d. | *Jones:* | 6 grapefruit and 0 avocado | (yielding 600 mg vitamin F) |
| | *Smith:* | 6 grapefruit and 12 avocado | (yielding 900 mg vitamin F) |
| \_\_\_\_e. | *Jones:* | 6 grapefruit and 6 avocado | (yielding 600 mg vitamin F) |
| | *Smith:* | 6 grapefruit and 6 avocado | (yielding 600 mg vitamin F) |
| \_\_\_\_f. | Some other distribution (specify): _____ | | |

These distributions are the respective "solutions" to problem $N_{2a}$ provided by the most prominent distribution mechanisms that have been studied in the economic literature on axiomatic distributive justice (see Yaari and Bar-Hillel, 1984).[4] For present purposes, it suffices to note that these distributions roughly correspond to several simple arguments or considerations that might guide intuitions about distributive justice. Two dichotomies are of particular interest: whether it is the fruits themselves or their vitamin content that should be divided equally, and whether the conflict between the two recipients extends to the entire bundle, or only to the part desired by both. Option e is the simplest division possible – to split the shipment straight down the middle and give each recipient exactly identical shares. Since, however, Jones has no interest in avocado, and Smith is indifferent between avocado and grapefruit, it is also possible to equalize their *total number* of fruits, if not the fruits themselves, thereby bettering the lot of Jones without detracting from that of Smith, as in a. Now, however, vitamin content is no longer equally divided. Option c restores equality of vitamin F allotment, while bettering the position of both recipients as compared with e. Option d is the result of giving Smith all of the avocado, in which Jones is not interested at all, and splitting the disputed grapefruit down the middle. Option b cannot be as simply argued for (and indeed, we shall see in the Results, was hardly ever chosen).

$N_{2a}$ is one of the more complicated questions we used. Other questions differed from it on one or more of the following dimensions (though not in a complete factorial design):

1. The shipment consisted of but one good (e.g., grapefruit).
2. The numerical parameters characterizing Jones and Smith were altered (e.g., "50 milligrams" was replaced by "20 milligrams").
3. Jones and Smith were said to differ not in their metabolic capacity, but rather in other attributes (to be elaborated below).
4. The distribution is to be carried out not by the respondent, but by the recipients themselves, with the respondent asked to predict its outcome.

There were other minor variations in problem formulation, which will be spelled out as their results are presented.

### Rationale and motivation

This study was an exploratory one, and at its inception was not guided by any well-defined set of hypotheses. The questionnaires were administered over some time, and later questions were often prompted by the responses to earlier questions. Readers may find, as they read through the tables of results, that they wish a certain question had been included that wasn't, or that they can think of a testable explanation for some result, or that they would like to take some notion a step further. We often encounter suggestions like that when presenting this study in lectures, as well as in some of the reviews this chapter underwent. Indeed, one of the exciting possibilities we see in this line of research is the ease with which new hypotheses can be tested by appropriate modifications of the problems. The results reported here represent a large body of data, but it is somewhat arbitrary in nature and scope. Our conclusions should be seen as interim, with no pretence to closure or completeness. Here, nonetheless, is the rationale behind the major choices and manipulations.

Though problems were set in a concrete context, it was deliberately schematic. In the problems we called Needs problems, calling the good "vitamin" was intended to induce respondents to think of it as answering a physiological need (though the vitamin is F, for "fictitious"), and to think of the recipients as differing only with respect to this need. In other problems, the recipients were portrayed as differing on other dimensions. One was their liking for the fruits (e.g., when operationalized by their willingness to spend money on them: "Jones likes grapefruit very much, and is willing to pay up to $1.00 per pound for them; he detests avocado, and never buys it. Smith likes both equally, though they are not his favorite fruits, and is willing to pay up to $.50 per pound for them"). We called these Tastes problems, and in them, the good was said to be consumed solely for its taste. This, of course, is the kind of stipulation that can only be asserted in artificial problems such as ours. Another was their beliefs about the vitamin F content of the fruits (e.g., "Jones believes that each grapefruit contains 100 milligrams vitamin F, whereas the vitamin F content of avocado is nil; Smith believes that each grapefruit and each avocado contain 50 milligrams of vitamin F"). We called these Beliefs problems.

The manipulation of the dimension on which the recipients were said to differ is the major manipulation of this study. Recall the formulations of the proportionality rule with which we opened. All three of them were context neutral, suggesting that the basic rule of distributive justice is determined by form rather than content. This is a very strong assumption, and one shared by economic theories of distributive justice as well, but it is by no means obvious. Clearly, some differences between people might justify a deviation from equal split in the allocation of goods while others might not (e.g., Needs seem more compelling than Beliefs). Also, the direction or the extent of the deviation might differ from context to context (e.g., when vitamins are extracted from fruit, less efficient extractors might be compensated by more fruit, but when pleasure is extracted, perhaps less efficient extractors ought to expect less fruit). Moreover, people might exhibit context sensitivity even to problems that lend themselves to the same abstraction in terms of utility. For example, it might matter to people whether Smith actually derives just as much vitamin F from a grapefruit as from an avocado, or whether Smith only thinks he does, and is in fact wrong. In both cases, Smith values the grapefruit and the avocado the same, though they really differ. Would people generally advocate a distribution based on the actual facts of the matter, even though it might appear unjust to Smith, or would they advocate the distribution that appears just to Smith? Insofar as they prefer "justice seen" to "justice done," they might advocate different distributions under different beliefs, even when the facts of the matter are unchanged. Alternatively, if they prefer "justice done" to "justice seen," they might advocate the same share for Smith even when Smith's subjective value for his share changes.

Most of the other manipulations were for purposes of control. The parametric manipulations were intended largely to test the robustness of particular quantitative aspects of the distribution rule. For example, it is reasonable in problem $N_{2a}$ to expect that it is the ratio of the metabolic capacities of the two recipients that matters, rather than the absolute numbers themselves, which represent arbitrary units in this fictitious context. By altering the numbers in a manner that either does or does not maintain the ratio, this expectation can be tested. Moreover, altering some parameters allows us to infer which properties of a particular distribution caused it to be chosen (e.g., is a chosen because it results in the maximum combined vitamin intake, or the maximum for Jones?), or to test the limits to which subjects will deviate from equal split when there seems to be cause for doing so. These things will be spelled out explicitly in the appropriate place in the Results section.

The decision to use no more than two-goods bundles was dictated by considerations of simplicity. Single-good bundles are the simplest there are, but they are so simple that they don't allow for certain tests. For example, in comparing any two divisions of a single good, the gain of one recipient is almost always accompanied by the loss of the other. Such divisions are known in the economics literature as "Pareto optimal." Two-goods bundles, on the other hand, allow for pairs of divisions in which both recipients are better off in one than in the other (e.g., c versus e in $N_{2a}$). Is the appeal of the equal split (which is the prima facie contender for embodying distributive justice) stronger when it is Pareto optimal than when it is not? This question cannot be studied with bundles consisting of a single good. Of course, there are research opportunities that are only provided by complicating the bundles even further, which we declined in this study.

The total number of minihypotheses that are tested in this study almost equals the large number of problems reported. It would be easier to discuss these alongside and in sequence with the corresponding results.

### Method

#### Subjects and procedure

The respondents were mostly applicants for admission to the Hebrew University of Jerusalem over a number of years. This population consists of roughly equal numbers of men and women, most between 18 and 24 years of age, of different socioeconomic and ethnic backgrounds, but all with a high school level education. They received the question (in Hebrew) in the context of their university entrance exams,[5] though it was clearly set apart from the rest of the exam. Each respondent received a single question, and was given just a few minutes to answer. (A pilot study determined that this time was amply sufficient, since the necessary computations were already done for the subjects. We also have data showing that respondents with no time limitations give essentially the same answers.[6]) Some of the subjects were given open-ended questions, but over 90% of their answers coincided with one of the options given in the closed versions, and most of the other 10% were computational errors. The number of respondents to each question ranged widely, but is typically between 60 and 80.

## Results and discussion

It is suggested that the readers peruse the appropriate table while reading this section, as tables will be discussed and explained practically row by row.

### Needs, one good

We start by seeing whether differences in needs are considered sufficient grounds for departure from equality, and – if so – whether the basic rule of distributive justice will govern the pattern of the departure. For this purpose, it is simplest to consider a one-good problem. Subjects were told, "Jones's metabolism is such that his body derives 100 milligrams vitamin F from each grapefruit, whereas Smith derives 20 milligrams from each grapefruit."

Of 73 respondents, 16% chose the equal split 6:6, and 82% chose the distribution 2:10 (see row a in Table 1). This distribution can readily be considered proportional: In order to extract a given amount of vitamin F Smith both needs (input) and gets (output) five times as many grapefruit as Jones.

Several others of the questions jointly support an estimate that close to 90% of people take "distributive justice" in such a problem to mean that the goods are to be divided in proportion to metabolic need, even if this leads to a deviation from equality. This was replicated when the parameters were doubled (to 200 mg and 40 mg, respectively, b); when only Smith's parameter was altered (from 20 mg to 50 mg, c); when subjects were asked to predict how Jones and Smith themselves would divide the grapefruit (d). (Similarly, p and r, to be described shortly, also differ only on the dividing agency, with little effect on their respective response distributions, although when we manipulated the dividing agency from the respondent to the recipients *within* subjects, as in t and u, the popularity of 6:6 rose quite a bit.) It also made no difference if the question was explicit on whether Jones and Smith know and like each other (e) or not (f).

Even when self-interest was introduced, this pattern persisted. When asked to imagine that they themselves were one of the recipients, 95% of those put in place of Jones (g), and 79% of those put in place of Smith (h), chose 2:10. Compared with the typical 90% favoring 2:10 over 6:6, it seems that the introduction of self-interest into this problem promoted generosity rather than greed. The combination of hypothetical questions, low stakes, and social desirability may render this tendency suspect, yet it is in line with the everyday courtesy of choosing the smaller of two pieces when one gets first choice, as well as with studies (e.g., Guth, Schmittberger, &

Table 1 *Needs, one good*

| Fruits (Jones: Smith): | | 6:6 | 2:10 | 12:0 | 0:12 | |
|---|---|---|---|---|---|---|
| Vitamin content: | Jones | 600 | 200 | 1,200 | 0 | |
| | Smith | 120 | 200 | 0 | 240 | N[a] |
| a. Prototype.[b] | | 16 | 82 | 0 | 1 | 73 |
| b. Both parameters are doubled.[c] | | 14 | 86 | 0 | 0 | 88 |
| c. 20 mg is changed to 50 mg.[c] | | 5 | 94 | 0 | 1 | 80 |
| d. Like a, but the recipients divide. | | 10 | 90 | 0 | 0 | 136 |
| e. The recipients like each other.[d] | | 8 | 92 | — | — | 63 |
| f. The recipients don't know each other.[d] | | 8 | 92 | — | — | 73 |
| g. You, the divider, are Jones. | | 3 | 95 | 3 | 0 | 74 |
| h. You, the divider, are Smith. | | 17 | 79 | 1 | 3 | 70 |
| i. The parameters are self-reported. | | 22 | 77 | 0 | 1 | 74 |
| j. The reported parameters are doubted. | | 43 | 55 | 2 | 0 | 49 |
| k. Smith's parameters are doubted. | | 45 | 52 | 2 | 0 | 44 |
| l. Minimum 100 mg. | | 8 | 92 | 0 | 0 | 73 |
| m. Minimum 200 mg. | | 8 | 91 | 1 | 0 | 65 |
| n. Maximum 200 mg. | | 8 | 91 | 0 | 1 | 85 |
| o. Minimum 240 mg. | | 11 | 53 | 11 | 25 | 64 |
| p. Minimum 600 mg. | | 38 | 20 | 42 | 0 | 65 |
| q. Minimum 1,200 mg. | | 16 | 26 | 59 | 0 | 70 |
| r. Minimum 600 mg, recipients divide. | | 30 | 29 | 41 | 0 | 73 |
| s. Vitamin F is easy to get elsewhere. | | 25 | 75 | 0 | 0 | 65 |
| t. Part 1 like a; | | 15 | 83 | 2 | 0 | 60 |
| Part 2 like d[c] (the recipients divide). | | 36 | 63 | 2 | 0 | 56 |
| u. Part 1 like q; | | 4 | 25 | 69 | 0 | 72 |
| Part 2 (the recipients divide). | | 27 | 39 | 34 | 0 | 70 |
| v. Part 1 like q; | | 9 | 27 | 64 | 0 | 82 |
| Part 2 like n. | | 15 | 82 | 3 | 0 | 74 |
| w. Part 1 like c + p[c]; | | 39 | 51 | 9 | 0 | 58 |
| Part 2: There are 18 grapefruits.[c] | | 0 | 100 | 0 | 0 | 60 |
| x. Smith needs 5 times more vitamin than Jones. | | 10 | 90 | 0 | 0 | 31 |

[a] The Ns do not include the subjects who gave some other answer. This number exceeded 5 for only two questions (k and o), and had an overall median of 1.5.
[b] "12 grapefruit are to be distributed between Jones and Smith. Jones derives 100 milligrams of vitamin F from each one, while Smith derives 50 milligrams."
[c] Whenever a change in the problem parameters necessitated a change in the answer parameters, the required change was naturally made.
[d] A dash indicates that this option was not spelled out for the subjects.
[e] A few subjects answered only one part of these questions, hence the N for the two parts may differ.

Schwarze, 1982) which found that subjects, when put in a position where they alone determine how some reward is to be distributed between themselves and another, "nearly never ask for more than their fair share . . . and if the rewards are rather low, they even deviate . . . to their own disadvantage" (Guth, 1988, pp. 6–7)

Of the manipulations attempted, only two altered the 90%:10% preference for proportionality. First, in three problems (i, j, and k), the information about the difference in metabolism between Jones and Smith was attributed to self-report by the recipients, and the problems hinted, more or
less strongly, that such reports might be self-serving. The questions added:
"You have no way of verifying Jones's and Smith's real metabolism," and
then went on to say one of the following: "but neither do you have any
reason to doubt their report" (i); or "but you have grounds for doubting
their report" (j); or "but you have grounds for doubting Smith's report"
(k). The popularity of the equal split 6:6 rose from the usual 10% to 22%,
43%, and 45%, respectively. (It is not surprising that there was so little
difference between j and k, given that only Smith's report, if doubted, is
self-serving.) This result supports a tenet of Guth's behavioral theory of
distributive justice: "To qualify for an investment . . . a variable must be
generally observable and measurable." Otherwise, "people would start to
pretend." So "one will often rely on the personal standard [i.e., equality]
if . . . inputs . . . cannot be easily observed" (p. 7).

The second manipulation involved stating alleged minimal or maximal
vitamin F levels required by the body, "according to scientific studies."
When this level was specified as being 200 mg (or 100 mg), then 2:10 –
which provides each recipient with exactly 200 mg of the vitamin – was
still the favorite of about 90% of the subjects (l, m, n). Opinions diverged
considerably, however, with higher minimum levels (o, p, q, r). Between
36% and 59% of the respondents chose 12:0 (or 0:12), which is the ultimate
departure from either equality or proportionality – presumably since any
other distribution is useless for one or both recipients. Nonetheless, there
was concurrently an increase in the popularity of the equal split 6:6, despite its wastefulness. Perhaps the subjects opting for 6:6 reasoned that if
no good were done to the recipients by deviating from equality to proportionality, then such a deviation should not be condoned. Note that if proportionality *is* useful (as in w part 2, where the number of grapefruit was
increased to 18) its appeal is restored – and with a vengeance (*all* subjects
chose it!).

Finally, if the need is made less acute, as when subjects are told that
"vitamin F is plentiful in many common foods, and can be bought cheaply
in pill form in any drug store" (s), the percentage of subjects who favor
proportionality over equality drops somewhat to 75%.

The results reported in Table 1 establish that Needs matter, in that they
bestow on recipients an entitlement for a share that is, where feasible, proportionately responsive to their need. Thus, when two recipients of some
medically required homogeneous good differ in the extent to which they
need the good, approximately 90% of subjects endorse a departure from
equality to meet this need. However, these problems fail to distinguish
between two senses of proportionality: (1) that *fruits* are divided in proportion to how much of them one needs to extract a given amount of vitamin

Table 2 *Needs, two goods*

| | 6:6 | 8:0 | 6:0 | 9:0 | 12:0 | |
|---|---|---|---|---|---|---|
| Grapefruit (Jones: Smith) | 6:6 | 8:0 | 6:0 | 9:0 | 12:0 | |
| Avocado (Jones: Smith) | 6:6 | 4:12 | 6:12 | 3:12 | 0:12 | |
| Vitamin content: Jones | 600 | 800 | 600 | 900 | 1,200 | $N^a$ |
| Smith | 600 | 800 | 900 | 750 | 600 | |
| a. Prototype (see text). | 11 | 80 | 1 | 6 | 2 | 84 |
| b. Like a, but the recipients divide. | 5 | 84 | 0 | 10 | 1 | 81 |
| c. 50 mg is changed to 20 mg.[b] | 4 | 82 | 6 | 6 | 1 | 83 |
| d. Like c, but the recipients divide.[b] | 5 | 80 | 3 | 8 | 5 | 64 |
| e. 50 mg is changed to 9.1 mg.[b] | 17 | 38 | 27 | 6 | 12 | 52 |

[a] The Ns do not include the subjects who gave some other answer. These numbers were 0, 2, 3, 4, 0, respectively.
[b] Whenever a change in the problem parameters necessitated a change in the answer parameters, the required change was naturally made.

(i.e., in inverse proportion to metabolic efficiency), or (2) that *vitamins* are divided in proportion to how much of them one needs (in these problems, recipients needed, and got, the same amount of vitamin). The final question, x, put this to the test. Smith was not less efficient in his metabolic capacity for extracting vitamin F, but he was said to require five times as much of it as Jones. If distribution were according to metabolic efficiency, 6:6 would thus have been the favored distribution. However, 90% of our respondents opted to give Smith five times as many grapefruit, in proportion to his vitamin requirements. We shall call this *N-proportionality:* The division gives each recipient the same proportion of the total needed to achieve a given welfare level.

*Needs, two goods*

*The case for N-proportionality.* In the set to which we now turn, the shipment is said to contain not one good but two – grapefruit and avocado. The prototype for this set is $N_{2a}$ (above). Of 84 respondents, 80% chose to give Jones 8 grapefruit, and Smith all the rest (a). This distribution gives each recipient an unequal share of the bundle, but one that ensures them an equal amount – 800 mg – of the vitamin F. Recall that in the single-good case, the favored distribution typically divided the fruits in inverse proportion to the recipients' metabolic efficiency: Smith, who extracts *less* vitamin from each fruit than Jones, was judged entitled to proportionately *more* fruits. Here, however, the fruits are no longer divided in inverse proportion to metabolic efficiency. Thus, although Jones metabolizes avocados more efficiently than Smith, he gets *more* than half of them. Clearly, it is vitamins rather than fruits that are divided in direct proportion to need, in accordance with $N$-proportionality. Since the recipients, though they differ in their metabolic characteristics, have an equal need for the vitamin, the shipment is divided proportionately to that need, namely, so as to equalize vitamin shares.

*Justice versus efficiency.* It is a coincidence of the present parameters that splitting both types of fruit down the middle also gives the recipients equal, though smaller (600 mg) amounts of vitamin F. When Smith's parameters are altered to indicate that he extracts 20 mg, rather than 50 mg, from each fruit, two notable changes occur. First, the equal split is no longer $N$-proportional – Jones gets 600 mg vitamin F, whereas Smith gets only 360 mg. Second, $N$-proportionality can now yield at most 400 mg vitamin F to each recipient – and this no longer Pareto-dominates the equal split (since Smith's lot improves, while Jones's decreases). It is noteworthy, therefore, that about 80% of the respondents still recommend $N$-proportionality (c, d).

The fact that upon departure from equal split, Smith's gain in terms of vitamin milligrams is less than Jones's loss in the same terms, entails that, in the limit, compensating Smith for his metabolic weakness sends both shares – and the value of the shipment in its entirety – plummeting to zero. This consideration is not lost on our subjects. When Smith is said to be able to metabolize but 9.1 mg vitamin F from each fruit (e), equalizing vitamin shares ceases to be the majority response. Only 38% of the respondents still recommend it. The appeal of the equal split is not, however, much enhanced thereby: Only 17% of the respondents recommend it. This is understandable when we realize how wasteful the equal split is. It gives Jones 6 avocados, in which he has no interest and which could profitably go to the weaker Smith. In other words, the equal-split distribution is not Pareto efficient, and most respondents seem to wish to give Pareto efficient recommendations. It is as if they were saying: "Even if we don't use $N$-proportionality, let's improve on strict equality. Let's resort instead to some more sensible version of equality." Some (27%) do so by splitting only the disputed part of the shipment (i.e., the grapefruit), leading to a share of 6 grapefruit for Jones, and all else for Smith, while others (12%), instead of splitting both types of fruits equally, split only the total number of fruits equally, resulting in 12 grapefruit for Jones and 12 avocados for Smith.

One might pause here and ask whether we have not tainted distributive justice considerations with distributive efficiency ones. Since the wording of our instructions did not change across the problems, we believe that our respondents were concerned with justice equally across the board. On the other hand, clearly the gross inefficiency of the $N$-proportional solution in some problems is affecting its appeal. It seems that many respondents feel that destroying the good being divided in the name of some formal principle (such as "to each in proportion to his need") is intuitively unacceptable.[7]

We encountered something similar in Table 1, where an impossibility of awarding both recipients their minimum vitamin F requirement decreased the appeal of the N-proportional solution considerably (o, p, q, r).

In conclusion, the results reported in Table 2 reconfirm that in distributing goods that are consumed to meet a need, such as some medical requirement, over 80% of people prefer N-proportionality to strict equality. This figure holds whether or not the favored distribution is Pareto-efficient. But efficiency also matters, since N-proportionality becomes less acceptable when it cannot be achieved without considerably diminishing the combined value of the distributed goods.

### Beliefs, one good

Hitherto, subjects were told, as an objective medical fact, that Jones and Smith extract different amounts of vitamin from the fruits being divided. Recall that the overwhelming willingness to take account of this difference was somewhat diminished at the suggestion that it is known with less than certainty, as when based on self-report (Table 1, i, j, k). What would happen if the difference between Jones and Smith were only in how much vitamin F each *believed* he could extract from the fruits, rather than in how much each actually extracted from them?

Hammond (1982) argued persuasively that such differences in people's beliefs are not sufficient to justify deviating from the equal split, because a distribution must strive to be considered just ex post (after all relevant information is known), not ex ante (under the conditions of uncertainty existing when it is made). Whether his apriori argument is intuitive was tested in the next set of problems, where the information regarding the recipients' metabolic capacities was replaced by information regarding their beliefs about grapefruit, as follows:

Jones believes that each grapefruit contains 100 milligrams vitamin F, whereas Smith believes each grapefruit to contain 20 milligrams.

It was stressed that the truth of the matter is not known. In response to the prototyical question, the equal split was preferred by 60% of 77 subjects (see Table 3, a). Since the problem implies that Smith and Jones do not differ in their need for vitamin F, the equal split here is also the N-proportional solution. Nonetheless, as many as 40% recommended a 2:10 split. This distribution fails not only to equate the amount of vitamin F that Jones and Smith get, but also to equate what each of them believes they both get – only the equal split can do that. But 2:10 can still be perceived as a kind of proportionality: It equates the vitamin level that each recipient *respectively believes* he gets, namely, both recipients believe their own share of vitamin F to be 200 mg. We shall label this RB-proportionality: The proportion that one recipient believes he obtained equals the proportion that the other recipient believes he got.

Table 3 *Beliefs, one good*

| Fruits (Jones: Smith): | | 6:6 | 2:10 | 12:0 | 0:12 | |
|---|---|---|---|---|---|---|
| Vitamin content: | Jones | 600 | 200 | 1,200 | 0 | |
| | Smith | 120 | 200 | 0 | 240 | $N^a$ |
| a. Protype.[b] | | 60 | 40 | 0 | 0 | 77 |
| b. Both parameters are doubled.[c] | | 60 | 40 | 0 | 0 | 45 |
| c. 20 mg is changed to 50 mg.[c] | | 61 | 37 | 0 | 3 | 71 |
| d. Like a, but the recipients divide. | | 72 | 28 | 0 | 0 | 54 |
| e. The recipients like each other.[d] | | 60 | 40 | — | — | 139 |
| f. The recipients don't know each other.[d] | | 60 | 40 | — | — | 126 |
| g. You, the divider, are Jones. | | 67 | 33 | 0 | 0 | 94 |
| h. You, the divider, are Smith. | | 58 | 42 | 0 | 0 | 53 |
| l. Minimum 100 mg. | | 60 | 38 | 2 | 0 | 97 |
| m. Minimum 200 mg. | | 42 | 54 | 1 | 3 | 78 |
| n. Maximum 200 mg. | | 38 | 62 | 0 | 1 | 66 |
| o. Minimum 240 mg. | | 62 | 22 | 7 | 10 | 73 |
| p. Minimum 600 mg. | | 65 | 20 | 15 | 0 | 60 |
| q. Minimum 1,200 mg. | | 37 | 27 | 36 | 0 | 67 |
| a'. Prototype + true content known. | | 74 | 26 | 0 | 0 | 73 |
| m'. Minimum 200 mg + truth known. | | 47 | 47 | 2 | 4 | 124 |
| n'. Maximum 200 mg + truth known. | | 65 | 34 | 0 | 1 | 82 |
| o'. Minimum 240 mg + truth known. | | 45 | 15 | 5 | 35 | 66 |
| p'. Minimum 600 mg + truth known. | | 71 | 21 | 8 | 0 | 76 |
| q'. Minimum 1,200 mg + truth known. | | 56 | 28 | 16 | 0 | 43 |
| x. Jones, 10; Smith, 14.[c,d] | | 64 | 36 | — | — | 83 |
| x'. Jones, 20; Smith, 4.[c,d] | | 72 | 28 | — | — | 71 |
| y. The disputed estate story. | | 52 | 48 | — | — | 62 |
| z. Belief concerns metabolic capacity, not vitamin content. | | 50 | 48 | 0 | 2 | 54 |

[a] The Ns do not include the subjects who gave some other answer. This number exceeded 5 for only three questions (c, q', and z), and had an overall median of 1.5.
[b] "12 grapefruit are to be distributed between Jones and Smith. Jones believes that each one contains 100 milligrams vitamin F, while Smith believes each contains 50 milligrams."
[c] Whenever a change in the problem parameters necessitated a change in the answer parameters, the required change was naturally made.
[d] A dash indicates that this option was not spelled out for the subjects.

Table 3 is constructed in a similar way to Table 1, and analogous questions are designated by the same letters, to facilitate comparison. Thus, as in Table 1, b doubles both recipients' parameters, c changes only Smith's parameter, in d the recipients divide the shipment themselves, and so on. The table shows 60% versus 40% to be a robust estimate of the appeal of N- versus RB-proportionality in this question type.

As in Table 1, we included problems with information about minimal or maximal levels of vitamin requirement. When the critical level is specified as 200 mg, then 2:10 – which indulges the recipients in allowing both to believe that they are at the critical value – becomes the favored response (m, n). When it is higher (o, p, q,), only one recipient can be so indulged, so 2:10 loses about half its popularity.

We were troubled by the high percentage of subjects choosing 2:10, RB-proportionality, over 6:6, N-proportionality: After all, it is still vitamins that are the focus of these distribution problems. In an effort to make it more apparent that only the equal split gives the recipients equal vitamin amounts, we repeated some questions along with a line stating that "each grapefruit actually contains 20 mg vitamin F, though you have no way of relaying this to Jones and Smith" (a', l', m', o', p', q', respectively). This addition caused a shift from 2:10 to 6:6. The sole exception is q', where the shift was to 0:12, the distribution that gives Smith – both according to his belief and in reality – his minimal level of 240 mg. In view of the fact that Jones and Smith cannot both be satisfied in this case, this is a reasonable answer. Likewise, it is reasonable that the distribution giving Jones all 12 grapefruit – chosen by 36% of the respondents to o – was chosen by only 16% of the respondents to o'.

The last four problems in this table are not analogues of Table 1. In x and x', beliefs about the fruits' vitamin content are replaced by beliefs about the very number of fruits in the shipment. Subjects were told that – though there are 12 fruits in the shipment – Jones erroneously believes there to be 10 (or 20), and Smith believes there to be 14 (or 4). Conveniently, this allows for a clean competition between the distribution that actually gives each recipient an equal share, and the one that leaves each recipient *believing* that he got an equal share of the shipment. In contrast to the earlier questions, only a nonequal distribution can here satisfy both Jones and Smith that their share is equal to their corecipient's. At 36% (x), this distribution, believed by both recipients to be proportional, seems no more popular than RB-proportionality; moreover, when it cuts considerably into Jones's share, its popularity drops to 28% (x').

A similar question, but with a different cover story, is y: Two estranged brothers believe that their father died leaving an estate worth $1,200 or $800, respectively, although its real worth is $1,000 (Yaari & Bar-Hillel, 1984). Close to half the respondents recommended $600:$400, preferring to give each son his believed share, rather than $500:$500, his true share.[8]

In the final problem, z, the recipients' beliefs refer to their respective metabolic capacities. This is our only Beliefs problem that doesn't rule out that both recipients hold true beliefs, since their beliefs are about different things. Still, only 48% of the respondents deviated from the equal split. Recall that in problem i of Table 1, the metabolic information was said to be based on self-report. Since that problem gave no reason to doubt the reporters' sincerity, it is rather similar to the present problem z. Nonetheless, the percentage choosing 6:6 there was a mere 22%. The difference between 22% and 50% may provide an estimate of the percentage of our subjects who are actually saying "Beliefs don't matter here at all," as opposed to those who are merely saying "Needs matter here more than beliefs."

Although we labeled this problem set Beliefs, it is more accurately labeled Beliefs-about-Needs, since the divided good is still a health requirement. So RB-proportionality competed here with N-proportionality, which was so prevalent in the Needs series. Although the majority of our respondents indicated that beliefs shouldn't matter to the distribution of needs – especially when the difference between ex ante and ex post utility was stressed – there is still a sizable and stable minority who wish to accommodate beliefs, even at the price of N-proportionality.

The way beliefs were accommodated makes more sense in some questions (y, z) than in others. Indeed, it is rather odd and somewhat arbitrary to try to equalize what one recipient believes himself to have obtained to what the other recipient believes himself to have obtained. Yet the intuition that vitamins, rather than fruits, are what really matter here, combined with the appeal of equality, may have led some subjects to recommend a distribution that is hard to defend normatively. Messick (this volume) has also found that equal split is so appealing a distribution that people will apply it even at the price of inconsistency. More work is clearly needed to study how and when people wish to honor differences in beliefs in distributive justice.

### Beliefs, two goods

When the shipment contains a single good, the equal split distribution can be altered to the "to each according to his belief" distribution only by making one of the recipients worse off. But when the shipment contains two goods, *both* recipients might benefit by deviating from equal split. How would this affect the distribution of responses? Whereas in the one-good case one could argue that it is unfair to penalize one recipient for the beliefs of the other – which is what happens when Jones's share dwindles in order to accommodate Smith's belief – with two goods neither recipient should feel penalized if both can be given a bundle believed to have high vitamin content instead of one believed to have lower vitamin content. Put differently, when equal split is not Pareto optimal, then although it is N-proportional, subjects may be more reluctant to impose it on recipients.

Table 4 presents the results of a series of questions on this issue. For ease of comparison with Table 2, with which it is analogous, comparable questions are labeled by the same letter. Note the stability of the percentage of subjects choosing by RB-proportionality (i.e., equating the amount of vitamins each recipient respectively believes himself to have received) versus the equal split (which is always also N-proportional, but is not always RB-proportional, e.g., in c and e). The former percentage ranges around 55%, from a low of 40% (d') to a high of 62% (a), and the latter ranges around 35%, from a low of 16% (a) to a high of 40% (a").

Table 4 *Beliefs, two goods*

| Fruits (Jones: Smith) | | 6:6 | 8:0 | 6:0 | 9:0 | 12:0 | |
|---|---|---|---|---|---|---|---|
| | Grapefruit | 6:6 | 8:0 | 6:0 | 9:0 | 12:0 | |
| | Avocado | 6:6 | 4:12 | 6:12 | 3:12 | 0:12 | |
| Vitamin content: | Jones | 600 | 800 | 600 | 900 | 1,200 | |
| | Smith | 600 | 800 | 900 | 750 | 600 | $N^a$ |
| a. Prototype. | | 16 | 62 | 2 | 6 | 14 | 63 |
| (HU professors[b]) | | 23 | 55 | 0 | 10 | 13 | 31 |
| a'. No trading allowed. | | 34 | 51 | 1 | 5 | 9 | 80 |
| a". Trading allowed. | | 40 | 51 | 5 | 4 | 0 | 75 |
| b. Like a, but the recipients divide. | | 35 | 51 | 8 | 3 | 3 | 65 |
| c'. 50 mg is changed to 20 mg, no trade.[c] | | 31 | 54 | 7 | 4 | 3 | 68 |
| c". 50 mg is changed to 20 mg, trade.[c] | | 28 | 51 | 5 | 4 | 11 | 148 |
| d. Like c', but the recipients divide.[c] | | 33 | 40 | 9 | 6 | 13 | 86 |
| (U. Penn professors[b]) | | 32 | 45 | 0 | 10 | 13 | 31 |
| e. 50 mg is changed to 40 mg.[c] | | 26 | 52 | 5 | 5 | 11 | 61 |
| f. Two parts; part 1 like a.', | | 38 | 54 | 2 | 2 | 4 | 52 |
| part 2 like a" | | 38 | 43 | 4 | 6 | 9 | 47[d] |

[a] The Ns do not include the subjects who gave some other answer. This number never exceeded 4, and the median and mode was 0.
[b] These are the results of a group of professors of economics, who were given the question during a lecture on distributive justice and allowed to ponder them as long as they wished, even to take the question home.
[c] Whenever a change in the problem parameters necessitated a change in the answer parameters, the required change was naturally made.
[d] Five subjects answered only part 1 of these two questions.

We could discern nothing systematic in the manner in which the fluctuations in these numbers related to variations in the problems. Indeed, it is remarkable how little the numbers change in response to some of these variations. For example, one would expect the popularity of the equal split to be higher when the recipients are allowed to trade than when they are not, but this is hardly the case (a' versus a":c' versus c":f).

Recall that in the Needs two-goods series, N-proportionality was favored over equal split by roughly 80% versus 10%. The difference may result from a moral conflict that exists only in the case of Beliefs – the conflict between the desire not to impose on the recipients a distribution which they both consider inferior, and the desire to ensure them both an ex post equal share of the bundle. In the Needs series, on the other hand, both desires can be met by a single distribution, inducing more intersubject consensus.

Another comparison of interest is with the results of the single-good series (Table 3). There, 40% of our respondents endorse a departure from equality (N-proportionality) to accommodate beliefs (RB-proportionality). Only 15% additional respondents join them here, although the equal split here has two major flaws – it is Pareto inefficient, and it is coercive.

In conclusion, we see that for Beliefs, the appeal of RB-proportionality versus equal split is somewhat different for the two-goods case than for the one-good case, in contrast to Needs, where the two cases differ less. This presumably reflects the fact that Needs provide very solid grounds for departure from equality, leaving little room for other considerations, whereas Beliefs are more shaky grounds, hence more sensitive to other considerations, such as the absence or presence of coercion.

### Tastes, one good

*The case of fruits.* The next series of questions explores a new possibility. Hitherto, we explored the extent to which people view differences between recipients in needs or in need-related beliefs as grounds for departure from equality, but there was not really any question as to which direction this departure would take. It seemed obvious that the "weaker" recipient – the one who extracts, or believes he extracts, fewer vitamins from the fruits – would receive more of them, so as to bring his vitamin quota up to a par with the "stronger," more efficient recipient. This is no longer obvious, however, when what is being extracted from the fruits is not vitamins, but, in a manner of speaking, hedons.

Without entering the thicket of the debate about the possibility (not to mention the very meaningfulness) of interpersonal utility comparisons, we offer the commonplace observation that people differ in the amount of pleasure they seemingly derive from various consumed goods, activities, and so forth. Now, if "Jones is absolutely crazy about grapefruit, they being his favorite fruit of all, whereas Smith just sort of likes them," how should a shipment of 12 grapefruit be divided between them? It is not senseless to argue that, if this difference is to be accommodated at all, it is Jones, who seems to value the grapefruit more, who should get (proportionately?) more of them. This possibility is the one advocated by utilitarianism – a distribution philosophy that allocates goods according to where they can be made the most of.

Indeed, utilitarian considerations seemed to guide the intuition of respondents to the present series of questions, summarized in the top half of Table 5. In this series of questions, we used an open-ended format, since no computations were called for. For presentation purposes, we lumped together all distributions giving Jones over half the grapefruit and Smith the rest, and separately counted all those doing the reverse. Of 70 respondents, 46% didn't consider the fact that Jones likes grapefruit more than Smith[9] grounds for departure from equal split, and recommended that the grapefruit be split 6:6. But the other 55% were unanimous in alloting Jones more grapefruit than Smith (a).

Concerned that perhaps our respondents inferred from our story that Smith doesn't really care whether he gets more or less grapefruit, we added

Table 5 *Tastes, one good*

| | % of Ss choosing distribution | | | |
|---|---|---|---|---|
| Grapefruits: | Same to both | More to Jones | More to Smith | N[a] |
| a. The prototype.[b] | 46 | 55 | 0 | 70 |
| b. Both want as many as possible. | 77 | 22 | 1 | 74 |
| c. Like a, but the recipients divide. | 48 | 52 | 0 | 50 |
| d. Like b, but the recipients divide. | 70 | 27 | 3 | 112 |
| g. You, the divider, are Jones. | 93 | 0 | 6 | 59 |
| h. You, the divider, are Smith. | 55 | 37 | 8 | 76 |
| t. Two parts; part 1 like b, | 70 | 21 | 9 | 80 |
| part 2 like c. | 70 | 20 | 11 | 80 |
| i. Jones can't bring his wife. | 78 | 2 | 20 | 78 |
| j. Jones doesn't have a wife. | 85 | 3 | 12 | 75 |
| k. Jones just lost his wife. | 81 | 7 | 12 | 91 |
| l. Jones can't take much sun. | 71 | 9 | 19 | 98 |
| m. Jones can't take any sun. | 78 | 0 | 22 | 79 |
| n. Jones is 60 years old. | 52 | 43 | 4 | 23 |
| i'. Jones can't bring his wife. | — | 23 | 77 | 82(1) |
| j'. Jones doesn't have a wife. | — | 48 | 52 | 61(9) |
| k'. Jones just lost his wife. | — | 57 | 43 | 54 |
| l'. Jones can't take much sun. | — | 25 | 75 | 53(20) |
| m'. Jones can't take any sun. | — | 10 | 90 | 61(17) |
| n'. Jones is 60 years old. | — | 87 | 13 | 54(8) |

[a] Numbers in parentheses indicate subjects who refused to choose between Jones and Smith.
[b] "Jones is crazy about grapefruit; it's his favorite fruit. Smith just sort of likes it."

an explicit statement to the effect that "Smith too would like to get as many grapefruit as possible, and would not voluntarily relinquish them in favor of Jones" (b). This statement indeed served to raise the percent of subjects who opt to give Smith his "fair share" of half the fruits from 46% to 77%, but still virtually none elected to give Smith *more* than half the fruits by way of compensation for his but moderate enjoyment of them.

As we found in the other series, our respondents' predictions about how Jones and Smith would divide the shipment themselves (c, d) matched the way they would have done so as disinterested third parties, even in a within-subject question (t). Also, the present respondents showed the same tendency remarked upon in Table 1 to be generous rather than greedy when asked to put themselves in place of either Jones (g) or Smith (h). Unfortunately, our data don't allow us to assess whether the nonsymmetric distributions were truly proportional in the strict quantitative sense.

*The case of the vacation.* We were sufficiently intrigued by these results to run another series of questions, which does not resemble the usual fruit shipment questions used throughout the rest of this study. This series was designed to test the generalizability of the finding that, where hedonic rather than health considerations are concerned, "just" deviations from equality are not compensatory, but the reverse: The party who enjoys the good in question more is deemed entitled to more of it. We used the following cover story:

A firm gives out rewards to its two most outstanding employees. The first prize is an all-expenses-paid two-week vacation in a modest seaside resort for the employee and his/her spouse, and the second prize is a one-week vacation in the same place.

The two employees selected for the rewards are Jones and Smith. In spite of many efforts, it is impossible to determine which of the two is the more outstanding employee, since both are evaluated equally.

Our respondents were asked which employee should *justly* get the two-week package. In terms of *deserving* the prizes (equity), we described the two employees symmetrically. But we aimed to describe them as differing in what might be construed as their capacity for *enjoying* the prize. This we did in several ways. In some questions, Jones was said to be unable to take his wife along with him (either because she just can't come, i; or because he isn't married, j; or because she recently died after a lengthy illness, k), whereas Smith could bring his wife; in some questions, Jones was said to be sensitive to sun, hence medically limited in his ability to spend time at the beach (the limitation was either mild, l; or severe, m), whereas Smith was under no such limitations; and in a final question, n, Jones was said to be 60 years old and close to retirement, whereas Smith's age was given as 30. Note that, in contrast to the other questions in this table, we did not explicitly tell our subjects whether Jones or Smith would derive more pleasure out of time spent at the resort, but we intended that in all cases they would infer that Smith is in a position to enjoy the prize more, or at least, that it is of more value to Smith.

There were two versions to each of these six questions. In the first, we didn't force our subjects to decide which employee should get which prize, but rather allowed them to opt for a lottery-based decision. However, this option was so popular that it left us with too few subjects making the choice that was of primary interest to us. So we ran a second version in which the lottery option was unavailable.[10] The results of all twelve questions appear in Table 5.

These questions didn't yield response distributions with the stability that we encountered up to now. Compare, for example, l with m (and l' with m'). The percentage giving the longer vacation to Smith is much higher in the m's than in the l's. This might well be a reflection of the disparity between Smith's and Jones's ability to take full advantage of the vacation in m versus in l. The same factor cannot account, however, for the variance in the percentages favoring Smith in questions i, j, and k. There, all that was varied were the reasons why Jones would vacation alone, while Smith would be accompanied by his wife (thereby presumably making his vacation more pleasurable, or at least enhancing its objective monetary worth). Although the upshot of all three reasons is the same, subjects seem to be influenced by *why* Jones would be vacationing alone. The percent of subjects giving the longer vacation to Smith rather than Jones seems to decrease as a function of something like Jones's "responsibility" for his circumstances, and this in both i, j, k and i', j', k'.

Most out of line are the n questions. Whereas in the other questions, deviations from equality tended to give more vacation days to Smith, in the pair n and n', Jones was seen as meriting a longer vacation than Smith (this was even the view of 43% of the subjects who were given the lottery option). After some reflection, we came up with several possible reasons for this: (i) Contrary to our original prediction, Jones may have been seen as getting more pleasure than the younger Smith from each vacation day; (ii) Jones may have been seen as *needing* the vacation more, due to his age; (iii) Smith may have been seen as having more of a chance to win the prize again in years to come.

We are quick to admit that all this is distinctly ad hoc. The point, however, is to note how sensitive people's intuitions about distributive justice are to variables that are infinitely subtle (contrast this with the robustness of the results portrayed in the previous tables). Regardless of how one interprets the differences we found, the differences are there. In our previous paper (Yaari & Bar-Hillel, 1984), we pointed out that "beliefs and tastes cannot very easily be separated from each other" (p. 17). The present problems point out, in addition, that needs and tastes cannot very easily be separated either.

### Tastes, two goods

In the final batch of questions, we are back to fruits, the bundles now consisting of two types of fruits. We included problems in which there was no attempt to quantify the differences in the liking for the fruits (top part of Table 6), alongside problems where there was (bottom part of the table). The manner in which we attempted to quantify liking was rather simple-minded. In addition to saying that "Jones likes grapefruit very much, and dislikes oranges,[11] whereas Smith likes grapefruit and oranges equally well," we gave the maximum buying price that these two are willing to pay for the fruits, making Jones's maximal price for grapefruit either twice as high as Smith's (h, i), or five times as high (j, k). The quantification thus mimicked that of the Needs and Beliefs series.

The quantified problems were all in a forced-choice format. The unquantified problems were mostly given in an open-ended format (except for a' and b'). It did not occur to us to include among the proferred alternatives in the closed questions any distributions – beside the equal-split one – that

Table 6 *Tastes, two goods*

| Grapefruits (Jones: Smith) Oranges (Jones: Smith) | % of Ss choosing distribution | | | | | |
|---|---|---|---|---|---|---|
| | 6:6 6:6 | i:0 12-i:12 | 6:0 6:12 | i:12-i 12-i:i | 12:0 0:12 | N^a |
| | | 7≤i≤11 | | 7≤i≤11 | | |
| a. Prototype. | 6 | 12 | 0 | 16 | 66 | 67 |
| a'. Closed version of a^b. | 8 | 38 | 4 | — | 51 | 77 |
| b. Smith likes both fruits so-so. | 12 | 15 | 0 | 15 | 58 | 59 |
| b'. Closed version of b. | 8 | 35 | 2 | 2^c | 53 | 130 |
| c. Smith adores both fruits. | 11 | 16 | 3 | 37 | 33 | 63 |
| d. Like b, but the recipients divide. | 7 | 9 | 1 | 28 | 56 | 78 |
| g. Like b, but you are Jones. | 12 | 7 | 6 | 37 | 37 | 67 |
| h. Like b, but you are Smith. | 1 | 3 | 0 | 18 | 77 | 66 |
| t. Two parts; part 1 like b, part 2 like d. | 10 | 15 | 0 | 33 | 42 | 60 |
| | 17 | 15 | 0 | 34 | 45 | 60 |

| | Cash-equivalence questions % of Ss choosing the distribution | | | | | |
|---|---|---|---|---|---|---|
| Grapefruits (Jones: Smith) Oranges (Jones: Smith) | 6:6 6:6 | 8:0 4:12 | 6:0 6:12 | 9:0 3:12 | 12:0 0:12 | N^a |
| Cash value to Jones | 60 | 80 | 60 | 90 | 120 | |
| Cash value to Smith | 60 | 80 | 90 | 75 | 60 | |
| i. Jones, 10:0; Smith, 5:5. | 7 | 29 | 4 | 23 | 38 | 56 |
| j. Like i, but they divide. | 10 | 19 | 5 | 32 | 34 | 62 |
| k. Jones, 10:0; Smith, 2:2. | 7 | 35 | 7 | 9 | 43 | 46 |
| l. Like k, but they divide.^d | 21 | 13 | 6 | 8 | 52 | 48 |

^a The Ns do not include the subjects who gave some other answer. This number had a median of 2.5.
^b A dash indicates that this option was not spelled out for the subjects.
^c This option was not offered, but these two subjects chose it anyway.
^d Whenever a change in the problem parameters necessitated a change in the answer parameters, the required change was naturally made.

give Jones fruits he detests, but such distributions cropped up in the open-ended questions (see column 4 of Table 6).

Two points emerge from a perusal of the table. First, the equal-split is nowhere as popular in the two-goods problems (about 10%) as it was in the one-good problems (about 75%). The second point concerns the emergence yet again of the tendency to distribute the fruits more heavily to the recipient who values them more. Less than half the subjects attempt to equalize the cash value of the recipients' shares (see columns 1 and 2 in bottom half of Table 6). With the mild exception of question c, the most

Table 7 *Summary of results*

|                  | Equality (%) | Proportionality (%)              |
|------------------|--------------|----------------------------------|
| Needs, one good  | 10           | 90 according to needs            |
| Needs, two goods | 10           | 80 according to needs            |
| Beliefs, one good| 60           | 40 according to beliefs          |
| Beliefs, two goods| 35          | 55 according to beliefs          |
| Tastes, one good | 75           | 20 utilitarian considerations    |
| Tastes, two goods| 10           | 50 utilitarian considerations    |

popular distribution throughout the table is the one that gives Jones all of his beloved grapefruit, leaving Smith with the rest (column 5). For half the questions, this is not only the modal, but even the majority choice (a, a', b, b', d, h, k). In the quantified problems, note that this distribution maximizes the bundle's (summed) cash value.

This table also repeats the by now familiar finding that self-division versus third-party division doesn't make much difference (see b, d, t), and that some measure of altruism is encouraged by putting oneself in place of one of the recipients (g and h).

In conclusion, we find that goods prized for their hedonic value are regarded quite differently than goods prized for their importance to one's health. If one extracts (or believes that one extracts) more vitamins from a given fruit shipment one might get less of the shipment than a less efficient metabolizer. But if one extracts more hedons (i.e., more pleasure), so to speak, then one gets more fruit than if one were less efficient a "pleasure machine." This trend means that pleasure is divided in a way that enhances total value over what the equal split allows, whereas necessities are divided compensatorily, even at the price of diminishing total value.

## General discussion

Schematic, hypothetical division-of-goods problems were used to study intuitions about distributive justice. The responses of thousands of subjects, who answered scores of questions, yielded robust estimates for the percentage of our study population that hold certain distributions to be "just" solutions to various distribution problems. These percentages may not prove invariant either under changes in subject population or under changes in the problem story, but the large – and interpretable – variance between problem-type as compared with the high stability within problem-type suggests that they reveal systematic trends, and not just demand characteristics. Table 7 presents a summary of the results of our six series of questions.

A primary objective of the present study was to see whether, insofar as departures from strict equality occur, they are governed by some basic rule of distributive justice, such as proportionality. In the introduction, we argued that the proportionality rule is both too broad and too narrow to serve as a useful rule of distributive justice. We are now in a position to propose a conceptual framework for distributive justice within which some of the well-known difficulties and seeming incompatibilities that have been discussed in the literature might be resolved. According to this framework, two interrelated considerations are relevant to distributive justice – the distribution units and the distribution ideal.

The first refers to whether one thinks of the distribution in terms of the goods as they occur in their natural, observable units or packaging, or whether one has in mind some other units – either because the observable ones are seen as arbitrary, or because they are imperfectly related to what is seen as the "essential" good being distributed. The second refers to whether one aims for some particular distribution – most notably, an equal one (either of the distributed good in itself, or of some integration of it with present holdings), or whether it is the allocation rule that is of concern (most notably, some form of proportionality) rather than the form of the ensuing distribution itself. In our questions, the two were often confounded.

*What is being distributed?* A simple example might illustrate. Suppose identical money bills are to be distributed to two recipients. What would be a just distribution? The observable units are the bills, but the essential good is the money, or cash value. In this particular case, it makes no difference if one performs the division in terms of the observable units (bills), or switches to essential units (dollars) – both methods agree. Suppose, however, that the bills come in two denominations. Then it makes a difference if the distribution problem is seen to be one that concerns bills or one that concerns dollars, because they don't correspond one-to-one. If the bills came in two colors, however, but in a single denomination, then two distributions that equalized the number of bills given to each recipient, even if not their colors, would be identical in terms of the essential units.

The relationship between the observable units and the essential units can be more complicated still, because the selfsame unit of packaging could correspond to different amounts of the essential unit according to who holds it. This is what happened in our background stories, where the vitamin content of a fruit depended on who consumed it. In this case, one can neither separate the fruits into types according to vitamin content (as one can do with bills), nor convert them into more essential units (since they don't have a fixed conversion rate). Thus, one is forced to conduct the distribution in terms of fruits, even though one might feel that vitamins are the essential unit. If one could divide vitamins directly, one might prefer an equal distribution (of the vitamins), but the necessity of dividing fruits might force a deviation from equality (of the fruits). So whether the distribution is seen as equal or not depends on the units in which it is described.

Other complications ensue if, for example, the vitamin requirements of the recipients differ (e.g., Table 1, b). In such a case, neither vitamins nor fruits may be the essential unit of concern, but rather something like percent of daily vitamin requirement. In our study, the distribution that equalized percent received of the total requirement divided the fruits proportionately to need, but this will not generally be the case (e.g., suppose vitamin intake is not linear with fruit consumption).

One can easily imagine compounding such considerations further, as when bills of different denominations are divided between recipients with different needs, who live in places with different costs of living, etc.

*Rule justice versus outcome justice.* We used the term "proportionality" to designate different kinds of distributions. For example, in our Needs questions with a single good, the distribution labeled "N-proportionality" divided the fruits in inverse proportion to metabolic efficiency, so that a recipient who extracted twice as much vitamin from each fruit received half as many of those fruits. Is this distribution judged as just because its form conforms to the basic rule of distributive justice, or because its outcome is equal vitamin shares? In the two-goods case, when there were two kinds of fruit to be distributed, "N-proportionality" applied to a distribution in which the fruits themselves were neither proportionately nor inversely proportionately divided, but rather were divided ad hoc so as to equalize vitamin shares between the two recipients. This suggests that in our study, allocation rules are considered just insofar as they produce just final distributions, but clearly the question of rule versus outcome is entwined with the question of essential units.

In the Beliefs series, a different kind of proportionality emerged, which we labeled RB-proportionality. This distribution provided the recipients neither with equal shares of fruits nor with equal shares of vitamin, but rather with equal *believed shares* of vitamin, a strange quantity indeed, and one clearly not directly distributable.

Finally, in problems involving Tastes, utilitarianism emerged. The recipient who extracts more pleasure from each fruit was typically awarded more than half of it – not, as in Needs, less than half. We did not have much opportunity to observe whether the quantitative rule governing the departure from equality had a proportional nature, because we didn't parameterize the recipients' pleasure except in questions i, j, k, and l of Table 6. But the results of these questions indicate that only a minority of the respondents recommended one of the two "proportional" distributions (namely, those that equalized cash value), while most preferred a distribution with a higher (or maximal) total cash value, in line with strict utilitarianism.

*Different standards of distributive justice.* The present framework gives us a way of seeing why equity, equality, and need are traditionally regarded as different standards of distributive justice, even though formally they all can often be cast into the mold of the basic rule of distributive justice. "Equality" concerns the shape of the distribution, insisting on the naturally given units, and disregarding all interpersonal differences between the recipients. "According to need" also concerns the shape of the distribution, but this time in terms of the resultant distribution's ability to meet the recipients' differing needs. Thus, it is a compensatory approach that seeks to correct certain interpersonal differences in needs, or in the ability to satisfy them, by assuring that they be equally met. It achieves equality on some desired dimension by departing from a strictly equal distribution of the given units. In this view, "according to belief" is similar to "according to need," in that it too upholds a principle of compensation for interpersonal differences. "Equity" is not concerned with distributing anything equally. It wishes the distribution rule, or the final outcome, to reflect – rather than to compensate for – the asymmetry in the variables to which it is sensitive, namely some criterion of desert. It is the most suited to the proportionality rule.

Efficiency considerations are often viewed as alternative or competing with justice considerations. This study has shown not only that efficiency considerations are often part and parcel of distributive justice, especially in setting constraints on compensatory schemes, but also that they actually constitute the essence of justice for some goods. In some contexts, a counter compensatory approach is advocated, namely one in which interpersonal differences are neither corrected for nor rewarded by the distribution, but rather capitalized upon to enhance the value of the distributed goods. Our Tastes series is surely but a small, and perhaps not very representative, sample of such contexts.

Typically, in the allocation of political or legal rights, equality is regarded as the standard of justice; in the allocation of basic necessities such as food or health services, compensation is regarded as the determinant of just allocation; in the allocation of economic rewards, distributive justice may be embodied in equity proportionately to contribution (see, however, Mellers, 1982, for nonproportional equity judgments); and in the allocation of tools and means of production, distributive justice may be indistinguishable from efficiency or utilitarianism.

Thus, the standards and rules that people bring to bear when considering any particular distribution problem depend not only on the differences between the recipients, but also on the differences in the perceived nature of the goods being distributed.

### References

Adams, J. S. (1965). Inequity in social exchange. In L. Berkowitz (Ed.) *Advances in experimental Social Psychology* (Vol. 2). New York: Academic Press.

Anderson, N. H. (1976). Equity judgments as information integration. *Journal of Personality and Social Psychology, 33,* 291–299.

Aristotle. (1967). *Politics.* H. Rackham (Trans.). Cambridge, MA: Harvard University Press (Loeb Classical Library).

Chomsky, N. (1957). *Syntactic structures.* The Hague: Mouton.

Furby, L. (1986). Psychology and justice. In R. L. Cohen (Ed.) *Justice: Views from social sciences.* New York: Plenum Press.

Guth, W. (1988). On the behavioral approach to distributive justice – A theoretical and experimental investigation. In S. Maital (Ed.) *Applied behavioral economics.* Brighton: Wheatsheaf.

Guth, W., Schmittberger, R., & Schwarze, B. (1982) An experimental analysis of ultimatum bargaining. *Journal of Economic Behavior and Organization, 3,* 367–388.

Hammond, P. J. (1982). Utilitarianism, uncertainty and information. In A. K. Sen and B. Williams (Eds.) *Utilitarianism and beyond.* Cambridge: Cambridge University Press.

Homans, G. C. (1961). *Social behavior: Its elementary forms.* New York: Harcourt, Brace, Jovanovich.

(1976). Commentary. In: L. Berkowitz and E. Walster (Eds.) *Equity theory: Toward a general theory of social interaction.* New York: Academic Press.

Jouvenel, B. de. (1957). *Sovereignty: An inquiry into the political good.* J. F. Huntington (Trans.). Chicago: University of Chicago Press.

Kahneman, D., Knetch, J. L., & Thaler, R. H. (1986a). Fairness and the assumptions of economics. *Journal of Business, 59,* S285–S300.

(1986b). Fairness as a constraint on profit seeking: Entitlements in the market. *American Economic Review, 76,* 728–741.

Komorita, S. S., & Chertkoff, J. M. (1982). A bargaining theory of coalition formation. *Psychological Review, 80,* 149–162.

Mellers, B. (1982). Equity judgment: A revision of Aristotelian views. *Journal of Experimental Psychology: General, 111,* 242–270.

Nydegger, R. V., & Owen, G. (1974) Two-person bargaining: An experimental test of the Nash axioms. *International Journal of Game Theory, 3,* 239–250.

Rawls, J. A. (1971). *A theory of justice.* Cambridge, MA: Harvard University Press.

Rescher, N. (1966). *Distributive justice.* New York: Bobbs-Merrill. London: Allen and Unwin.

Roth, A. E., & Malouf, W. M. K. (1982). Scale changes and shared information in bargaining: An experimental study. *Mathematical Social Sciences, 3,* 157–177.

Roth, A. E., & Murnighan, K. J. (1982) The role of information in bargaining: An experimental study. *Econometrica, 50,* 1123–1142.

Selten, R. (1978) The equity principle in economic behavior. In W. Gottinger and W. Leinfellner (Eds.), *Decision theory and social ethics.* Dordrecht, Holland: D. Reidel.

Sen, A. (1970) *Collective choice and social welfare.* San Francisco: Holden Day.

Tversky, A., & Kahneman, D. (1986). Rational choice and the framing of decisions. *Journal of Business, 59,* S251–S278.

Walster, E., Berscheid, E., & Walster, G. W. (1973). New directions in equity research. *Journal of Personality and Social Psychology, 23,* 151–176.

Walster, E., Walster, G. W., & Berscheid, E. (1978). *Equity theory and research.* Boston: Allyn & Bacon.

Yaari, M. (1979) Distributive justice. Lecture in memory of Elisha Pazner, presented in Hebrew in the annual meeting of the Israeli Economic Society. *Iyyunim be'calcala* (a Hebrew periodical in Economics)

Yaari, M., & Bar-Hillel, M. (1984). On dividing justly. *Social Choice and Welfare, 1,* 1–24.

### Notes

1 We do not wish to defend this difference as holding universally and clearly; it is quite possible for some cases to combine elements of more than one category, as well as to combine differences in utilities with differences in entitlements.

2 We thank R. Thaler for suggesting this term.

3 N2a stands for Needs, two-goods, problem a.

4 It is possible to devise other questions where other solutions will emerge, by choosing parameters appropriately, and also to have a one-to-one correspondence between mechanisms and solutions.

5 With changes in testing procedures in Israel, it is today impossible to use applicants for experimental purposes.

6 Nonetheless, see footnote b of Table 4.

7 Recall, in this context, the famous story of King Solomon and the two women claiming the same baby. His ploy of "dividing" the baby equally between the two served merely as a "lie detection" device, not as a serious contender for justice.

8 This percentage might be somewhat inflated by some considerations particular to this story, such as wishing to avoid bad feelings between the brothers, bitterness against the dead father, etc.

9 We express ourselves this way here, though we were careful to avoid interpersonal utility comparisons in the actual question formulation.

10 Admittedly, it is a weakness of our results that most of the nonsymmetric solutions to these problems were given only when symmetric distributions were disallowed. The crucial point of these problems, however, was to see which direction nonsymmetry would take.

11 We switched from avocados to oranges in these problems for realism's sake: At the time, the market prices of grapefruit and oranges were highly similar, whereas avocados were considerably more expensive.

# Part III

# Economic perspectives

# 5 Fairness in groups: Comparing the self-interest and social identity perspectives

*Tom Tyler and Robyn M. Dawes*

### Overview

In both their evaluations and their behavioral choices, people are sensitive to issues of fairness. First, people in this culture and in others evaluate individual actions and social procedures in terms of fairness. A judgment that an action or a procedure is unfair provides us with one reason for modifying it. Some people even maintain that life itself is – or at least "should be" – fair, to the point that President John F. Kennedy's declaration during the 1961 Berlin crisis that "life is not fair" was widely considered to be an act of political courage.

Considerations of fairness also constrain behavioral choice. People often eschew egoistically satisficing or maximizing behaviors in favor of those judged to be fair. For example, people with greater power take less than they might in ultimatum bargaining games (Guth, Schmittberger, & Schwarze, 1982; Ochs & Roth, 1989); people choose to work for less pay in an organization where pay is distributed fairly (Schmitt & Marwell, 1972); and, when people have control of scarce resources, they do not sell those resources at their market price, an action which would be personally advantageous, but is widely viewed as unfair (Kahneman, Knetsch, & Thaler, 1986a, b; Okun, 1981; Solow, 1980).

The central question to which this chapter is addressed is whether these attitudinal and behavioral constraints can be explained in terms of egoistic incentives. One possibility, for example, is that individual and cultural acceptance of fairness norms involves the sacrifice of small egoistic payoffs in order to achieve the larger egoistic gains that can be accrued by living in a society in which the actions of all are constrained by the norms of fairness. Behavior in accord with these norms oneself would thus be egoisti-

We would like to thank Barbara Mellers, David Messick, and Philip Tetlock for their comments on a draft of this chapter.

cally rational by providing protection against the individually disastrous Hobbesian "war of alle against alle" – without the cost and potential cruelty of an imposed Leviathan (although, of course, cheating and "getting away with it" would be egoistically optimal). Another closely related possibility is that fairness norms evolve as a compromise between the egoistic strivings of a society's individual members. While such egoistically based explanations cannot be definitively supported or rejected by a single group of findings reviewed in a single paper, we present evidence here that does not support them.

Our evidence is obtained from studying people in our own culture at the present time. We believe, however, that it has general relevance to understanding conceptions of fairness norms and explanations of following them, because any theory about such norms must – to be empirically testable – have implications about the here and now. Moreover, theories about the "emergence of norms" involving hypothetical historical or evolutionary development must as well. And it is the here and now that we are most capable of examining.

### What is egoism?

Historically, the concept of egoistic, or self-interested, motivation has had a wide variety of definitions (Mansbridge, 1990). We draw our definition from recent discussions in the public choice literature. These discussions distinguish two elements of economic theory: a theory of utility or value, and a theory of evaluation and choice.

The theory of utility embodied within economic models makes two assumptions about the nature of human values. The first is that people attempt to maximize their own personal gains – however they define them – in their interactions with others. This is a key assumption of public choice theories. This concept of personal utility maximization has a long history within economics (Stigler, 1950). People are assumed to maximize personal self-interest, or to behave egoistically, by acting in ways that are responsive only to their own gains and losses.

The second assumption of economic models is that actors are primarily motivated by a desire for material rewards. Although actions could conceivably be motivated by social utilities, such as the desire for prestige or respect, this will occur only when these secondary values are instrumental means linked to material gains (Laver, 1981). Economic theory also assumes that actors discount future gains and losses.

One way in which the model of utility underlying economic theory has been expanded is to regard a wider variety of actions as having personal utility. One possible such extension is to regard social rewards, like prestige and honor, as personally rewarding (Kelley & Thibaut, 1978). Another extension of utility theory is to regard others' gains as personally rewarding or disgusting. For example, I may find it personally rewarding to see you eating an apple that I have given you. Hence, my self-interest is advanced by your happiness (see Kelley & Thibaut, 1978). In this discussion we will focus on the more limited conception of personal utility that has dominated the tradition of public choice theory. In it people are regarded as focused on their own personal self-interest and its advancement through the attainment of material resources.

The second aspect of economic models is a methodology for evaluating and choosing among behavioral alternatives. The major model of evaluation and behavioral choice is the subjective expected-utility model. It suggests that actions can be modeled by calculations involving the combination of expectancies and values.

As is true of the economic theory of utility, the theory of evaluation and judgment underlying economic analysis can also be reexamined. It has been recognized that people seldom behave as if they engage in the type of calculations suggested by the subjective expected utility model. Instead, they use a variety of simplifying heuristics (Dawes, 1988).

Economic theories of evaluation also assume that the valence of gains and loses is determined individually, based on the degree to which a resource meets personal needs. In other words, the value of gains and losses is *not* determined by judgments about what is gained or lost relative to what is gained and/or lost by others. Studies of evaluation, in contrast, have found that the value placed on gains and losses is influenced by judgments of relative gain/loss (Loewenstein, Thompson, & Bazerman, 1989; Messick & Sentis, 1985). Hence, your well-being influences my well-being because I evaluate my happiness by judging my outcomes relative to your outcomes. As a consequence, the same gain or loss will take on different subjective values in different situations.

The evaluative aspect of economic models is distinct from assumptions about whether people are egoistical. It describes how people translate their values into choices. Any type of values – egoistic, altruistic, moral, group-based – can be included within the context of subjective expected-utility models and, as a consequence, can influence behavioral choices. Hence, it is the theory of utility underlying economic theory that is key to this discussion. Our concern in this chapter is with the finding that people's judgments and behavioral choices depart from self-interest in ways that seem consistent with a desire to be responsive to issues of justice.

### Does justice matter in organized groups?

Psychological theories of distributive and procedural justice have received strong support. Within groups people are sensitive to both issues, reacting to allocation and conflict-resolution decision making by judging their fairness, not their personal favorability. When they are within groups, people's evaluations of their outcomes, as well as their views about groups and group authorities, are influenced by judgments about what is just.

Exchanges of rewards and resources in groups are typically governed by the principles of distributive justice, primarily equity, equality, and need. Large research literatures on both relative deprivation and equity have demonstrated that people both expect others to follow principles of distributive justice when allocating resources within groups and follow those principles themselves (see Crosby, 1976, 1982; Masters & Smith, 1987; Olson, Herman, & Zanna, 1986; Walster, Walster, & Berscheid, 1978).

The distributive justice literature suggests that people restrain themselves in groups; that is, they "work out a compromise" (Walster, Berscheid, & Walster, 1976, p. 2), in which fairness norms define the apportionment of rewards, with the goal of facilitating social interaction. They do so to maximize their attainment of rewards from the group. Concerns about distributive justice naturally emerge when resources are allocated within groups (Deutsch, 1985).

More recent justice research has suggested that, in addition to concerns about distributive justice, people evaluate the fairness of the procedures by which allocations are made (Thibaut & Walker, 1975). Since the publication of *Procedural Justice* by Thibaut and Walker (1975), a substantial body of research has been conducted on issues of procedural justice (see Lind & Tyler, 1988, for a review). The findings of the initial Thibaut and Walker research have been widely confirmed in subsequent studies of legal trial procedures (e.g., Lind, Kurtz, Musante, Walker, & Thibaut, 1980), in studies of other nontrial procedures used in resolving legal disputes, such as plea bargaining (Houlden, 1980; Casper, Tyler, & Fisher, 1988) and mediation (Adler, Hensler, & Nelson, 1983; Lind et al., 1989; MacCoun, Lind, Hensler, Bryant, & Ebener, 1988), as well as in studies of police officer dealings with citizens (Tyler, 1988, 1990; Tyler & Folger, 1980). In addition, researchers have found that concerns about procedural justice extend to organizational (Folger & Greenberg, 1985; Greenberg, 1990; Greenberg & Folger, 1983), political (Tyler & Caine, 1981), interpersonal (Barrett-Howard & Tyler, 1986), and educational (Tyler & Caine, 1981) settings. In fact, wherever procedural justice issues have been studied they have emerged as an important concern. (See Tyler & Lind, 1990, for possible limits to the procedural justice effect.)

Procedural concerns have emerged as especially important in the evaluation of group authorities and institutions. Studies of legal authorities (Tyler, 1984, 1990), political authorities (Tyler & Caine, 1981; Tyler, Rasinski, & McGraw, 1985), and managerial authorities (Alexander & Ruderman, 1987; Folger & Konovsky, 1989) all suggest that procedural issues shape evaluations of authorities and commitment or loyalty to groups.[1]

## Concerns about justice and the egoistical model of the person

The results of both the distributive and procedural justice literatures initially appear to violate self-interest because they suggest that people are not reacting to their experiences by evaluating the favorability of the outcomes they personally receive from them. Instead, they are primarily concerned about issues of justice.

In fact, however, the extensive findings of concern about justice are not inconsistent with a model of the person as basically egoistic, pursuing self-interest. Even if people make judgments based on fairness, this does not demonstrate that they are not egoistical. Past models of distributive justice have linked people's motivation for using fairness in deciding how to behave to their interest in obtaining valued resources through social exchange. In other words, they "rest on the assumption that man is selfish" (Walster et al., 1976, p. 2). Equity models, for example, suggest that people focus on distributive justice in allocations in an effort to balance their desire to maximize their personal gain in dealing with others against their fears of provoking destructive conflict by trying to take too much from others (Walster et al., 1978). This model suggests that people believe that they can gain the most for themselves in the long run by following distributive justice rules in making social exchanges.

As was true with theories of distributive justice, the egoistic theory of procedural justice presented by Thibaut and Walker (1975) – control theory – flows directly out of social exchange theory. Control theory suggests that the distribution of direct and indirect control over outcomes is the primary element of procedures that shapes judgments about their desirability and fairness. To the extent possible, people seek to keep control over the outcome of a procedure so that they can maximize their pursuit of self-interest. If they must give up direct outcome control to a third party in order to resolve a dispute, people attempt to maximize their outcome control through the indirect means of maximizing their control over the presentation of evidence to the decision making third party (process control). As with distributive justice, the underlying assumptions about the justice motive contained within procedural justice theory develop from social exchange theory (Thibaut & Kelley, 1959), which focuses on people's use of groups as a source of resources.

### Constraining behavioral choices

Theories of self-interested motivation emphasize people's desire to be free of constraints, so that they can maximize their personal outcomes in their behavior. Such a desire suggests that people would resent and resist social and other constraints on their behavior.

The suggestion that people resent and resist rules and other social constraints is not a new one. It was Rousseau, not Marx or Engels, who first wrote that: "Man is born free, and everywhere he is in chains." In his discussion of eighteenth-century French society, Rousseau contrasted his image of the savage, who lived freely in the uncivilized wilderness, to those who lived within his own society. He suggested that those within civilized societies were constrained by the rules and authorities who dominated their lives and were unable to live the desirable state of unfettered freedom attained by the "savage."

In contrast to this image of the person as an unwilling and unhappy prisoner of the social group, social psychologists typically find that people willingly join groups and spontaneously create rules and authority structures to govern their lives. People in unstructured situations create rules or seek out social organization to regulate their lives and resolve conflicts that arise in social interaction. For example, in a classic study by Thibaut and Faucheux (1965), and in a follow-up study by Thibaut and Gruder (1969), it is demonstrated that when people enter profitable, but unstable, relationships they create rules to stabilize interaction and lessen the possibility of disruption.

Another example of the creation of rules and authority structures in a situation of potential social conflict is provided by recent research in social dilemmas. Using an experimentally created renewable resource pool Messick studied how groups respond to the possibility that some group members will deplete a resource that benefits all members of the group. One response he found is for groups to create an authority structure in which one member is empowered to regulate the behavior of others (Messick et al., 1983; Samuelson, Messick, Rutte, & Wilke, 1984).

Given that people want to be free to behave in ways that maximize their self-interest, it is surprising that people support the creation of rules and authority structures that constrain their behavior. It is not surprising that people want rules and authorities to constrain the behavior of others, since such constraints protect them. Hence, it is possible that, seeing the value of having rules controlling others, people may regard having to follow rules themselves as a reasonable cost to pay for having rules to constrain others. In other words, people may be more focused on what they gain in protection from others than on what they lose in opportunity for themselves.

Although people may see the value of self-constraint as part of a package in which everyone is constrained, self-interest motivations are best served by a situation in which everyone else is constrained but I am free. Hence, egoistic theories postulate a persistent tendency for individuals to "free-ride," allowing others to follow rules, but ignoring those rules in shaping their own behavior. Hence, a key concern is not whether people support the creation of rules for all, but whether they alter their own behavior to accord with rules.

### Cooperation in social dilemmas

The social dilemmas literature focuses directly on people's willingness to change their behavior to accord with group rules and needs. That literature is concerned with the behavioral choices that people make in groups. We have outlined evidence suggesting that people appear to make judgments about outcomes obtained in groups using nonegoistic criteria of fairness. It demonstrates that people who are placed in groups often stop behaving egoistically. Instead, they cooperate (Dawes & Thaler, 1988). One example of cooperative behavior is found in the context of the provision of public goods. Dawes and Thaler (1988) review the literature on single- and multiple-trial public goods experiments and find that cooperation occurs, especially in single-trial experiments.

Our review of research findings indicates that people frequently engage in cooperative actions in groups, actions that appear inconsistent with an egoistic orientation toward the group. Instead of people acting in their own interest, people's motivations are transformed to a concern with the welfare of their group (Kramer & Brewer, 1986). Is the fact that people cooperate really evidence against self-interest? Again, not necessarily. We must also recognize that it may be in a person's self-interest to act in the group's interest. If the group succeeds, its members are successful as well. Hence, finding evidence of cooperation does not, in and of itself, illustrate the operation of nonegoistic motives.

### Why does cooperation occur?

Research suggests that the key to acting for the group is forming a sense of group identity. After reviewing the literature on cooperation Dawes and Thaler (1988) suggest that "group identity appears to be a crucial factor in eschewing the dominating strategy [competition]" (p. 195). If, for example, the researcher creates a common identity among participants, or otherwise encourages people to think of themselves as being in a group, individual actions on behalf of the group are facilitated. Studies show that group identity enhances cooperation (Brewer & Kramer, 1986; Kramer & Brewer, 1984, 1986). When their common identity as a group is made salient, people in groups are more likely to act in ways that benefit the group as a whole, rather than acting out of personal self-interest.

Such findings suggest that developing a group identity is central to willingness to act in the group's interest rather than one's own. The key psychological question is why this effect occurs. Is group membership important because groups provide their members with a sense of social identity, or are groups important because they provide resources? If people value groups as a source of resources, they should be most protective of the group when it is giving them high levels of resources. If people value groups as a source of identity, they should act most strongly in the group's interest under conditions that promote identity, not under conditions of high resource dependence.

Some operationalizations that create group identity do not allow the identity and resource links to groups to be distinguished. For example, Brewer and Kramer (1986) created group identity by linking the individual's obtained resources to the actions of the group. This may lead people to act in the group's interest because the group's interest is their own interest. Ideally, identity and resource dependence can be distinguished as motivations for acting in the group's interest.

One judgment that has been examined is the expectation of reciprocity, an issue linked to resource dependence. If people do not expect others to act to their benefit, they stand to gain fewer resources from the groups of which they are members. Hence, they should not cooperate with the group. Studies suggest that one effect of creating a sense of group identity is to increase expectations that others will reciprocate cooperative behavior (Brewer, 1981).

Messick et al. (1983) and Kramer and Goldman (1988) both examined the influence of such expectations on behavior. They measured trust in reciprocity and found that those people with low trust acted less in the interests of the group and more in self-interest. Brann and Foddy (1988) replicated this finding using a scale measuring trust in others.

While the findings outlined would seem to support a resource dependence perspective on acting in the group's interest, Kramer (in press) points out that they contain an interesting anomaly. In Messick et al. (1983) high trusters – people who expected reciprocity – cooperated irrespective of whether others actually reciprocated. Similarly, Brann and Foddy (1988) found that the behavior of high trusters was not linked to how others in their study behaved. Kramer (in press) suggests that trusters are cooperating out of a sense of "moral duty or commitment," rather than because they are seeking the benefits of mutual cooperation. In other words, a set of moral or ethical values is involved. Orbell, Schwartz-Shea, and Simmons (1984) similarly found that cooperators did not leave groups, when it was in their interest to do so, because of their ethical concerns.

A consistent finding emerges from studies of the development of group identity in natural settings. Dawes suggests that a key is allowing members of the group to talk to each other (Dawes, 1980). The combination of group identity and discussion leads to cooperation. Why? Because people make promises to each other that they feel obligated to keep (Dawes, van de Kragt, & Orbell, 1988; Kramer & Goldman, 1988; Orbell, van de Kragt, & Dawes, 1988). Again it is the ethical feeling of obligation that drives the behavioral effects observed.

These findings suggest that there is more to group identity effects than expected resource gains from acting in the group's interest. It is not expected personal rewards that are shaping the extent to which people cooperate in groups. Instead, people seem to be focusing on ethical commitments. Further, those concerns seem to be distinct from concerns about personal gain. As Dawes, van de Kragt, and Orbell (1990) suggest: "Our experiments have led us to conclude that cooperation rates can be radically affected by one factor in particular, which is independent of the consequences for the choosing individual. That factor is group identity: Such identity – or solidarity – can be established and consequently enhance co-

operative responding in the absence of any expectation of future reciprocity, current rewards or punishments, or even reputational consequences among other group members" (p. 199). The strongest evidence
that group identity is necessary for people to feel obligated to keep promises is that individual promises to cooperate are related to subsequent cooperation when promising is universal within a group. (In fact, there was
no relationship at all between promising and subsequent behavior when
promising was *not* universal – no relationship either between groups or
within.)

### Does self-interest explain the importance of justice judgments?

As has been noted, both people's evaluations and their behaviors are altered when they are in groups. Evaluations become responsive to justice
concerns, and behaviors become responsive to issues of group interest.
Further, the social dilemmas literature suggests that the latter, behavioral,
effect is linked to the effects of identification with the group. In other words,
the behavioral change does not occur for self-interested reasons. How can
these findings in support of identity theories in the social dilemmas literature be reconciled to the previously outlined psychology of justice? That
psychology links concerns about distributive and procedural justice to self-
interested motives. For example, equity concerns are linked to the desire
to maintain long-term exchange relationships, while procedural justice
concerns are linked to the desire to control the outcome of distributive
procedures.

Recent studies of procedural justice have supported a different psychological model of justice that is much more consistent with the findings of
the literature on social dilemmas.[2] Those studies have compared the control model of procedural judgments, which links reactions to procedures
to issues of control over outcomes, to a model that links such reactions to
relational issues (Lind & Tyler, 1988; Tyler, 1989; Tyler & Lind, 1992).

The relational perspective focuses not on the resources that groups supply to their members, but on the importance of the group in defining people's identities. This model is similar to the work of Tajfel (Tajfel & Turner,
1979, Turner & Giles, 1981) in that it focuses on groups as sources of information that people can use to construct their self-identities, rather than as
a source of resources. The key to comparing the control view of justice
against a relational perspective is to test for noncontrol influences on judgments about justice.

Following Thibaut and Walker's articulation of a control model, research
focused on the distinction between process control (the opportunity to present information) and decision control (influence over outcomes). In their
original presentation of control theory Thibaut and Walker (1975) suggested that people value process control because it leads to outcome control. In other words, it suggested that people believed that by presenting

evidence on their own behalf they could lead the third party to decide a dispute in their favor. Hence, they valued process control because it was linked to decision control.

Research on control does not support the Thibaut and Walker prediction. Instead, it suggests that people value process control even when it is not linked to decision control (Lind, Lissak, & Conlon, 1983; Tyler, 1987; Tyler, Rasinski, & Spodick, 1985). A striking illustration of this effect is found in a study by Lind, Kanfer, and Early (1990). In that study people were allowed to present their arguments after a decision had already been made. This produced a "pure" process effect, with people feeling more fairly treated than if they could not present their arguments, even though they clearly could not affect the outcome.

If people do not care about control over outcomes, as suggested by exchange theory, what do they care about? An alternative perspective suggests that people care about their relationship to the social group. That perspective develops from group-value theory (Lind & Tyler, 1988; Tyler, 1989; Tyler & Schuller, 1990). It suggests that people's self-identity is strongly related to their status, or standing, in the groups of which they are members. According to the group-value perspective it is evidence about status, rather than information about control over resources, which shapes people's reactions to their experiences in social groups.

Tyler (1989) suggests that information about one's status in the group is communicated by three aspects of experience with groups: standing, trust, and neutrality. Information about standing is communicated by the interpersonal quality of treatment by others in the group. Whether people are treated politely and with dignity and whether respect is shown for their rights is linked to social status (Tyler & Bies, 1990). Respectful treatment conveys high status, whereas disrespect indicates that one is not a full member of the group, equal in value to others.

Trust or benevolence involves beliefs about the intentions of others. People are concerned about the benevolence of those they are dealing with. Inferences about trustworthiness are especially important because they are used to predict both the future behavior of that person and the behavior of others.

When considering neutrality, people are focusing on the dispute or problem, not on the favorability of its outcome or on their control over that outcome. Instead, they are focusing on whether that outcome occurs through a "level playing field." Neutrality involves honesty and a lack of bias. Neutral decision making also uses facts, not opinions, leading to decisions of objectively high quality.

We will use the results of two recent studies (Tyler, 1989; Tyler & Schuller, 1990) to contrast a control perspective on procedural justice to the relational model. Control influences are represented by the influence of control judgments on assessments of procedural justice. The analysis also includes the other potentially important outcome dimensions of outcome favorability, outcome quality, and outcome consistency. Group-value influences are reflected by the influence of neutrality, trust and standing (Tyler, 1989; Tyler & Lind, 1992).

Tyler (1989) contrasted control and relational influences in a study of people's reactions to personal experiences with legal authorities. He conducted a regression analysis that used judgments of control, neutrality, trust, standing, outcome favorability, decision quality, and decision consistency to predict evaluations of procedural justice. His results indicate that each of the relational factors had an independent influence on justice judgments (beta = .22, $p < .001$, for neutrality; beta = .30, $p < .001$, for trust; beta = .24, $p < .001$, for standing). Control judgments also mattered (beta = .20, $p < .001$), as did outcome favorability (beta = .15, $p < .001$). Overall relational judgments explained 20% of variance in procedural justice judgments that could not be explained by outcome variables, while outcome variables explained only 4% of variance in procedural justice that could not be explained by relational concerns. Tyler and Schuller (1990) contrasted control and relational influences in a study of worker's reactions to personal experiences with their supervisors. They conducted a regression analysis that used judgments of control, neutrality, trust, standing, outcome favorability, decision quality, and decision consistency to predict evaluations of procedural justice. Their results indicate that each of the relational factors had an independent influence on justice judgments (beta = .27, $p < .001$, for neutrality; beta = .35, $p < .001$, for trust; beta = .13, $p < .01$, for standing). Control judgments also mattered (beta = .09, $p < .05$), as did outcome favorability (beta = .09, $p < .05$) and decision quality (beta = .12, $p < .001$). Overall relational judgments explained 19% of variance in procedural justice judgments that could not be explained by outcome variables, while outcome variables explained only 3% of variance in procedural justice that could not be explained by relational concerns.

The results of these studies indicate that in both settings definitions of procedural justice are dominated by relational issues. This dominance is illustrated by the proportion of independent variance explained by each model. Outcome issues explain approximately 4% of such variance, group-value variables 20%.[3] Thus, at least insofar as predicting interindividual *differences* in judgments of procedural justice, individual differences in judgments of relational, group-value variables were much more important than individual differences in judgments of outcome.

As this review makes clear, findings in both the social dilemma and the justice literatures suggest that people's judgments and behaviors in groups cannot easily be explained by arguing that people are egoistically motivated. It is clear that people regard groups as more than a valuable source of resources. People also clearly regard groups as a source of self-identify. When they take on the identity of the group, people act out of group interest.

In addition to noting the convergence in the conclusion of the social dilemmas and the procedural justice research paradigms, it is also important to emphasize the differences in the two approaches. In the social dilemmas literature people are typically making choices among different behaviors. In the procedural justice literature, people are evaluating and reacting behaviorally to decisions made by third parties. Hence, the issues of concern are quite different. The social dilemmas literature focuses on choices among behaviors. The procedural justice literature focuses on the choice to accept or reject a decision. Further, the procedural justice literature focuses on evaluations of third parties and the organizations they represent, issues not necessarily important in social dilemmas studies.

An interesting extension of current procedural justice research would be to study choices among procedural alternatives. Such choices among procedures were studied in the original research of Thibaut and Walker (1975) but have been less central to subsequent studies. If given the choice of: (1) a procedure that involved treatment with respect, neutrality, and benevolence and (2) a procedure likely to yield more favorable outcomes, what would people choose? Such a study would parallel the work of Schmitt and Marwell (1972) on distributive justice. That research offered people the choice of working in an organization in which rewards were fewer, but were fairly distributed (5 for me / 5 for you) or an organization in which they received more, but the distribution was unfair (8 for me / 6 for you). They found that people generally chose fairness over favorability. (Suppose you were absolutely convinced that the probability a jury would acquit you of a crime you didn't commit was 80%. Would you rather go to trial expecting a 20% chance of being unfairly found guilty, or be judged guilty if you drew a black ball from an urn containing 90% white and 10% black balls, thereby halving your chance?)

## When are people egoistical? Limits to the use of justice principles

### Group identity

Our view is that both the egoistic and the nonegoistic models are probably dominant in some settings. We believe, further, that one dimension that distinguishes those settings is the extent to which the people involved define themselves as members of a common group. We distinguish interactions among three types of people: strangers or marketplace competitors, people with weak interpersonal ties, and people who strongly identify themselves as members of a common group.

The situation among strangers is often depicted in books and movies whose theme is life outside of civilization. Whether traveling in uncivilized lands and dealing with bandits and thieves, living in a postnuclear-war world, or buying from a traveling salesman, interactions among strangers are "conflicts without rules" (Brickman, 1974). In such settings people seek to gain all that they can from others and evaluate their interactions in self-interested terms. The economic marketplace in contrast represents an extension of conflicts without rules to a partially structured conflict setting. In such a setting self-interested competition occurs within a framework of rules. For example, you would not expect someone selling you a used car to tell you about its defects ("Let the buyer beware!"), but you would be surprised if they pulled out a gun and robbed you. In economic bargaining situations of the type widely studied in negotiation experiments the parties are motivated to obtain all that they can for themselves, without breaking the framework of rules that prohibit extreme forms of coercion and lying. Sometimes, these distinctions can be quite subtle, or even outwardly irrational. For example, it is considered improper for a seller to take advantage of a temporary shortage of a product (e.g., gasoline) by radically increasing prices ("gouging"), while it is considered perfectly proper for people selling real estate, even their own house to a close friend to make a gigantic profit when they sell at greatly increased "market values" (Kahneman, Knetsch, & Thaler, 1986a). What constitutes "coercion" is itself subject to social norms concerning procedural fairness.

Key to the interactions that have been described is the lack of a social bond or sense of group identity among the parties to the interaction. The people involved are strangers, involved in one-shot interactions. Hence, their motivation is self-interested. People in such settings both behave and evaluate their outcomes in egoistical terms.

In the real-world settings, however, many interactions occur over time. People repeatedly buy gasoline at the same station, groceries at the same store, and go to the same doctors, dentists, and lawyers over time. This has two consequences. First, people think about how to maintain their interactions over time, so that they have access to resources from the group. Second, people develop social bonds and feelings of common identity with those with whom they share exchange relationships. People define themselves and their identity in terms of group membership and group values. The first issue is linked to resource dependency, the second to the desire for self-identity.

### Rules

As has already been noted, people respond to being in ongoing relationships by creating rules to maintain those relationships. People tend to make their interactions more fully structured (Brickman, 1974), increasingly defining both rules of acceptable conduct and fair rules of outcome distribution. The work of Kahneman, Knetsch, and Thaler (1986a, b) illustrates the extensive set of rules that constrain marketplace freedom within real-world economic transactions. Interestingly, these rules are generally linked to existing social relations. For example, companies owe fairness to current employees, not to new hires, and landlords owe fairness to current tenants, but not to new tenants. (But consider the example of selling one's house to a friend at "market value" – whatever it happens to be. When and how a social relationship is relevant is itself subject to a sometimes complex set of norms.)

The findings of the social dilemmas and procedural justice literatures both suggest that the concept of egoism becomes problematic when we are talking about the members of groups. To the extent that people have a group identity, group outcomes become personal outcomes. People derive personal pleasure from the achievements and happiness of others in their group. It may be less that people act in the group's interest, rather than acting in their own self-interest when in groups, than it is that people no longer distinguish between groups and self-interest. Hence, these findings suggest a need to fundamentally rethink the concept of self-interest as an explanation for people's evaluations and behaviors in organized groups.

### Commitment

It is also possible to distinguish among group members, identifying subgroups likely to be especially concerned about issues of self-interest. We would like to consider three groups: those of high, intermediate, and low commitment to the group.

The first group consists of people people who are central, committed group members. Our concern is with how such people evaluate their commitment or loyalty to the group and how they behave. Our prediction is that committed group members are those who will behave out of group concern, seeking to maximize the resources obtained by the group. We expect such people to have high levels of loyalty to the group, accepting that group procedures are fair, and to focus on distributive justice issues, such as the equitable split of rewards.

This acceptance of the fairness of allocation procedures represents a cushion of support for authorities and their decisions, with group members predisposed to accept decision making procedures as fair. Panel studies have demonstrated that people with prior commitment are, in fact, more likely to interpret their outcomes in favorable ways (Conley & O'Barr, 1990; Tyler, 1990; Tyler, Casper, & Fisher, 1989).

A second subgroup are those whose commitment and loyalty is intermediate. We would continue to expect these people to behave out of a concern for the group. However, we suspect that it is those members who have intermediate or uncertain status who focus most directly on whether or not the procedures of the group are fair. This suggestion is consistent with the finding in social psychological research that it is those of intermediate status in the group – that is, those with basically positive feelings toward the group, but some uncertainty about their status in the group – who care the most about whether or not group procedures are fair.[4] Finally, people of low status will be the least likely to behave based on group interest and are also the least likely to evaluate outcomes in justice terms.

This does not mean that this group will be indifferent to issues of justice. Even members of marginal social groups, like poor blacks, who have experienced a lifetime of evidence that the procedures of society are biased against them, retain high levels of loyalty to the procedures of the political and legal system (Tyler et al., 1989; Tyler & McGraw, 1986). Our argument is that, relative to others, this group will be the most strongly motivated by self-interest.

### Relative advantage versus disadvantage

Another principle underlying how people react to their outcomes in groups is their feeling that, if there is unfairness in the distribution of rewards, they do not want to be on the downside. Hence, we predict that people will react to experiencing deprivations due to injustice by becoming more egoistical and focusing on the quality of their own outcomes.

Experimental studies support the suggestion that people focus more strongly on avoiding disadvantage than on seeking advantage. Such studies find that "Most subjects preferred that rewards or costs be equitably shared, [but] they were more averse to disadvantageous inequality than to advantageous inequality" (Loewenstein et al. 1989, p. 432). In other words, if there must be injustice, people prefer to be advantaged than disadvantaged (also see Messick & Sentis, 1985, and Pritchard, Dunnette, & Jorgenson, 1972).[5]

Other studies as well support the suggestion that people react to unfairness by focusing on the favorability of their own outcomes. For example, Lind and Lissak (1985) examine the effects of flaws in the enactment of a fair procedure on reactions to it. They expose participants to an adversary trial procedure that does or does not include evidence of procedural unfairness. In the flawed procedure condition participants see evidence that the "neutral" decision maker has a friendly social relationship with the other side, while in the unflawed procedure no such interaction occurs. Participants are also randomly assigned to win or lose their case. When the procedure is enacted without the hint of unfairness, its outcome does not influence litigant's feelings about the fairness of the trial. When the procedure is enacted unfairly, however, the outcome of the trial shapes views about the procedure's fairness. In other words, in the face of unfairness, self-interest shapes procedural evaluations.

The suggestion that people are especially concerned with avoiding the downside of unfairness is also supported by the results of a study of behavioral choices by Greenberg (1987). In that study participants in work groups receive either high, medium, or low levels of outcome through a fair or an unfair allocation procedure. Following the allocation participants are given the opportunity to take action against the allocator by contacting a supervisory authority. If the allocation procedure is unfair, those participants who receive unfair outcomes are more likely to complain. Again, in the face of unfairness, self-interest shapes behavior. However, this effect occurred only among those who are "one-down" – that is, who receive too little. While those who receive unfairly high levels of reward recognize that the procedure is unfair, they take no action. Only those who are unfairly disadvantaged complain.

These findings of asymmetry due to advantage or disadvantage suggest that there is an interaction between self-interest and justice concerns. If people cared only about justice, they would be equally upset by unfair advantage or disadvantage. However, both people's judgments and their behaviors suggest that injustice is more troubling to people who are in a disadvantaged position vis-à-vis others.

## Summary

The social dilemmas and the justice literatures represent two very different research traditions within social psychology. Nonetheless their findings converge to support two suggestions about human motivation. The first is that people act in ways that appear discrepant from their self-interest. In the justice literature there is extensive evidence that people evaluate and react to decisions based on justice judgments. In the social dilemmas literature there is evidence of cooperation that is difficult to explain by reference to egoistical concerns. Neither the occurrence of cooperation nor the importance of justice issues demonstrates unambiguously that people are nonegoistical. An exploration of the psychology underlying these effects, however, provides considerable evidence that the pattern of people's judgments and behaviors is not easily explained by reference to their self-interest. People's cooperative behavior, for example, is ethically based and is not linked to the behavior of other group members (and, hence, the likelihood that cooperation will be personally rewarding). That ethical obligation is, in turn, linked to solidarity with the group. Similarly, people's justice judgments are not linked to assessments of outcome favorability. Instead, such judgments are linked to the social bond between the person and the group.

What emerges as important in these studies is the role of the group in providing the person with self-identity, above and beyond resource-based links to the group. Having taken on a self-identity linked to the group, people voluntarily behave in ways that benefit the group.

Our argument is that it is the nature of the social bond between exchange partners that determines the extent to which people's behavior in groups and their evaluations of groups themselves will be governed both by egoistical and by group-centered motives. We doubt that either an egoistical or a group-centered model can explain behavior in all situations. In situations without strong social bonds, people are egoistical. Once a group identity is created, however, people are increasingly responsive to group-centered motives.

## Postscript on fairness, concerns for group, and evolutionary theory

Modern evolutionary theory rests on two observations. The first is that organisms vary – both within and between species – in characteristics that are inherited across generations (genetically). The second is that not all organisms survive to reproduce. Evolutionary change then results if there is any statistical relationship between these inherited characteristics and selective reproduction of the individual organism or of other allied organisms having the same heritable characteristics (genes). Such changes can be labeled "survival of the fittest" (although with Simon, 1983, we prefer the term "fitter"). It must be kept in mind, however, that "fitness" is a tautological term in this description, a term that implies nothing about progress, optimality, or conscious striving among organisms capable of planning. In particular, it is not possible to infer any motivational characteristics such as egoistic individualism from the mere fact of evolution. (See Caporael, Dawes, Orbell, & van de Kragt, 1989a and the comments and replies, 1989b). It may turn out on the basis of other evidence that people consciously strive to survive and reproduce – or even to acquire wealth – but these conclusions would not follow directly from evolutionary theory.

A constraint on human behavior and social procedures to be fair or substitute their group's welfare for their own does not, therefore, contradict evolutionary theory; nor does the acceptance of evolutionary theory imply egoistic individualism as the basis of such constraint. All that can be predicted apriori from evolutionary theory is that those inherited characteristics that relative to others yield a decreased probability of (genetic) replication across generations will eventually disappear. Thus, to make an evolutionary argument against the human concern for fairness or group success independent of egoistic motivations and payoffs, it would be necessary to show that, across human history, such concern would consistently be extinguished – independent of the societies people themselves create (or allow to evolve). We have seen no such demonstration. In contrast, we have observed consistent concern for acting in a fair manner toward others, at least toward other members of one's own group. And the people we observe have evolved.

### References

Adler, J. W., Hensler, D. R., & Nelson, C. E. (1983). *Simple justice: How litigants fare in the Pittsburgh Court Arbitration Program*. Santa Monica, CA: Rand.
Alexander, S., & Ruderman, A. (1987). The role of procedural and distributive justice in organizational behavior. *Social Justice Research, 1*, 177–198.
Barrett-Howard, E., & Tyler, T. R. (1986). Procedural justice as a criterion in allocation decisions. *Journal of Personality and Social Psychology, 50*, 296–304.
Brann, P., & Foddy, M. (1988). Trust and the consumption of a deteriorating common resource. *Journal of Conflict Resolution, 31*, 615–630.

Brewer, M. (1981). Ethnocentrism and its role in interpersonal trust. In M. B. Brewer and B. E. Collins (Eds.), *Scientific inquiry and the social sciences.* San Francisco: Jossey-Bass.

Brewer, M., & Kramer, R. M. (1986). Choice behavior in social dilemmas: Effects of social identity, group size, and decision framing. *Journal of Personality and Social Psychology, 50,* 543–549.

Brickman, P. (1974). *Social conflict.* Lexington, MA: D. C. Heath.

Caporael, L., Dawes, R. M., Orbell, J. M., & van de Kragt, A. J. C. (1989a). Selfishness examined: Cooperation in the absence of egoistic incentives. *Behavioral and Brain Sciences, 12,* No. 4, 683–699.

(1989b). Thinking in sociality. Replies to "Selfishness examined: "Cooperation in the absence of egoistic incentives." *Behavioral and Brain Sciences, 12,* No. 4, 727–739.

Casper, J. D., Tyler, T. R., & Fisher, B. (1988). Procedural justice in felony cases. *Law and Society Review, 22,* 483–507.

Conley, J. M., & O'Barr, W. (1990). *Rules and relationships.* Chicago: University of Chicago Press.

Crosby, F. (1976). A model of egoistical relative deprivation. *Psychological Review, 83,* 85–113.

(1982). *Relative deprivation and working women.* Oxford: Oxford University Press.

Dawes, R. M. (1980). Social dilemmas. *Annual Review of Psychology, 31,* 169–193.

(1988). *Rational choice in an uncertain world.* San Diego, CA: Harcourt, Brace, Jovanovich.

Dawes, R. M., & Thaler, R. H. (1988). Anomalies: Cooperation. *Journal of Economic Perspectives, 2,* 187–197.

Dawes, R. M., van de Kragt, A. J. C., & Orbell, J. M. (1988). Not me or thee but we: The importance of group identity in eliciting cooperation in dilemma situations: Experimental manipulations. *Acta Psychologica, 68,* 83–97.

(1990). Cooperation for the benefit of us – not me, or my conscience. In J. Mansbridge (Ed.), *Beyond self-interest.* Chicago: University of Chicago Press.

Deutsch, M. (1985). *Distributive justice.* New Haven, CT: Yale University Press.

Folger, R., & Greenberg, J. (1985). Procedural justice: An interpretive analysis of personnel systems. In K. Rowland & G. Ferris (Eds.), *Research in personnel and human resources management* (Vol 6, pp. 3, 141–183). Greenwich, CT: JAI Press.

Folger, R., & Konovsky, M. (1989). Effects of procedural and distributive justice on reactions to pay raise decisions. *Academy of Management Journal, 32,* 115–130.

French, J. R. P., Jr., & Raven, B. (1959). The bases of social power. In D. Cartwright (Ed.), *Studies in Social Power.* Ann Arbor, MI: Institute for Social Research.

Greenberg, J. (1987). Reactions to procedural justice in payment distributions: Do the means justify the ends? *Journal of Applied Psychology, 72,* 55–61.

(1990). Organizational justice: Yesterday, today, and tomorrow. *Journal of Management, 16,* 401–434.

Greenberg, J., & Folger, R. (1983). Procedural justice, participation, and the fair process effect in groups and organizations. In P. Paulus (Ed.), *Basic group processes,* New York: Springer-Verlag, pp. 235–266.

Guth, W., Schmittberger, R., & Schwarze, B. (1982). An experimental analysis of ultimatum bargaining. *Journal of Economic Behavior and Organization, 3,* 367–388.

Houlden, P. (1980). The impact of procedural modifications on evaluations of plea bargaining. *Law and Society Review, 15,* 267–292.

Kahneman, D., Knetsch, J. L., & Thaler, R. (1986a). Fairness as a constraint on profit seeking: Entitlements in the market. *American Economic Review, 76,* 728–741.

(1986b). Fairness and the assumptions of economics. *Journal of Business, 59,* 285–300.

Kelley, H. H., & Thibaut, J. (1978). *Interpersonal Relations: A Theory of Interdependence.* New York: Wiley.

Kelman, H. C., & Hamilton, V. L. (1989), *Crimes of obedience,* New Haven, CT: Yale University Press.

Kramer, R. M. (in press). Helping the group or helping one's self. In D. Schroeder (Ed.), *Social dilemmas.*

Kramer, R. M., & Brewer, M. (1984). Effects of group identity on resource use in a simulated commons dilemma. *Journal of Personality and Social Psychology, 46,* 1044–1057.

(1986). Social group identity and the emergence of cooperation in resource conservation dilemmas. In H. Wilke, D. Messick, & C. Rutte (Eds.), *Experimental Social Dilemmas* (pp. 205–234). Frankfort am Main: Springer-Verlag.

Kramer, R. M., & Goldman, L. (1988). Expectations that bind: Group-based trust, causal attributions, and cooperative behavior in a commons dilemma. Unpublished manuscript, Stanford University, Stanford, CA.

Lamm, H., Kayser, E., & Schwinger, T. (1982). Justice norms and other determinants of allocation and negotiation behavior. In M. Irle (ED.), *Studies in decisionmaking.* New York: Walter de Gruyter.

Laver, M. (1981). *The politics of private desires.* New York: Penguin.

Lind, E. A., Kanfer, R., & Earley, P. C. (1990). Voice, control, and procedural justice: Instrumental and noninstrumental concerns in fairness judgments. *Journal of Personality and Social Psychology, 59,* 952–959.

Lind, E. A., Kurtz, S., Musante, L., Walker, L., & Thibaut, J. (1980). Procedure and outcome effects on reactions to adjudicated resolutions of conflicts of interest. *Journal of Personality and Social Psychology, 39,* 643–653.

Lind, E. A. & Lissak, R. I. (1985). Apparent impropriety and procedural fairness judgments. *Journal of Experimental Social Psychology, 21,* 19–29.

Lind, E. A., Lissak, R. I., & Conlon, D. I. (1983). Decision control and process control effects on procedural fairness judgments. *Journal of Applied Social Psychology, 4,* 338–350.

Lind, E. A., MacCoun, R. J., Ebener, P. A., Felstiner, W. L. F., Hensler, D. R., Resnik, J., & Tyler, T. R. (1989). *The Perception of Justice: Tort Litigants' Views of Trial, Court-annexed Arbitration, and Judicial Settlement Conferences.* Santa Monica, CA: Rand.

(1990). In the eye of the beholder: Tort litigants' evaluations of their experiences in the civil justice system. *Law and Society Review, 24,* 953–996.

Lind, E. A., & Tyler, T. R. (1988). *The social psychology of procedural justice.* New York: Plenum.

Loewenstein, G., Thompson, L., & Bazerman, M. H. (1989). Social utility and decision making in interpersonal contexts. *Journal of Personality and Social Psychology, 57,* 426–441.

MacCoun, R. J., Lind, E. A., Hensler, D. R., Bryant, D. L., & Ebener, P. A. (1988).

*Alternative adjudication: An evaluation of the New Jersey Automobile Arbitration Program*. Santa Monica, CA: Institute for Civil Justice, Rand.

Mansbridge, J. (1990). The rise and fall of self-interest in the explanation of political life. In J. Mansbridge (Ed.), *Beyond self-interest*. Chicago: University of Chicago Press.

Masters, J. C., & Smith, W. P. (1987). *Social comparison, social justice, and relative deprivation*. Hillsdale, NJ: Erlbaum.

Mathieu, J. E., & Zajac, D. M. (1990). A review and meta-analysis of the antecedents, correlates, and consequences of organizational commitment. *Psychological Bulletin, 108*, 171–194.

Messick, D. M., & Sentis, K. P. (1983). Fairness, preference, and fairness biases. In D. M. Messick and K. S. Cook (Eds.), *Equity theory*. New York: Praeger.

(1985). Estimating social and nonsocial utility functions from ordinal data. *European Journal of Social Psychology, 15*, 389–399.

Messick, D. M., Bloom, S., Boldizar, J. P., & Samuelson, C. D. (1985). Why we are fairer than others. *Journal of Experimental Social Psychology, 21*, 480–500.

Messick, D. M., Wilke, H., Brewer, M. B., Kramer, R. M., Zemke, P. E., & Lui, L. (1983). Individual adaptations and structural change as solutions to social dilemmas. *Journal of Personality and Social Psychology, 44*, 294–309.

Mikula, G., & Schwinger, T. (1978). Intermember relations and reward allocation. In H. Brandstatter, J. H. Davis, & H. Schuler (Eds.). *Dynamics of group decisions*. Beverly Hills, CA.: Sage.

Ochs, J., & Roth, A. E. (1989). An experimental study of sequential bargaining. *American Economic Review, 79*, 335–385.

Okun, A. (1981). *Prices and quantities: A macroeconomic analysis*. Washington, DC: The Brookings Institute.

Olson, J. M., Herman, C. P., & Zanna, M. P. (1986). *Relative deprivation and social comparison*. Hillsdale, NJ: Erlbaum.

Orbell, J. M., Schwartz-Shea, P., & Simmons, R. T. (1984). Do cooperators exit more readily than defectors? *American Political Science Review, 78*, 147–162.

Orbell, J. M., van de Kragt, A. J. C., & Dawes, R. M. (1988). Explaining discussion-induced cooperation. *Journal of Personality and Social Psychology, 54*, 811–819.

Organ, D. W. (1988). *Organizational Citizenship Behavior: The Good Soldier Syndrome*. Lexington, MA: D. C. Heath.

Pritchard, R. D., Dunnett, M. D., & Jorgenson, D. O. (1972). Effects of perceptions of equity and inequity on worker performance and satisfaction. *Journal of Applied Psychology Monograph, 56*, 75–94.

Samuelson, C. D., Messick, D. M., Rutte, C. G., & Wilke, H. (1984). Individual and structural solutions to resource dilemmas in two cultures. *Journal of Personality and Social Psychology, 47*, 94–104.

Schmitt, D. R., & Marwell, G. (1972). Withdrawal and reward allocation in response to inequity. *Journal of Experimental Social Psychology, 8*, 207–221.

Seigel, S., & Fouraker, L. E. (1960). *Bargaining and group decision making: Experiments in bilateral monopoly*. New York: McGraw-Hill.

Simon, H. A. (1983). *Reason in human affairs*. Stanford, CA: Stanford University Press.

Solow, R. M. (1980). On theories of unemployment. *American Economic Review, 70*, 1–11.

Stigler, G. J. (1950). The development of utility theory. *Journal of Political Economy,* 58, 307–321, 373–396.

Tajfel, J., & Turner, J. C. (1979). An integrative theory of intergroup conflict. In W. Austin & S. Worchel (Eds.), *The social psychology of intergroup relations,* Monterey, CA: Brooks/Cole, pp. 33–47.

Thaler, R. M. (1988). Anomalies: The ultimatum game. *Journal of Economic Perspectives,* 2, 195–206.

Thibaut, J., & Faucheux, C. (1965). The development of contractual norms in a bargaining situation under two types of stress. *Journal of Experimental Social Psychology,* 1, 89–102.

Thibaut, J., & Gruder, C. L. (1969). Formation of contractual agreements between parties of unequal power. *Journal of Personality and Social Psychology,* 11, 59–65.

Thibaut, J., & Kelley, H. H. (1959). *The social psychology of groups.* New York: Wiley.

Thibaut, J., & Walker, L. (1975). *Procedural justice.* Hillsdale, NJ: Erlbaum.

Turner, J. C., & Giles, H. (1981). *Intergroup behavior.* Chicago: University of Chicago Press.

Tyler, T. R. (1984). The role of perceived injustice in defendant's evaluations of their courtroom experience. *Law and Society Review,* 18, 51–74.

(1987). Conditions leading to value-expressive effects in judgments of procedural justice: A test of four models. *Journal of Personality and Social Psychology,* 52, 333–344.

(1988). What is procedural justice?: Criteria used by citizens to assess the fairness of legal procedures. *Law and Society Review,* 22, 301–355.

(1989). The psychology of procedural justice: A test of the group value model. *Journal of Personality and Social Psychology,* 57, 830–838.

(1990). *Why people obey the law.* New Haven, CT: Yale University Press.

Tyler, T. R., & Bies, R. (1990). Interpersonal aspects of procedural justice. In J. S. Carroll (Ed.), *Applied social psychology in business settings.* Hillsdale, NJ: Erlbaum.

Tyler, T. R., & Caine, A. (1981). The role of distributional and procedural fairness in the endorsement of formal leaders. *Journal of Personality and Social Psychology,* 41, 642–655.

Tyler, T. R., Casper, J. D., & Fisher, B. (1989). Maintaining allegiance toward political authorities: The role of prior attitudes and the use of fair procedures. *American Journal of Political Science,* 33, 629–652.

Tyler, T. R., & Folger, R. (1980). Distributional and procedural aspects of satisfaction with citizen-police encounters. *Basic and Applied Social Psychology,* 1, 281–292.

Tyler, T. R., & Lind, E. A. (1992). Intrinsic versus community-based justice models: When does group membership matter? *Journal of Social Issues,* 46, 83–94.

Tyler, T. R. & McGraw, K. (1986). Ideology and the interpretation of personal experience: Procedural justice and political quiescence. *Journal of Social Issues,* 42, 115–128.

Tyler, T. R., Rasinski, K., & McGraw, K. (1985). The influence of perceived injustice on support for political authorities. *Journal of Applied Social Psychology,* 15, 700–725.

Tyler, T. R., Rasinski, K., & Spodick, N. (1985). The influence of voice on satisfaction with leaders: Exploring the meaning of process control. *Journal of Person-ality and Social Psychology, 48,* 72–81.

Tyler, T. R., & Schuller, R. (1990). Comparing the control and group value models of procedural justice: Instrumental vs. relational perspectives on authority in groups. Unpublished manuscript, Northwestern University.

Walster, E., Berscheid, E., & Walster, G. W. (1976). New directions in equity re-search. In L. Berkowitz (Ed.), *Advances in experimental social psychology* (Vol. 9). New York: Academic.

Walster, E., Walster, G. W., & Berscheid, E. (1978). *Equity: Theory and research.* Boston: Allyn & Bacon.

### Notes

1 Such commitment is important because it has been shown to influence both whether people join and stay in groups (Mathieu & Zajac, 1990) and whether they follow group rules (Or-gan, 1988; Tyler, 1990).

2 While the findings of the social dilemmas literature are similar on this point to those of the procedural justice literature, it is important to recognize that Dawes does not equate the ethical behavior he finds associated with group solidarity to a moral concern. In fact he suggests, "we wish to point out that group identity does not equal morality (Dawes, van de Kragt, & Orbell, 1990, p. 119). for an extended discussion of the distinction between personal morality and feelings of obligation to social groups see Kelman and Hamilton (1989).

3 We are presenting the results of the regression analyses to illustrate the importance of group identification issues. It is important to remember, however, that the strength of the coefficients is influenced both by the range and variance to the variables and by other factors in the situation. We have some confidence in the coefficients in these studies be-cause the naturally occurring range of variables in the "real world" was established through random sampling of respondents. Nonetheless, then we can only be confident in these findings after they have been replicated in a variety of settings.

4 This argument is consistent with the past suggestion that fairness issues will matter most in profitable, but unstable, relationships (Barrett-Howard & Tyler, 1986; Lamm, Kayser, & Schwinger, 1982; Mikula & Schwinger, 1978; Thibaut & Faucheux, 1965; Thibaut & Gruder, 1969; Tyler & Lind, 1990). However, we are suggesting that it is procedural justice issues which are likely to be key to people of intermediate status in groups.

5 The preference of self over others may reflect the application of equity theory – i.e., the balancing of outcomes and deservedness. Research demonstrates that people see them-selves as acting more fairly than others (Messick, Bloom, Boldizar, & Samuelson, 1985; Messick & Sentis, 1983), suggesting that preferring oneself over others is typically acting out of fairness – that is, giving more to the more deserving person.

# 6 Heuristics and biases in equity judgments: A utilitarian approach

*Jonathan Baron*

Human judgments and decisions have been compared to normative models that specify how judgments and decisions should be made. Such comparisons often find discrepancies between people's goals and the decisions meant to achieve those goals. These discrepancies are often called *biases*, and the informal ways of thinking that lead to them are called *heuristics*. Evidence of biases is useful because we can often find ways of teaching people better ways of thinking, better heuristics, or we can learn when we need to work around the biases by using more formal methods of analysis. In these ways, the discovery of human error leads to ways to improve the human condition.

In this chapter, I shall apply this comparative approach to the study of equity judgments. Of course, even the earliest studies of equity judgments were implicitly concerned with criticizing and improving them. However, by making the interest in criticism more explicit than previous writers, I am forced also to be more explicit about the normative theory to which the judgments are compared. The normative theory I shall defend is utilitarianism, the view that the best decision is the one that maximizes expected utility over all who are affected. I take *utility* to be the extent to which goals are achieved in fact. Utility in this sense need not be the same as utility as expressed in decisions or judgments, which usually involve implicit *predictions* of utility in my sense (Kahneman & Snell, 1990).

Utilitarianism has been criticized over the last two centuries for leading to conclusions that seem unjust. For example, it can permit hurting people who are already unfortunate if the benefit to those who are more fortunate is sufficiently great. Most modern philosophers (e.g., MacIntyre, 1984; Sen

The research described here was supported by grant SES-8809299 from the National Science Foundation. I thank Robyn Dawes, Jon Elster, Clark McCauley, Barbara Mellers, and Jay Schulkin for comments on drafts of this chapter.

& Williams, 1982; Williams, 1985) think that these kinds of criticisms have stuck.

On the other hand, economists and other social scientists (e.g., Landes & Posner, 1987; Shavell, 1987) often accept some form of utilitarianism. Some philosophers (e.g., Hare, 1981; Singer, 1979) think that recent, more carefully developed forms of utilitarianism can answer the criticisms, so that the theory now represents the most defensible and complete normative approach to questions of policy as well as individual moral decision making. In general, these writers deal with apparent counterexamples by either reinterpreting them as consistent with a more thorough utilitarian analysis (e.g., Singer, 1977) or arguing that a generally good intuitive principle (e.g., "Do no harm") is being overgeneralized. The latter reply challenges the critics to provide some other justification than their intuitive judgments about what is just. So far, the critics have not met this challenge and have, instead, retained a degree of faith in human intuition that recent psychological findings (reviewed by Baron, 1988a) would lead us to question.

If utilitarianism is the correct normative theory, the exercise of asking where our judgments differ from utilitarianism tells us where our judgments are in need of improvement (if improvement is possible). If, on the other hand, the critics are correct, then this exercise tells us why our judgments – correct or not – could fail to bring about the best consequences in the utilitarian sense. This sort of knowledge will at least help utilitarians understand our current situation.

In this chapter, I shall outline the implications of utilitarianism for equity judgments. Although I shall sketch some arguments that might be made for it, I cannot provide a complete defense here. (See Baron, in press, and Hare, 1981, for that.) Then, I shall discuss some apparent departures of decisions and judgment from these implications. These are the purported biases. At the end, I shall discuss the implications of these biases for public policy.

Utilitarianism is a normative theory – a standard for evaluating our decisions – not necessarily a prescriptive theory – a set of practical guidelines (Baron, 1985). It need not apply to everyday judgments such as how to treat a student who asks for an extension on an assignment. Such judgments are typically made on the basis of intuitions – moral heuristics, as it were – or fixed rules, such as, "No extensions, because they are unfair to those who need them and don't request them." In general, we feel that these intuitions and rules are morally right, and we tend to feel guilty when we go against them, even when we know that they are normatively wrong. These intuitions and rules constitute our "naive theories" of morality (in the sense of McCloskey, 1983, and others).

We might maximize utility better by using our naive theories even if they disagree with the results of our best effort to maximize utility in a given case (Hare, 1981). Certainly, if I considered in great detail every student who asks for an extension, I would find a few who seem to deserve it. But I could be wrong: For example, I could misestimate probabilities. I might make fewer mistakes in the long run to say, "No extensions, period," than to try to pick out those deserving cases. To paraphrase the late Hillel Einhorn, I must accept error to avoid more error. In some cases, then, following strict rules is a better way to maximize utility than trying to maximize utility. In other cases, though, our naive theories might not maximize utility. We might do better by trying, or by using different naive theories or heuristics.

Equity judgments are often based on these kinds of intuitions or naive theories. In showing that these judgments depart from the normative standard, we must not jump to the conclusion that they should not be used. Instead, we are led to ask whether any alternative set of intuitions or ways of making judgments can bring us closer to the normative model. Often, the answer to this question will be affirmative, but we cannot assume that it is in all cases. In this sense, showing that something is nonnormative makes only a prima facie case that it is irrational. The rest of the case involves showing that a better way can be found.

### Utilitarianism as normative theory

Utilitarianism is about choosing best options. It allows us to evaluate one option against another. It ignores whether one is an "action" and the other an "inaction." It holds that decisions should be made on the basis of future differences between outcomes of different options. The past is relevant only if it affects the future. For example, the existence of an agreement (a past event) sets up a situation in which violation of the agreement sets a precedent (in the future) for other violations.

Utilitarianism often conflicts with our intuitive beliefs about what is morally right. This is, indeed, the main phenomenon I shall discuss. Other moral theories are often defended on the basis of appeal to intuitions (or the systematization of intuitions, as in Rawls, 1971). Most utilitarians cannot accept this approach, because it puts us in danger of begging the question by confirming our present moral beliefs. To think about moral theory, we must put aside our present moral intuitions so that we can question them. We must find some other way to justify moral conclusions aside from appeal to our own prior intuitions.

My own approach to justification (Baron, in press) argues that the best moral principles are those that we would each have reason to endorse for others to follow for the sake of the achievement of our nonmoral goals. (The limitation to nonmoral goals avoids begging the question.) These principles must be impartial across people, so that we can endorse them convincingly for others. The goals that we already have give us our only reasons to endorse these principles. We do not need the intuitive moral beliefs that we have put aside. The best principle for us to endorse consistently, in order to achieve our goals as well as possible, is that everyone should act so as to maximize the achievement of everyone's goals, that is, maximize total utility. By endorsing this principle, we are acting to ensure the achievement of our own goals as well as the goals of others.

### Interpersonal comparison

An important difference between utilitarianism and other theories is its reliance on interpersonal comparison of utility. Utilitarianism assumes that consequences can be evaluated and that differences in consequences can be compared, ideally if not in practice. In some simple cases, we have two options. One option is better for one person and the other option is better for another person. For example, a couple is trying to decide whether to go to a movie or a play. The husband wants the movie, and the wife wants the play. To make an interpersonal comparison, we must compare the utility differences for each person. Hare (1981) suggests that we do this by imagining that the decision were being made by a single person who had all the goals of both the husband and wife. If the wife prefers the play strongly – so that the difference is large for her – and the husband prefers the movie only weakly – so that the difference is small for him – then the couple does better on the whole to go to the play. The utility loss to the husband (relative to the movie) is smaller than the utility gain to the wife (relative to the movie).

The ability to make such comparisons requires understanding of the goals of other people and willingness to put aside one's own goals for the purpose of achieving such understanding. These conditions are often absent in adversarial situations such as simple bargaining (with mediation or arbitration).

More generally, utilitarianism assumes that we can make judgments of whether a loss (or forgone gain) for one or more people is compensated by a gain (or forgone loss) for one or more others. If we judge that a loss is compensated, then we can justify the loss by pointing to this judgment: "Yes, by choosing this option, I hurt you, but I would hurt others more if I chose the alternative." (Of course, the judgment can be challenged.) This kind of comparison of losses and gains can be used to define the utility scale itself (Hare, 1981, ch. 7.3), thus avoiding the problems of inferring utility from preferences among gambles faced by individuals (Weymark, 1991).

Importantly, any theory that leads to different conclusions cannot always appeal to this justification in terms of comparison of relative harm. It must sometimes countenance harm to some (relative to other options) *without* compensating gain for others. (Examples are given later.) Various principles are often invoked for this purpose, such as rights, fairness, retribution, honor, and so on. But these principles cannot derive their authority from any considerations of consequences for the achievement of people's goals. Compared to the utilitarian decision, any other theory yields decisions that achieve people's goals less well.

Several competing theories try to do without interpersonal comparisons. For example, some conceptions of economic efficiency rely on *Pareto optimality*. By this criterion, a situation is optimal if it is impossible to improve matters for one person without making matters worse for someone else. Notice that, in our example, both the movie and the play could be Pareto optimal.

Sometimes this principle is used in a way that puts the burden of proof on the side against the status quo. If the couple had "planned" to go to the movie, then, by this rule, it would be wrong to change the plan because the change would make matters worse for the husband. This rule creates a bias toward inaction, even when action could increase total utility. Here, the past, the prior plan, is affecting the outcome in ways that need not be relevant to future effects on goal achievement. Nozick (1974) seems to endorse such a principle.

Another competing theory, proposed by Kaldor (1939) and Hicks (1939), holds that a change is optimal if the winners could compensate the losers so that nobody loses. This rule does not lead to a bias toward inaction. But it does not require the compensation to be provided, so it could make things worse. If the wife very much wants something that the husband could easily provide (agreement to go to dinner at a certain restaurant that the husband likes too), so that she might accept it as compensation for attending the movie, then, by this rule, the couple should go to the movie, even if the husband does not in fact provide the compensation.

These competing theories often start from the assumption that interpersonal comparison is impossible or impractical. Although it is indeed impractical in many cases, its theoretical possibility has been defended (Baron, 1988b, in press; Griffin, 1986; Hare, 1981). What matters is not whether it is easy to do, but rather whether it makes sense for us to try to do it. When we try to compare one person's gain with another's, does it make sense to say that we are accurate or inaccurate in this judgment?

In many cases, it clearly does make sense. For example, certain medical policies, such as vaccination, will hurt a few (who get serious side effects) to help many others. In such cases, we can think of the desires of the "typical person" affected by such a policy. If some of the people affected happen to be "utility monsters," with utilities 100 times as sensitive to different outcomes as those of other people, we do not know who these monsters are. If each person has an equal chance of being such a monster, then the conclusion that we should base our judgment on the typical person is unaffected (on the basis of expected utility).

In other cases, we must consider differences in tastes. Although this is more difficult, we do know something about the development of tastes, and the errors in our knowledge are as likely to be in one direction as in another (if we are unbiased), so we are better off trying to apply what we know than ignoring it. In the extreme, if identical twins have identical experiences, then we can be sure that their utility functions are the same. (If we can't be sure of this, then we are slipping into a kind of skepticism that would make all normative inquiry impossible.) If we know something about the effects of experience on desires, we can adjust for differences in experiences. Perhaps genetic differences do make people differentially sensitive to certain experiences. In the absence of understanding of such effects, however, the earlier argument about utility monsters applies, and we can neglect genetic differences on the grounds that they are as likely to go one way as another, and we can take a probability-weighted average of all their possible effects.

Interpersonal comparison is not a proof procedure designed to beat down alternative theories. We can usually imagine a set of utility functions that yields decisions compatible with any alternative theory. These functions need not be the ones we would arrive at, however, if we focus our attention on the question of what achieves the goals of those affected. Utilitarianism tells us what to attend to when trying to make difficult judgments as best we can, not how to justify judgments we have already made.

## Issues in the application of utilitarianism

Although the basic principle of utilitarianism can easily be stated while standing on one foot, applications require a number of intermediate devices. This section reviews a few of the more common ones.

### Declining marginal utility versus incentive

In general, the utility of one additional unit of a good (e.g., a dollar or an apple) becomes smaller the more units one has already. We say that *marginal utility* declines. This is because goods are essentially means to the achievement of more fundamental goals. We use money, for example, to buy food, and we use food to nourish ourselves. Money is a flexible good, in that we can use it to satisfy many different goals. If we are poor, we use money to satisfy only the goals that can be most easily satisfied with money, such as food and shelter. If we are rich, additional spending to achieve these goals has little effect, and we try to find other ways to spend money to achieve our goals, but these are bound to be less efficient uses of money, for we have already done the things that money can do most easily.

Declining marginal utility is an important utilitarian justification for provision of compensation for injury, whether the compensation comes from personal insurance, social insurance, or liability law. If you suffer a loss that can be made up with money (such as a house fire), then you can obtain greater utility from money than you could before the loss. (You can rebuild.) If utility is marginally declining and insurance is "actuarily fair" (i.e., the insurer makes no long-run profit), then you maximize expected utility by insuring yourself fully against the loss.

This principle does not necessarily apply when losses cannot be replaced with money or goods. Unless the death of one's child increases one's marginal utility for money, compensation for such a death is not justified (Friedman, 1982). Penalties for death caused by negligence are justified by the need to deter negligence, but the penalty need not, in principle, be paid to the victim or the victim's parents. This is nonintuitive, as are many conclusions derived from utilitarianism. But, in fact, people do not generally buy life insurance on their children.

Because the marginal utility of money (and other goods) is usually declining, we can generally increase total utility by taking from the rich and giving the same amount to the poor, other things equal. The poor can make use of money to achieve their goals more easily. Of course, other things are not equal. But this argument pushes us toward equal division of goods.

One utilitarian argument against equal division is that goods can be used as rewards and punishments. The market rewards those who produce goods and services that others want. The availability of this reward causes people to try to provide goods and services that others want. Similarly, we can penalize people for behavior that we want to discourage. I mean "reward" and "punishment" in the general sense of anything that affects the frequencies of certain behavior, if only through expressing consistency with avowed social norms.

The principle of declining marginal utility and the principle of incentive are the major utilitarian considerations in allocating goods (including money), for example, through wages or taxation. If taxation is not progressive enough, then the poor will suffer too much; matters would be better on the whole if we took more from the rich and less from the poor. If, on the other hand, taxation is too progressive (so that, for example, everyone received the same after-tax income), incentive to produce would be reduced too much; matters would be better on the whole to allow some inequality. Some optimal balance can usually be found, but the correct distribution of goods need not follow any simple rule. Research is required to study both the utility of money for different groups and the incentive effects of extra income. From a utilitarian perspective, rules such as "To each according to her contribution" or "To each the same" are at best crude approximations to an optimum. When the relevant data are not worth collecting, however, use of such rules may be the best we can do.

The deterrence principle is the major utilitarian justification of punishment, including criminal law and tort law. Punishment is a harm, and it therefore must be justified by compensating gains. For utilitarians, two wrongs do not make a right, unless the second wrong prevents even greater wrongs in the future. In some cases, deterrence is optimal if an injurer is required to compensate the victim fully for a loss (Landes & Posner, 1987;

Shavell, 1987). In other cases, additional "punitive" penalties are justified (e.g., if the offense is difficult to detect). It might make sense to make someone who kills a child negligently pay a penalty – as deterrence – even if it does not make sense to give that penalty to the child's parents. For utilitarians, compensation and deterrence are not necessarily linked, although for practical purposes it might make sense to link them.[1]

Competing theories (e.g., Cohen, 1989; Rawls, 1971) often make some sort of distinction between different kinds of goods. The idea is that equalization should apply mainly to certain goods, such as adequate nutrition, medical care, educational opportunity, opportunity to compete for positions, and opportunity to participate politically. Other goods – such as expensive cars, vacation homes, pornographic movies, or, more generally, the things that people spend their money on once they have satisfied their basic "needs" – should be left to the incentive system, if anywhere.

Utilitarianism does not begin with any distinction of this sort, but a similar distinction can be derived from the competing principles of incentive and declining marginal utility. Both sorts of goods achieve people's goals. The principle of declining marginal utility says that, other things equal, we should try to eliminate discrepancies in all of these things. A progressive income tax could still be justified even in a world in which everyone's basic needs were completely satisfied and money was spent only on luxuries. But in the real world, this principle alone gives us no particular reason to equate the distribution of basic needs rather than the money that people could use to satisfy them or to achieve any other goals.

But goods in the first category – the basic needs – allow people to take part most effectively in a competition based on incentive. Efforts to equate the distribution of these goods – beyond simply giving people the money to pay for them – increase the general effectiveness of an incentive system. (I assume that the effectiveness of money spent on these goods at making people sensitive to incentive is also marginally declining.) People who are poorly educated, in poor health, or malnourished cannot be induced to contribute much even by fairly heavy incentives. Their production is therefore lost to the rest of us. So we have additional reason to equate these basic goods, aside from the fact that people want them very badly.

Moreover, some of the "luxuries" (e.g., pornography, or buying gas guzzlers) that people pursue with wealth derive from goals that people should be discouraged from developing, because they impair the achievement of other people's goals more than most goals do. We might tolerate some of these goals by allowing them as part of an incentive system, but we surely do not want to encourage them by making them part of a system of basic entitlements.

Although utilitarianism presupposes equal consideration of everyone, it is, in another sense, not a theory of justice at all, for it tries to subsume all other considerations of justice under other headings. In doing this, it can account for some of the intuitions about justice that inspire competing theories.

## Tastes

A second utilitarian argument against equal division of all goods is the existence of individual tastes. If I like apples and you like oranges, it is better for me to get more of the apples and you to get more of the oranges. The market, as an institution, allows us to satisfy our individual tastes, insofar as we can predict them.

## Envy and comparison

Certain emotions are connected with distributions, particularly envy, a desire that those who are perceived as coming out ahead unjustly should suffer (Elster, 1989; Sabini & Silver, 1982). Envy is most likely to arise when the comparison between self and others is clear, and this is most likely to happen when people are near each other, working together, in the same family, and so on.

Envy can be an unpleasant consequence of decisions about distribution. It must therefore be included in the evaluation of options. One way to avoid envy is to use simple rules of equal division, or any rules that everyone agrees should be used. Another way is to teach people not to be envious, as traditional Christianity has tried to do.

We often find decision makers paying careful attention to equity within their groups, ignoring gross inequity between members of different groups. Reduction of envy is a possible justification of such concerns.

Another possible justification of such concern is that many goods are evaluated through comparison to the goods possessed by others (Sen, 1987). Clothing, automobiles, and houses are, for many people, valued to the extent to which they are up to (or above) the level of the owner's reference group. Lawyers must dress like other lawyers, not like professors, so even a public-interest lawyer needs a collection of suits. People might be able to overcome such comparative evaluation, just as they can overcome envy, but, until they do, it is a relevant concern.

Many have argued that certain goals, such as those resulting from envy, should be ignored in a utilitarian calculus. I shall not assume this, for these goals are real.[2] However, ignoring envy might be one way to teach people not to be envious. If it is, then we might well be justified in ignoring envy in our decisions.

## Expectations

In the second grade, my son was given a story of the "fair bears," who went out to collect berries. The baby collected the most berries, the (large) father the next most, and the mother the least. All three worked equally hard. The children were asked how the bears should divide up the berries.

Clearly, this is one of several episodes of the same type. The bears have probably worked out a system, and, in the long run, a great variety of systems could be approximately optimal from a utilitarian point of view. My own answer is "not enough information given." (If it were people and not bears, I might be able to make some reasonable guesses about what had happened before.) If the bears expected to keep the berries that each of them collected, then it would seem unfair to divide the berries equally. Likewise, if they expected to divide the berries equally, it would seem unfair to keep what was found.

Expectations have a role in utilitarian theory. They coordinate social interaction, and their violation weakens the general trust that people have in them, forcing people to take precautions against their violation by others. It does not matter much whether we drive on the left or right side of the road, provided that we all drive on the same side. If even a few people start driving on the other side, then everyone must be extra cautious, and this is costly. Likewise, people make plans based on expectations of how goods will be distributed. They suffer if they cannot make or carry out these plans. A nonoptimal system of distribution that fits everyone's expectations can be better than an otherwise optimal system that is introduced unexpectedly, without giving people adequate time to modify their plans.

### Rights

Here is a story based on Foot (1978): Five people are in a hospital, dying. One can be saved only by a kidney transplant, another by a heart transplant, another by a brain transplant, and so on. They are all young and will lead full lives if they are saved. But no donors are available. Then, one day, Harry wanders into the emergency room to ask directions. . . .

So the question for a utilitarian is, why not? The answer could be that this is one of those cases in which our intuitions are wrong, so that Harry really ought to be sacrificed, although a good person would not do it.

Another answer is that Harry, and all of us, have a right not to be sacrificed in this way. But what is a right and where does it come from? A possible utilitarian answer is that a right is a social rule that saves people certain costs of worry and protective behavior. If Harry were sacrificed, we would all have to take precautions against being sacrificed for the benefit of others. We would also worry about it. In the end, the sacrifice might not be justified in utilitarian terms.

More generally, many rights can be seen as social institutions or norms that are reliably enforced, so that people can depend on certain things not happening to them. If rights are violated, people have to change their plans – taking steps to protect themselves against things they thought they were protected against – and they have something new to worry about. These effects, although perhaps small, are spread over *many* people, and they might therefore outweigh a substantial net good that would be done otherwise.

In a utilitarian analysis, rights are never absolute. They can always be outweighed. As a practical matter, though, our judgments are prone to error, and we are properly suspicious of those who lightly take it upon themselves to violate someone's rights for someone else's imagined good. On the other hand, we should also be suspicious of those who raise the banner of rights on behalf of questionable practices. As Mill (1859) argued, rights are worth enforcing because they serve a utilitarian purpose. Some practices put forward as rights might not be justifiable in terms of their consequences for goal achievement.

### The need for adequate information

To test for antiutilitarian biases, we need to provide subjects with sufficient information so that utilitarianism provides an answer to the question we ask. Many experiments in equity theory are like the fair-bears story described above. Too little information is given, and many different responses are normatively reasonable. These experiments cannot tell us whether antiutilitarian biases exist. (Some of the experiments I discuss can be faulted on these grounds too, but I include them because I think that more information would not change the results.) For example, Bar-Hillel and Yaari (1987, and their chapter in this book) asked subjects to divide a shipment of 12 grapefruits and 12 avocados between Jones and Smith. Jones derives 100 mg of "vitamin F" from each grapefruit, and Smith derives 50 mg from each grapefruit and from each avocado. Smith and Jones are interested only in vitamin F.

A utilitarian would need to make some explicit assumptions about each person's utility function for vitamin F. If utility were linear with vitamin F, then Jones should get all the grapefruit and Smith, the avocados. But if the minimum requirement for staying alive were 800 mg from this shipment, or if envy were a strong consideration, then Smith should get four of the grapefruit too. (This solution, which also equated the amount of vitamin F for Smith and Jones, was preferred by most subjects.) If utility functions were marginally declining and similar for both people, the optimal solution would be somewhere in this interval. The utilitarian solution is even less clear in several variants of the basic cases – for example, those in which the subject is told only Smith's and Jones's *beliefs* about their ability to extract vitamin F, with their true ability unstated.

When relevant information about utility functions is withheld, we can learn about the heuristics that subjects use in the absence of such information. We cannot tell whether subjects regard these heuristics as sufficient even when the relevant information is provided. True, subjects rarely complain about the lack of information, but they are not usually asked whether they think the information is adequate, and they have come to expect psychologists to require judgments to be based on minimal cues.

In the rest of this chapter, I shall argue that many people have nonutilitarian intuitions about equity. Moreover, their heuristics have, in many cases, solidified into moral intuitions that are resistant to counterargument. People are not at all monolithic in these intuitions. Many people *do* bring utilitarian intuitions to bear on the same cases. All this makes for lively disputes in debates about public policy.

### Probability, ex ante and ex post

When no incentive effects are present, it seems equitable to divide costs or risks equally among similar individuals, and this is justified by declining marginal utility. But what seems equitable before a risk is resolved (ex ante) may not be equitable (ex post) (Keller & Sarin, 1988; Ulph, 1982). If I give each of my two nephews a lottery ticket, they are both being treated equally. If one wins, the situation is then unequal. But suppose that my only choices are to give 10 tickets to one nephew or 1 ticket to each. To get envy out of the picture while they are waiting for the results of the draw, suppose that neither nephew will ever know that I have given them the tickets, and that, if one wins, he will simply be told that someone gave him the winning ticket. Many people might still think that it is wrong to give more tickets to one nephew. The intuition that ex ante equity is important in its own right has inspired some (e.g., Sarin, 1985) to develop nonutilitarian normative models of equity. (Note that ex post equality is supported by declining marginal utility. Utilitarianism conflicts only with the intuition that ex ante equity is justified beyond its effect on ex post equity.)

In the end, though, only one of them can win, and giving one of them 10 tickets makes such an event more likely. The expected utility is greater for the unequal solution. The expected achievement of my nephew's goals – and mine insofar as I care about theirs – is greater with the unequal division. If I were to choose one ticket for each, I must deprive one nephew of an additional chance to win, and I could not justify this by saying that I had given the other a *compensating* gain.

One possible utilitarian justification of ex ante equality is that equal division follows a good general rule, and breaking this rule – even when doing so seems to maximize utility in a given case – would weaken support for the rule, so that, in the long run, the consequences would be worse. Notice that this argument presupposes that people will not distinguish between uses of the equality rule that do and do not maximize utility in the specific case.

Another possible utilitarian justification is that arbitrary ex ante inequality – not justified by incentive – weakens or dilutes the use of inequality of distribution for incentive. If distribution of anything, risks included, is seen as arbitrary, then people will not work so hard to gain benefits or avoid risks.

It is also possible, though, that the equal-chance principle is sometimes an overgeneralization, a true error. Chances to win are not the same as winnings. An equal-division rule for winnings is justified by the declining marginal utility of winnings themselves. But the utility of *chances* to win is not marginally declining. People still apply the equal division rule because they do not know its justification.

Keller & Sarin (1988) gave subjects hypothetical options like the following:

Option 1:   Person 1 dies, person 2 lives.
Option 2:   50% chance:   Person 1 dies,  person 2 lives.
            50% chance:   Person 2 dies,  person 1 lives.
Option 3:   50% chance:   Person 1 dies,  person 2 dies.
            50% chance:   Person 1 lives, person 2 lives.

Options 1 and 2 differ in *ex ante* equity, that is, equity determined before the uncertainty is resolved. Option 2 differs from option 3 in *ex post* equity, determined after the uncertainty is resolved. Subjects preferred more equal distributions in both kinds of situations, that is, option 3 is preferred to option 2, and option 2 is preferred to option 1.

According to a *simple* utilitarian analysis, all three options are equivalent. Emotional considerations could account for the pattern of choices that subjects make, however: Option 2, compared to option 1, leaves both potential victims with some hope until the uncertainty is resolved. (On the other hand, a 50% chance of death may provoke more than half of the anxiety of certain death, in which case option 1 would be better.) Option 2 might seem worse than option 3 because the person who lived might grieve for the person who died in option 2, and this could not happen in option 3.

For many cases of dispersed risk, however, these considerations are irrelevant, or they work in the opposite direction. In the case of small ex ante environmental risks from chemicals, for example, doubling the risk level and halving the number of people exposed would probably have little effect on the amount of anxiety in each exposed person, so that it would, on the whole, decrease anxiety (rather than increase it) by reducing the number of people exposed. Likewise, most decisions about risk have no effect on the amount of grief per death. This issue would arise only if the risk were such as to annihilate a substantial portion of some community.

Issues of equity in risk of discrete events such as death are somewhat separate from equity issues involving money. The utility of money is marginally declining. The utility of probability of death is, normatively, linear with probability (putting aside such issues as the effects of deaths on communities, and assuming constant grief per death). Our intuitions about equity in risk bearing – despite their strength – are probably unjustifiable. If we must give up something in order to follow them, then the intuitions themselves harm the achievement of other goals. This may be happening in our judgments about equality of ex ante risk.

### Punishment, deterrence, and compensation

To compare people's judgments to utilitarian theories of punishment and compensation, we (Baron and Ritov, 1992) devised a questionnaire concerning liability law for medical products. The questionnaire addressed, among other issues, respondents' understanding of deterrence as a rationale for penalties, and their understanding of the justification of compensation. Respondents were told:

Imagine that, a few years from now, the United States has a new law concerning medical misfortunes, such as injuries or diseases. According to this law, anyone who suffers such a misfortune can request compensation from the government. This compensation is in addition to medical expenses, which are paid out of universal medical insurance.

*If the misfortune might be caused by a medical product made by a company*, the person who suffered the misfortune can file a complaint. For each complaint, two questions will be decided separately, each by a different panel:

* One panel will decide whether the company will be fined, and, if so, how much. All fines go to the government, not the injured person. The panel that decides the fines considers only the justice of imposing the fines. It ignores the needs of the government for money, and it ignores how the money will be spent.
* The second panel will decide how much the injured person will be compensated. If any compensation is paid, the government pays it, not the company. This panel takes into account only the situation of the injured person. It ignores the cost to the government, and it ignores the responsibility of the government, if any, for causing or preventing the misfortune.

Compensation can be provided even if the company pays nothing, and the company can be fined even if no compensation is provided. The government does *not* have to break even in the long run.

The panel that decides on compensation to the victim does not know how much the company has been fined, if anything, and the panel that decides on fines does not know how much compensation has been given to the injured person.

*If the misfortune was not caused by a product*, the person who suffered the misfortune can still ask for compensation. Only the second panel will hear the case.

This situation allowed us to examine the determinants of compensation and penalties separately.[3]

Two cases were then presented. In the first, a woman becomes sterile as a result of taking a new (but well-tested) birth control pill. In the second, a child dies from a vaccine against a disease that is far more likely to kill the child than the vaccine is (based on real cases – see Inglehart, 1987). Each case was followed by several questions, which were then compared to each other. Questions were directed at both penalties and compensation for the victim (the parents, in the case of the child). Each question asked for a justification as well as a response.

We gave the questionnaire to members of Judicate, a group of arbitrators who are mostly retired judges, a group of environmental activists, a group of members of the American Economic Association, and a group of undergraduate students, and a few law students, 93 respondents in all. In general, the groups did not differ greatly in their responses, and I shall not discuss the group differences here.

*Do people see deterrence or incentive – future consequences – as a reason for increasing or decreasing penalties?* One test for this was the comparison of penalty judgments in questions in which the penalty would bring about improved behavior (making a safer product) versus questions in which the penalty would bring about a less desirable state (no product). For example, one question stated, "The company knew how to make an even safer pill but had decided against producing it because the company was not sure that the safer pill would be profitable. If the company were to stop making the pill that the woman took, it would make the safer pill." A matched question stated, "If the company were to stop making the pill that the woman took, it would cease making pills altogether." Analyses are restricted to those respondents who said that the company should pay some penalty in the first question.

If respondents said that the company should be punished less in the second question, then they were sensitive to the future effects of the penalties. Of 74 respondents who would fine the company in one case or the other and who answered these questions, 31% did think that the company should be punished less in the second case in at least one of the two cases, and 4% thought the company should be punished more.[4] Most of the subjects who would punish less in the second case explicitly mentioned incentive in their justifications, but only one of the other subjects mentioned it (arguing that incentive was optimal). Most respondents did not seem to notice the incentive issue.

A second test for incentive was the question in which the penalty would have no future effect at all because the penalty was secret (and those who would know were retiring) and, in any case, the company was insured by a long-term policy with fixed rates. "These two facts together mean that decisions about payment to the government could have no effect on future decisions by this company or other companies about which pills to produce." This stipulation ruled out any more general effect of fines on the deterrence of future behavior, if subjects accepted it (and none explicitly denied it as part of a deterrence rationale). Of 72 respondents who penalized the company in one case or the other and who answered this question, 24% did penalize the company less in this question, and 10% penalized the company more. Again, most respondents were not sensitive to incentive effects here.

*Does compensation depend on the cause of the injury?* In each case, the particular injury (sterility, death of a child) was held constant across the questions. Differences in the need for penalties could not serve as a reason for differences in compensation, because these two decisions were independent. We examined three different factors that could affect compensation in the absence of differences in the victim's need for compensation: whether the injury was caused by an omission or a commission; whether it was caused by nature or a company; and whether the company that caused it was negligent. In the negligence case, the company did not follow regulations in producing the product, but the negligence itself did not lead to the injury. Most analyses are restricted to those respondents who thought that some compensation should be provided in the first question.

In the omission questions, the company did not produce the product in question, and the injury would not have occurred if the company had produced it: the woman became sterile because she took a different, more risky, pill; or the child died from the flu. Of the 63 respondents who compensated the victim in the first question in at least one case and who answered this question, 32% provided less compensation (in at least one case) when the harm was caused by an omission and 2% provided more compensation. The effect was found in both cases. (Arguably, the victim should not have taken the risky pill, but the parents of the child who received the vaccine had no alternative vaccine.) People seem to feel that compensation should be greater when injury is caused by an act than when it is caused by an omission or by nature.

In other questions, the injury was simply caused by nature and could not have been prevented. Of 69 respondents who provided compensation in at least one case and who answered the questions about compensation for natural injuries, 58% provided less compensation for natural injuries than those caused by a company (in at least one case), 42% provided equal compensation in both cases, and none provided more compensation for natural injuries. People seem to feel that more compensation should be provided for injuries caused by people than for those caused by nature. This issue is discussed further subsequently.

Finally, of 76 respondents who provided compensation in at least one case and who answered the questions about negligence, 13% provided more compensation when the company was negligent and 1% provided less compensation. Note, however, that the provision of extra compensation did not help to punish the company, for that was handled in the penalty question. In sum, people seem to be influenced by nonutilitarian considerations having to do with establishing some sort of balance between compensation and penalty, as if the two could not be separated.

*Does direct compensation have special status?* In our cases, penalties and compensation were determined separately and did not have to be equal. Typically, however, injurers pay victims directly. We thought that people might have a very basic intuition about the need to "undo" a harm that would lead to greater payment when the compensation was paid directly. In other words, people might see the provision of compensation as more than just the assessment of a penalty and the provision of compensation. We tested this by asking how much compensation should be provided to the victim if the injurer pays directly, in the case in which the penalty was secret and the injurer was insured.

Of 83 respondents who answered the relevant question at least once, 29% provided more compensation when the company paid the victim directly and 5% provided less compensation. Moreover, 50% of the 82 respondents who answered the relevant questions provided more compensation here than when the injury was naturally caused. Of 79 subjects who answered all the relevant questions, 28% showed both of these effects together and only 1% showed the reverse effects (more compensation from nature and less compensation with direct payment).

This pattern of responses cannot be justified in terms of compensation or incentive. The need for compensation does not change as a function of the direct payment. Incentive is absent because of the insurance and the secrecy. We conclude, then, that a substantial proportion of respondents are inclined to ask injurers to pay more and victims to receive more when the payment is direct, as it is in most cases in the real world. Such a pattern of responding would lead to excessive use of the tort system, compared to what could be justified by the functions of compensation and deterrence.

### More on personal versus natural causation

In another study, not reported elsewhere, I examined a potential alternative explanation of the finding that compensation was greater when the injury was caused by people rather than by nature. Specifically, victims might feel more emotionally upset when their misfortune was caused by a person, thus needing extra compensation.

To test this, I asked subjects to decide on appropriate compensation for victims of injuries. Subjects were told that the victims never knew the cause of their accident and that the injurers never knew the effect of their carelessness on the victim (so they did not know about the compensation either). The latter stipulation ruled out any possible deterrent effect of the compensation provided. Thirty-two student subjects (paid for their time) completed the questionnaire.

Subjects were told:

Imagine that you are the executor of the estate of an eccentric multimillionaire, whose estate is to be used to compensate people who have suffered some misfortune. It is your task to decide how much to compensate each person. The highest award can be $100,000, but you should feel free to give less if you want to save the money for more deserving cases.

Please compare the cases in each group to each other. We are interested in why you give different amounts to different cases in each group, or why you give the same amounts, so please provide brief explanations. We are not interested in the absolute levels of compensation, so if you prefer simply to rank the cases (including ties, if any), that is fine.

When we do not provide details (such as the age of the people), assume that you cannot take these details into account, or that they are the same for all the cases within a group.

Finally, please imagine that all these events occur in a country in which *lawsuits are prohibited*. The compensation that you award is therefore the only compensation that people can get for their suffering, even when, in our country, they might be able to sue. (They are, however, insured for their medical expenses.)

In the first scenario,

The people in this group have all suffered a permanent back injury that causes severe pain when they are engaged in strenuous activity. During the course of a normal day they experience some pain in the back. In all cases, the injury resulted from tripping over a rock lying on the sidewalk.

In Case 1, the rock "rolled onto the sidewalk from a nearby hill, as a result of a rainstorm." In Cases 2 and 3, it "rolled onto the sidewalk because a construction crew, which was working on a nearby building, had violated safety rules for the use of rocks in construction." Cases 2 and 3 were distinguished by whether those responsible for the violation were caught and punished (Case 2) or not (Case 3). Greater compensation in Case 3 than in Case 2 would suggest that subjects applied an intuition about retribution even when there was in fact no effect of the compensation on the perpetrator.

The second scenario involved blindness from an infection caused either by a mosquito bite, in Case 1, or by violation of sanitary rules by the kitchen staff in a restaurant in Cases 2 and 3, which were again distinguished by whether those responsible were caught and punished. The third injury was loss of a job caused either by normal business competition (Case 1) or by the unfair and illegal practices of another business firm (Cases 2 and 3, distinguished as before).

In each scenario, subjects were told that the victim did not know the cause of his injury (e.g., "The injured person never learned how the rock got where it was"), and in each case with a perpetrator they were reminded that the perpetrator did not know that the injury had occurred (e.g., "Those responsible . . . did not know about the injury").

Table 1 shows the ranking patterns of the three cases within each injury. Of 32 subjects, 16 provided equal compensation for all cases within each injury. Fifteen of the remaining 16 provided more compensation in Case 2 or Case 3, where carelessness was to blame, than in Case 1, where nature

Table 1 *Number of subjects who showed each pattern of ranking in the experiment on compensation*

| | Injury | | |
|---|---|---|---|
| | Back | Blindness | Job loss |
| 3>2>1 | 2 | 0 | 2 |
| 2>3>1 | 1 | 1 | 1 |
| 1>3>2 | 0 | 1 | 0 |
| 3>1>2 | 1 | 0 | 0 |
| 2=3>1 | 7 | 7 | 8 |
| 3>1=2 | 1 | 1 | 0 |
| 1>2=3 | 1 | 1 | 0 |
| 1=2=3 | 19 | 21 | 21 |

*Note:* In Case 1, the misfortune was caused by nature; in Cases 2 and 3, it was caused by negligence. In Case 2, those who were negligent were caught and punished; in Case 3, they were not. Higher ranks reflect greater compensation.

was to blame, in a majority of comparisons ($p < .001$ by a Wilcoxen test on the number of scenarios per subject, for each comparison). Of the subjects who compensated Cases 1 and 2 differently, 10 of 12, 8 of 10, and 11 of 11 were in the predicted direction for the three injuries, respectively. For Cases 1 and 3, the analogous results were 11 of 12, 8 of 10, and 11 of 11.

There was no significant difference in the compensation provided to Cases 2 and 3 (carelessness vs. accident). This result conflicts, inexplicably, with the result of the last study, in which compensation was greater when the company was negligent. Apparently, that phenomenon is not robust.

Typical justifications of lower compensation in Case 1 were: "In Case 1, no compensation should be awarded because no one is at fault. . . . it was a freak of nature and no one is to blame." "Case 1 – lowest amount → uncontrollable Natural Act – unpreventable unless person himself hadn't tripped." "Both people in Cases 2 & 3 are victims of people's carelessness so we decide to give [them] more than Case 1." "Case 1 should be awarded $10,000 only, because the rock came loose because of nature and it was inevitable that it would come apart." Cases 2 & 3: "A person eating in a restaurant should be able to assume that the food will not make her blind, so [I] awarded these two more than Case 1 where the blindness was from natural cause." One subject referred to victim incentive in the business scenario: "Case 1 should get less money because he could have done something to contribute to the company going out of business. . . ."

This experiment indicates that the heuristic of providing less compensation for misfortunes caused by nature than for those caused by people is not dependent on subjects' beliefs about victims' or injurers' knowledge or emotions. This person-causation bias could lead to inequity in the provision of compensation. We are more inclined to compensate those who are injured by others than those who are victims of natural accidents such as the unfortunate circumstances of their birth. Such inequity is nonoptimal for maximizing utility because it leaves some people uncompensated who could benefit greatly from a relatively small amount of compensation, while those who are injured by people sometimes get compensation that does them less good.

### Inequity and change in public policy

Other equity biases often seem to inhibit reform. Most reforms help some people and hurt others. For example, a higher tax on gasoline in the United States will help the whole world by reducing $CO_2$ emissions, and it will help most Americans by reducing traffic, pollution, and the budget deficit. But it will hurt those few Americans who are highly dependent on gasoline, even when we take the other benefits into account. Some of those who would be hurt are poor, who would suffer considerably. Congress might try to craft some sort of compensation for those who are hurt, but it is difficult to target them accurately.

The problem of uncompensated harm arises in practically any sort of reform in energy and environmental policy. The argument is basically in the form of a heuristic rule or intuition, "Don't hurt people." This argument has been made against increased gasoline taxes. Very likely, the same argument will be raised when other needed environmental reforms, such as those occasioned by global warming or the population explosion, are considered seriously. It is even made when the ultimate effect is to reduce inequity: I once almost convinced someone that the United States ought to abolish its sugar quotas in order to help the impoverished families who work on sugar plantations in Jamaica and the Philippines, until I mentioned that a much smaller number of sugar workers in the United States would lose their jobs as a result of such a move.

Most positions in public policy can be supported by some rational argument, so we cannot simply write off the opponents of gasoline taxes or supporters of sugar quotas as irrational. (For example, it is possible that abolition of sugar quotas will not really help the workers, although I suspect that those who say this have no particular reason to believe it.) It is possible, however, that part of the basis of their position is unjustifiable and that, if this part were removed, many opponents of truly beneficial reforms would not hold their position, or they would not fight for it so strongly.

Opposition to reform on grounds of uncompensated harm alone is a bias. Uncompensated harm is also caused by *failure* to make reforms. If we do *not* raise the gasoline tax, then – compared to the alternative at issue – we will rapidly exhaust natural reserves of petroleum, more people will get emphysema, more people will live in poverty as a result of economic stagnation, and so on. And if I am right that abolishing sugar quotas will help many families in foreign countries, then failure to abolish these quotas, relative to the alternative, is hurting these people. We must decide which hurt is smaller. What matters is the future achievement of goals, for that is what our decision can affect. The status quo is normatively irrelevant, as is the distinction between action and inaction.

In several studies (Ritov & Baron, 1990, 1992; Spranca, Minsk, & Baron, 1991) my colleagues and I have demonstrated a bias toward inaction, especially in cases in which both action and inaction can cause some harm. I am suggesting here that this bias tends to inhibit change in public policy because we attend to changes rather than ultimate results, and we attend more to harms than to benefits. When some people are hurt in order to help others, we view the change as unfair, even if we would prefer the result to the status quo if given a straightforward choice between the two (with neither functioning as the status quo).

### Resistance to voting for coerced reform

Some evidence for such an effect comes from a study (Baron and Jurney, in press) in which we presented subjects with six proposed reforms, each involving some public coercion that would force people to behave cooperatively, that is, in a way that would be best for all if everyone behaved that way. The situations involved abolition of TV advertising in political campaigns, compulsory vaccination for a highly contagious flu, compulsory treatment for a contagious bacterial disease, no-fault auto insurance (which eliminates the right to sue), elimination of lawsuits against obstetricians, and a uniform 100% tax on gasoline (to reduce global warming).

Most subjects thought that things would be better on the whole if the reforms, as we described them, were put into effect, but many of *these* subjects said that they would not vote for the reforms. (A much smaller group of subjects made the opposite kind of "reversal," saying they would vote for a proposal they thought would make things worse.) A status quo effect was also found: Subjects who thought that the reforms were beneficial were less likely to vote to repeal the reforms, once they were in effect, than comparable subjects were to vote against the reforms at the outset.

Subjects who voted against proposals that they saw as improvements cited several reasons (among a list of reasons that we gave them). The following three reasons (shown in the form used here in one of the studies) played a major role in such resistance to reform, as indicated both by correlations with resistance (among subjects who saw the proposals as improvements) and by subjects indicating that these were reasons for their votes:

Harm. "The law [or rule] would make some group worse off than they were before the law."

Rights. "The law would take away a choice that people ought to be able to make."

Fairness. "The law would unfairly distribute the costs of the change. That is, some people would suffer more than they should, relative to other people."

For example, in one study, 39% of subjects said they would vote for a 100% tax on gasoline, but 48% of the *non*voters thought that the tax would do more good than harm on the whole. Of those subjects who would vote against the tax despite thinking that it would do more good than harm, 85% cited the unfairness of the tax as a reason for voting against it, 75% cited the fact that the tax would harm some people, and 35% cited the tax as taking away a choice that people should be able to make.

Unfairness was generally the most consistent of these reasons for resistance, across different experiments and different cases. This result provides some evidence for the role of equity judgments in resistance to reform. Note that, in this study, we deal with subjects who saw reform as an improvement in utilitarian terms. We essentially asked subjects this directly.

### Resistance to inequality: Experiment 1

To examine further the role of fairness and harm in policy evaluation more quantitatively, I carried out two experiments using hypothetical situations. The first experiment examined trade-offs between, on the one hand, the total gain or loss in income of two groups, and, on the other hand, increases or decreases in the inequality of outcome or in the change from the status quo.

Twenty-four paid subjects (students) were given a questionnaire, which began,

Imagine that you are the president of a small island republic. You have the power to make treaties by yourself. You are engaged in trade negotiations with your sole trading partner, a much larger nation. Your entire economy is dependent on agricultural exports. Crops are grown by small farmers who own their own farms. Half are bean growers, and half are wheat growers. Bean growers and wheat growers are equally needy and equally deserving.

Each of the following cases represents a final offer made by your trading partner. For each offer, you are shown the present average annual income of each group, and the income that would result from accepting the offer. If you decline an offer, the current situation will stay in effect for at least two years.

Please indicate whether you would accept each offer ("yes") or not ("no"). Feel free to comment on the reasons for your policy in each part.

Part A, with 21 cases, began with the following case.

| 1. | Income of bean growers | Income of wheat growers |
|---|---|---|
| Decline | $30,000 | $30,000 |
| Accept | $40,000 | *$20,000* |

The income of the wheat growers for "Accept" (italicized here but not in the original) was incremented by $1,000 per case up to Case 21, where it reached $40,000. Case 2 is therefore the first case in which a net improvement is possible. Case 11 is the first case in which no harm is done to the wheat growers by accepting. The critical measure here is the minimum income of wheat growers at which the subject accepts the offer, minus $20,000. We can think of this net gain (roughly) as the minimum that the subject is willing to accept to give up equity (WTA).

In part B, with 11 cases, the first case was as follows.

| 1. | Income of bean growers | Income of wheat growers |
|---|---|---|
| Decline | $40,000 | *$20,000* |
| Accept | $30,000 | $30,000 |

The income of wheat growers for *Decline* (italicized here) was incremented in $1,000 steps until it reached $30,000 in Case 11. Case 1 entails no net loss. The remaining cases entail greater net loss for removing less initial inequality. Notice that Part B is identical to Cases 1–11 in part A, except that the "Decline" and "Accept" are reversed. At issue here is the highest income of wheat growers, minus $20,000, at which the subject accepts the offer. We can think of this net loss as the maximum that the subject is willing to pay for equity (WTP).

In parts A and B, one of the options is always equality of income. The value of such equality is therefore confounded with the value of equality or inequality in the *change* from the status quo that results from accepting an offer. Parts C and D were identical to parts A and B, respectively, except that the income of the wheat growers was everywhere shifted upward by $5,000, and part C had 16 cases instead of the 21 in part A. Hence, the gains or losses of each group from the status quo were the same as in parts A and B. In part C, however, initial equality never occurred, and final equality occurred in Case 16 (the last case) rather than Case 21. In part D, neither initial nor final equality occurred. Comparison of parts C and D to parts A and B therefore tells us about the role of inequality of results (initial or final) as opposed to inquality of changes (which are the same in both conditions).

Table 2 shows the statistics for WTA and WTP for the four parts. In general, about half the subjects gave the indicated modal response in each condition and the remaining responses were spread out over the range. The modal (and median) response in parts A and C represent the first case in which the wheat growers do not lose at all in order to help the bean

Table 2 *Statistics for four conditions of island experiment ($ thousands)*

| Part | A | B | C | D |
|---|---|---|---|---|
| Income | | | | |
| Bean decline | 30 | 40 | 30 | 40 |
| Wheat decline | 30 | 20–30 | 35 | 25–35 |
| Bean accept | 40 | 30 | 40 | 30 |
| Wheat accept | 20–40 | 30 | 25–40 | 35 |
| Measure | WTA | WTP | WTA | WTP |
| Mean | 9.2 | 2.0 | 8.1 | 1.0 |
| S.D. | 5.4 | 3.9 | 4.1 | 3.0 |
| Median | 10 | 0 | 10 | 0 |
| Mode | 10 | −1 | 10 | −1 |
| N at mode | 10 | 11 | 11 | 11 |

*Note:* The WTA measure is the increase in income of the wheat growers required to accept the change. The WTP measure is the greatest acceptable loss
in order to increase equality. For WTP, a value of −1 indicates that the subject
declined all offers, including the first (which had no net loss). "N at mode"
indicates the number of subjects, out of 24, who gave the modal response.

growers gain. (In part C, this case is also the one at which the overall group
difference of $5,000 is not increased.) Apparently, most subjects are un-
willing to hurt one group at all in order to help the other, even if the hurt
is as small as 10% of the gain.[5] The same heuristic accounts for the modal
unwillingness to accept any offers in parts B and D.

Note that these responses lead to a large discrepancy between WTA and
WTP as measures of the value of equality ($t = 6.68$, $p = .000$, combining parts
A and C and parts B and D). The removal of equality from one of the
options (parts C and D versus parts A and B) reduces the value of equity
somewhat ($t = 2.60$, $p = .016$). This reduction is not significantly different
for part A versus C and B versus D. Together, these results indicate that
subjects are most concerned about changes in the status quo, although
there is some value placed on a state of equality as well. The unwillingness
to hurt one group in order to help another group leads to large failures to
maximize net benefit.

*Resistance to inequality: Experiment 2*

The last experiment provided evidence for the "harm" heuristic: that it is
wrong to hurt some people for the benefit of others. The present experiment looks for additional evidence for the "fairness" heuristic (equal distribution) applied to changes, as well as initial and final states.

Subjects (students) were given a questionnaire beginning:

You are the principal of an elementary school with 200 children, 100 boys and 100 girls, in a small town. An epidemic of flu is approaching your town. The aches and fever typically last for about a week.

In the following cases, you are given statistics on the number of boys and the number of girls expected to get the flu if a vaccination program is undertaken in your school and if it is not. What is the greatest amount of money that you would spend from the school budget in each case on a vaccination program?

Subjects were told to use any units – dollars, percentages, or dollars per child – but to do so consistently, in terms of the total or average amount spent for both boys and girls.

The first case read:

| 1. | Boys | Girls |
|---|---|---|
| Do nothing | 15 | 15 |
| Vaccinate | 10 | 10 |

Twenty-two cases differed so as to manipulate the following variables: BEGINDIFF, the beginning difference (without vaccination) between the groups (ranging from 0 to 10); CHANGEDIFF, the difference in the change resulting from the vaccination (0 to 20); ENDDIFF, the end difference if the vaccinations are given (0 to 10); TOTALCHANGE, total reduction in disease resulting from the vaccine (10 to 20); and END, the final overall disease rate with vaccination (30 to 20). (The cases also varied from 30 to 50 in BEGIN, the initial number without vaccination, but BEGIN could be deduced from END and TOTALCHANGE.) Each case in which boys or girls were treated differently was repeated with the sexes reversed. Beginning levels varied from 15 to 25 for one sex or the other, and ending levels varied from 15 to 5. In six cases, the vaccine affected only one sex. In six cases, it affected both sexes equally.

An additional 22 cases were made up in which "the program was already planned" and "you could save money for your school by canceling the program." Subjects were asked, "What is the smallest amount of savings you would have to receive by canceling the program in each case?" These cases were identical to the initial 22 cases except that "Do nothing" was replaced with "Cancel," and "Vaccinate" was replaced with "Do not cancel." The two groups of 22 cases were distinguished by an additional dichotomous variable, SQ (for "status quo").

Thirty-three subjects received this form of the questionnaire, and 35 subjects were given the same questionnaire with the two SQ conditions reversed. Thirteen Ss in the original condition and 14 in the reverse condition were eliminated from analysis, either because they did not follow instructions (9 subjects, e.g., simply said whether they would vaccinate or not), responded only to TOTALCHANGE (14), or gave the same response to all cases in a group (2).

Data were analyzed by regressing each subject's responses on BEGIN,

END, BEGINDIFF, CHANGEDIFF, and ENDDIFF, separately for each SQ condition. The effect of inequality was assessed as the standardized coefficients for BEGINDIFF, CHANGEDIFF, and ENDDIFF. Across all subjects, the means of the BEGINDIFF and ENDDIFF coefficients were not significantly different from zero, nor were they different as a function of SQ. The CHANGEDIFF coefficient was significant in the hypothesized direction, with greater inequality in the change leading to lower value (mean = 0.100, $t = 2.46$, $p = .009$, one-tailed, for the mean coefficient of both SQ conditions; the result was the same in both SQ conditions, with means of 0.103 and 0.096).

Examination of individual regression coefficients confirmed the overall results. Sixteen (of 43) subjects had at least one coefficient for CHANGEDIFF significant at $p < .025$. Four subjects had one CHANGEDIFF coefficient significant in the wrong direction. Only five subjects showed any other significant coefficients.

There was no status quo effect overall, as determined from the constant terms in the regressions. This contrasts sharply with the last experiment, in which the status quo effect was extremely large. In that experiment, however, changes from the status quo involved hurting one group in order to help another. In the present experiment, all groups were helped by the vaccinations. Still, a status quo effect is often found (Samuelson & Zeckhauser, 1988), and it remains a puzzle why it was not found here.

In sum, the present experiment revealed that some subjects were concerned about inequality in the distribution of the benefits of a vaccination program. Inequality reduced the value they placed on the program. Once again, use of this heuristic could lead to failure to maximize the total benefits of a program.

These experiments are preliminary because I have not ruled out a possible alternative explanation of the results. Specifically, subjects might take into account not only the direct costs and benefits of options but also the indirect costs and benefits that result from the emotional response of those affected. Wheat growers might resent having their income cut, and this resentment might increase the disutility of the cut itself. It is more difficult to make this argument in the case of the children, for they would be unlikely to know how much the vaccine helped each of the sexes. But anticipated resentment could again have some role.

On the basis of the experiment reported in the last section, in which I have tried to explicitly remove the possibility of such emotions, I doubt that this sort of explanation accounts for the results. More likely, I think, subjects are applying heuristics without explicitly evaluating the consequences of the options. Further research must be done, but, in the meantime, I believe that the present results make more plausible the claim that many people do not evaluate options in terms of their expected utilities, but, rather, in terms of heuristics that yield the best solution only some of the time.

## Conclusion

In this chapter, I have summarized the utilitarian approach to distribution, and I have described several studies suggesting that people's intuitions often contradict utilitarian theory. Many people seem to think that punishments or penalties are inherently deserved, so that they should be applied even when deterrence is absent. People also tend to think that compensation should be greater when harm is caused by people than when it is caused by nature, especially (in one study) when injurers are negligent. Greater compensation is also provided when the injurer compensates the victim directly; this seems to fit into a schema for compensation. Also in contrast to utilitarian theory, people are reluctant to harm one person in order to help another, and they are reluctant to initiate reforms when the benefits of reform are unequally distributed, even when the reforms are beneficial on the whole.

In all studies, these biases (departures from the theory) were by no means universal. People differ in the extent to which they subscribe to utilitarian theory in each case. Many subjects follow the theory. (The number who follow the theory depends heavily on the question, and very likely also on the wording of the question.) It does not seem to be beyond our cognitive power to follow it. Most people seem to have utilitarian intuitions alongside of others. The findings of Larrick, Nisbett, & Morgan (1990) suggest that subjects who follow this sort of theory are at least no worse off personally than those who do not.

My own view (Baron, 1990) is that people should be taught to understand the utilitarian approach. If instruction in the kind of principles I have outlined were widespread, then I think that people would have a common language for discussing their differences about matters of social policy, and we would be able to reduce many of our differences to empirical questions (or to judgments about the answers to these questions, when we must decide in the absence of data). The need for a common language is particularly important in the years immediately ahead, when the world must collectively decide (if only by default) how to respond (or not respond) to an interrelated set of issues concerning population growth, environmental degradation, and global warming. The question of how the burden of global warming will be distributed among different people and people of different nations will raise very serious questions of equity (Baron & Schulkin, in press).

If utilitarianism were better understood, those who reject it would do so on the basis of understanding, not on the basis of ignorance. These critics would be encouraged to work out alternative theories more thoroughly, so that they provided solutions to real problems just as well as utilitarian theory does.

**References**

Bar-Hillel, M., & Yaari, M. (1987). Judgments of justice. Unpublished manuscript, The Hebrew University, Jerusalem.

Baron, J. (1985). *Rationality and intelligence.* Cambridge: Cambridge University Press.

(1988a). *Thinking and deciding.* Cambridge: Cambridge University Press.

(1988b). Utility, exchange, and commensurability. *Journal of Thought, 23,* 111–131.

(1990). Thinking about consequences. *Journal of Moral Education, 19,* 77–87.

(in press). *Morality and rational choice.* Dordrecht, Holland: Kluwer.

Baron, J., & Jurney, J. (in press). Norms against coerced reform. *Journal of Personality and Social Psychology.*

Baron, J., & Ritov, I. (1992). Intuitions about punishment and compensation in the context of tort law. Unpublished manuscript, University of Pennsylvania.

Baron, J., & Schulkin, J. (in press). Equity, moral judgments, and global warming. *Environment.*

Cohen, G. A. (1989). On the currency of egalitarian justice. *Ethics, 99,* 906–944.

Elster, J. (1989). *The cement of society.* Cambridge: Cambridge University Press.

Foot, P. (1978). The problem of abortion and the doctrine of the double effect. In P. Foot, *Virtues and vices and other essays in moral philosophy.* Berkeley: University of California Press, pp. 19–32. (Originally published in *Oxford Review,* no. 5, 1967.)

Friedman, D. (1982). What is "fair compensation" for death or injury? *International Review of Law and Economics, 2,* 81–93.

Griffin, J. (1986). *Well being.* Oxford: Oxford University Press (Clarendon Press).

Hare, R. M. (1981). *Moral thinking: Its levels, method and point.* Oxford: Oxford University Press (Clarendon Press).

Hicks, J. R. (1939). The foundations of welfare economics. *Economics Journal, 49,* 696–712.

Inglehart, J. K. (1987). Compensating children with vaccine-related injuries. *New England Journal of Medicine, 316,* 1283–1288.

Kahneman, D., & Snell, J. (1990). Predicting utility. In R. Hogarth (Ed.), *Insights in decision making.* Chicago: University of Chicago Press.

Kaldor, N. (1939). Welfare propositions of economics and interpersonal comparison of utility. *Economic Journal, 49,* 549–552.

Keller, L. R., & Sarin, R. K. (1988). Equity in social risk: Some empirical observations. *Risk Analysis.*

Landes, W. M., & Posner, R. A. (1987). The economic structure of tort law. Cambridge, MA: Harvard University Press.

Larrick, R. P., Nisbett, R. E., & Morgan, J. N. (1990). Who uses cost-benefit reasoning? Unpublished manuscript, University of Michigan, Ann Arbor.

MacIntyre, A. (1984). *After virtue: A study in moral theory* (2nd ed.). Notre Dame, IN: University of Notre Dame Press.

McCloskey, M. (1983). Naive theories of motion. In D. Gentner & A. L. Stevens (Eds.), *Mental models* (pp. 299–324). Hillsdale, NJ: Erlbaum.

Mill, J. S. (1859). *On liberty.* London: Parker & Son.

Nozick, R. (1974). *Anarchy, state, and utopia.* New York: Basic Books.

Rawls, J. (1971). *A theory of justice.* Cambridge, MA: Harvard University Press.

Ritov, I., & Baron, J. (1990). Reluctance to vaccinate: Omission bias and ambiguity. *Journal of Behavioral Decision Making, 3,* 263–277.

(1992). Status-quo and omission bias. *Journal of Risk and Uncertainty, 5,* 49–61.

Sabini, J., & Silver, M. (1982). *Moralities of everyday life.* Oxford: Oxford University Press.

Samuelson, W., & Zeckhauser, R. (1988). Status quo bias in decision making. *Journal of Risk and Uncertainty, 1,* 7–59.

Sarin, R. K. (1985). Measuring equity in public risk. *Operations Research, 33,* 210–217.

Sen, A. (1987). *The standard of living.* Cambridge: Cambridge University Press.

Sen, A., & Williams, B. (Eds.) (1982). *Utilitarianism and beyond.* Cambridge: Cambridge University Press.

Shavell, S. (1987). *Economic analysis of accident law.* Cambridge, MA: Harvard University Press.

Singer, P. (1977). Utility and the survival lottery. *Philosophy, 52,* 218–222.

(1979). *Practical ethics.* Cambridge University Press.

Spranca, M., Minsk, E., & Baron, J. (1991). Omission and commission in judgment and choice. *Journal of Experimental Social Psychology, 27,* 76–105.

Ulph, A. (1982). The role of ex ante and ex post decisions in the valuation of life. *Journal of Public Economics, 18,* 265–276.

Weymark, J. A. (1991). A reconsideration of the Harsanyi-Sen debate on utilitarianism. In J. Elster & J. E. Roemer (Eds.), *Interpersonal comparisons of well-being,* pp. 255–320. New York: Cambridge University Press.

Williams, B. (1985). *Ethics and the limits of philosophy.* Cambridge, MA: Harvard University Press.

### Notes

1 We should not assume this, however. New Zealand has been experimenting with a compensation system totally separate from the tort system.
2 In saying this, I do not imply that we should invoke such goals to explain every deviation from utilitarian theory. Rather, in making decisions, we should honestly decide whether such goals are relevant. In experimental work, we should try to eliminate them.
3 The story is not entirely unrealistic. New Zealand now has a system something like this.
4 These results are unlikely to result from confusion of compensation and deterrence, for the proportions were essentially identical in subjects who did not think that the victim should be compensated and in those who did think so.
5 It is unlikely that subjects believe that the utility loss of a $1,000 loss is greater than a utility gain of a $10,000 gain. Previous studies of the utility of gains versus losses have not found such large differences, but this was not checked here.

# 7 Trade-offs in fairness and preference judgments

*Lisa D. Ordóñez and Barbara A. Mellers*

At the heart of many debates about distributive justice is the widely assumed trade-off between equality and efficiency (Okun, 1975). In the present chapter, *equality* refers to the distribution of income within a society. Equality increases whenever income variability is reduced. *Efficiency* refers to the goods and services that result from a given input – production, physical capital, or human labor. Efficiency increases whenever society produces more from the same input. Trade-offs between equality and efficiency occur because increases in one often lead to decreases in the other. An egalitarian society satisfies basic needs by establishing programs that redistribute wealth. But those programs can reduce efficiency when they introduce bureaucratic waste or diminish financial incentives. A reduction in efficiency can lead to fewer investments, fewer jobs, and declining productivity.

### Theories of distributive justice

Is there an ideal point along the equality–efficiency continuum? Political and moral philosophers have articulated a number of positions about what constitutes justice and how to arrive at just distributions of resources and rewards. These positions place differential emphasis on equality and efficiency.

Utilitarians believe that society should be arranged to maximize the total (or sometimes average) utility of all individuals (Bentham, 1961/1789). If utility is identical to profit, then profit maximization occurs when efficiency

We thank Jon Baron, Karen Biagini, Michael Birnbaum, John Carroll, Shi-jie Chang, Alan Cooke, Robyn Dawes, and Philip Tetlock for helpful discussions and comments on drafts of this chapter. We also thank Kim Gallegus and Katty Ho for help with data collection. This research was supported by an NSF grant (BNS-90-16526) to the first author and another NSF grant (SES-89-08698) to the second author. The first author was also supported by a Ford Foundation Predoctoral Fellowship (880-0765).

is greatest. This version of utilitarianism might emphasize efficiency over equality. On the other hand, if utility is a negatively accelerated function of income, the poor benefit more from any given dollar. This form of utilitarianism might strike a compromise between equality and efficiency in an attempt to provide both assistance at the bottom and incentives at the top.

Egalitarians argue that society should be arranged to provide food, shelter, and essential medical care for all concerned. These basic needs are satisfied by means of redistributive policies that minimize income inequality. In this framework, the emphasis is on equality rather than efficiency.

More recently, Rawls (1971) developed a philosophical theory of justice based on a social contract. Rawls asks what would happen if the framers of society operated behind a "veil of ignorance," so that they knew nothing about their future socioeconomic position. Rawls contends that two principles of justice would emerge. The first is the principle of greatest equal liberty; each person would have an equal right to the most extensive system of liberties and freedoms. The second is the difference principle, which asserts that societal and economic institutions should be arranged to benefit the worst off. This principle is a *maximin* rule. Disparities in wealth are assumed to be just when they improve the welfare of the poorest members of society. This theory focuses on the incomes of the least advantaged members of society.

### Compromises between equality and efficiency

Researchers have posited that, for an assortment of cognitive and political reasons, people have difficulty making trade-offs between strongly held values such as environmental protection and economic growth (Abelson & Levi, 1985; Einhorn & Hogarth, 1981; Tetlock, 1986). Hadari (1988) notes that some philosophical theories of distributive justice structure society to avoid trade-offs between basic values. Utilitarians escape trade-offs by reducing all values to a single scale of utility or welfare. Rawls avoids trade-offs by lexicographically ordering values. Only after a society has established basic liberties for everyone does the maximin rule apply.

The present chapter investigates how people make trade-offs when judging societal fairness and preference. It builds on earlier work by Mitchell, Tetlock, Mellers, and Ordóñez (1992) that examined the judged fairness of hypothetical societies. In those experiments, societies were displayed as income distributions, that is, average incomes in each quartile. Equality and efficiency were manipulated using income variance and average income, respectively. Societies with more income variance had greater income inequality. Societies with higher average income had greater efficiency. Subjects were told to assume that the distribution of inputs was held constant across all societies, so greater profits resulted from greater efficiency.

A fairness ranking over societies was derived for each individual. When the effort-reward correlation was low, rankings correlated higher with income variance (equality). When the effort–reward correlation was high, rankings were better predicted from average income (efficiency). Mitchell et al. (1992) concluded that the effort–reward correlation or level of meritocracy was a moderator of equality–efficiency trade-offs.

In Mitchell et al. (1992), income variance was confounded with minimum income (i.e., average income in the lowest quartile). We manipulate both factors and investigate whether the predictability of income variance is due to a concern for the overall income variability or the floor of the income distribution. Furthermore, we manipulate the effort–reward correlation in such a way that subjects can make trade-offs between this factor and others. We also investigate judged preferences to examine whether people prefer to live in societies they judge more fair. Finally, do trade-offs made at the societal level also occur at the individual level? We ask subjects to judge the extent to which an individual within different societies is overbenefited or underbenefited. Of interest is whether the same factors influence fairness judgments at the micro and macro levels (Brickman, Folger, Goode, & Schul, 1981).

### Macro fairness and preference

Two experiments examined judgments of societal fairness and preference. Societies were displayed as scatterplots with salary plotted against work index. Work index, ranging from 0 (lowest contribution) to 4 (highest contribution), was said to reflect merit, seniority, effort, productivity, experience, etc. The distribution of work was held constant across societies.

In Experiment 1, eight societies were constructed from variations along three factors: minimum salary, mean salary, and salary standard deviation.[1] Figure 1 presents two societies that differ in salary mean and salary standard deviation. Society A has a lower mean salary, but less salary variability; Society B has a higher mean salary, but more salary variability.

In Experiment 2, sixteen societies were formed by manipulating the three factors in Experiment 1 and the effort–reward correlation. Figure 2 shows two societies that differ in correlation and minimum salary. Society A has a higher minimum salary but a lower work–salary correlation, and Society B has a higher correlation but a lower minimum salary.

Table 1 gives information about the eight societies in Experiment 1. The correlation between work and salary ranged from .19 to .77 across societies. Table 2 provides information about the sixteen societies in Experiment 2. In both experiments, the distribution of work was held constant.

Subjects were presented with all possible pairs of societies. In the fairness conditions, subjects judged which society was more fair. In the preference conditions, subjects selected the society in which they preferred to live. Subjects were told that the poverty level was $15,000.[2] After comple-

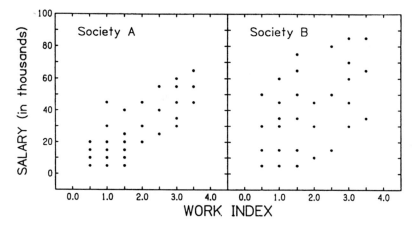

Figure 1   Trade-offs between measures of equality and efficiency in Experiment 1.
Society A has a narrow salary standard deviation and a low mean salary. Society B
has a wide salary standard deviation and a high mean salary.

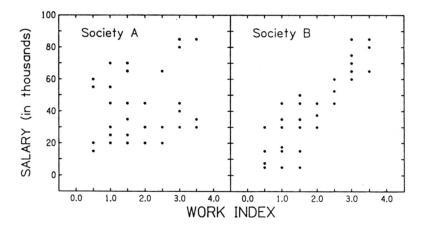

Figure 2   Correlation and minimum salary trade-offs in Experiment 2. Society A
has a high minimum salary but low correlation, and Society B has a high correlation but a low minimum salary.

tion of the two tasks, subjects answered a questionnaire requesting information about sex, socioeconomic status, political party affiliation, and political views (rating on a seven-point conservative/liberal scale). In Experiment 2, subjects were also asked to state their anticipated socioeconomic
status and rank the importance of each experimental factor in their fairness
and preference judgments. Participants were undergraduates at the University of California at Berkeley who received credit in a lower division
psychology course. There were 80 and 70 subjects in Experiments 1 and 2,
respectively.

Table 1 *Societies in Experiment 1 (in thousands)*

| Society | Minimum salary | Mean salary | Salary std. dev. |
|---------|----------------|-------------|------------------|
| LLW | 5 | 31 | 23 |
| LLN | 5 | 30 | 18 |
| LHW | 5 | 41 | 25 |
| LHN | 5 | 40 | 18 |
| HLW | 15 | 34 | 19 |
| HLN | 15 | 33 | 12 |
| HHW | 15 | 43 | 21 |
| HHN | 15 | 42 | 18 |

*Note:* The first letter in the society label refers to the minimum salary (L = low and H = high). The second represents mean salary (L = low and H = high). The third letter refers to the salary standard deviation (W = wide and N = narrow).

Table 2 *Societies in Experiment 2 (in thousands)*

| Society | Correlation | Minimum salary | Mean salary | Salary std. dev. |
|---------|-------------|----------------|-------------|------------------|
| LLLW | 0.22 | 5 | 31 | 23 |
| LLLN | 0.27 | 5 | 30 | 18 |
| LLHW | 0.19 | 5 | 41 | 25 |
| LLHN | 0.25 | 5 | 40 | 18 |
| LHLW | 0.19 | 15 | 34 | 19 |
| LHLN | 0.21 | 15 | 33 | 12 |
| LHHW | 0.22 | 15 | 43 | 21 |
| LHHN | 0.18 | 15 | 42 | 18 |
| HLLW | 0.87 | 5 | 31 | 23 |
| HLLN | 0.79 | 5 | 30 | 18 |
| HLHW | 0.87 | 5 | 41 | 25 |
| HLHN | 0.83 | 5 | 40 | 18 |
| HHLW | 0.79 | 15 | 34 | 19 |
| HHLN | 0.88 | 15 | 33 | 12 |
| HHHW | 0.87 | 15 | 43 | 21 |
| HHHN | 0.86 | 15 | 42 | 18 |

*Note:* The first letter in the society label refers to the correlation between work index and salary (L = low and H = high). The second represents minimum salary (L = low and H = high). The third letter refers to the mean salary (L = low and H = high). The fourth represents standard deviation (W = wide and N = narrow).

*Did subjects make trade-offs?*

For each subject, two societal rankings were derived – one for fairness and one for preference. These rankings were computed by counting the number of times a society was judged as more fair (or more preferred) than the others. Scores could range from 0 to 7 in Experiment 1 and from 0 to 15 in Experiment 2. The higher the score, the higher the rank of that society. If two or more societies received the same score, ranks were tied.

Trade-offs were assumed to occur if societal rankings were *inconsistent* with a lexicographic order of any of the experimental measures. For example, a lexicographic order of minimum salary would be one in which all societies with high minimum salaries were ranked above those with low minimum salaries. Societies with the same minimum salary might be distinguished on the basis of other factors, but this ordering would be secondary to considerations of minimum salary.

In Experiment 1, 57% and 52% of the subjects had fairness and preference rankings that were *inconsistent* with any of the lexicographic orders. In Experiment 2, 38% and 70% had fairness and preference rankings that were inconsistent with the lexicographic orders. These subjects appeared to make trade-offs.

It could be argued that these percentages are too high, since they do not allow for error or unreliability in the data. Therefore, subjects whose rankings were *almost* consistent with a lexicographic order were reclassified. Whenever a subject's ranking was consistent with a lexicographic order after the ranks for two societies were reversed, that subject was assigned to the lexicographic group. With this revised count, 40% and 39% of the subjects in Experiment 1 had fairness and preference rankings that were inconsistent with lexicographic orders. In Experiment 2, 29% and 60% had fairness and preference rankings that were inconsistent with lexicographic orders. Thus, an average of 42% of the subjects in each condition appeared to make trade-offs.

*Which factors accounted for the most variance?*

Individual fairness and preference rankings were correlated with three orthogonal rankings, each based on the experimental measures (i.e., low and high mean salary, low and high minimum salary, or wide and narrow salary standard deviation). Table 3 shows the percentage of individuals whose rankings correlated highest with each experimental measure. In the fairness condition, the largest percentage of subjects had rankings that correlated highest with salary standard deviation. In the preference condition, the largest percentage of subjects had rankings that correlated highest with minimum salary. However, the most striking result in Table 3 is that there are no clear winners. Subjects used a variety of different strategies in their judgments.

Table 3 *Percentage of subjects best fit by experimental measures*

| Response | Minimum salary | Salary std. dev. | Mean salary |
|---|---|---|---|
| Fairness | 34 | 41 | 25 |
| Preference | 43 | 28 | 30 |

Table 4 *Median correlations of subject rankings with experimental measures shown for subject groups*

| | Fairness groups | | | Preference groups | | |
|---|---|---|---|---|---|---|
| Measures | Minimum salary | Salary std. dev. | Mean salary | Minimum salary | Salary std. dev. | Mean salary |
| Minimum salary | 0.82 | 0.22 | 0.38 | 0.77 | 0.11 | 0.36 |
| Salary std. dev. | 0.28 | 0.77 | 0.44 | 0.22 | 0.72 | 0.33 |
| Mean salary | 0.35 | 0.28 | 0.66 | 0.44 | 0.44 | 0.78 |

Table 4 provides information about the average correlations of subjects in each of the three groups and additional information about the extent to which their rankings correlate with other measures. Rows are the three experimental measures, and columns are the three groups of subjects whose fairness and preference rankings correlated highest with each experimental measure. Entries are median correlations. Correlations should be high down the diagonals, since subjects in those groups had rankings that were best-fit by that measure. Those correlations ranged from .66 to .82 for fairness and .72 to .78 for preference.[3]

Correlations on the off-diagonals show average predictability of the measures. These correlations are lower than those on the diagonals, ranging from .22 to .44 for fairness and .11 to .44 for preference. Although they are considerably smaller, these off-diagonal correlations differ significantly from zero. In sum, other factors also contribute to the predictability of the rankings.

How do societal rankings differ across the three groups? Figure 3 presents median fairness rankings for subjects in each best-fitting group. Numbers range from 1 (least fair society) to 8 (most fair society). In each box, rows are salary means, and columns are salary standard deviations. A box represents a set of societies with the same minimum salary; different boxes show societies with different minimum salaries.

Upper boxes, center boxes, and lower boxes present median rankings for the mean salary, the salary standard deviation, and the minimum salary group, respectively. Rankings differ considerably across groups. Subjects whose rankings were best fit by mean salary assigned lower ranks to low-mean societies and higher ranks to high-mean societies. Subjects whose rankings were best fit by salary standard deviation assigned lower ranks to wide-standard-deviation societies and higher ranks to narrow-standard-deviation societies. Finally, subjects whose rankings were best fit by minimum salary tended to assign lower ranks to low-minimum-salary societies and higher ranks to high-minimum-salary societies.

Despite these differences, certain patterns are common across all three groups. Within a box, the low-mean, wide-standard-deviation society is always ranked lowest. Furthermore, the high-mean, narrow-standard-deviation society is always ranked highest. Of interest are the rankings in the other two cells. Subjects whose rankings were best predicted by salary mean (upper boxes) judged the high-mean, wide-standard-deviation society as more fair than the low-mean, narrow-standard-deviation society for both levels of minimum salary. Subjects whose rankings were best predicted by salary standard deviation (center boxes) judged the low-mean, narrow-standard-deviation society as more fair than the high-mean, wide-standard-deviation society. Subjects whose rankings were best described by minimum salary (lower boxes) did not have a consistent set of rankings. In sum, Figure 3 shows systematic differences in trade-offs across groups. Similar patterns were found for preference rankings.

### Effects of the work–salary correlation

Experiment 2 investigates societies that vary in work–salary correlations as well as minimum salaries, salary means, and salary standard deviations. Table 5 presents the percentage of subjects whose fairness and preference rankings correlated highest with the four experimental factors. Approximately 75% of the subjects had fairness rankings that correlated highest with the work–salary correlation. The remaining 25% had rankings that were best described by minimum salary. Approximately 50% of the subjects had preference rankings that were best described by the correlation and the other 50% were best predicted by the minimum salary. Almost no subjects had fairness or preference rankings that were best predicted from measures of equality or efficiency.

Table 6 shows median correlations for best-fitting groups, as in Table 4. Rankings of subjects in the correlation and minimum salary groups were correlated with all four experimental measures. Once again, correlations were highest for the best-fitting measures. The other correlations were lower, but not zero. These correlations ranged from .16 to .52 for fairness and .12 to .44 for preference. Salary mean and standard deviation also contribute

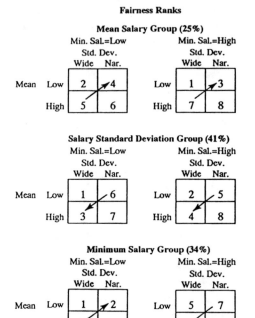

**Fairness Ranks**

**Mean Salary Group (25%)**

**Figure 3** Median rankings of societies from Experiment 1 for each group of subjects best fit by an experimental measure. Upper boxes, center boxes, and lower boxes show mean salary, salary standard deviation, and minimum salary groups, respectively. Numbers range from 1 (least fair society) to 8 (most fair society).

Table 5 *Percentage of subjects best fit by experimental measures*

| Response | Correlation | Minimum salary | Salary std. dev. | Mean salary |
|---|---|---|---|---|
| Fairness | 74 | 26 | 0 | 0 |
| Preference | 50 | 44 | 0 | 6 |

to the predictability of fairness and preference rankings, although they are not the best predictors.

Figure 4 presents median fairness rankings for subjects in the correlation and minimum salary groups. Numbers range from 1 (least fair society) to 16 (most fair society). Within each box, rows are minimum salaries and columns are work–salary correlations. Different boxes reflect societies with different levels of salary mean and salary standard deviation. Once again, certain patterns are consistent across groups. Within a box, the low-correlation, low-minimum-salary society is always ranked lowest. The high-correlation, high-minimum-salary society is always ranked highest. Subjects in the correlation group (upper boxes) judged the high-correlation,

Table 6 *Median correlations of subject rankings with experimental measures shown for subject groups*

| Measures | Fairness groups | | Preference groups | |
|---|---|---|---|---|
| | Correlation | Minimum salary | Correlation | Minimum salary |
| Correlation | 0.87 | 0.40 | 0.80 | 0.35 |
| Minimum salary | 0.25 | 0.77 | 0.44 | 0.75 |
| Salary std. dev. | 0.16 | 0.19 | 0.12 | 0.12 |
| Mean salary | 0.20 | 0.52 | 0.25 | 0.27 |

*Note:* Mean salary and salary standard deviation groups are not presented because there were either none or very few subjects in these groups.

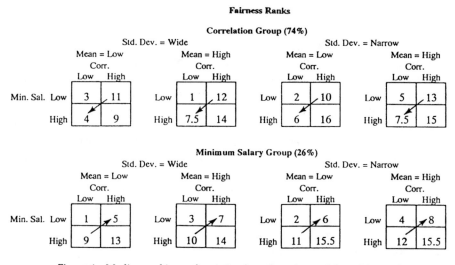

Figure 4   Median rankings of societies from Experiment 2 for subjects whose rankings were best fit by the correlation (upper boxes) and the minimum salary (lower boxes). Numbers range from 1 (least society) to 16 (most fair society).

low-minimum-salary society as more fair than the low-correlation, high-minimum-salary society in all four boxes. Subjects in the minimum-salary group (lower boxes) showed the opposite pattern. Preference rankings were similar to fairness rankings.

*Discussion*

Results from these experiments suggest that many people make trade-offs when judging societal fairness and preference. When equality and efficiency are varied in conjunction with other factors, trade-offs tend to occur between minimum salary and work–salary correlation. These measures are better predictors of fairness and preference judgments. Approximately 75% and 50% of the subjects had fairness and preference rankings that were best described by work–salary correlation, respectively. Virtually none of the subjects had fairness or preference rankings that were best predicted by equality and efficiency.

Why might people focus on the minimum salary and the work–salary correlation? Minimum salary might be viewed as a safety net beneath which people should not fall. The work–salary correlation may reflect the incentive system within the society. A high correlation implies that greater effort will lead to greater rewards. It also implies equal pay for equal work. But is societal fairness simply a high effort–reward correlation? Correlations could be high due to extreme outliers. Consider the salaries of some chief executive officers that are several hundred times more than those of the average workers. Effort–reward correlations could be low for most of the workers, but the overall correlation could be high due to a single point, the CEO. It would be interesting to investigate the extent to which societies with identical correlations but different outliers are judged fair.

As far back as Aristotle, justice has been thought to depend on the relationship between deservingness (effort, work, or productivity) and reward. Mellers (1982) examined fairness ratings of faculty members in hypothetical departments and found quite different deservingness functions between salary and merit in departments with the same salary–merit correlations. Deservingness functions were positively accelerated, linear, and negatively accelerated, depending on the joint distribution of salary and merit. Deservingness functions are not captured by correlations alone. However, in many situations, correlations may be a good first approximation. In fact, the correlation is a special case of Birnbaum's (1983) adjustment model of fair salaries. Birnbaum suggested that fair salaries might be determined by a context-dependent relationship between deservingness and reward. Salaries are assumed to be fair to the extent that they are determined by this relationship.

Results from these experiments also suggest that the societies in which people prefer to live are not necessarily judged as most fair. Many people judge societies with high correlations as fair, but they prefer to live in societies with high minimum salaries. Differences between fairness and preference judgments have also been found by Messick and Sentis (1979), who investigated judged allocations in situations where subjects assigned payments to themselves and another. In one condition, subjects divided rewards fairly, and in the other condition, they allocated rewards as they wished. Amounts that subjects preferred to give *themselves* were larger than amounts they judged to be fair.

What motivates societal preferences? One possibility is self-interest. People may be concerned about their own position in society. When their status

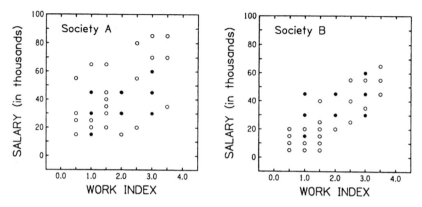

Figure 5   Two illustrative societies from Experiment 3. Common members (solid circles) are nested within different societies. Additional members (open circles) are varied across societies.

is uncertain, it may be prudent to prefer societies that help the least advantaged. Rawls develops this point in his theory of distributive justice. Another possibility is altruism. People may be genuinely concerned about the plight of the poor and prefer to live in societies that care for the needy. Research on social dilemmas indicates that some percentage of people act in altruistic ways, even when it entails personal sacrifice (Caporael, Dawes, Orbell, & van de Kragt, 1989). See Tyler and Dawes (this book) for a further discussion of this topic.

### Micro fairness

Experiment 3 examines whether factors that describe fairness judgments at the individual level resemble those at the societal level. Societies in Experiment 1 were constructed such that eight individuals (points in the scatterplots) were common to each society. Other points were added to manipulate the minimum salary, salary mean, and salary standard deviation. Figure 5 shows two illustrative societies. Solid points are the common members; open points are individuals who differ across societies. Society A has a high salary mean and a high minimum salary, but a wide salary standard deviation. Society B has a narrow salary standard deviation, but a low salary mean and low minimum salary.

Subjects were asked to rate the extent to which an individual was underbenefited or overbenefited on an 80 to −80 scale (where 80 = very very overbenefited, 0 = fairly treated, and −80 = very very underbenefited). As in the other experiments, they were told that the poverty level was $15,000. Subjects were given eight societies and judged 15 randomly ordered individuals in each society (the eight solid points in each panel of Figure 5 and seven points that differed for each society). After completing the experimental trials, subjects answered the same questionnaire used in Experi-

Figure 6    Mean overbenefited ratings for common members averaged over societies. Ratings are plotted against salary with a separate curve for each level of work.

ment 1. Participants were 88 undergraduates at the University of California at Berkeley who received credit in a lower division psychology course for their participation.

Figure 6 presents ratings for the eight common individuals, averaged over all eight societies. Judged overbenefitedness increased with salary and decreased with work index. Similar means were obtained for each society. Average ratings for the common individuals never changed sign across societies; an individual who appeared overbenefited in one society was never judged as underbenefited in another. But despite the fact that the signs did not change, the magnitudes of the ratings varied systematically across societies.

To illustrate the contextual effects, Table 7 presents average ratings of the common individuals in each of the eight societies. Common individuals were judged more overbenefited as mean salary, salary standard deviation, and minimum salary decreased. All three factors were statistically significant.[4]

### Which factors accounted for more variance?

For each subject, eight ratings were computed, one for each society, by averaging responses for the common individuals. These ratings were correlated with three orthogonal rankings based on salary mean, salary standard deviation, and minimum salary. Table 8 shows that for the largest

Table 7 *Mean overbenefitedness ratings for common members in different societies*

| Salary std. dev. | Low minimum salary | | High minimum salary | |
| | Mean salary | | Mean salary | |
| | Low | High | Low | High |
|---|---|---|---|---|
| Wide | 0.51 | −3.53 | 0.67 | −6.58 |
| Narrow | 5.76 | −1.92 | 2.54 | −3.28 |

*Note:* Mean ratings are averaged over common members. The response scale ranged from −80 to 80.

Table 8 *Percentage of subjects best fit by experimental measures*

| Response | Minimum salary | Salary std. dev. | Mean salary |
|---|---|---|---|
| Rating | 23 | 32 | 45 |

percentage of subjects, overbenefitedness ratings correlated with salary mean, followed by salary standard deviation, and then minimum salary. Correlations were also computed for each common member in all eight societies, and results were similar to those based on averages; for the largest percentage of subjects, overbenefitedness correlated with decreases in salary mean.

### Discussion

Experiments 1 and 3 allow a comparison of societal and individual fairness judgments. At the societal level, the largest percentage of subjects had fairness rankings that correlated highest with salary standard deviation. Minimum salary came in second, and salary mean took third place. At the individual level, the largest percentage of subjects had fairness rankings that correlated highest with salary mean. Salary standard deviation came in second place, followed by minimum salary.

Differences between individual and societal fairness might occur because people use different criteria to assess macro and micro justice. Subjects may make different trade-offs between equality and efficiency at different levels. If so, trade-offs could come into conflict; it may be impossible to make optimal trade-offs simultaneously.

### Individual differences

The present experiments demonstrate individual differences in fairness and preference judgments. Several studies have examined individual differences in fairness. In a review on sex and gender differences, Kahn and Gaeddert (1985) noted that men tend to endorse distributions of rewards in which ratios of outcomes to inputs are equal across individuals, whereas women tend to allocate rewards in a more uniform fashion. Major and Adams (1983) reported that women tend to have less variability than men in their reward allocations. Other studies have investigated individual differences in political ideology. Rasinski (1987) found that perceptions of fairness correlated with political orientation. Those scoring high on efficiency (proportionality rules for fair divisions) tended to be more conservative, whereas those scoring high on equality (egalitarian rules for fair divisions) tended to be more liberal.

Subjects in the present experiments were UC Berkeley undergraduates, and one might expect the vast majority to be liberal Democrats. However, only 60% of the subjects described themselves as Democrats. The average conservative/liberal rating was at the center of the scale. Roughly half were men, and half were women. The average self-report of socioeconomic status was 3.3 on a scale from 1 (lower class) to 5 (upper class).

Membership in a best-fitting group correlated significantly with the judged importance of that measure. However, group membership did not correlate significantly with demographic variables and political opinions, with a few notable exceptions. In Experiment 1, subjects with lower socioeconomic status tended to have fairness rankings that were best predicted by minimum salary. In Experiment 2, men tended to have preference rankings that were best predicted from the effort–reward correlation. Democrats, liberals, and women tended to have preference rankings that were best predicted from the minimum salary.

### Conclusions

Results from the present experiments suggest that some people make trade-offs between economic measures of equality and efficiency when judging societal fairness and preference. However, trade-offs tend to occur more often between the minimum salary and the work–salary correlation. These measures predict fairness and preference judgments to a greater extent than equality and efficiency. Furthermore, trade-offs tend to differ for fairness and preference judgments. The percentage of subjects best fit by minimum salary was greater for preference rankings than fairness rankings. Interestingly, preference rankings seemed more in line with Rawls's theory of justice than fairness rankings. Fairness rankings were not entirely consistent with Rawls's theory, egalitarianism, or utilitarianism.

Finally, factors that determine fairness at the individual level differ from those that describe fairness at the societal level. Micro and macrojustice can come into conflict whenever we think it is fair to treat individuals and groups differently. It may be one thing to vote for overall cuts in welfare programs, and another thing to refuse assistance to a homeless person who lost his job due to illness. Understanding the nature of these differences may ultimately help us reach more acceptable trade-offs between economic and psychological factors.

### References

Abelson, R. P., & Levi, A. (1985). Decision making and decision theory. In G. Lindzey and E. Aronson (Eds.), *Handbook of social psychology* (3rd ed.). New York: Random House.

Bentham, J. (1961/1789). *Principles of morals and legislation.* New York: Doubleday.

Birnbaum, M. H. (1983). Perceived equity of salary policies. *Journal of Applied Psychology, 68,* 49–59.

Brickman, P., Folger, R., Goode, E., & Schul, Y. (1981). Microjustice and macrojustice. In M. J. Lerner and S. C. Lerner (Eds.), *The justice motive in social behavior.* New York: Plenum.

Caporael, L. R., Dawes, R. M., Orbell, J. M., & van de Kragt, A. (1989). Selfishness examined: Cooperation in the absence of egoistic incentives. *Behavioral and Brain Sciences, 12,* 683–739.

Einhorn, H. J., & Hogarth, R. M. (1981). Behavioral decision theory: Processes of judgment and choice. *Annual Review of Psychology, 32,* 53–88.

Hadari, S. A. (1988). Value trade-off. *Journal of Politics, 50,* 655–676.

Kahn, A. S., & Gaeddert, W. P. (1985). From theories in equity to theories in justice: Deliberating consequences of studying women. in V. E. O'Leary, R. E. Unger, & B. S. Wailston (Eds.), *Women, gender, and social psychology.* Hillsdale, NJ: Erlbaum.

Major, B., & Adams, J. B. (1983). Role of gender, interpersonal orientation, and self-presentation in distributive-justice behavior. *Journal of Personality and Social Psychology, 45,* 598–608.

Mellers, B. A. (1982). Equity judgment: A revision of Aristotelian views. *Journal of Experimental Psychology: General, 111,* 242–270.

Messick, D. M., & Sentis, K. P. (1979). Fairness and preference. *Journal of Experimental Social Psychology, 15,* 418–434.

Mitchell, G., Tetlock, P. E., Mellers, B. A., & Ordóñez, L. (1992). Judgments of social justice: Compromises between equality and efficiency. Unpublished manuscript.

Okun, A. (1975). *Equality and efficiency: The big tradeoff.* Washington, DC: Brookings Institute.

Rasinski, K. A. (1987). What's fair is fair – or is it? Value differences underlying public views about social justice. *Journal of Personality and Social Psychology, 53,* 201–211.

Rawls, J. (1971). *A theory of justice.* Cambridge, MA: Harvard University Press.

Tetlock, P. E. (1986). A value pluralism model of ideological reasoning. *Journal of Personality and Social Psychology, 50,* 819–827.

Notes

1 Subjects were given pairs of societies and judged which society had: (1) a higher mean salary, (2) a larger salary variance, and (3) a higher correlation between salary and effort. All subjects properly detected differences in the manipulations.
2 Half of the subjects were presented with scatterplots showing the poverty line as a horizontal line, and half were not. There was no significant effect of poverty line, and all analyses were collapsed over the two groups.
3 These correlations are point-biserial correlations that cannot exceed .87.
4 All tests of significance were done at an alpha level of .01.

# 8 Information, fairness, and efficiency in bargaining

*Colin F. Camerer and George Loewenstein*

Economic theory assumes people strive for efficient agreements that benefit all consenting parties. The frequency of mutually destructive conflicts such as strikes, litigation, and military conflict, therefore, poses an important challenge to the field.

Among economists, game theorists have devoted the most attention to inefficiency and have proposed a number of theories to explain why inefficient agreements occur. Most of these revolve around a common theme: Inefficiencies arise because parties possess incomplete information. Bargainers often lack information about how much other parties value an agreement (Babcock, 1991; Hayes, 1984; Tracy, 1987), about the personal characteristics (e.g., impatience) of the other party (Rubinstein, 1985), or the likely consequence of nonsettlement as determined by the ruling of an arbitrator or the existence of other parties willing to make a deal (Priest & Klein, 1984).

Incomplete information impedes settlement for two reasons. First, when bargainers lack information about the other party, they may use the bargaining process to find out the missing information. For example, a union might call a strike to assess management's ability to withstand a strike. Second, when bargainers lack information about the other party's tastes or opportunities, they may overestimate the other party's willingness to make concessions. For example, the seller of a used car may hold out for an unrealistically high price in the erroneous belief that the buyer really likes the car or is impatient to buy it.

All models that explain inefficiency as a consequence of information imperfections imply that increasing the amount of information shared by the two parties will increase efficiency. Indeed, such models imply that if disputants were perfectly informed about one another's values, all agree-

We thank Maya Bar-Hillel, Jon Baron, Max Bazerman, Robin Keller, and Barbara Mellers for helpful comments. NSF grant SES 90-23531 provided support to the first author.

ments would be efficient. In this essay we challenge this prediction. We show that increasing the amount of information sometimes improves efficiency, as the game theoretic models predict, but in other situations has the opposite effect.

Shared information can interfere with settlement because people care about fairness and their view of what is fair is biased in a manner that favors themselves.[1] When people lack information about the values of others, it is difficult for them to judge agreements by how fair they are. As a result, fairness cannot inhibit bargaining and create inefficiency. But when people do know how much others value an agreement, their concern for fairness – and different interpretations of what is fair based on the same information – may cause them to reject agreements, creating inefficiency.

For example, suppose two people contribute different amounts of time to a joint project. The person who worked less will typically think that equal compensation is fair, while the person who worked more will think that payments should be proportional to effort (Messick & Sentis, 1983). If the parties bargain over how to split the proceeds from the project, and each knows how much the other worked, they may have difficulty agreeing upon a split since the one who worked more will demand a larger share of the proceeds, while the one who worked less will demand an equal share. If the parties did not know how much the other put in, however, they could not base compensation on input levels and they might be *more* likely to settle. In this situation, sharing information about effort can *interfere* with efficient settlement (precisely the opposite of the economic prediction).

We illustrate the mixed impact of information on bargaining with three experimental studies. In two of these, giving the bargainers more shared information leads to greater inefficiency, contrary to the broad game theoretic prediction. The third study shows that the effect of information on efficiency is the opposite: In a bargaining situation in which complete information is accompanied by a clear definition of a fair agreement, reducing information can create competing definitions of fairness and create inefficient disagreements.

The chapter has four sections. In the next section we describe some game theoretic models which predict that inefficiency results from incomplete information. We then present two new studies showing how incomplete information can reduce inefficiency and one showing the opposite result. Finally we discuss the results and a variety of implications.

## Information and efficiency in game theoretic analysis

Game theory is a formal way of modeling social situations in which the payoffs people earn from choices are interdependent. Rasmusen (1989) is an excellent introduction.

A game consists of several *players* who choose *strategies*. The choice of strategies, one by each player, determines an outcome that yields payoffs to each player. In most applications of game theory to natural situations, players are assumed to care only about their own payoffs; they are not envious or altruistic, nor do they care about whether an agreement is fair (as long as it is fair enough to them). This self-interest assumption is usually made just for analytical convenience. Theorists recognize that envy, altruism, and fairness matter, but are not certain how to capture their effects in formal models. Self-interest is a kind of analytical fuel used to power the machinery of game theory (much like risk aversion in expected utility theory). Game theory is not proved false if players are fair-minded or altruistic, because the theory can run on other fuels.

Until about 20 years ago, game theorists were not sure how to model situations in which players had different information or perceptions about the choices or outcomes in a game. Harsanyi (1967–68) suggested a method that is now widely used: Assume that "nature" chooses a "type" for each player before the game begins. A player knows her own type, but others know only the distribution of probability over what her type might be. A type includes all the player's private information – the largest sum she would pay for an antique, how impatient she is, how much a strike would cost her firm each week, and so on. In a game of "complete information," a player's type is known to everyone.[2] In a game of "incomplete information" (à la Harsanyi), players know only their own types. We will use the informal terms *shared information* and *asymmetric information* to refer to complete and incomplete information.

We now give examples to illustrate two situations in which inefficiency can arise when information is asymmetric.

### Inefficiency from strategic delay

In the first example, Burt is thinking of buying a house from Sally. Another buyer offered $125,000 for Sally's house; she will sell to the other buyer if a deal with Burt falls through and is therefore willing to sell to Burt at any price higher than $125,000 – her "reservation price." Burt's reservation price is $145,000; he will pay no more than that for the house. Since Burt's reservation price is $20,000 above Sally's, it would be efficient for them to strike a deal: At any price $P$ between $125,000 and $145,000, both would prefer the deal and the sum of their gains would be ($145,000 − P$) + ($P$ − $125,000$), or $20,000.

Suppose Sally is eager to sell, so it costs her $1,000 a week to delay the agreement with Burt. It costs Burt something to delay, too, but Sally is not sure how much: Either it costs Burt $200 a week (if his other house is sold) or $2,000 a week (if not). Sally guesses the two delay costs are equally likely. (The game involves asymmetric information because Sally does not know Burt's cost of delay, but Burt does.)

Suppose they bargain in the following simple way: Sally offers a price to

Burt, who accepts or rejects it. If he rejects it, he mulls it over for a week then proposes a new price. If Sally rejects that, she proposes another price in a week, and so on. Much bargaining has this simple "alternating offer" structure.

Game theory makes the following precise prediction: Sally will offer a price of $127,000. If Burt's cost of delay is high ($2,000/week) then he will accept the price because he cannot afford to wait. If his cost of delay is low ($200), he will wait a week, counteroffer $125,000, and Sally will accept it.

Notice that waiting a week is inefficient; it costs Burt $200 and Sally $1,000. If they could have agreed in the first week, they would have saved $1,200 between them. But neither had an incentive to agree in the first week. If Burt's delay cost is low, waiting a week cost him $200 but saved him $2,000 on the price of the house. Sally figured she had a 50% chance of making $2,000 (above her $125,000 outside offer) if Burt settled right away, and a 50% chance of making no profit and incurring a $1,000 delay cost if Burt waited a week. Unless she is very risk averse, she prefers to take that gamble (its expected value is $500) and risk a delay. Even though both behaved rationally, the outcome of their behavior is inefficient.[3]

Game theory predicts that if Sally knew Burt's cost of delay, she would make an offer he would accept right away. There would be no reason for Sally to risk a delay, or for Burt to cause one because Burt could not send a message to Sally by delaying. When his delay costs are unknown, Burt's one-week delay is *strategic:* By waiting, he is able to show that his cost of delay is low, not high, and get a lower price.

*Strategic delay* is one way to convey information about how patient you are to others that you bargain with, which improves your bargaining position.[4] But delay inevitably creates inefficiencies. Asymmetric information is the real culprit, because it creates a motive for strategic delay (which creates inefficiency).

### Inefficiency from strategic misrepresentation

Selina owns a piece of folk art (a whittled pipe, of some value) that Byron would like to buy. Neither is sure how valuable the object is to the other.

To satisfy the modeling conventions of asymmetric information game theory, suppose Byron and Selina know what the object is worth to each of them, but neither is sure how much the other values it. Selina figures that Byron's value for the pipe is somewhere between $5 and $100, roughly uniformly distributed. Byron figures Selina's value is between $5 and $100, also uniformly distributed. Assume their values are independent.

They agree to use the following simple bargaining technique (see Chatterjee & Samuelson, 1983): Each writes down a price, a multiple of $5, simultaneously. If Byron's bid $B$ is less than Selina's offering price $S$ then no exchange takes place. But if $B \geq S$ the pipe changes hands at a price $(B + S)/2$ that splits the difference between $B$ and $S$.

Suppose the pipe is actually worth $60 to Selina. It would be foolish to write down a value of $S$ less than \$60 (then she might sell the pipe for less than it's worth). So she considers whether to bid $S = 60$ (a *truthful bid*) or a value of $S$ greater than 60 (*strategic misrepresentation*). If Selina picks the higher price, it is less likely the pipe will be sold at all, but if it is sold she will make more profit. It turns out that Selina will maximize her expected value by strategically misrepresenting her value as long as it is below \$75; in other words, it is usually in her interest to state a price higher than her true value.[5] The same is true for Byron; he will strategically misrepresent his value as long as it is above \$25.

By bidding truthfully, the parties guarantee that they will always trade the pipe when they should (truthful bidding is efficient). Strategic misrepresentation introduces the inefficient possibility that they will fail to arrive at a settlement even though Byron values the pipe more highly. Bidding strategically may be inefficient, but it is more profitable in an expected value sense for both parties. As in the house-buying example of Sally and Burt, asymmetric information sometimes causes inefficiency.


### Inefficiencies from shared information

These examples show how different kinds of uncertainty about what the other person gets from an agreement – their cost of delay, value, or profit – can harm efficiency in bargaining, according to game theoretic analysis. Roughly speaking, game theory predicts that bargaining should be more efficient when information is shared than when it is asymmetric.

Information may, however, have another effect that game theoretic analyses typically ignore. Lacking information about another person's values, it is difficult to tell whether outcomes are fair (since fairness involves some comparison of how much each bargainer gets). Fairness judgments are easier to make, and more likely to influence agreements, when information is shared. If disagreements about fairness reduce the efficiency of bargaining, then bargaining is likely to be more efficient when information is asymmetric (so fairness matters less), contrary to the game theoretic view.

Consider our earlier examples. When Sally sells her house to Burt, her uncertainty about Burt's delay cost makes it difficult to tell whether her initial offer is fair (since she does not know what the deal will cost Burt in the end). Sally's delay cost is \$1,000/week. If she knew Burt's delay cost was only \$200/week then the game theoretic analysis says she should offer \$125,000 initially (giving her no profit beyond the amount the other buyer had offered) (Rubinstein, 1982). We predict she would consider that offer unfair and would make a much higher offer that Burt would be likely to reject.[6]

The story about Selina selling her whittled pipe to Byron suggests a different conclusion. Suppose the pipe is worth \$60 to Selina and \$80 to Byron. Trading the pipe for \$70, splitting the difference in their values, seems extremely fair. In sufficiently simple cases, shared information may not harm efficiency because bargainers agree on what is fair. Instead, asymmetric information may harm efficiency by making fairness judgments more difficult or creating dispersion in what players think is fair.

Others have pointed out the subtle interactions between information, fairness, and efficiency (Foddy, 1989; Roth & Murnighan, 1982; Roth, 1987; Smith, 1982). And of course, there are large literatures in several fields on judgments of fairness and their impact (e.g., Kahneman, Knetsch, & Thaler, 1986; Messick & Sentis, 1979; Yaari & Bar-Hillel, 1984). Our main contribution is the argument – and experiments to support the claim – that asymmetric information can cut either way, improving efficiency, or reducing it depending on whether shared information causes more disputes about fairness or fewer disputes.

### Three experimental studies

#### Study 1: Appleton-Baker

The first study is about bargaining over a plot of land. The Appletons are moving; they would like to sell a strip of land, measuring 100 feet by 200 feet, adjacent to their house. The land lies between the Appletons' house and the house owned by their neighbors, the Bakers. The land is too small for anyone else to use or build on (because of zoning restrictions in the neighborhood) and the people who bought the Appletons' house expressed little interest in buying the land. So the Appletons begin bargaining with the only sensible buyer, the Bakers.

The Appletons bought the land for $7,000 several years earlier. Unbeknownst to the Bakers, the buyer of the Appletons' house offered $5,000 for the land. (The $5,000 represents the reservation price or BATNA – best alternative to a negotiated agreement – of the Appletons.)

The Appletons do not know how much the Bakers would like the land. In fact, the Bakers would *love* to buy the land, so they can build a new kitchen and greenhouse. The amount they would pay for the land – the Bakers' BATNA – is a treatment variable in our experiment. In one condition they would pay $18,000, in the other condition they would pay $25,000.

*Methods.* Subjects were 70 Wharton MBA students in two classes on negotiations. Each subject was randomly paired with another and randomly assigned to the buyer (Baker) or seller (Appleton) role. Part of their course grade depended on how cheaply they bought the land or how high a price they sold it for.[7]

Students read a one-page description of their role (in a case available from the Harvard Business School) before class, and negotiated during a class period. The negotiation lasted about 20 to 40 minutes. They were allowed to bargain and exchange information (except for their BATNA values) any way they liked.

After negotiating, students reported the prices they agreed on (if they agreed). Class discussion revealed the BATNA values and the range of prices that were agreed upon. The students were generally surprised at how low or high the other party's BATNA was. (The case is useful for teaching students to avoid overconfidence in judging the other side's BATNA.)

After the initial agreements were discussed, students were instructed to meet again with the same person and renegotiate the case in 10 to 20 minutes. Both the initial and renegotiated agreements counted toward their course grade.

The experimental design has two treatment variables. One treatment is distribution of information: In the initial agreement, information is asymmetric (in the game theorists' sense). In the renegotiated agreement, information is shared (because of the class discussion). The information treatment was manipulated within subjects. Notice that information is confounded with order of negotiation, but the confound is inevitable because the order cannot be reversed (after giving shared information *first*, information cannot be made asymmetric without changing the stimuli in some other way).

The second treatment variable, buyer BATNA (either $18,000, $n = 19$, or 25,000, $n = 16$) was varied between subjects.

*Results.* Each subject *pair* is a data point. Figures 1 and 2 show the two prices each pair agreed on in the two negotiations. The Y axis shows the price initially agreed upon (asymmetric information) and the X axis shows the price agreed upon during the renegotiation (shared information). If they failed to agree in either negotiation, the price is plotted as zero.

Consider Figure 1 first (BATNA = $18,000). Several effects are apparent in the graph. The initial prices are much more widely scattered (s.d. = $3,750) than the renegotiated prices (excluding zeros) (s.d. = $1,434) but the means are not different (M = $10,821 vs. M = $10,404). The same effect is apparent in Figure 2 (BATNA = 25,000), in which the means are $13,684 (initial) and $13,714 (renegotiated) and the standard deviations are $4,119 and $2,213.

One can define three decision rules for picking a renegotiation price: Pick the equal split between the buyer and seller BATNA ("Equal Split"); pick the same price as in the initial negotiation ("Same"), or pick a price on the opposite side of the equal split ("Opposite") (as if to compensate one side for making a bad deal, relative to the equal split, initially). The three bold lines in Figures 1 and 2 show prices that pairs using each of these rules would pick. Each point is plotted as a shaded (equal split), open (opposite), or closed (same) circle depending upon which of the three lines it is closest to. Most of the points (shaded) cluster around the equal split price during the renegotiation. Slightly more pairs seem to use the opposite-price rule (open circles, 7 pairs in total) than use the same-price rule (closed circles, 4 pairs).

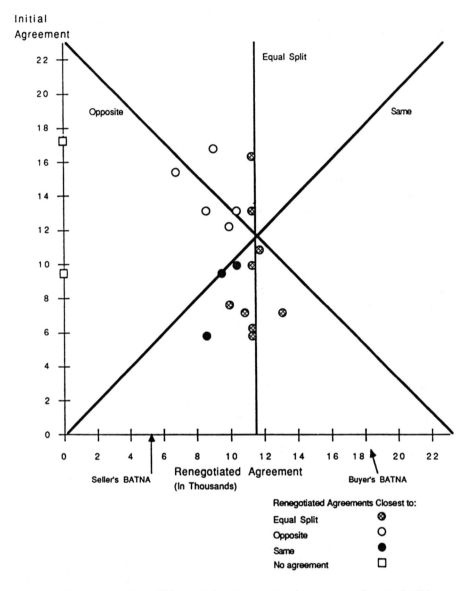

Figure 1    Appleton-Baker initial and renegotiated agreements (buyer's BATNA = 18).

Most strikingly, there are *no* disagreements during the initial bargaining (under asymmetric information) but there are 7 disagreements during the renegotiation (under shared information). The difference is small in magnitude but highly significant.[8]

*Discussion.* The subjects negotiated twice. Revealing the other side's values (BATNAs) to subjects in the second negotiation effectively transformed the

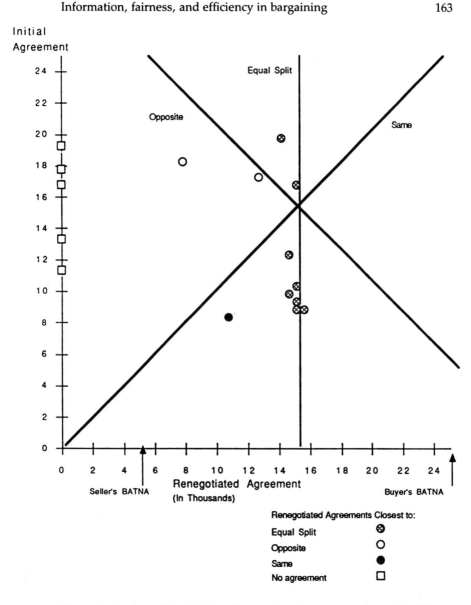

Figure 2   Appleton-Baker initial and renegotiated agreements (buyer's BATNA = 25).

game from one of asymmetric information to one of shared information. The average negotiated price did not change across the information conditions, but the variation in prices was roughly half as large when information was shared (excluding disagreements). The number of disagreements also rose dramatically, from none to 7 (out of 35 pairs), though disagreement was uncommon in both conditions.

Most of the disagreements happened quickly and emotionally. A typical pattern was that one side felt it had been wronged in the initial agreement, then demanded an equal split or opposite-price settlement. When the other side disagreed, they argued briefly, angrily scrawled "disagree" on their reporting forms, and stormed off.

Our interpretation is that adding shared information caused disagreement by suggesting *three* fair ways to renegotiate the initial price (equal split, same-price, opposite-price). Two of these rules – the equal split and opposite-price rules – cannot be applied without shared information. Sharing information therefore gave subjects two more standards of fairness (besides equal split) to disagree about.

Our conclusions from Study 1 are speculative. We did not test whether different parties actually preferred fairness rules that benefited them (i.e., Were their assessments self-serving?). The second study fills in one of the gaps in the Appleton-Baker study by measuring fairness directly. We also tie disagreements to fairness measures and test whether the perceptions of case information are self-serving.

### Study 2: "Sudden impact"

"Sudden Impact"[9] is based on a lawsuit filed by a motorcyclist against a driver whose car hit him. The plaintiff (the motorcyclist) claimed that he sat at a light waiting to make a left turn when the car hit him from behind. The defendant (the driver) claimed that the plaintiff turned suddenly in front of him and he could not stop. The plaintiff is suing for $100,000 in damages. The lawsuit was filed in Texas; we excerpted actual court documents and disguised some confidential details. We had a professor at the University of Texas Law School judge the case (in the excerpted form given to subjects) and decide how much he would award in damages.

*Methods.* Subjects were 38 graduate students from Carnegie-Mellon's School of Urban and Public Affairs and 38 law students from the University of Texas at Austin. They participated voluntarily in exchange for money.

Subjects read 27 pages of excerpted material, including depositions of key witnesses and a police accident report.[10] The depositions give conflicting testimony, some supporting the plaintiff, and some supporting the defendant. After reading the material, subjects recorded how large an out-of-court settlement they thought was fair. They also predicted what they thought the judge would award. They earned a $1 bonus if their guess was within $5,000 of the judge's actual award. The actual value of the judge's award was withheld until after the negotiation ended, and was revealed only to those who failed to settle.

Each subject then attempted to negotiate a settlement with a randomly assigned partner in six 5-minute rounds. In each round, five minutes of discussion were followed by each subject writing a settlement figure on a slip of paper and exchanging them. If the plaintiff was willing to settle for an amount the defendant was willing to pay, the bargaining was over. If the proposed settlements did not overlap, both sides incurred $5,000 in "legal fees" and the next round began. (Notice that every period without settlement decreases bargaining efficiency, since it incurs legal fees that reduce the sum of the plaintiff's net award and the defendant's expenses.) After six rounds, the plaintiff was awarded the judge's predetermined figure ($30,560).

Subjects were paid cash according to their settlements and legal fees. Plaintiffs received a dollar payment equal to the settlement they negotiated (minus any legal fees incurred) divided by 10,000. For example, a plaintiff who got $45,000 in the third round (incurring two rounds of legal fees, or $10,000) would earn $3.50. Defendants were given $10 to begin with and paid back the amount of the settlement *plus* legal fees, divided by 10,000.

After negotiating, each subject was given a list of eight arguments favoring the plaintiff and eight arguments favoring the defendant. Subjects were asked to "rate the importance that you think a fair judge would place on each of the arguments" using an 11-point scale.

Notice that the bargaining game has no asymmetric information (in the usual sense) because both subjects read exactly the same court documents. But we conjectured that subjects might interpret the evidence in the case in a self-serving manner, depending on their roles. We tested this by studying whether perceptions of argument importance, ratings of fair settlements, and predictions of the judge's settlement vary between plaintiff subjects and defendant subjects.

We also tested the self-serving interpretation hypothesis with a subtle treatment: In the *known-role* condition ($n = 18$) subjects knew whether they were plaintiffs or defendants when they read the case. In the *unknown-role* condition ($n = 20$) subjects did not know which role they were until *after* they read the case and stated what they thought was a fair settlement and the judge's likely award. (They knew their role when they negotiated, of course, and when they rated importance of arguments after negotiating.) We thought encoding of case information might be affected by knowledge of their role, leading to more self-serving interpretations, slower settlement, and inefficiency in the known-role condition.

*Results.* Table 1 summarizes results from bargaining pairs. First notice the substantial self-serving differences (plaintiff minus defendant) in judgments in the known-role condition: Plaintiffs thought a fair settlement was about $20,000 more than what the defendants thought was fair, and predicted that judges would award $13,000 more than defendants predicted. These differences are unlikely to be due to chance (they are 2–4 standard errors from zero). The differences in the unknown-role condition are not significantly different from zero, which was to be expected, since the parties did not know their roles when they assessed fairness and predicted the judge.

Table 1 *Bargaining results in Sudden Impact Study*

| | Condition | |
|---|---|---|
| | Known role | Unknown role |
| Statistic | ($n = 18$) | ($n = 20$) |
| Difference in | $20,527 | -$4,900 |
| fair settlement | ($5,588) | ($6,208) |
| Difference in | $12,667 | $7,125 |
| predicted award | ($6,461) | ($5,915) |
| % Settling | 61% | 100% |
| Mean no. of periods | 3.5 | 2.1 |
| before settlement | (.52) | (.18) |
| Mean settlement | $35,864 | $39,038 |
| | ($4,025) | ($3,621) |
| Difference in | 21.2 | 8.2 |
| importance-rating | (4.4) | (5.0) |

*Note:* Standard errors are in parentheses. All differences are plaintiff value minus defendant value. "Difference in importance ratings" is the difference in importance of proplaintiff and prodefendant arguments as rated by plaintiffs, minus the difference as rated by defendants.

Table 2 *Self-serving biases and settlement in Sudden Impact Study*

| | Settlement outcome | |
|---|---|---|
| | Did not settle | Did settle |
| Statistic | ($n = 7$) | ($n = 31$) |
| Difference in | $32,357 | $451 |
| fair settlement | ($6,918) | ($4,958) |
| Difference in | $33,143 | -$4,725 |
| predicted award | ($8,416) | ($4,474) |
| Difference in | 33.1 | 10.1 |
| importance-rating | (5.0) | (3.8) |

The differences in fairness and predicted awards are strongly correlated with differences in bargaining behavior. Table 2 compares the differences in fairness and predicted judgment for those who settled and did not settle. For those who settled, these differences are small and not significantly different from zero. For those who failed to settle, the plaintiff's fairness figure and prediction of the judge was, on average, approximately $33,000 more than the defendant's. The experimental manipulation also had a significant effect. All pairs in the unknown-role condition settled before the sixth period (taking about 2 periods), but only 61% of the known role pairs settled, taking 3.5 periods. There was no substantial difference in the average settlement amount in the two conditions.

The last row of Table 1 shows a measure of self-serving (or egocentric) bias in the ratings of argument importance made after the negotiation. The measure takes the difference in total importance ratings given by plaintiffs to proplaintiff and prodefendant arguments, and subtracts the difference given by defendants. Known-role subjects clearly rated the arguments in a more self-serving manner, even though unknown role subjects also rated the arguments *after* negotiating, knowing their role.

*Discussion.* In the Appleton-Baker study we did not measure fairness directly or relate it to disagreement. In the Sudden Impact study we did. Differences in perceptions of fairness strongly predicted the propensity to settle and time to settlement. Plaintiffs thought the difference in importance of proplaintiff and prodefendant arguments was greater than defendants did, and the difference in their importance ratings strongly predicted whether a bargaining pair would settle.

The data paint a picture in which incomplete information (in the game theoretic sense) is hardly a necessary ingredient for disagreement. Even when two sides receive a common pool of information, inefficient disagreements can arise if the information is rich enough and their roles encourage them to interpret the information in a self-serving manner.

The first two studies, Appleton-Baker and Sudden Impact, illustrated how adding information could increase disagreement in bargaining (and hence reduce efficiency). In both studies, more shared information created multiple notions of what outcomes were fair. Then disagreements were caused by egocentric judgments of fairness (people chose the fairness rule that benefited themselves). The third study demonstrates an opposite conclusion, which sharpens our account of how information and fairness interact to determine efficiency.

### Study 3: Ultimatum games

In the *ultimatum game*, two people divide an amount $S$. ($S$ could represent the potential gains from a trade, like the distance between the buyer and seller's BATNAs). Their only communication is through offers. Player 1 suggests that she take $x$ and player 2 take the rest, $(S-x)$, an offer denoted $(x, S-x)$. If player 2 agrees, the bargaining is over. If player 2 disagrees neither gets anything (an inefficient outcome). The game got its name because player 2's offer is a take-it-or-leave-it ultimatum.

There are several experimental studies of ultimatums under shared information (i.e., both sides know the value of $S$) (e.g., Thaler, 1988). People typically offer an average of 40% of $S$. Offers of 20% or less are considered insulting or unfair and often get rejected. Only 10–20% of the offers are rejected, so efficiency is very high.

In the ultimatum game, splitting $S$ equally is a fair offer with widespread appeal. Nearly half the offers in experiments are equal splits and they are rarely rejected. We conjectured that making the value of $S$ uncertain might increase the frequency of rejected offers (harming efficiency), by introducing variation into what people thought was fair.

To illustrate, consider the certain case in which $S = \$5$ and both players know it. An offer of \$2.50 is fair; an offer of less than \$1 seems unfair. In the uncertain case, suppose $S$ is either \$1, \$3, \$5, \$7, or \$9 (all are equally likely). Player 1 knows the value of $S$ before making an offer, but player 2 must evaluate 1's offer without knowing $S$. Fairness in the certain ultimatum game is clear but uncertainty about $S$ creates dispersion in rules of fairness. Several rules suggest themselves; no single rule is especially appealing. One rule is to split $S$ equally. However, this rule is difficult to implement since player 2 will not be able to determine whether an offer by player 1 of, say, \$1.50 is an equal split of \$3.00 or a disadvantageous split of \$7 or \$9. Another rule is that player 1 should offer at least the minimum value of $S$ (\$1). However, if $S$ turns out to be \$1, player 1 is unlikely to view this as fair, since it gives her nothing. A more extreme rule is that player 1 should offer \$2.50, half of the *expected value* of $S$; however, this imposes a nontrivial risk that player 1 will actually have to absorb a loss if $S = \$1.00$.

In this situation, self-serving assessments about the fair way to deal with the uncertainty can create disagreement. In contrast, the fair thing to do in the full information condition is straightforward, at least to most subjects. Thus, in this situation, we expect full information to produce more efficient outcomes than partial information.

*Methods.* The subjects were 46 Carnegie-Mellon University (CMU) undergraduates (66% male) and 46 University of Pennsylvania undergraduates (70% male) taking classes on decision making. The experiment was conducted in the two classes on the same day; it took about 15 minutes. Each CMU student was randomly, and anonymously, paired with a Penn student. Their responses were collected on one day, and money amounts were paid (in sealed envelopes) on the next day each class met.

CMU students made offers and Penn students stated the minimum offer they would accept. Note that Penn students were *not* told a specific offer, then asked whether they would accept it. (This method is more cumbersome to implement and gives up the opportunity to find out what is the least a person would accept). Instead, the minimum acceptable offer each Penn student stated was actually used to determine whether the specific offer by the paired CMU student would be accepted or not.

There were two treatments, *certain amount* and *uncertain amount*, which were varied between subjects. In the certain-amount treatment, CMU subjects decided how much they would offer the Penn students contingent upon a particular amount to be split (either \$1, \$3, \$5, \$7, or \$9). They were told that one of these amounts would be picked at random, and would count as the actual amount to be split. Penn students stated the minimum offer they would accept for each specific amount to be split. Notice that while they bargained over five different amounts, for each of the possible amounts both the CMU and Penn students knew the amount when making offers and deciding how much to accept.

In the uncertain-amount treatment, CMU students also decided how much they would offer for each of the five amounts. However, Penn students stated the minimum offer they would accept, *but they did not know the amount (as the CMU students did)*. In both conditions, CMU and Penn students completed identical forms, which made explicit to them the choice that their counterpart at the other institution would face. Forms for both conditions are included in an appendix to this chapter.

In both conditions, one of the five amounts was actually chosen for each pair of subjects. Then bargaining was carried out (by the experimenters) using the subjects' offers and minimum acceptable offers, and subjects were paid whatever they earned.

*Results.* Table 3 shows summary statistics for offers and minimum acceptable offers. First consider the offers by CMU students (top panel). Mean offers increased with the money amount, in a slightly curvilinear way (e.g., the offers at $S = 9$ were 8.2 times as large as the $S = 1$ offers, not 9 times as large). About half of the offers were equal splits. (In the two conditions, 7 and 9 subjects offered equal splits for every amount.) Fewer offers were equal splits in the uncertain-amount condition, and the standard deviation of offers was slightly larger, but those differences were not significant.

Next consider the minimum acceptable offers stated by Penn students. Like CMU students' offers, these minimums increased slightly curvilinearly. The standard deviations indicate more variance in minimum acceptable offers than in offers, suggesting the application of more varied standards of fairness by player 2s (Penn students).

Now compare the minimums stated in the uncertain-amount condition with those in the certain-amount condition.[11] Compared to their certain-amount counterparts who knew the amount was $5, the uncertain-amount subjects demanded more on average (1.88 vs. 1.46) and their demands were more dispersed (standard deviations of 1.72 vs. 1.23). Ten subjects demanded 2.50 or more in the uncertain-amount condition, compared to only two in the certain-amount condition. A Kolmogorov–Smirnov nonparametric test (which is sensitive to several differences in distribution moments) indicated the two distributions of demands were only weakly significantly different (K–S statistic = .27, $p = .12$, one-tailed test).

So when they did not know the amount being bargained over, the player 2s (Penn students) generally asked for more, and their demands were more variable. Their demands also led to higher disagreement rates[12] (see Table 4). When the amount was actually $1, for instance, 65% of the subjects in the uncertain-amount condition demanded more than was offered, result-

Table 3 *Offers in ultimatum bargaining*

| Information condition | Statistic | Amount of money S | | | | |
|---|---|---|---|---|---|---|
| | | 1 | 3 | 5 | 7 | 9 |
| *Offers by CMU subjects* | | | | | | |
| Certain amount | mean | .48 | 1.34 | 2.23 | 3.12 | 3.91 |
| (n = 23) | median | .50 | 1.50 | 2.50 | 3.50 | 4.50 |
| | mode | .50 | 1.50 | 2.50 | 3.50 | 4.50 |
| | (n at mode) | (17) | (13) | (13) | (12) | (12) |
| | std. dev. | .11 | .38 | .64 | 1.00 | 1.27 |
| Uncertain | mean | .42 | 1.30 | 2.21 | 3.12 | 3.93 |
| amount (n = 23) | median | .50 | 1.50 | 2.50 | 3.50 | 4.00 |
| | mode | .50 | 1.50 | 2.50 | 3.50 | 4.50 |
| | (n at mode) | (16) | (11) | (11) | (9) | (8) |
| | std. dev. | .17 | .59 | .75 | 1.12 | 1.37 |
| *Minimum acceptable offers by Penn subjects* | | | | | | |
| Certain amount | mean | .32 | .85 | 1.46 | 2.00 | 2.62 |
| (n = 22) | median | .38 | 1.00 | 1.75 | 2.00 | 3.00 |
| | mode | .10 | 1.00 | 2.00 | .1, 3 | .1, 3, 4 |
| | (n at mode) | (6) | (7) | (6) | (4) | (4) |
| | std. dev. | .25 | .71 | 1.23 | 1.73 | 2.26 |
| Uncertain | mean | | | 1.88 | | |
| amount (n = 24) | median | | | 2.00 | | |
| | mode | | | 0, 2.50 | | |
| | (n at mode) | | | (4) | | |
| | std. dev. | | | 1.72 | | |

Table 4 *Disagreement rates in ultimatum bargaining*

| Information condition | Amount of money S | | | | | Overall |
|---|---|---|---|---|---|---|
| | 1 | 3 | 5 | 7 | 9 | |
| Certain | .11 | .15 | .14 | .15 | .17 | .15 |
| Uncertain | .65 | .57 | .35 | .23 | .17 | .39 |

ing in inefficient disagreements. (Fourteen of 24 subjects demanded more than $1, which CMU subjects could not offer without losing money.) Overall, 39% of the uncertain-amount bargaining ended in disagreement, more than double the 15% disagreement rate in the certain-amount condition.

*Discussion.* In the study of simple "ultimatum" games, when information is shared there is a single clear standard for fair outcomes. Half the offers are equal splits, and disagreements are relatively rare (15%). Under asymmetric information about the amount being bargained over, offers are still centered around the equal split, but demands are now highly dispersed (reflecting competing notions of fairness created by the uncertainty), causing many more disagreements (39%). The ultimatum results suggest that it is dispersion in assessments of fairness, not information per se, that creates disagreement. Sometimes more information creates more dispersion (in the Appleton-Baker and Sudden Impact studies) and sometimes it reduces dispersion (in the ultimatum study).

Some recent studies of ultimatum bargaining report related findings. In a design much like ours, Mitzkewitz and Nagel (1991) found *no* difference in efficiency in complete- and incomplete-information ultimatum games. Efficiency also rose as they repeated the game, because subjects learned to accept less and less. The difference between their results and ours could be due to differences in subjects or instructions and is worth exploring further.

In two studies (Straub and Murnighan, 1991; Croson, 1992) subjects were asked the amounts they would offer or accept if the amount being divided was known (complete information) or unknown. Subjects appear to be more fair-minded when they know how much the other person is getting, consistent with our general point that more information can increase fairness concerns (or make them calculable).

Hoffman, McCabe, Shachat, and Smith (1991) found that ultimatum offers are somewhat sensitive to details of experimental procedure (e.g., whether subjects earn the right to make the offer by winning a trivia contest). Their results can be interpreted as evidence that fairness norms are sensitive to the way in which bargaining positions are determined.

Roth & Murnighan (1982) report results similar to ours. In their studies, pairs of players bargained over 100 chips that determined their chances of winning a dollar prize. (For example, 37 chips give a .37 chance of winning). One player's prize was $20 and the other's prize was $5. Notice that there are *two* ways to split the chips equally: Give 50 chips to each (equal chance of winning); or give 20 chips to the $20-prize player and 80 chips to the $5-prize player (equal expected dollar winnings).

When neither player knew the prize amounts, they agreed to divide the chips about equally; only about 10% of the pairs disagreed. When information was asymmetric, disagreement rates were much higher. For example, when the $5-prize players knew both prize amounts, they insisted on getting 80 chips (to equalize dollar winnings) but $20-prize players wanted 50 chips (to equalize chances of winning); about 30% of the pairs disagreed. Thus, asymmetric information produced disagreement because players focused self-servingly on the kind of equal split that favored themselves.[13]

## Conclusions and implications

Game theory offers the most prominent formal approach to bargaining in social science. Game theory is also increasingly popular, finding application in biology (Maynard Smith, 1982), economics (Kreps, 1990; Rasmusen, 1989), law (Ayres, 1990), business management (McMillan, 1992), and political science (Ordeshook, 1986).

In game theoretic analyses of bargaining, asymmetries in information can reduce efficiency in several ways. In some cases (like Burt buying Sally's house) the bargaining process is used to credibly convey asymmetric information, which inhibits achievement of the more important goal – agreement. In other cases (Byron and Selina) uncertainty about the other side's values makes strategic misrepresentation of one's own information worthwhile, which risks the chance of missing opportunities to make mutually beneficial trades. All these inefficiencies resulting from asymmetric information should, according to the game theoretic analyses, disappear when information is shared.

Our research shows that sharing information can replace the inefficiencies that asymmetries cause with new inefficiencies. There are several ingredients in our formula for new inefficiencies. One ingredient is shared information, which is necessary for many rules of fairness to apply to proposed agreements. Another ingredient is *competing* fairness rules. In the Appleton-Baker study, competing rules arose because the initial negotiation in the experiment created an initial price; in the renegotiation subjects argued over whether they should choose the same price, an opposite one, or an equal split. The final ingredient is self-serving assessments of fairness (Thompson & Loewenstein, 1991): In Appleton-Baker, those who did well in the initial agreement think that sticking to the same agreement is fair; those who did poorly want an opposite agreement or an equal split. In the Sudden Impact study, self-serving interpretations of conflicting facts in a case caused subjects to disagree on what out-of-court settlement was fair, creating inefficient delays in settlement.

Of these ingredients, our third study shows that disagreement about fairness is the most essential. In *ultimatum bargaining*, shared information does *not* cause disagreements because shared information makes an equal split of gains uniformly appealing. In that case, making information asymmetric creates variation in perceptions of fairness, raising the rate of disagreement from 15% to 39%.

The notion that more information can impede settlement has significant practical ramifications because many institutions and techniques are designed to improve bargaining by promoting information exchange. Discovery rules in legal systems require opposing parties to share information. (For example, prosecutors and defense attorneys must list the witnesses they will call during a trial beforehand to enable both sides to share the information conveyed by witness testimony.) In some large firms, when one division buys a part from another, the selling division must tell the buying division how much the part costs to make. In financial markets several rules are imposed to reduce information asymmetries between investors and managers: Insider trading is prohibited, certain corporate data must be disclosed, and buyers must declare their motives when their ownership of a firm exceeds 5% of its shares.

The widespread belief in the beneficial effects of information is also evident in studies of mediation, which emphasizes the mediator's function as a conduit for information exchange between the parties (Kolb, 1983; Raiffa, 1982). Many of the techniques used by mediators to facilitate negotiations, such as "active listening" (Athos & Gabarro, 1978), are intended to promote information exchange. If the central assumption that information facilitates settlement is incorrect, or correct only in specific situations, then these institutions and techniques that promote information sharing might backfire.

Our evidence implies that requiring bargainers to share information, through discovery rules and the like, may backfire because sharing information makes unfairness apparent. If parties disagree on what makes an agreement fair, they may disagree more when information is shared. We do not deny the importance of game theoretic accounts in which asymmetric information causes disagreement (for reasons unrelated to fairness). Whether information-sharing rules help, on balance, is an empirical question that depends on whether the efficiency-inhibiting effect of asymmetry or the fairness-evoking effect of shared information (which also reduces efficiency) is stronger.

Our main point is that information sharing does not automatically create perspective sharing (in fact, the opposite may occur if information is interpreted self-servingly). But when information sharing backfires, simple treatments to promote perspective sharing may work well. In the Sudden Impact study, subjects who absorbed the facts of the case before knowing whether they were plaintiffs or defendants were much less biased in their judgments and came to settlements quicker and more often than others. The data suggest that role-playing exercises encouraging people to take the perspective of others (e.g., Bazerman & Neale, 1991; McMillan, 1992) could improve bargaining efficiency, especially in conjunction with sharing of information. The improved efficiency from perspective sharing also reminds us that one important service attorneys and other agents can perform is to supply objectivity when the people they represent interpret evidence self-servingly.

Our results contribute new evidence to an emerging revisionist perspective on the role of information in decision making. Economists typically assume more information is preferred to less, because information that is not beneficial can always be ignored. But some situations have been identified in which accurate information hurts those who have it or impedes economic efficiency. Smith (1982, p. 946) reports that certain experimental markets tend to converge to competitive equilibrium more rapidly when participants do *not* know what goods are worth to others. Camerer, Loewenstein, and Weber (1989) found that subjects who were rewarded for accurately guessing other subjects' predictions of several companies' earnings were hurt by being given information about actual earnings. In a game theory context, Brams (1980) has shown that in strategic games, if one party is omniscient (can predict the other's behavior) and both parties are aware of this, then the omniscient party can be at a disadvantage. The nonomniscient party can choose the noncooperative option, forcing the other party (who knows this) to choose a cooperative option that yields less. Information clearly plays an important role in bargaining, but whether it helps or hurts efficiency in a particular situation depends on the complex interplay of economic and psychological factors.

### References

Athos, A. G. and Gabarro, J. J. (1978). *Interpersonal behavior: Communication and understanding in relationships.* Englewood Cliffs, NJ: Prentice-Hall.

Ayres, Ian. (1990, May). Playing games with the law. *Stanford Law Review, 42,* 1291–1317.

Babcock, Linda. (1991). *Impasses in contract negotiations: Why do bargainers use arbitration?,* Carnegie-Mellon School of Urban and Public Affairs working paper.

Babcock, Linda, Loewenstein, George, Issacharoff, Sam, & Camerer, Colin. (in press.). Self-serving assessments of fairness and bargaining impasse. *American Economic Review.*

Bazerman, Max, & Margaret A. Neale. (1991). *Cognition and rationality in negotiation.* Oxford: Oxford University Press.

Binmore, Ken, Shaked, Avner, & Sutton, John. (1988). A further test of noncooperative bargaining theory: Reply. *American Economic Review, 78,* 837–839.

Bolton, Gary. (1992). A comparative model of bargaining: Theory and evidence. *American Economic Review, 81,* 1096–1136.

Brams, Steven. (1980, November). Mathematics and theology: Game-theoretical implications of god's omniscence. *Mathematics Magazine.*

Camerer, Colin F. (1990). Behavioral game theory. In R. M. Hogarth (Ed.), *Insights in decision making: A tribute to Hillel J. Einhorn.* Chicago: University of Chicago Press.

Camerer, Colin F., Loewenstein, George, & Weber, Martin. (1989). The curse of knowledge in economic settings: An experimental analysis. *Journal of Political Economy, 97,* 1232–1254.

Chatterjee, Kalyan, & Samuelson, William. (1983). Bargaining under incomplete information. *Operations Research, 31,* 835–851.

Croson, Rachel T. A. (1992, October). Information in ultimatum games: An experimental study. Department of Economics, Harvard University working paper.

Foddy, Margaret. (1989). Information control as a bargaining tactic in social exchange. *Advances in group processes* (Vol. 6, pp. 139–178). Greenwich, CT: JAI Press.

Guth, Werner, & Tietz, Reinhard. (1990, September). Ultimatum bargaining behavior: A survey and comparison of experimental results. *Journal of Economic Psychology, 11,* 417–449.

Harsanyi, John C. (1967–68). Games with incomplete information played by 'Bayesian' players. *Management Science*, 14: 159–182, 320–334, 486–502.

Hayes, Beth. (1984). Unions and strikes with asymmetric information, *Journal of Labor Economics*, 2, 57–83.

Hoffman, Elizabeth, McCabe, Kevin, Shachat, Kevin, & Smith, Vernon L. (1991, October). Preferences, property rights and anonymity in bargaining games. University of Arizona, Department of Economics, working paper.

Kahneman, Daniel, Knetsch, Jack L., & Thaler, Richard H. (1986). Fairness and the assumptions of economics. *Journal of Business*, 59, S285–S300.

Kolb, Deborah M. (1983). *The Mediators*. Cambridge, MA: MIT Press.

Kreps, David M. (1990). *A Course in Microeconomic Theory*. Princeton, NJ: Princeton University Press.

Loewenstein, George, Issacharoff, Sam, Camerer, Colin, & Babcock, Linda. (in press). Self-serving assessments of fairness and pretrial bargaining. *Journal of Legal Studies*.

Maynard Smith, John. (1982). *Evolution and the theory of games*. Cambridge: Cambridge University Press.

McMillan, John. (1992). *Games, strategy, and managers*. Oxford: Oxford University Press.

Messick, David M., & Keith P. Sentis. (1979). Fairness and preference. *Journal of Experimental Social Psychology*, 15, 418–434.

    (1983). Fairness, preference, and fairness biases. In D. M. Messick and K. S. Cook (Eds.), *Equity theory: Psychological and sociological perspectives*. New York: Praeger.

Mitzkewitz, Michael, & Nagel, Rosemarie. (1991, March). Envy, greed, and anticipation in ultimatum games with incomplete information: An experimental study. Department of Economics, University of Bonn, Discussion Paper No. B-181.

Ordeshook, Peter C. (1986). *Game theory and political theory*. Cambridge: Cambridge University Press.

Osborne, Martin J., & Rubinstein, Ariel. (1990). *Bargaining and markets*. San Diego: Academic Press.

Prasnikar, Vesna, & Roth, Alvin E. (1992). Considerations of fairness and strategy: Experimental data from sequential games. *Quarterly Journal of Economics, 107*, 865–888.

Priest, George L., & Klein, Benjamin. (1984). The selection of disputes for litigation. *Journal of Legal Studies, 13*, 1–55.

Rabin, Matthew (in press). Incorporating fairness into game theory and economics. *American Economic Review*.

Radner, Roy, & Schotter, Andrew. (1989, June). The sealed-bid mechanism: An experimental study. *Journal of Economic Theory, 48*, 179–221.

Raiffa, H. (1982). *The art and science of negotiations*. Cambridge, MA: Harvard University Press.

Rapoport, A., Weg, E., & Felsenthal, D. (1990). "Effects of fixed costs in two-person bargaining." *Theory and Decision, 28*, 47–71.

Rasmusen, Eric. (1989). *Games and information: An introduction to game theory*. Oxford: Basil Blackwell.

Roth, Alvin E. (1987). Bargaining phenomena and bargaining theory. In A. E. Roth

(Ed.), *Laboratory experimentation in economics: Six points of view*. Cambridge: Cambridge University Press.

Roth, Alvin E., & Keith J. Murnighan. (1982, September). The role of information in bargaining: An experimental study. *Econometrica, 50*, 1123–1142.

Rubinstein, Ariel. (1982). Perfect equilibrium in a bargaining model. *Econometrica, 50*, 97–109.

——— (1985). A bargaining model with incomplete information about time preferences. *Econometrica, 53*, 1151–1172.

Selten, Reinhard. (1987). Equity and coalition bargaining in experimental games. In A. E. Roth (Ed.), *Laboratory experimentation in economics: Six points of view*. Cambridge: Cambridge University Press.

Smith, Vernon L. (1982, December). Microeconomic systems as an experimental science. *American Economic Review, 72*, 923–955

Straub, Paul G., & Murnighan, Keith. (1991, October). Ultimatums, utility, minimum acceptable offers, and fairness: An experimental investigation. University of Illinois at Urbana Champaign.

Thaler, Richard. (1988). Anomalies: The ultimatum game. *Journal of Economic Perspectives, 2*, 195–206.

Thompson, Leigh, & Loewenstein, George. (1992). Egocentric interpretations of fairness and interpersonal conflict. *Organizational Behavior and Human Decision Processes, 51*, 176–197.

Tracy, Joseph. (1987). "An empirical test of an asymmetric information model of strikes." *Journal of Labor Economics, 5*, 149–173.

Weg, E., Rapoport, A., & Felsenthal, D. S. (1990). "Two-person bargaining behavior in fixed discounting games with infinite horizon." *Games and Economic Behavior, 2*, 76–95.

Yaari, Menahem, & Bar-Hillel, Maya. (1984). On dividing justly. *Social Choice and Welfare, 1*, 1–24.

### Notes

1  There have been some attempts to incorporate fairness concerns into game theoretic models (e.g., Rabin, in press). German experimentalists, most notably Selten (1987) and Guth and Tietz (1990), have developed empirically based theories of bargaining with fairness norms as a central feature. And experimental evidence of fair-minded divisions in sequential bargaining games (Rubinstein, 1982) has provoked an important debate about fairness (e.g., Binmore, Shaked, & Sutton, 1988; Bolton, 1992; Prasnikar & Roth, 1992; Thaler, 1988).

2  This is not quite true, since players might not be sure of their own types. Complete information means no single player has more information than another; everyone has the same information.

3  The Prisoner's Dilemma is the most famous example of how individual rationality can lead to collective irrationality.

4  The game theory underlying the example is described by Rubinstein (1982, 1985) and Osborne and Rubinstein (1990, ch. 5).

5  The unique equilibrium bidding strategy is for sellers to ask $\max(v_s, 25 + (2/3)v_s)$, where $v_s$ is the value of the pipe to the seller, and for buyers to bid $\min(v_b, 25/3 + (2/3)v_b)$ where $v_b$ is the value of the pipe to the buyer (Chatterjee & Samuelson, 1983). Thus, sellers will bid their true value only if it is above 75 and will strategically misrepresent their value otherwise. Buyers will bid their true value only if it is below 25. Radner & Schotter (1989) report experimental tests roughly confirming that bids are a linear function of values, but report less misrepresentation of values, and thus *more* efficiency, than game theory predicts.

6  This prediction is consistent with findings from experimental studies of "shrinking pie

games" in which two parties bargain over how to split a resource pool that diminishes in value if they are unable to agree. Researchers have found that, when each side's pie shrinks at a different rate, the parties take longer to settle (Raiffa, 1982, p. 52; Rapoport, Weg, & Felsenthal, 1990; Weg, Rapoport, & Felsenthal, 1990).

7 Although the exercise did not incorporate explicit financial incentives, the students' grades in the course depended, in part, on their performance on the exercise. Students are generally motivated to get good grades, apart from the financial ramifications; however, it is nonetheless instructive to perform a very rough calculation of the financial implications of their performance in Appleton-Baker, and thus their pecuniary incentive to obtain an advantageous price. If they do not agree, they get an exercise grade of 0, compared to a class average of .5. That decreases their course average by .0183 (since 12 exercises are 40% of the grade, and $(-.5/12)(.4) = .0183$). Assume a standard deviation in course averages of .10 (a good approximation) and suppose a .624 average (1.24 standard deviations above the student mean of .50) is required to get a grade of A in the course. Students with averages between .6423 and .624 would be *prevented* from getting an A by not agreeing (which reduces their average by $-.0183$); a student has a .03 chance of falling in that interval.

A student with three As in four courses (the usual load) makes the "director's list." Since about 25% of the course grades are As, an average student has a 14% chance of getting exactly 2 of 3 As. Thus, a student who fails to agree has a 14% chance of *needing* a third A to make the director's list, and a 3% smaller chance of not getting it because of failing to agree. Suppose making the director's list earns an incremental $1,000 in starting salary, or around $10,000 in discounted salary over many years. Then the financial impact of failing to agree is (.14)(.03)($10,000), or $42. This amount is considerably larger than the stakes typically employed in experimental games.

8 By Fisher's exact test, null hypothesis that the disagreement rates are the same can be rejected at $p < .01$ (relative frequencies are 7/35 and 0/35). A within-pair test of the null hypothesis that a disagreement is equally likely in both conditions rejects the null at $p < .01$ too.

9 Three experiments based on sudden impact, including the one discussed here, are reported in Babcock, Loewenstein, Issacharoff, and Camerer (in press), and in Loewenstein, Issacharoff, Camerer, and Babcock (in press).

10 The materials are available from the authors.

11 The table gives only one column in the uncertain-amount condition. Subjects stated only one minimum acceptable offer because they did not know what the amount was when they stated their respective minimum offers.

12 Disagreement rates were calculated by pairing each CMU subject with *every* Penn subject, even though each student was only paired with one other to calculate her actual payoff.

13 However, when both players knew the prize amounts, and knew that the other player knew them too, disagreements were slightly fewer (18%). This suggests that competing equal-split points contribute something to inefficiency (from 10% to 18%), and asymmetry of information contributes a little bit more (from 18% to 30%).

## Appendix

### (Complete information condition)

We are conducting an experiment with two undergraduate classes, one at Carnegie Mellon University and one at the University of Pennsylvania. You will be making decisions about the division of amounts of money. Penn and Carnegie students will be randomly paired with one another. Each student at Carnegie will propose a division – $X to me, $Y to you – to a student at Penn. If the Penn student rejects $Y, then neither student will receive any money. If the Penn student accepts $Y, then the Carnegie student will actually receive $X and the Penn student will actually receive $Y. We will give you money in an envelope with your social security number on it after the experiment is finished (in the next class).

Below are five money amounts. For each amount, Carnegie students will state the offer to the paired Penn students. Penn students will receive the same five amounts, but they will state the *lowest* offer they will accept, for each of the five amounts. Amounts must be multiples of ten cents ($.10).

For each pair, we will randomly pick one of the five amounts, and actually pay you using that amount. If the offer by the Carnegie student is higher than (or equal to) the Penn student's lowest acceptable offer, then the Penn student will receive the amount offered by the Carnegie student, and the Carnegie student will receive the balance. If the offer by the Carnegie student is below the Penn student's lowest acceptable offer, then both students receive nothing.

| Amount | Carnegie students | Penn students |
|---|---|---|
| $1 | Offer $_____ to me,<br>$_____ to Penn student<br>total  $1_____ | Lowest acceptable offer $_____ |
| $3 | Offer $_____ to me,<br>$_____ to Penn student<br>total  $3_____ | Lowest acceptable offer $_____ |
| $5 | Offer $_____ to me,<br>$_____ to Penn student<br>total  $5_____ | Lowest acceptable offer $_____ |
| $7 | Offer $_____ to me,<br>$_____ to Penn student<br>total  $7_____ | Lowest acceptable offer $_____ |
| $9 | Offer $_____ to me,<br>$_____ to Penn student<br>total  $9_____ | Lowest acceptable offer $_____ |

### (Incomplete information condition)

We are conducting an experiment with two undergraduate classes, one at Carnegie Mellon University and one at the University of Pennsylvania. You will be making decisions about the division of amounts of money. Penn and Carnegie students will be randomly paired with one another. Each student at Carnegie will propose a division – $X to me, $Y to you – to a student at Penn. If the Penn student rejects $Y, then neither student will receive any money. If the Penn student accepts $Y, then the Carnegie student will actually receive $X and the Penn student will actually receive $Y. We will give you money in an envelope with your social security number on it after the experiment is finished (in the next class).

Below are five money amounts. For each amount, Carnegie students will state the offer to the paired Penn students. Penn students will state the *lowest* offer they will accept. Amounts must be multiples of ten cents ($.10).

For each pair, we will randomly pick one of the five amounts, and actually pay you using that amount. If the offer by the Carnegie student is higher than the Penn student's lowest acceptable offer, then the Penn student will receive the amount offered by the Carnegie student, and the Carnegie student will receive the balance. If the offer by the Carnegie student is below the Penn student's lowest acceptable offer, then both students receive nothing.

Penn students
Lowest acceptable offer $_____

Carnegie students

| $1 | Offer $_____ to me, |
| | $_____ to Penn student |
| | total  $1_____ |
| $3 | Offer $_____ to me, |
| | $_____ to Penn student |
| | total  $3_____ |
| $5 | Offer $_____ to me, |
| | $_____ to Penn student |
| | total  $5_____ |
| $7 | Offer $_____ to me, |
| | $_____ to Penn student |
| | total  $7_____ |
| $9 | Offer $_____ to me, |
| | $_____ to Penn student |
| | total  $9_____ |

# Part IV

# Variations in perspectives on justice

# 9 The unfolding of justice: A developmental perspective on reward allocation

*Colleen F. Moore, Sheri E. Hembree,*
*and Robert D. Enright*

"Social peace must spring from economic justice."
   – Martin Luther King, Jr. (as quoted in Garrow, 1986)

This quote from a winner of the Nobel Peace Prize expresses a hope that many people hold in common. The hope is for a world where peace is secure because it is based on a just distribution of goods. The problem with this vision is that people and nations seem to disagree about what constitutes a just distribution. In this essay we take a developmental approach to the issue of fairness in reward distribution. By doing so, we hope to illuminate some of the potential sources of disagreement about what constitutes a just distribution.

To developmentalists, how concepts of fairness of reward distribution develop in people is intrinsically interesting. We think that a developmental viewpoint on justice should be of interest to researchers who normally deal only with adult subjects. First, because we are looking for developmental differences among people, a developmental perspective emphasizes that not everyone has the same view of what constitutes fairness. Thus, a developmental view sensitizes the researcher to the possibility of individual differences and encourages the search for evidence of the use of a variety of strategies or concepts. In contrast, nondevelopmentalists sometimes seem to assume that all subjects in their experiments are behaving in the same manner. Our viewpoint is that uniformity of strategies and concepts in judgment and decision making should not be taken for granted. A developmental look at any phenomenon immediately disabuses a researcher of such an assumption.

The authors thank James A. Dixon for helpful conversations about the material. Preparation of this chapter was supported in part by a grant to the first author from the Graduate School, University of Wisconsin–Madison.

Second, according to any developmental view a psychological phenomenon is regarded as not well understood unless the life history of that phenomenon is included. Even where there are alternate developmental paths to the same point, knowing the developmental history of a phenomenon may help predict its future course. This is important when researchers are interested in influencing how subjects make a given type of judgment or decision.

The developmental history of a phenomenon can also help elucidate the psychological processes involved in it, whether those processes are particular experiences that lead to particular attitudes or certain cognitive abilities. For example, the general viewpoint that humans have a limited capacity for information processing might be used as one justification for a theory positing the use of simple heuristics for making reward allocations (Messick, this book). A developmental approach immediately presses two issues on such a viewpoint. What is the origin of the person's repertoire of heuristics? As Kuo (1976) said, if a behavior was not present at birth then it must have developed. Yet such heuristics are often taken as almost preexistent. If the heuristics develop, the degree to which they are modifiable and the circumstances in which they are used might depend on their developmental source. If limited information-processing capacity is a major motivation for the use of simple heuristics in judgment and decision making, what happens if the same task is put before a presumably more limited (immature) information processor? So we see that some implications of our theories may not be clear until they are considered developmentally. It is our view that for a theory of adult concepts of equity to be viable, it should at least be capable of accommodating (if not predicting) observed developmental changes. Thus, developmental phenomena can be regarded as providing constraints on theories of judgment and decision making.

On the other side, it is also the case that nondevelopmental theories provide important ideas for developmental research and theory, especially about the mature state of a concept or endpoint of development. This is certainly true in the case of concepts of fairness of reward distribution. In many developmental studies, the proportional distribution rule of equity theory (Adams, 1965; Bar-Hillel & Yaari, this book) has been used as a benchmark against which children's reward distributions are judged (see Hook & Cook, 1979, for a review). When a nondevelopmental theory is adopted in developmental research as a representation of maturity, it is necessary to supplement it with descriptions of the developmental steps leading toward the mature point described by the nondevelopmental theory. Sometimes this can be done simply by allowing certain parameters in the original theory to change with development (Surber, 1977, 1982).

Another option for accommodating developmental change in judgment and decision making is to hypothesize a sequence of rules or heuristics that increase in complexity and/or amount or type of information used (Anderson & Butzin, 1978; Hook & Cook, 1979; Moore, Dixon, & Haines, 1991; Siegler, 1976). For example, Siegler's (1976) theory of the development of the ability to solve balance scale problems consists of a set of decision rules. The rule representing developmental immaturity uses only one source of information (amount of weight on each side of the scale), while the rule representing mastery of the task uses more information in a more complex manner (torque = weight × distance is calculated for each side of the scale and the values are compared). In a similar way, an equality rule for reward distribution can be regarded either as a special case of the proportional distribution rule of equity theory[1] (Messick, this book), or as a reward distribution rule which uses fewer sources of information than the proportional rule. The equality rule requires consideration of only the number of people and the total amount of reward. In contrast, proportional reward distribution also requires considering the contribution, work, or "deservingness" of each person. In fact, developmental theories (Damon, 1975; Hook & Cook, 1979; Piaget, 1965) regard the equal distribution rule as a developmental precursor to the proportional rule because it can be regarded as cognitively simpler than proportional distribution (see Baron, this book, for a description of how complex the process of deciding to use equal distribution might be).

This brings us to what we see as a serious problem in many developmental theories in the realm of social cognition. Because the goal of developmental research is to describe the sequence of steps, levels, or stages through which one passes en route to the putatively mature point, there is a strong tendency to assume that there is a *single* sequence of steps, levels, or stages leading toward a single mature point. Thus, although the developmental approach emphasizes the search for age differences in strategies and concepts, it is commonly assumed that there is only one developmental path to maturity, and that maturity constitutes a single strategy. The single-sequence hypothesis has different implications for the modifiability and flexibility of reward allocation strategies than does a view that includes branches in the developmental pathway and/or the possibility of more than one mature state. Although the single developmental sequence idea is important as a testable null hypothesis, developmental studies rarely *test* it (for exceptions in the moral domain, see Davison, Robbins, & Swanson, 1978, and Kuhn, 1976). Instead, the indirect evidence provided by age-group differences in performance is often accepted as support for a claim about a single developmental pathway.

The single developmental pathway hypothesis is based largely on the idea that a person cannot choose to use a reward allocation principle unless it is understood. It is really the understanding of such principles that is expected to show a single developmental pathway. However, once a variety of reward allocation principles are understood, the one that is most difficult to understand (and presumed to be late developing) will not necessarily be the one chosen and will not necessarily be regarded as ethically preferable. This distinction between understanding and preference has been somewhat neglected in developmental research, partly due to the difficulty of empirically distinguishing between competence and performance in any context. In the case of social concepts such as fairness of reward allocation, the confusion of understanding (competence) and preference can lead to a prescriptive use of a descriptive theory. That is, *preferences* for reward allocation principles that are represented in the developmental theory as immature (early in the developmental sequence) are sometimes regarded as undesirable, or at least as evidence of a developmental lag that needs to be ameliorated (Enright, Enright, & Lapsley, 1981). It should be noted, however, that such a prescriptive use of a descriptive developmental theory is based on the assumption that preferences reflect understanding and that immature understanding is undesirable.

In this essay we use unfolding theory (Coombs, 1964) and a data set based on the cognitive-developmental or Piagetian approach to test empirically the hypothesis that there is a single developmental sequence in the development of distributive justice concepts. Given that our results contradict the hypothesis of a single developmental pathway, we discuss the implications of this finding for the existence of a diversity of viewpoints on what constitutes fair reward distribution and also for the impossibility of defining development in this domain as having a single mature endpoint. Thus, we argue that the lack of a single developmental pathway suggests that concepts of fair reward distribution are essentially matters of values and attitudes and that diversity of viewpoints among people should be expected to be the rule rather than the exception. Before we present the unfolding test of the single-sequence hypothesis, we present a brief review of the developmental literature on reward distribution. Two main theoretical approaches have dominated the study of distributive justice development: equity theory and the cognitive developmental or Piagetian approach. Interestingly, *both* approaches have accepted proportional reward distribution as the desirable mature point of development, and writers from both approaches have hypothesized a unidimensional developmental sequence.

## Equity theory adopted for development

Developmental research derived from equity theory has typically asked children to allocate rewards to two or more people who did different amounts of work. The division of the rewards is then examined to see the extent to which it conforms to the proportional rule of equity theory, versus the equality rule, or if the subject is a worker, a self-interest rule. A variety of variables that influence the degree to which children's allocations conform to the proportional equity norm have been studied. For example, Lerner (1974) found that kindergarten age children showed an equality norm in their reward allocation responses, showing an equity norm only when told they were "co-workers" rather than working as a team. Nelson and Dweck (1977) found that preschool children demonstrated a self-interest response (keeping most of the rewards for oneself) when told to distribute rewards " 'any way you want to' " but conformed to a proportional equity rule when told more explicitly to distribute rewards " 'so that you get the right amount for doing this much work and he/she gets the right amount for doing this much work' " (p. 194). Gender and cultural differences in performance on distribution tasks have also been found (Murphy-Berman, Berman, Singh, Pachauri, & Kumar, 1984).

Hook and Cook (1979) reviewed the literature on the development of reward distribution using equity theory as their basic framework and focusing on extracting the main developmental trends from the literature. They claim that the evidence supports the existence of a developmental sequence proposed by Hook (1978). According to this view, at a young age (4–5 years) children think about allocations "unidimensionally," ignoring the amount of work. At this level, children make reward distributions reflecting either self-interest or strict equality. Next, children adopt an "ordinal" approach to allocation (i.e., more work implies more reward), but without the ability to allocate rewards in numerical proportion to amount of work. Finally, children distribute rewards proportionally to amount of work.

The bulk of the studies in Hook and Cook's 1979 review seemed to support what they called "ordinal equity." For example, if following an equality norm would lead to allocating 10 units of reward to a person and following an equity norm to 15 units of reward, a mean of 12 or 13 was interpreted by Hook and Cook as evidence that children were following an ordinal equity norm. However, their conclusions, like those drawn by the original authors of the studies, were based on age-group means rather than on patterns of individual performance. Group means are not necessarily representative of the individual performance patterns. Furthermore, reward distribution consistent with what Hook and Cook call "ordinal equity" could reflect a proportional distribution with a marginally decreasing function for work (Anderson & Butzin, 1978; Baron, this book). An ordinal equity reward distribution could also result from an allocation rule that does not involve proportions, as when the difference in rewards is determined by the difference in work contributions (Mellers, 1982).

We wish to emphasize two aspects of the developmental research that has been based on the equity theory framework. First, the literature shows that children's reward allocations are sensitive to contextual variables such as instructions or the social meaning of the situation (cf. Messick, this book). Second, in spite of the influence of contextual variables, this literature shows some broad developmental trends. Hook and Cook (1979) concluded that there is evidence of a developmental sequence from self-interest and equality to ordinal equity, culminating in the proportional rule of equity theory. Thus, the developmental research based on equity theory has yielded the hypothesis that there is a single developmental sequence.

### The Piagetian approach

The cognitive-developmental or Piagetian approach has also been used to study the reward allocations and reasoning of children (Damon, 1975; Enright, Franklin, & Manheim, 1980; Piaget, 1965). In contrast to the equity theory approach, in which children are asked to allocate rewards, the cognitive-developmental approach has used predominantly interview methods to provide evidence that there are qualitative developmental changes in how people reason about reward allocation. According to the cognitive-developmental approach, it is children's cognitive abilities that are of import in understanding children's allocation behavior.

Piaget (1968) suggested that children develop concepts of fairness out of the general concept of reciprocity and the requirement for reciprocity in peer interaction. By interviewing children about their responses to hypothetical distribution dilemmas (both of loss and reward), Piaget proposed that at first, distributive justice decisions demonstrate a reliance on authority and external circumstances, and a preference for self-serving outcomes. Next, children demonstrate "equalitarianism," a preference for equality over obedience to authority and a lack of a punishment orientation. Finally, there is a preference for "equitable" judgments that take into account a variety of extenuating circumstances, that is, how an individual is situated.

Damon (1975, 1977, 1980) extended Piaget's general theory of the development of the concept of justice with a narrower focus on positive justice or "that aspect of justice that is concerned with problems generated in prosocial interaction" (Damon, 1975, p. 302). Although Damon's 1977 book addressed a variety of aspects of the development of social knowledge, his theory of fair distribution deals with reward allocation. Damon, following Piaget's methods, interviewed children, examining their justifications in hypothetical and real-life distribution dilemmas. As a result of these interviews, Damon posited six levels of positive justice development. Each stage represents a particular pattern of reasoning or justification associated with distributive justice choices. According to Damon, "Perhaps the best way to conceptualize these levels is as a sequence of unfolding confusions in the mind of the child. Each mental confusion is less sophisticated than the following one" (Damon, 1977, pp. 74–75).

At the first stage (labeled 0-A) Damon regarded the child as confusing fairness with desire. Justice choices are derived from the child's wishes and reasoning consists of asserting choices ("I should have it because I want it"). At the next level (0-B), self-serving choices are justified by arbitrary and irrelevant external characteristics such as height, age, or other physical characteristics (e.g., "I should get it because I'm the oldest").[2] A child at

Damon's third level of distributive justice development (1-A) is said to confuse fairness with strict equality. Justice decisions at this stage are rigidly equal and reflect a strict egalitarian principle (e.g., "Everyone should get the same"). The theory specifies that at level 1-B the child confuses fairness with deserving. Decisions are more "meritarian" in nature and reflect an understanding of inflexible reciprocity (e.g., "She should get the most because she works the hardest"). In progressing to Stage 2-A, fairness is "confused" with compromise. The child's decisions are based more on consideration of special needs and are often an attempt at quantitative compromise. Damon called this a "benevolent" mode that reflects a kind of moral relativity coming out of an understanding that certain individuals may have a special claim to resources (e.g., "He should get the most because he is poor, but she should get some too.").

Finally, at Damon's Stage 2-B the child is said to confuse fairness with a kind of "situational ethic," recognizing that there are many competing justice claims. All of these claims (need, equality, deserving, compromise) are considered, with certain claims being weighed more heavily depending on the individual's situation. According to Damon, "often these children sound like utilitarians" (Damon, 1977, p. 76) with their clear-cut decisions justified with a recognition that all should be given their due. One example of utilitarian reasoning at Stage 2-B found by Damon was the argument that basing rewards on work productivity provides an incentive to everyone to work harder in the future, so that in the long run all would benefit (see Baron, this book, for an insightful description of the many nuances of utilitarianism).

In an effort to test the cognitive-developmental hypothesis that level of cognitive functioning is related to positive justice reasoning, Damon (1975) used his interview dealing with positive justice as well as a set of Piagetian logic tasks with a sample of 4- to 8-year-olds. The results showed the expected association between level of performance on the Piagetian mathematical and physical reasoning tasks and reasoning in the positive justice interviews. Damon concluded that the development of logical and positive justice reasoning occurs in parallel.

To investigate whether his proposed stages of positive justice development form an invariant sequence (that is, whether all children follow the same pattern of stage development), Damon (1980) conducted a two-year longitudinal study with 4- to 9-year-old children. The positive justice reasoning of each child was assessed three times at one-year intervals with interviews. The study revealed a "gradual progression" along the proposed reasoning levels with age so that by the end of the study most of the children had demonstrated progress through the proposed stages. The majority of the children (56%) showed a theoretically more advanced stage level at the end of the two-year period than at the beginning, a substantial number (44%) showed either no change or reversal of change. According to Damon (1980, p. 1016), "The results of this study confirmed the progressive, stepwise nature of children's social-cognitive development." Damon qualified this conclusion by adding that, "Although stages of social cognition express important qualitative differences among various social reasoning patterns appearing successively throughout childhood, actual day-to-day development is gradual, mixed, and often uneven" (p. 1017). Although he acknowledged the possibility of developmental regression to an earlier stage, Damon seemed to take his results as evidence that his stages of positive justice constitute an ordered unidimensional developmental sequence.

### Enright's distributive justice scale

With its emphasis on the underlying reasons and principles behind reward distribution decisions, the cognitive-developmental approach has usually examined verbal protocols gathered during interviews about reward distribution dilemmas (e.g., Piaget, 1965; Damon, 1975, 1980). Despite the ability of this method to discover the reasoning behind children's decisions, the approach has the obvious disadvantages of relying on verbal expression (which in itself is expected to change developmentally). Other problems are possible unreliability of coding verbal protocols into categories and lack of standardization of the interview.

In an effort to eliminate some of the weaknesses of the verbal protocol procedure, Enright and his colleagues developed an objective and standardized measure of justice development, the Distributive Justice Scale (DJS), based on Damon's stages (Enright et al., 1984; Enright, Enright, & Lapsley, 1981; Enright, Enright, Manheim, & Harris, 1980; Enright, Franklin, & Manheim, 1980). While Damon's interview technique requires that the interviewer offer alternatives to a child's justice decision, its relatively unstructured format does not exhaust every comparison between stages. In contrast, the DJS is a paired comparison task, requiring the child to choose between solutions representing all six possible stages in solving a justice dilemma.

The DJS consists of two separate dilemmas with pictures and statements representing each of Damon's six stages of distributive justice development. The child is read a dilemma "story" and asked to choose the better of two "endings" that represent two stages. The statement and picture for each stage is then presented paired with every other for a total of 15 comparisons.

In one dilemma, four children at a camp make paintings and are paid nickels for them. The child must decide how the nickels are to be divided among the four children, based on their different characteristics: Betty is the "oldest one at camp"; Jennifer's family "does not have much money"; David "made the most paintings"; and Mathew has no special circumstance. Ending statements representing the different stages are read and the child is asked to choose, "Which one of these ends the story better?"

For example, a child would choose whether "Betty gets the most nickels because she is older than the others at camp" (stage 0-B), or "Jennifer gets the most nickels because she does not have much money and needs the nickels" (Stage 2-A). The second dilemma is similar in format but is based on a story of four children making crayon drawings and selling them at the school fair. The order of pairings is randomized, as is which stage in the pair is presented first.

Enright and his colleagues scored the DJS by finding the child's most preferred stage for each dilemma, then converting stage level to a numerical score (0 for Stage 0-A, .5 for Stage 0-B, and so on), and taking the mean for both dilemmas to yield a final score. If a child was intransitive in choices on a dilemma, the lowest score of the intransitive set of stages was selected to represent his or her level.

### Unfolding analysis of developmental sequence

Damon's theory of the development of distributive justice postulates a unidimensional sequence of stages. Because subjects choose for all possible paired comparisons which of two stage representative reward distributions they prefer, Enright's DJS provides data suitable for Coombs's (1964) unfolding theory. With unfolding theory it is possible to use data from Enright's DJS to test Damon's postulated unidimensional stage sequence. Any developmental theory that hypothesizes a single unbranching sequence can be examined by testing the hypothesis that a single common dimension underlies the responses of all subjects. Unfolding theory in one dimension is one method for testing the unidimensional model (McIver & Carmines, 1981).

Because unfolding theory is not used very often, a brief description may be helpful. Our description is similar to that found in Coombs (1964). Assume for the moment that Damon's (1975, 1977) stage theory is correct and that the stages are ordered along a single developmental dimension as shown in the top section of Figure 1. The common dimension that is hypothesized to underlie the preference orders of all subjects is called the J-scale in unfolding theory. Notice that we have spaced the stages out arbitrarily along the J-scale to emphasize that the distances between them are unknown.

A person's observed preference order will be determined by the person's position on the developmental dimension. To see how preference orders are determined, imagine that the developmental dimension is a string and the position of each stage is a knot on the string. If a person's current developmental position is precisely at Stage 1, then the string is picked up (or "folded") at the Stage 1 location. As the two sides of the string dangle from the Stage 1 knot, the person's preference order is determined by the order in which the knots are encountered as one moves down the string. This is shown in the bottom of Figure 1, although we show the string clipped at the preference point and the two sections laid side by side horizontally.

Theoretical Stage Order or J-Scale

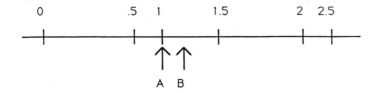

Observed preference order or I-scale for Person A:

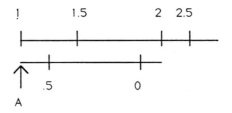

Observed preference order or I-scale for Person B:

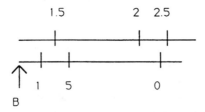

Figure 1    Examples of relationship between theoretical stage order (*J*-scale) and observed preference orders (*I*-scales).

For the example of person A in Figure 1, the observed preference order (or I-scale in Coombs's terms) is 1, .5, 1.5, 0, 2, 2.5. A person need not be precisely *at* a given stage, however. A person's current position on the developmental dimension might be partway between two stages, for example, about a third of the way between Stage 1 and Stage 1.5 at a point labeled B in the upper portion of Figure 1. Imagine the string picked up at point B. As we move down the dangling string, the knots we encounter will be, in order, 1, 1.5, .5, 2, 0, 2.5. This is also shown in the bottom of Figure 1.

Table 1 *Percentages of transitive and intransitive choice patterns*

| Age group | Transitive | Intransitive |
| --- | --- | --- |
| Kindergarten | 20 (12) | 80 (48) |
| 2nd Grade | 58 (35) | 42 (25) |
| 4th Grade | 68 (41) | 32 (19) |
| 6th Grade | 82 (49) | 18 (11) |
| Total | 57 (137) | 43 (103) |

*Note:* Numbers of patterns are given in parentheses. Each subject contributed two choice patterns, one for each scenario.

The reader can also imagine how changing the metric properties of the J-scale, or spacing between the stages, permits different observed preference orders to be consistent with it. Nevertheless, the qualitative or ordinal features of the J-scale do provide some constraints on the preference orders which are permissible. The easiest way to understand the constraints provided by a qualitative J-scale is to imagine that the developmental dimension is a rubber band with knots tied in it. It can be stretched to change the intervals between the stages, but the order of the stages on the rubber band remains fixed. For a 6-item stage theory, there are 32 preference orders that will be qualitatively consistent with it (Davison, 1979).

The empirical question is whether the set of observed preference orders (I-scales) is consistent with the hypothesized stage order (J-scale). In the description that follows, we considered only the qualitative, ordinal aspects of the data. Thus, in unfolding theory terms we attempted to determine whether there is a single qualitative J-scale that is consistent with the observed preference orders, or I-scales.

The data set we reanalyzed consisted of the second, fourth, and sixth grade U.S. sample of Study 1 of Enright et al. (1984), and also the kindergarten sample of Study 2. This data set was chosen because it includes all six of Damon's hypothesized stages. Earlier versions of the DJS omitted Stage 2-B. First, we determined whether each subject's pattern of choices formed a transitive preference order. Unfolding theory requires that each subject's paired comparison choices be collapsed into a preference order. This requires transitivity. Table 1 presents the percentages of subjects in each grade level showing transitive patterns on the DJS. The overall percentage of transitive patterns was 57%. The percentage of transitive patterns increases with increasing age. The kindergarten sample had 20% transitive patterns, but by sixth grade 82% of patterns were transitive. With 15 paired comparisons, there are $2^{15} = 32768$ choice patterns possible. Three hundred sixty of those patterns are transitive preference orders of the six stages. Thus, the apriori probability of a totally random chooser yielding a transitive choice pattern is approximately .01. Thus, all the age groups perform better than chance in terms of transitivity.

These developmental changes in transitivity are interesting in themselves. Intransitivity might be expected to come from a variety of sources. One possibility is that some of the youngest children do not really comprehend the stage scenarios, and so their choices are somewhat random. From a stage theory perspective, comprehension would be expected to be best for the lower stages and worst for the higher stages that are beyond the child's current level of functioning. In designing the DJS, Enright and his colleagues assumed that subjects would show a clear preference for dilemma solutions representing their current stage, but that choices between dilemma solutions not involving the subject's current stage might be random. For younger children the randomness might result from lack of understanding of the higher stages, while older children might see solutions representing theoretically lower stages as equally poor, be uninterested, and choose randomly. Enright's idea that subjects will have a clear preference for their current stage but will choose randomly between other pairs of stages says that 10 of the 15 choices will be random. There are $2^{10} = 1,024$ choice patterns possible, and 60 of these will be transitive orders. Thus, the apriori probability of a transitive order is approximately .06 under Enright's idea of clear preference for only the subject's current stage. The data of all age groups exceed this probability of occurrence of transitive patterns. Nevertheless, Enright's idea of partially random choices would be expected to decrease the reliability of the observed preference orders. Low reliability of the preference orders would question the conclusions based on our unfolding analysis (see also Coombs, 1964, for a probabilistic version of unfolding theory).

A second possible source of intransitivity is developmental change in the ability to order the stimuli. Research has shown developmental changes in both the ability to order a set of stimuli (seriation) and to make transitive inferences from a set of ordered stimuli (Braine, 1959, Kingma, 1984, Siegel, 1972). Memory for the previous stimuli and choices would also be expected to change developmentally, and might contribute to intransitivity.

A third possible source of intransitivity is that the younger children may not yet have developed clear preferences about fairness. Without clear preferences, choice responses would not be expected to be consistent over the set of stimuli. Enright's DJS includes three repeated trials as a consistency check in each scenario. All subjects whose data were included were consistent on at least 4 of 6 repeated trials (a total of only 5 subjects, all kindergarteners were excluded based on this criterion). Since the data set we examined included only those who passed the consistency check, lack of genuine preferences seems unlikely. A final possibility is that the younger children evaluate the stimuli according to different criteria on different trials, depending on the comparison context. One of the longstanding puzzles of the literature on decision making is how to account for intransitive choices (Bar-Hillel & Margalit, 1988; Gehrlein, 1990; Tversky, 1969, 1977).

After determining the preference orders implied by each transitive choice pattern, we evaluated the consistency of the obtained preference patterns with the qualitative (ordinal) scale hypothesized by Damon. We excluded the intransitive patterns, and we also ignored reversals of the .5 and 0 stage items in examining the fit of the preference patterns to Damon's stage model. In a very large percentage of obtained preference patterns (92%), these two items fell together at the least preferred end of the continuum. We judged that a reversal of the ordering of these two items did not represent a serious deviation from Damon's theory.

We found that only 11% (15 of 137) of the observed transitive patterns were qualitatively consistent with Damon's stage ordering. Considering that 32 of the 360 possible preference patterns will fit Damon's theory (8.9%), the finding that 11% of the observed patterns fit the theoretical order is not impressive. Furthermore, in order for a set of observed preference patterns to be consistent with a unidimensional common developmental scale, it is necessary that there be only one observed order with the highest stage on one end and the lowest stage on the other end (i.e., the hypothesized order and its mirror image). We found seven distinct preference patterns beginning with Stage 2.5 and ending with either Stage 0 or .5. These seven patterns encompassed 26% (35 individuals of 137) of the transitive patterns. Of those 35 individuals with patterns that began with 2.5 and ended with 0 or .5, only 11% (4 of 35) had patterns that corresponded to Damon's hypothesized stage order. Thus, the data are inconsistent with the hypothesis that there is a unidimensional developmental scale from Stage 0 or .5 to Stage 2.5.

If Damon's postulated order is not consistent with the data of Enright et al. (1984), is there another qualitative unidimensional scale that is consistent with the observed preference patterns? With six stage items, there are 360 qualitative unidimensional J-scales (orderings of the six stages) possible. We examined three of these possibilities that were suggested by the data. It appeared that Stage 1.0 was often close to Stage 2.0 or 2.5 in the observed preference patterns. Therefore, we tried qualitative J-scales that have Stage 1.0 (equal distribution) placed closer to Stage 2.5 (balancing competing claims) than in Damon's theory. Table 2 presents the percentages of patterns consistent with each of these three other qualitative J-scales, as well as with Damon's order. Because we examined only the qualitative J-scales rather than metric J-scales, an observed preference order can be consistent with more than one hypothesized stage order, or J-scale. Also, an observed preference order need not agree with any of the four possible stage orders in Table 2, since there are 360 possible stage orders. Therefore, the percentages in Table 2 do not add up to 100.

As can be seen in Table 2, all three alternative stage orders outperform Damon's order, and are consistent with 46% to 58% of the observed pref-

Table 2 *Percentages of transitive patterns consistent with four possible orderings*

| Order | Grade level | | | | |
|---|---|---|---|---|---|
| | K | 2nd | 4th | 6th | Total |
| Damon's Theory | 25 (3) | 20 (7) | 7 (4) | 4 (2) | 11 (15) |
| Alternative A | 42 (5) | 43 (15) | 56 (23) | 53 (26) | 50 (69) |
| Alternative B | 33 (4) | 40 (14) | 68 (28) | 67 (33) | 58 (79) |
| Alternative C | 50 (6) | 34 (12) | 63 (26) | 39 (19) | 46 (63) |

*Note:* Numbers of patterns are given in parentheses.
  *Stage orders:*
  Damon's Theory:  0–.5–1–1.5–2–2.5
  Alternative A:  1–2.5–2–1.5–.5–0
  Alternative B:  2–2.5–1–1.5–.5–0
  Alternative C:  2.5–1–2–1.5–.5–0
  *Stage descriptions:*
  0 – Desire; .5 – Physical characteristics; 1 – Equality; 1.5 – Work; 2 – Need;
  2.5 – Balancing competing claims

erence patterns. However, the observed preference patterns are also qualitatively inconsistent with these alternative unidimensional hypotheses. For example, Alternative C, which begins with Stage 0 and ends with Stage 2.5, is also disconfirmed as a unidimensional hypothesis for these data by the multiplicity of observed preference patterns with 0 and 2.5 on the ends. The same thing is true for Alternatives A and B. There are several observed preference patterns beginning and ending with Stages 1 and 0 or Stages 2 and 0.

We also split the data according to Enright's two subscales, one involving the camp scenario and the other the school fair scenario. The results were comparable to those described above for the two subscales combined. The percentages of patterns fitting Damon's hypothesized order were 17% and 6% for the two scenarios, and the percentages fitting the alternatives in Table 2 ranged from 40 to 63%. Thus, the unidimensional developmental path hypothesis does not fare well in the data of Enright et al. (1984). That the same results hold across the two scenarios of the DJS suggests that the finding is robust.

A statistical approach based on unfolding theory that can be used to test the predictions of a hypothesized stage theory has been described by Davison (1979). In Davison's approach it is not necessary to use the entire preference order of each subject. Instead, the predictions of unfolding theory can be tested for the first two items (or the first $n$ items) of the preference orders. Unfolding theory makes a simple qualitative prediction for the first two preferences; the first two preferred items should be adjacent on the developmental dimension. To test this prediction the investigator needs to construct a two-way First Preferred Stage × Second Preferred Stage con-

Table 3 *Frequencies of subjects for the first two preferred stages*

|  |  | First stage preference | | | | |
|---|---|---|---|---|---|---|
|  |  | 1 | 1.5 | 2 | 2.5 | Total |
|  | 1 | 0 | 6 | 11 | 17 | 34 |
| Second stage | 1.5 | 9 | 0 | 1 | 8 | 18 |
| preference | 2 | 18 | 2 | 0 | 13 | 33 |
|  | 2.5 | 32 | 2 | 16 | 0 | 50 |
|  | Total | 59 | 11 | 30 | 38 | 135 |

*Note:* Subjects with a first or second preference for Stage 0 or .5 were excluded.

tingency table of frequencies of subjects. The contingency table is then tested in a two-step process. First, the table is tested to see if it violates quasi-independence. Because the diagonal is empty by definition, the usual test of independence does not apply. Davison (1979) described how to use one log-linear model to test quasi-independence, that is, to test whether there is any structure in the data beyond that imposed by the empty diagonal. If quasi-independence is rejected, then one can proceed to test to see if a hypothesized developmental order can account for the structure in the data.

We applied Davison's (1979) method to the first two stage preferences of the subjects in the present study. This type of test is in keeping with Enright's original idea that the top preferences of the subjects would be more reliable than the lower preferences. Table 3 presents the contingency table for the first two preferences of those subjects with transitive orders. A test of quasi-independence using the log-linear model was not significant, $x^2 = 6.23$, $p > .20$. (This test was done using BMDP-4F, Dixon (1988), and defining the diagonal as containing structural zeros.) We repeated the test of quasi-independence including those subjects with intransitive patterns who showed clear preferences for their first two preferred stages. This added 11 subjects, but did not change the result of the test of quasi-independence, $x^2(5) = 6.76$, $p > .20$. There is no evidence for structure in even the first two stage preferences. Inspection of Table 3 shows that there were 47 adjacent stage preferences (e.g., 2–2.5 or 2.5–2) and 88 nonadjacent stage preferences. Thus, even if quasi-independence could be rejected, Damon's sequence hypothesis would not account for the structure.

The data of Enright et al. (1984) are inconsistent with the existence of a unidimensional developmental scale ordered as hypothesized by Damon. Two conclusions that could be drawn from this result are: (a) that Enright's DJS is invalid as a measure of Damon's hypothesized stages, or (b) that Damon's hypothesized order of stages should be rejected.

The validity of Enright's DJS as a measure of Damon's stages depends on the degree to which the scenarios and stage items instantiate the essential features of Damon's stages. Because Damon's theory evolved out of the Piagetian framework, it deals primarily with the reasoning the subject gives in support of a given reward distribution. Damon (1975, 1977, 1980) used the Piagetian *method clinique* in which children are interviewed in depth about reward distribution dilemmas. The goal of the interview is to pin down the child's understanding and reasoning process (see Baron, this book, for the collection of written justifications with adults to tap fairness reasoning). Thus, from a structuralist, cognitive-developmental viewpoint, Enright's DJS would be criticized because it is a recognition measure, not a production measure. From the structuralist perspective, an objective recognition measure fails to capture the richness of the subject's thinking.

Other empirical evidence provides grounds for the validity of Enright's DJS, however. Enright and his colleagues have shown that stage score on the DJS is related to age, performance on Piagetian logic tasks, and social class in predictable ways (Enright, Enright, Manheim, and Harris, 1980; Enright, Franklin, and Manheim, 1980). In addition, in three different countries (the United States, Sweden, and Zaire) similar age trends were observed in stage scores on the DJS (Enright, Franklin, and Manheim, 1980; Enright et al., 1984). In a one-year longitudinal study Enright et al. (1984, Study 3) found age changes that replicated those obtained in their cross-sectional study (1980a). These types of evidence are similar to those used by Damon (1975, 1980) to support his stage theory. The relationship of the DJS to Piagetian logical reasoning tasks found by Enright, Franklin, and Manheim (1980) is especially noteworthy because the relationship is as predicted by Damon's theory and is similar to that found in Damon (1975). Overall, the pattern of results lends support to the validity of Enright's DJS as a measure of the constructs of Damon's theory of the development of distributive justice.

The other conclusion that can be drawn from the results of our unfolding analysis of the data of Enright et al. (1984) is that Damon's hypothesized stage order is incorrect. In fact, the data suggest that there is *not* a unidimensional stage order of any sort underlying the DJS. Damon (1980) expressed caution about attributing stagelike features to his levels of distributive justice development. Enright et al. (1984) observed regressions from Stage 2.0 (Need) to Stage 1.0 (Equality) in the longitudinal part of their study and took those regressions as evidence that "distributive justice is not rigidly stagelike." The authors suggested that preadolescent tendencies toward peer conformity could be responsible for some of the observed regressions from Stage 2.0 to Stage 1.0. Thus, our unfolding analysis adds further evidence that distributive justice does not show a unidimensional stage sequence.

There is, however, an important caveat in this conclusion. Damon's (1975) theory deals primarily with the development of children's *understanding* of reward allocation principles. The central idea behind Damon's theory is that the capacity for certain logical operations is necessary in order to understand different reward allocation principles. Enright's DJS measures preferences, not understanding. In the cognitive-developmental approach it is sometimes argued that subjects should show preferences for principles that are just slightly ahead of their current level of understanding (Rest, 1983). (This argument is based on Piagetian notions of how cognitive change occurs, and requires the assumption that more advanced stages are intrinsically better than less advanced stages.) Thus, cognitive-developmentalists have argued that preferences can be a valid measure of understanding.

For reward allocation, or other social domains, it is possible that preferences would show a unidimensional sequence during the development of understanding. The underlying dimension would be the cognitive difficulty of the principles. Once a person understands the full range of principles, however, the reward allocation principles need not be arrayed on a dimension of cognitive difficulty. Once understanding is established, subjects would be expected to evaluate reward allocation principles according to some *moral* dimension or dimensions. Thus, based on the data we analyzed it is still possible that there is a unidimensional sequence for the development of the *understanding* of reward allocation principles, but that there is not a single common moral dimension used by people to evaluate those reward allocation principles once they are understood. Such a conclusion requires assuming that the understanding of the principles represented in the DJS occurs fairly early.

In a series of three experiments, Anderson and Butzin (1978) asked children 4 to 11 years of age to distribute rewards based on information and need, work, or both need and work of pairs of story characters. Their results showed that even the majority of 4-year-olds consistently used the need and work information in allocating rewards. A study by Nelson and Dweck (1977) also found that 4-year-olds distribute rewards proportionately to work under some conditions. Studies such as these provide evidence that an understanding of the reward allocation principles that are designated as the highest stage in Damon's theory may occur quite early.

## Developmental trends versus developmental sequence

We are faced with a somewhat puzzling pattern of findings. The evidence we have presented here based on our unfolding analysis of the preference data of Enright et al. (1984) suggests that there is little ground for asserting a unidimensional developmental ordering of stages of reward distribution. Nevertheless, studies by both Damon and Enright have shown consistently in group data that average stage score increases with age, and Hook and Cook's 1979 review also showed age changes. Clearly there is something developmental occurring, but it does not seem to be development along a single dimension.

Elsewhere the first author has argued that developmental research should consider the possibility of the existence of several alternative paths of development in any domain (Moore, Dixon, & Haines, 1991). Individuals need not follow a fixed path of development in order for there to be general developmental trends. For example, in the study by Moore et al. (1991) there were age changes in the percentages of subjects who understood two different principles of a temperature mixture task. However, further analyses showed no evidence for a developmental ordering of the two principles. If the two principles were part of a unidimensional developmental sequence, then subjects should be observed who have mastered the first principle or both the first and second principles, but no subjects should be found with mastery of only the second principle. (See Froman & Hubert, 1980, for ways to use cross-sectional data of this sort to test developmental sequences.)

The temptation for the developmental researcher is to oversimplify the facts about development by assuming a single fixed sequence. The unfolding analysis, the frequency of regression to Stage 1.0 (Equality) in the longitudinal study of Enright et al. (1984), evidence of early competence in proportional reward allocation (Anderson & Butzin, 1978), the existence of cross cultural (Nisan, 1984) and social class differences (Enright et al., 1981), and the influence of a variety of contextual variables all provide evidence that the development of distributive justice is a phenomenon that cannot be simplified as a unidimensional sequence. Nevertheless, unidimensional stage theories provide an important starting place and testable null hypothesis for developmental research. That development does not often follow unidimensional sequences is disappointing in some ways, but encouraging in others. If reward allocations are not constrained to follow a unidimensional sequence, then children's reward allocations can be viewed as malleable and other sources for developmental trends should be examined. Some of those sources might include culture, social class, and specific reward allocation practices and teaching in children's homes and schools.

## Contributions of the developmental approach

We began by arguing that nondevelopmental researchers should be interested in developmental work on distributive justice. How does the developmental work enrich our understanding of reward allocations by people, regardless of their ages? We think that an important contribution of Damon's stage theory is that it articulates several philosophies of reward allocation which he borrowed from Frankena (1963): egalitarian (Stage 1-A), meritarian (Stage 1-B), benevolence (Stage 2-A), and the attempt to strike a balance among these three approaches (Stage 2-B). The developmental work shows that children do differ in the degree to which they subscribe to these different principles. We know of little nondevelopmental work that has probed specifically for the presence of such differences, though Singh (1985) showed differences in the reward allocation strategies of college students versus managers. Also Messick's review (this book) shows that a variety of variables can influence whether an egalitarian or meritarian approach is taken.

It is interesting that Damon (1977, p. 77) eschewed any relationship between the proposed developmental order of his stages in childhood and the adult use of the reward distribution principles represented by those stages. Damon felt that in the context of the complexities of adult life that include politics and economics, "Positive justice reasoning takes on an entirely different form. . . . the primitive . . . uses that young children in the present study make of the egalitarian, meritarian, and benevolent philosophies have no direct relation to similar-sounding ideas when applied by adults. . . ." (p. 77). It is not completely clear to us why Damon posits developmental discontinuity between childhood and adulthood, but the task context and difficulty seemed to have a role in his thinking: "But it would be a mistake to expect, for example, an eight-year-old child, demonstrating 2-A benevolence, to construct a benevolent solution to a problem in adult social welfare" (p. 77).

We think a more important issue is what influences different people to adopt different reward allocation principles in different situations. A decade ago Payne (1982) reviewed evidence showing that decision strategies depend on a variety of task variables. Although the field has continued to accumulate evidence of how a variety of variables influence decision strategies, an attractive theoretical integration of those results has yet to be developed. A possible approach to this, we propose, would be a mentalistic one in which the goal is to construct a theory which describes the interrelations among conscious states and their modes and contents (Dulany, 1991). In a mentalistic approach a theory would be constructed in which one's beliefs about the social context, the behavior and social expectations of others, the results of different reward allocations, and so on, combine to yield a chosen reward allocation strategy in a given context. That the contents of a person's conscious states could be influenced by variables such as age, cognitive ability, social and cultural background, and current task situation goes almost without saying. But the claim of the mentalistic view is that conscious states have a more orderly relationship among themselves than do stimulus conditions and conscious states. In a mentalistic approach, it is the conscious state a stimulus produces that theoretically influences other conscious states, which in turn yield behavior. Thus, a more fully articulated mentalistic approach should be capable of describing both developmental and individual differences in judgment and decision making. Our view is that the field of judgment and decision making is in need of an approach that will predict how judgment and decision strategies are chosen by individuals for specific situations.

### References

Adams, J. S. (1965). Inequity in social exchange. In L. Berkowitz (Ed.), *Advances in experimental social psychology* (Vol. 2). New York: Academic.

Anderson, N. H., & Butzin, C. A. (1978). Integration theory applied to children's judgments of equity. *Developmental Psychology, 14,* 593–606.

Bar-Hillel, M., & Margalit, A. (1988). How vicious are cycles of intransitive choice? *Theory and Decision, 24,* 119–145.

Braine, M. D. S. (1959). The ontogeny of certain logical operations: Piaget's formulation examined by nonverbal methods. *Psychological Monographs, 27* (Whole No. 475).

Coombs, C. H. (1964). *A theory of data.* New York: Wiley

Damon, W. (1975). Early conceptions of positive justice as related to the development of logical operations. *Child Development, 46,* 301–312.

—— (1977). *The social world of the child.* San Francisco: Jossey-Bass.

—— (1980). Patterns of change in children's social reasoning: A two-year longitudinal study. *Child Development, 51,* 1010–1017.

Davison, M. L. (1979). Testing a unidimensional, qualitative unfolding model for attitudinal or developmental data. *Psychometrika, 44,* 179–194.

Davison, M. L., Robbins, S., & Swanson, D. B. (1978). Stage structure in objective moral judgments. *Developmental Psychology, 14,* 137–146.

Dixon, W. J. (Ed.). (1988). *BMDP statistical software.* Berkeley: University of California.

Dulany, D. E. (1991). Conscious representation of thought systems. In R. S. Wyer & T. K. Srull (Eds.), *Advances in social cognition* (Vol. 4). Hillsdale, NJ: Erlbaum.

Enright, R. D., Bjerstedt, A., Enright, W. F., Levy, V. M., Lapsley, D. K., Buss, R. R., Harwell, M., & Zindler, M. (1984). Distributive justice development: Cross-cultural, contextual, and longitudinal evaluations. *Child Development, 55,* 1737–1751.

Enright, R. D., Enright, W. F., & Lapsley, D. K. (1981). Distributive justice development and social class: A replication. *Developmental Psychology, 17,* 826–832.

Enright, R. D., Enright, W. F., Manheim, L. A., & Harris, B. E. (1980). Distributive justice development and social class. *Developmental Psychology, 16,* 555–563.

Enright, R. D., Franklin, C. C., & Manheim, L. A. (1980). Children's distributive justice reasoning: A standardized and objective scale. *Developmental Psychology, 16,* 193–202.

Folger, R. (1977). Distributive and procedural justice: Combined impact of "voice" and improvement on experienced inequity. *Journal of Personality and Social Psychology, 35,* 108–119.

Frankena, W. K. (1963). *Ethics.* Englewood Cliffs, NJ: Prentice-Hall.

Freeman, E. B., & Daly, J. (1984). Distributive justice in children: Its relationship to immanent justice and egocentrism. *Early Child Development and Care, 16,* 185–194.

Froman, T., & Hubert, L. J. (1980). Application of prediction analysis to developmental priority. *Psychological Bulletin, 87,* 136–146.

Garrow, D. J. (1986). *Bearing the cross: Martin Luther King, Jr., and the Southern Christian Leadership Conference.* New York: W. Morrow.

Gehrlein, W. V. (1990). The expected likelihood of transitivity of preference. *Psychometrika, 55,* 695–706.

Grant, J. E., Weiner, A., & Rushton, J. P. (1976). Moral judgment and generosity in children. *Psychological Reports, 39,* 451–454.

Hook, J. G. (1978). The development of equity and logico-mathematical thinking. *Child Development, 49,* 1035–1044.

(1982). Development of equity and altruism in judgments of reward and damage allocation. *Developmental Psychology, 18.*

(1983). The development of children's equity judgments. In R. Leahy (Ed.), *The child's construction of social inequality.* New York: Academic Press.

Hook, J. G., & Cook, T. D. (1979). Equity theory and the cognitive ability of children. *Psychological Bulletin, 86,* 429–445.

Kingma, J. (1984). The sequence of development of transitivity, correspondence, and seriation. *Journal of Genetic Psychology, 144,* 271–284.

Kourilsky, M., & Kehret-Ward, T. (1984). Kindergarteners' attitudes toward distributive justice: Experiential mediators. *Merrill-Palmer Quarterly, 30,* 49–64.

Kuhn, D. (1976). Short-term longitudinal evidence for the sequentiality of Kohlberg's early stages of moral judgment. *Developmental Psychology, 12,* 162–166.

Kuo, Z. Y. (1976). *The dynamics of behavior development: An epigenetic view.* New York: Plenum.

Lane, I. M., & Coon, R. C. (1972). Reward allocation in preschool children. *Child Development,* 1382–1389.

Lerner, M. J. (1974). The justice motive: "Equity" and "parity" among children. *Journal of Personality and Social Psychology, 29,* 539–550.

Leventhal, G. S., Popp, A. L., & Sawyer, L. (1973). Equity or equality in children's allocation of reward to other persons? *Child Development, 44,* 753–763.

McIver, J. P., & Carmines, E. G. (1981). *Unidimensional scaling.* Newbury Park, CA: Sage.

Mellers, B. (1982). Equity judgment: A revision of Aristotelian views. *Journal of Experimental Psychology: General, 111,* 242–270.

Moore, C. F., Dixon, J. A., & Haines, B. A. (1991). Components of understanding in proportional reasoning: A fuzzy set representation of developmental progressions. *Child Development, 62,* 441–459.

Murphy-Berman, V., Berman, J. J., Singh, P., Pachauri, A., & Kumar, P. (1984). Factors affecting allocation to needy and meritorious recipients: A cross-cultural comparison. *Journal of Personality and Social Psychology, 46,* 1267–1272.

Nelson, S. A., & Dweck, C. S. (1977). Motivation and competence as determinants of young children's reward allocation. *Developmental Psychology, 13,* 192–197.

Nisan, M. (1984). Distributive justice and social norms. *Child Development, 55,* 1020–1029.

Payne, J. W. (1982). Contingent decision behavior. *Psychological Bulletin, 92,* 382–402.

Piaget, J. (1965). *The moral judgment of the child.* Tr. by Marjorie Gabain. New York: Free Press.

Rest, J. R. (1983). Morality. In P. H. Mussen, J. Flavell, & E. Markman (Eds.), *Handbook of child psychology* (Vol. III): *Cognitive development* (pp. 556–629). New York: Wiley.

Siegel, L. S. (1972). Development of the concept of seriation. *Developmental Psychology, 6,* 135–137.

Siegler, R. S. (1976). Three aspects of cognitive development. *Cognitive Psychology, 8,* 481–520.

Simons, R., & Klaassen, M. (1979). Children's conceptions and use of rules of distributive justice. *International Journal of Behavioral Development, 2,* 253–267.

Singh, R. (1985). A test of the relative-ratio model of reward division with students and managers in India. *Genetic, Social, and General Psychology Monographs, 111,* 363–384.

Surber, C. F. (1977). Developmental processes in social inference: Averaging of intentions and consequences in moral judgment. *Developmental Psychology, 13,* 654–665.

   (1982). Separable effects of motives, consequences, and presentation order on children's moral judgments. *Developmental Psychology, 18,* 257–266.

Tompkins, B. M., & Olejnik, A. B. (1978). Children's reward allocations: The impact of situational and cognitive factors. *Child Development, 49,* 526–529.

Tversky, A. (1969). Intransitivity of preferences. *Psychological Review, 76,* 31–48.

   (1977). Features of similarity. *Psychological Review, 84,* 327–352.

### Notes

1 It can be shown that equal distribution is a special case of Mellers's distributional theory of reward distribution.
2 It might be argued that distributing rewards, especially food, according to physical size is a type of proportional distribution.

# 10 Of ants and grasshoppers: The political psychology of allocating public assistance

*Linda J. Skitka and Philip E. Tetlock*

A grasshopper that had merrily sung all the summer was almost perishing with hunger in the winter. So she went to some Ants that lived nearby, and asked them to lend her a little of the food they had put by. "You shall certainly be paid before this time of year comes again," said she. "What did you do all summer?" asked they. "Why, all day long, and all night long too, I sang, if you please," answered the grasshopper. "Oh! you sang, did you?" said the Ants. "Well, now then, you can dance."

–Aesop's fable (Rundell, 1956)

The United States is still one of the most prosperous countries in the world. However, millions of people are destitute and rely on the generosity of the community for their survival. What obligations does the community have to these people? What responsibilities do these people have to the community? Answers to these fundamental questions depend largely on one's political point of view. In the 1960s, the Johnson administration declared "war on poverty" and the welfare state proliferated. During the 1980s and early 90s, many political leaders concluded that the welfare state was a failure, and attempted (sometimes successfully, sometimes not) to dismantle social programs and to stress the virtues of self-reliance and free markets.

Neil Christiansen, Laura Stephens, Richard Eaves, Bruce Aebel, and Elaina Edwards deserve thanks for their assistance with data collection at Southern Illinois University for the Setting limits, Thought, and Reform studies. Likewise, Charles McGuire, Jr., deserves thanks for collecting data at the University of California for the same studies. Laura Stephens will be using portions of the Thought data to write an Honors thesis and Neil Christiansen will be using portions of the Reform data for his Master's thesis at Southern Illinois University at Edwardsville.

Preparation of this chapter was facilitated by a Southern Illinois University Fourth Quarter Research Fellowship to the first author.

All correspondence should be directed to Linda J. Skitka, Department of Psychology, Southern Illinois University, Edwardsville, IL, 62026-1121 or SM01@SIUEMUS.BITNET.

The United States is both a democratic and capitalistic society. However, the marriage between capitalism and democracy is often tense (Dahl, 1989). On the one hand, capitalism fosters a belief in individualism and self-determination. Through hard work and ability, people should strive to cultivate marketable skills and products (skills and products of value to others). In the process, enormous inequalities emerge. Some people amass great power over others (e.g., employers over employees; landlords over tenants; creditors over debtors). On the other hand, our government was founded on the democratic ideal of equality of citizenship and its attendant rights. These core rights of citizenship (voting, freedom of speech and association) cannot be bought or sold in markets. Democracy "blocks" certain exchanges (Walzer, 1983).

These conflicting value orientations lead to different positions regarding the obligations of the collective to help the disadvantaged (Dionne, 1991; Mead, 1988). Should we allow the market – with its well-known efficiencies – free rein? Or should the government intervene and redistribute income through taxation and specially targeted income transfers? If so, from whom should the money be taken, and to whom should it be given? Should standards of deservingness be applied equally to all citizens? Is someone who is personally responsible for losing a job (e.g., due to substance abuse or low effort) as deserving of public support as someone laid off because of an economic recession? What if the substance abuser successfully kicks his or her habit, or the lazy person reforms?

As we explore in this essay, social psychological theories make a variety of predictions about how people will allocate public assistance. However, the literature is badly fragmented with many "minitheories" but no overall integrative framework. The current chapter will explore how existing theories of attribution, distributive justice, and political ideology can be brought together to generate testable predictions concerning perceptions of the fair allocation of collective resources.

## The contingency model of distributive justice

We have recently developed a contingency model of allocation decisions that incorporates predictions based not only on abstract norms and values (e.g., equity, equality, and need), but also on causal attributions for why people need help, emotional reactions to claimants, and political point of view (Skitka & Tetlock, 1992; see Figure 1). Stage I in this model requires assessing resource availability. If there are sufficient resources to help everyone, the decision making process ends, and the allocator aids all

Figure 1   A four-stage contingency model of allocation. Depending on resource scarcity and the match between resource constraints and the number of personally responsible claimants, allocators go through one to four stages in deciding who to assist within a pool of claimants.

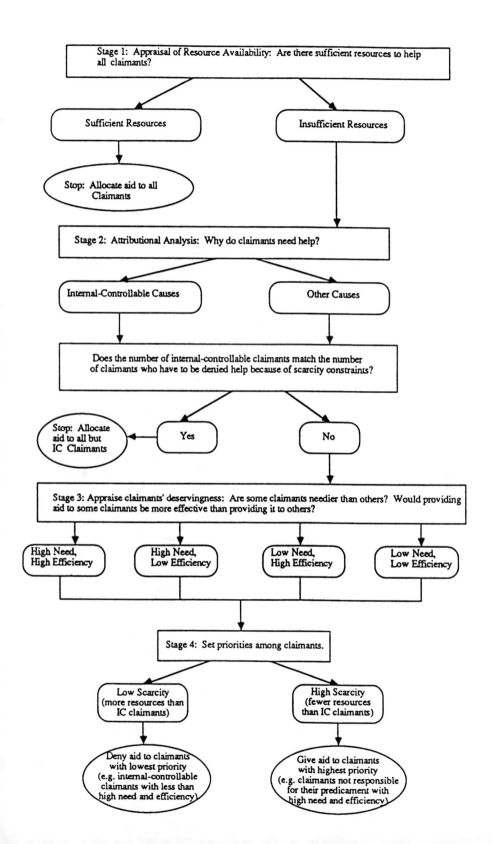

Stage 1: Appraisal of Resource Availability: Are there sufficient resources to help all claimants?

Sufficient Resources

Insufficient Resources

Stop: Allocate aid to all Claimants

Stage 2: Attributional Analysis: Why do claimants need help?

Internal-Controllable Causes

Other Causes

Does the number of internal-controllable claimants match the number of claimants who have to be denied help because of scarcity constraints?

Stop: Allocate aid to all but IC Claimants

Yes

No

Stage 3: Appraise claimants' deservingness: Are some claimants needier than others? Would providing aid to some claimants be more effective than providing it to others?

High Need, High Efficiency

High Need, Low Efficiency

Low Need, High Efficiency

Low Need, Low Efficiency

Stage 4: Set priorities among claimants.

Low Scarcity (more resources than IC claimants)

High Scarcity (fewer resources than IC claimants)

Deny aid to claimants with lowest priority (e.g. internal-controllable claimants with less than high need and efficiency)

Give aid to claimants with highest priority (e.g. claimants not responsible for their predicament with high need and efficiency) claimants (although this expectation is moderated by the political ideology of the allocator, as we discuss later). If resources are scarce, allocators move to stage II: attributional analysis. If allocators perceive claimants to be personally responsible for their predicament (an internal-controllable attribution), they consider whether there is a match between the number of personally responsible claimants and the number of claimants who cannot be helped because of resource constraints. If there is such a match, the decision making process stops, and allocators distribute aid to all but personally responsible claimants. If there is not an exact fit between resource constraints and the number of personally responsible claimants, the allocator moves to stage III. Here allocators rely on abstract norms and values to evaluate claimants' relative deservingness and try both to minimize suffering (a need criterion) and to minimize waste (an efficiency criterion). Allocators will give higher priority to claimants as a function of both severity of need and likelihood of help proving effective.

Stage IV requires setting priorities among claimants as a joint function of their cause of need and relative deservingness. When there are sufficient resources to help almost everyone (low scarcity), allocators will deny aid only to those claimants with the lowest overall priority: Internal-controllable claimants whose needs are not urgent and whose chances of being effectively helped are slim. When there are insufficient resources (high scarcity), allocators will initially respond by denying aid to all personally responsible claimants. However, if even this step is not sufficient to bring resources and needs into balance, allocators will also deny aid to those claimants who are not responsible for needing assistance, in particular those whose needs are not urgent, and whose chances of being helped are slim.

### Why do people need assistance? Attributions of responsibility

Attribution theorists maintain that arousal of normative pressure to help others depends critically on attributions of responsibility (i.e., judgments of moral accountability, or blame). Weiner (1986), for instance, has specified how cognitive appraisal and affect influence decisions to help. According to his three-stage model, initial explanations (such as, "The grasshopper needs assistance because she sang away the summer") are processed according to the following sequence: (1) causal analysis (attribution of cause along the dimensions of locus and control); (2) affective arousal (different explanations trigger different affective reactions); and (3) behavioral or policy decision (in this case, to provide or withhold resources). The guiding metaphor has shifted from the person (in this case, allocator) as a scientist to the person as a judge. A judge must appraise the responsibilities and intentions of others to make evaluative decisions that involve rewards and punishments (Weiner, 1991).

Researchers have already demonstrated linkages between causal analysis, affective arousal, and behavioral decisions in several domains (see review in Weiner, 1986). The work on helping is especially relevant and points to a clear-cut conclusion: People are less likely to help victims whose need is attributed to internal-controllable causes, such as carelessness, laziness, or self-indulgence, than people whose need for assistance is due to other causes (e.g., internal-uncontrollable, external-controllable or external-uncontrollable causes).

Research also suggests that ideology moderates these effects. Attitudes toward social welfare (a prototypical redistributive program) are consistently linked to ideologically driven attributions for why people are poor. Conservatives blame poverty on self-indulgence and lack of moral standards and intelligence. Liberals see the poor as victims of unjust social practices and structures. These ideological differences in attributions for poverty prove to predict differences in willingness to expand social programs: Liberals generally favor, whereas conservatives oppose, increased spending on social programs (Feather, 1985; Kluegel & Smith, 1986; Sniderman & Tetlock, 1986; Williams, 1984).

### Distributive justice

Current psychological theories of distributive justice focus on multiple normative rules that guide allocation decisions (e.g., the equity rule: Outcomes should be distributed in proportion to contributions; a need rule: Outcomes should be distributed in proportion to people's needs; and the equality rule). Which rule or standard is activated depends on the social context and goals of the allocator (e.g., Deutsch, 1985; Leventhal, 1976; Leventhal, Karuza, & Fry, 1980; Mikula, 1980); the relationship between the allocator and recipient (e.g., Lerner, 1977); and the personality and political ideology of the allocator (e.g., Major & Deaux, 1982; Rasinski, 1987). Although multivalue theories of justice organize a wide range of findings, there is no guarantee such theories give either the right weights to competing values or capture the conditions under which competing values or rules are primed or activated.

The goal-orientation approach of Leventhal (1976), however, leads to a number of testable hypotheses. Leventhal argues that allocators determine outcomes by a weighted averaging formula that includes contributions, need, equality, and other distributive norms. The weight attached to each distributive norm varies as a function of the "goal orientation" of the social system. For instance, the goals of public assistance are based on need norms (the "safety net" of welfare state capitalism). The aim is to minimize suffering due to illness, mishap, or extreme poverty. However, if public assistance is limited by technology or budgetary constraints, people will also weight efficiency (minimization of waste) heavily in judging deservingness and making allocation decisions (cf. Leventhal et al., 1973).

*Resource constraints on the capacity to provide aid*

Resource constraints pose painful problems for allocators. In a world of finite resources, allocators must "winnow" the competing claimants (Ross & Ellard, 1986) to determine who shall receive assistance. In an economy of scarcity, justice defined as equality or equity is often beyond our grasp. If everyone is given an equal share, or a "share proportional to their contributions" some may not get what they need to survive (Greenberg, 1981; Rescher, 1966). For example, imagine it takes 3 milligrams of drug X to cure an otherwise fatal disease. What if two people contract the disease, and only 4 milligrams of the drug is available? An equal or equitable distribution of drug X might be "just," but would save no one's life. Consistent with this reasoning, research indicates that equity becomes less important as resources become increasingly scarce (e.g., Coon, Lane, & Lichtman, 1974; Lane & Messé, 1972), and both need (minimize suffering) and efficiency (minimize waste) become more important (cf. Greenberg, 1981).

In addition to priming need and efficiency as guides to decision making, scarcity may motivate cognitive appraisal. Assuming most people are cognitive misers (cf. Fiske & Taylor, 1991) who prefer simple solutions to difficult decisions, allocators may simply treat claimants as approximately equal whenever it is possible to satisfy everyone. In contrast, scarcity should motivate cognitive work as allocators search for reasons to deny some claims, but not others.

*Ideological differences in allocation preferences*

In addition to ideological differences in attributions for why people need assistance, there are ideological differences in allocation preferences. For example, Rasinski (1987) found that fairness judgments of social policies or support for presidential candidates who ran on egalitarian versus individualistic platforms depended on the personal values people placed on individualism (the work ethic, personal freedom, and competition in free markets) versus egalitarianism (basic human needs and opportunities should be provided for all). In other words, value orientations predict support for public policies that determine the distribution of public resources.

Drawing on the findings of Carroll, Perkowitz, Lurigio, and Weaver (1987), we expect two clusters of personality and ideological variables to shape allocation preferences: (1) cognitive conservatism, a combination of political conservatism with personality measures of dogmatism, authoritarianism, and internal locus-of-control; and (2) liberal humanism, a combination of liberal ideals and the principled stage of moral development. We expect personality and ideology to have direct effects on allocation preferences, as well as to moderate the cognition-affect-behavior link. Conservatives should experience especially negative affect toward, and therefore withhold more resources from, claimants whose needs are due to internal-controllable causes. Liberals are expected to recognize that people with internal-controllable causes of need are responsible for their predicament, but to remain sympathetic to their plight, and to allocate resources to personally responsible claimants when there are sufficient resources to do so.

Allocation preferences and perceptions of fairness are probably shaped by an interaction of social context and individual values. Given that most people hold complex (sometimes contradictory) mixtures of liberal and conservative values (Nilson, 1981; Tetlock, 1986), situational factors (e.g., the state of the economy) often determine which beliefs are primed or activated. This explanation is consistent with our hypothesis that there will be minimal ideological differences in allocation preferences when resources are scarce. Liberals cannot allocate equally when resources are scarce; by definition, some claimants cannot be assisted. We don't expect, however, that liberals will randomly select claimants to go without assistance; rather they will be compelled by the situation to think more like conservatives and to deny aid to those personally responsible for their predicament. By contrast, other situations will prompt conservatives to think more like liberals. For example, reactions to natural disasters (e.g., earthquakes, fires, or hurricanes) – situations in which it is difficult to assign personal blame – typically evoke quick and overwhelming humanitarian responses that are relatively free of political ideology.

### Research support for the contingency model of distributive justice

Skitka and Tetlock (1992) tested the contingency model of distributive justice by investigating allocation preferences under low and high scarcity (Study 1) as well as no scarcity (Study 2) across three resource domains: AZT for AIDS patients; organs for people needing transplants; and low-income housing for the poor. We derived claimant descriptions for each policy domain from a four-factor design of locus (internal, external cause) by control (controllable, uncontrollable cause) by need (high, low) by efficiency (high, low), yielding a total of 16 claimants per resource domain. Under high scarcity, subjects could select only 3 of 16 claimants to receive assistance, and under low scarcity they could select 13 of 16 claimants to receive assistance (none of the subjects allocated less assistance than the maximum they were allowed). Under no scarcity, subjects could select as many or as few claimants as they thought fair. In addition, subjects reported emotional reactions to each claimant on 1 to 9 Likert-response scales (emotions such as sympathy, disgust, anger, and pity).

Subjects also completed a packet of personality and attitudinal measures to assess conservatism and liberalism (conceptually replicating Carroll et al., 1987) including Rotter's Internal-External Locus of Control Scale (Rotter, 1966); the Shortened F for Political Surveys (Authoritarianism – Janowitz & Marvick, 1953) and the Short Dogmatism Scale (Trodahl & Powell,

1965), a scale assessing attitudes toward proportional and egalitarian public polices (Rasinski, 1987), as well as a single, bipolar, 10-point measure of liberalism-conservatism. Using principal components analysis, we identified two components that largely replicated the Carroll et al. (1987) solution. The conservatism component included high dogmatism, authoritarianism, and endorsement of individualistic values. The liberalism component included endorsement of egalitarian values, and self-reported political liberalism. Unlike Carroll et al. (1987), locus-of-control did not load with the conservatism component.[1]

Predictions derived from the contingency model held up well. Under scarcity, when claims arose from internal-controllable causes, allocators devalued their deservingness, and withheld resources. Consistent with hypotheses, under high scarcity, allocators (liberals and conservatives alike) denied assistance to people personally responsible for their plight. Claimants not personally responsible for their predicament received assistance if the need was urgent, and there was a high likelihood that help would be effective. Under low scarcity, allocators helped all claimants who were not responsible for their need, as well as personally responsible claimants who were in dire need and for whom help would be most effective. In other words, there were significant four-way interactions of locus, control, need, and efficiency on choices under high scarcity [$F$ (1, 98) = 25.84] and low scarcity [$F$ (1,97) = 51.95], averaging across resource domains (see Table 1).[2] Also consistent with predictions, under scarcity conservatives reported more negative affect and less positive affect toward personally responsible claimants than did liberals.[3]

Under no scarcity (Skitka & Tetlock, 1992, Study 2), conservatives continued to withhold assistance from claimants personally responsible for their predicament, whereas liberals tended to help everyone. In other words, the ants described in Aesop's fable must have been conservatives: Even though they had plenty of food stored for the winter, they refused to help the self-indulgent grasshopper.

The results from these two studies provided preliminary support for the model: Under no, low, and high scarcity, allocators reacted as predicted. In contrast to predictions from other theories, the results indicate that distributive norms are never sufficient to predict how people allocate public aid. Attributions of responsibility are critical determinants of allocation preferences under scarcity, regardless of the political ideology of the allocator. Under no scarcity, liberals and conservatives diverged dramatically: Liberals were egalitarian and helped everyone, whereas conservatives continued to withhold assistance from people personally responsible for their plight.

Further support for the importance of attributions of responsibility, scarcity, and political ideology in allocation decisions was provided by a study of willingness to provide postwar assistance to help rebuild Iraq and Kuwait after the Persian Gulf war (Skitka, McMurray, & Burroughs, 1991).

Table 1 *Average number of times claimants were chosen to receive available aid*

### High scarcity

| Locus of responsibility | Need/Efficiency | | | |
|---|---|---|---|---|
| | High need High efficiency | High need Low efficiency | Low need High efficiency | Low need Low efficiency |
| Internal-controllable | 0.16 | 0.01 | 0.03 | 0.01 |
| Internal-uncontrollable | 1.97 | 0.23 | 0.56 | 0.19 |
| External-controllable | 2.07 | 0.15 | 0.58 | 0.06 |
| External-uncontrollable | 2.22 | 0.12 | 0.53 | 0.05 |

### Low scarcity

| Locus of responsibility | Need/Efficiency | | | |
|---|---|---|---|---|
| | High need High efficiency | High need Low efficiency | Low need High efficiency | Low need Low efficiency |
| Internal-controllable | 2.20 | 0.89 | 1.51 | 0.42 |
| Internal-uncontrollable | 2.97 | 2.72 | 2.95 | 2.78 |
| External-controllable | 2.95 | 2.76 | 2.94 | 2.54 |
| External-uncontrollable | 3.00 | 2.86 | 2.91 | 2.66 |

*Note:* Boldfaced borders indicate the claimants predicted to have highest priority under high scarcity, and double borders indicate the claimants predicted to have lowest priority under low scarcity.

Subjects completed questionnaires either within two days after the start of ground war or within 24 hours after the cease-fire was announced. Subjects allocated the amount of the total needed to rebuild Iraq ($80 billion) and Kuwait ($40 billion) that they thought was fair after being primed with either a pessimistic or optimistic forecast for the American economy (a scarcity manipulation); provided open-ended explanations for their allocations; and completed a number of scales.

Although there are historical precedents for assisting war-torn nations after the shooting stops (e.g., the United States provided a great deal of support to Japan, Germany, and most of Europe after World War II, as well as to South Korea after the Korean conflict), people were reluctant to help either Iraq ($M = 22.1\%$ of amount needed) or Kuwait ($M = 39.5\%$).

Stepwise multiple regression indicated that only scarcity and timing explained significant variance in allocations to Kuwait, total $R^2 = .08$. Other variables included in the analysis were affective reactions toward the citizens of Iraq and Kuwait (e.g., sympathy, anger), perceptions of responsibility on the part of Iraq, Kuwait, and the United States as well as their leaders, the economic forecast, Saddam Hussein assumed to be in- versus out-of-power, and timing of data collection (beginning or end of the ground war). Open-ended explanations for aid allocations indicated that unwillingness to help Kuwait was due to two factors: (1) the perceived shared responsibility to help Kuwait on the part of coalition members, or diffusion of responsibility (cf. Darley & Latane, 1968), and (2) the perceived ability of Kuwait to help itself, or lack of legitimate need (cf. Berkowitz, 1969).

Consistent with predictions, however, Iraqi responsibility for the war was the most frequent explanation for refusing aid to Iraq, and accounted for the most variance in allocations to this country ($R^2 = .11$; high responsibility, less aid). Liberal-humanism (more liberal, more aid and lower perceptions of Iraqi responsibility) and scarcity (optimistic economic forecast, more aid) contributed an additional 4% explained variance each. Of those subjects who cited Iraqi responsibility as a justification for their aid allocations, 63% provided *no* assistance to Iraq as compared to 23% of those who cited some other justification. These results further support the idea that distributive values are not sufficient to explain allocation preferences in the political domain, and underscore the importance of attributions of responsibility, scarcity, and political ideology in allocation decisions.

We have shown that the variables identified by the model are critical determinants of aid allocations in a variety of domains. When asked to make policy decisions, people take into account the relative availability of resources, attributions of responsibility, and only to a minor degree, distributive norms. Under no scarcity, the political ideology of the judge emerges as an important predictor of allocation preferences. Although this is not a formal model (in its present form it does not predict how people will integrate information), it is useful in generating testable hypotheses about how people will allocate public resources, and how allocators will make allocation decisions. Future research needs to investigate the implied order of cognitive processes in allocation decisions and the way these variables are integrated to form general impressions of deservingness.

Ideological differences in allocations also pose some interesting empirical questions. The political orientation of the allocator turns out to be an important predictor of allocations of AZT, body organs, low-income housing, and postwar foreign aid: Liberals provide more assistance to claimants than conservatives. But how exactly do conservatives and liberals differ? Although the current model predicts ideological differences, it is agnostic concerning where in the decision making process liberals and conservatives diverge. The model identifies a number of possible points of divergence, including attributional proclivities, thresholds for different emotional reactions (e.g., anger or sympathy), differences in basic values, and decision avoidance.

### Flattering and unflattering explanations of ideological differences in allocations under no scarcity

Our recent research has explored the cognitive and motivational roots of ideological differences in allocation preferences. We will describe three studies here. The first study (Skitka & Tetlock, 1991) examines how liberals and conservatives cope with pressures to expand or limit public resources. The second ("thought") and third ("reform") studies examined allocations to individual claimants. The "thought" experiment (Skitka, 1992a) tests whether liberal egalitarianism is the result of careful thought or scripted ideological reactions. The "reform" study (Skitka, 1992b) probes the limits of punitiveness among conservatives: Will conservatives withhold resources from personally responsible claimants who have reformed, even though withholding aid from these claimants no longer serves efficiency or deterrence goals?

*Setting limits and living with them: Ideological differences in reaction to scarcity and change*

Subjects in the Skitka and Tetlock (1992) studies could not control scarcity of public resources. This situation is typical of many allocation situations. For example, physicians cannot control organ donation rates or the cost of drugs. But it is sometimes possible in the political world to influence the availability of public resources – for example, policymakers can opt to decrease scarcity by increasing taxes, or vice versa. An open question concerns feedback relationships between the size of the public purse and the perceived deservingness of recipients.

Skitka and Tetlock (1991) extended previous research by giving subjects additional options for coping with scarcity beyond deciding who should be denied assistance. We also examined a variety of psychological processes that may explain ideological differences in how people cope with these issues. In contrast to the earlier studies, subjects began by making allocations to social programs (divided a budget to different health and social programs) rather than individuals, as well as rating these programs on such dimensions as cost effectiveness, and the perceived personal responsibility of program claimants. Afterward, subjects learned that one program was not allocated enough money (always AZT for AIDS patients). Subjects then had an opportunity to vote to expand the resource pool to help all claimants, with the idea that if the vote failed to pass, subjects would have to decide which individual claimants should be denied assistance. In the political world, decisions to expand the resource pool usually involve costs, e.g., higher taxes, or deficit spending. To capture this contingency, half the subjects were told that they would have to sacrifice a large portion of their pay if they expanded the budget; the other half heard no mention of costs. The primary dependent measures were how much aid people allocated to specific spending programs and whether people voted to expand the budget to help all claimants. Political ideology was assessed with Altemeyer's (1988) Right-Wing-Authoritarianism (RWA) scale.[4]

We chose AIDS patients as the claimant population for a variety of reasons. Resource allocations to AIDS patients have recently become the focus of intense public policy debates. In particular, the high costs of caring for AIDS patients – federal spending is expected to reach $4.3 billion in 1992 (Winkenwerder, Kessler, & Stolec, 1989) – has raised concern that needed funding for other diseases has been diverted to AIDS related research and treatment (Krieger, 1988). Others claim, however, that AIDS has not been overfunded based on econometric analyses of mortality data (e.g., Hatziandreu, Graham, & Soto, 1988; Winkenwerder et al., 1989). Still others argue that hostile reactions toward populations at special risk for AIDS (e.g., homosexual men, intravenous drug users, and minorities) severely limit public support for AIDS treatment and research (Chapman, Levin, & Kuhn, 1991; Rogers, 1989).

Research indicates that reactions to AIDS patients are driven in large part by attributions of personal responsibility to homosexuals and intravenous drug users for their illness (e.g., Kite, Whitley, Michael, and Simon, 1991; Levin & Chapman, 1990; Weiner, 1992; Weiner, Perry & Magnusson, 1988). Although these investigators have demonstrated a clear linkage of attributions of responsibility to derogation of AIDS patients, they have yet to demonstrate linkages of attributions of personal responsibility to withholding resources at either the individual or programmatic level.

We anticipated that liberals would vote to expand the resource pool to help all claimants, whereas conservatives would not. We also tested several psychological hypotheses to explain this predicted difference, including: (1) punitiveness; (2) homophobia, (3) value expression; (4) cognitive avoidance; and (5) self-interest.

*Punitiveness.* Conservatives are more motivated than liberals to punish violators of traditional values and norms, and may even relish the opportunity to do so (cf. Altemeyer, 1988). In support of this hypothesis, Skitka and Tetlock (1992) found that conservatives had more negative emotional reactions toward targets, made stronger attributions of personal responsibility, and withheld more aid from personally responsible claimants under both scarcity and no scarcity. The affective data (e.g., anger and disgust ratings) were consistent with the idea that conservatives wanted to punish personally responsible claimants for breaking an implicit social contract. If people want to enjoy the benefits of society, then they should behave responsibly; if not, they should absorb the natural consequences of their actions. In contrast to conservatives, liberals were more sympathetic to personally responsible claimants, even when they denied these claimants aid under scarcity. Under no scarcity, liberals tended to aid all claimants. Liberals, then, showed little evidence of punitiveness toward personally responsible claimants.

The punitiveness hypothesis is also consistent with Tomkins's (1965) theory of ideo-affective scripts – the notion that ideological points of view contain emotional scripts that dictate our reactions to people and situations. Conservatives are posited to have a generalized negative affective stance, whereas liberals are posited to have a generalized positive affective stance toward people and situations.

Other research also reveals linkages between ideology, attributions, and punitiveness: For example, conservatives are more likely to attribute crime to individual greed and self-interest and to assign harsher sentences. Liberals, on the other hand, tend to believe that causes of crime are largely external, due to environmental and macroeconomic factors, and impose more lenient sentences (Carroll et al., 1987).

*Homophobia.* Conservatives withhold assistance from AIDS patients under no scarcity because homosexuals violate sexual norms in addition to social contract norms. AIDS is stereotypically associated with homosexual males (Herek & Glunt, 1988; Triplet, 1989; Turner et al., 1989). Therefore it is important to explore the relative roles of locus of responsibility and defensiveness (feelings of revulsion toward homosexuality) in conservatives' reactions to requests for resources from AIDS patients.

In support of the homophobia hypothesis, Altemeyer (1988) reports that conservatives do indeed react "defensively" toward homosexuals; that is they project unacceptable motives to homosexual persons, and express open hostility toward them (cf. Herek, 1987). However, Skitka and Tetlock (1992) found that under no scarcity, conservatives denied aid not only to AIDS patients, but also to people personally responsible for needing housing and organ transplants, or who are perceived as responsible for starting a war (Skitka et al., 1991). In a similar vein, research has found that attributions of responsibility are better predictors of reactions toward homosexual AIDS patients than homophobia (e.g., Kite et al., 1991; Mallery, 1990, as cited in Weiner, 1992), but other researchers have reported homophobic reactions to AIDS victims even when controlling for source of infection (Triplet & Sugarman, 1987).

*Avoidance.* Because of tension among competing values, liberals try to *avoid*, whenever possible, situations that require assigning specific weights to these values and arriving at a specific resolution. Assuming liberals especially dislike placing a specific monetary value on human lives or suffering, they will show a decided preference for aiding everyone. In support of the trade-off avoidance hypothesis, studies of both ordinary citizens and political elites indicate that liberals are more likely to think in complex trade-off terms than are other ideological groups (e.g., Tetlock, 1986; Tetlock, Skitka, & Boettger, 1989). This finding does not mean, however, that liberals like trade-offs. In support of the avoidance hypothesis, most indications are that decision makers generally find trade-offs unpleasant and try to avoid them by relying on noncompensatory choice rules or even by buck-passing and procrastination (Abelson & Levi, 1985; Einhorn & Hogarth, 1981; George, 1980; Jervis, 1976; Steinbruner, 1974; Tetlock, 1986; Tetlock & Boettger, 1992). If liberals especially dislike placing a monetary value on human lives, they should be especially likely to help all claimants in order to avoid this trade-off.

*Value expression: Egalitarianism versus efficiency.* Ideological differences in allocating aid stem from the desire to express one's fundamental values. Liberals might be more inclined to distribute aid equally to all who require it (regardless of why they need it) because of an ideological commitment to social equality, whereas conservatives withhold aid to uphold their commitment to self-reliance and efficiency (see Rasinski, 1987).

*Self-interest.* Conservatives are also less willing than liberals to pay for social programs, and refuse to expand the resource pool because they want to avoid higher taxes or incurring other personal costs. This unwillingness may reflect the greater value conservatives place on personal wealth, or the greater likelihood that liberals place on needing government help in the future (fear of falling).

*Results.* Consistent with research indicating derogation or social distancing from AIDS patients, the AZT for AIDS patients' program received the lowest funding of any program (other programs included a nutritional counseling and food supplemental program for pre- and postnatal nursing mothers and their children; an independent living program that provides special devices for the handicapped; and Medicare/Medicaid programs that provide health care for welfare recipients). Subjects were instructed to assume equal numbers of claimants in each program. Regression analysis indicated that subjects' perceptions of personal responsibility for claimants' needs (e.g., the people served by this program "try hard to help themselves") and the effectiveness of the AZT program (e.g., "the benefits of this program are equal to or exceed the costs of the program") explained the most variance in the amount of the budget allocated to the AZT program. Recall that assessments of program effectiveness, responsibility of program recipients for needing help, and so on, were made *before* subjects allocated resources to different programs. This fact weakens the likelihood that these judgments were post hoc justifications for underallocating to any particular program.

Only defensive attitudes toward homosexuals (Herek, 1987) explained additional variance in allocations to the AZT program. Path analysis indicated, however, that the effects of ideology were mediated by attributions of causality and efficiency. That is, ideological beliefs were associated with different attributions for why AIDS patients needed help and the effectiveness of the AZT program, which in turn predicted the funding provided to the AZT program.

Of special interest was how subjects coped with an opportunity to increase their AZT program budget in order to help all claimants. The majority of the subjects (58%) voted to increase the budget, regardless of cost to themselves. People who voted to expand the resource pool were more liberal than those who did not.

Why do conservatives withhold assistance from people who need help, when they have an opportunity to help everyone? Analyses indicated that attributions of personal responsibility for need explained the most variance in ideological differences in voting behavior (more responsible, less aid), followed by a desire to avoid making painful allocation decisions (more decision avoidance, more aid). Egalitarianism and perceptions of program efficiency had little independent effect on the decision to increase the resource pool, but when considered in isolation, each was a significant covariate of the vote–ideology relationship. Personal cost had no effect on willingness to help all claimants.

Together, these results indicate that conservatives are more tolerant of scarcity and less likely to act to alleviate shortages. It is interesting to note the comparatively minor role of homosexual defensiveness in willingness to help AIDS patients, a result consistent with other research (Mallery, 1990, as described in Weiner, 1992). Instead, ideological differences are best explained by different attributions for AIDS patients' responsibility for infection and the desire to avoid deciding who should be helped. Conservatives made more internal attributions for why claimants needed help; they perceived AIDS patients as "people who just want a free ride" and who needed help because "they don't try hard enough to help themselves" – perceptions, by the way, that were independent of the effectiveness of the AZT program in prolonging life and of judgments of the cost effectiveness of the AZT program. Given that assessments of high personal responsibility factored out separately from perceived program effectiveness and cost efficiency, the punitiveness hypothesis gains increased support as an underlying motive for conservative allocation behavior.

Liberals showed almost the opposite pattern of results. Liberals found the prospect of making individual-level allocation decisions to be both painful and socially awkward, consistent with the idea that liberals find it especially aversive to trade lives for money. In short, ideological differences in willingness to expand the resource pool seem motivated by a combination of conservative punitiveness and liberal trade-off avoidance.

*Liberal egalitarianism: Thoughtful moral judgment or ideological reflex?*

The previous study indicated that liberals felt more awkward about decid-ing which individual claimants should receive assistance than conserva-tives, supporting the idea that liberals want to avoid making trade-offs between important values. But are higher ratings of decision avoidance post hoc rationalizations masking a desire for cognitive simplicity? In short, are liberals "mindlessly" egalitarian? Equal allocations have the virtue of cognitive simplicity; they do not require careful scrutiny of the strengths and weaknesses of competing claims on resources. One simply helps everyone. The "egalitarian" and "generous" behavior of liberals is con-sistent with both a value trade-off (implying thoughtfulness and cog-itive complexity, cf. Tetlock, 1986) and a mindless egalitarian interpreta-tion.

The "mindlessness" hypothesis is consistent with considerable research that indicates most behavior, even complex social interaction, can be en-acted without attending to it (Langer, 1978; Abelson, 1976), and that peo-ple have to be spurred by unexpected events to engage in detailed attri-butional analysis (Hastie, 1984). Conservatives may therefore follow a script that dictates "reward hard workers" and "punish free-riders" – a script that works well regardless of resource scarcity. Similarly, liberals may plug in an egalitarian script whenever there is no scarcity.

To investigate the competing portraits of liberals as thoughtful versus mindless, the "Thought" experiment (Skitka, 1992a) varied the amount of thought subjects were required to devote to individual claimants before making allocations. Two resource domains were included: AZT for AIDS patients, and vocational training for the unemployed. In the thought con-dition, subjects were required to respond to detailed rating scales for each claimant. In the no-thought condition, subjects simply read descriptions of claimants, without making any ratings, before making allocation decisions. As an additional check for "mindless" responding, an additional claimant was listed on subjects' selection sheets (person Q), when in fact, no person Q had been described in the claimant pool. If subjects selected person Q, it would indicate response set allocation behavior. Selecting person Q im-plies that allocators were not considering claimant descriptions carefully when selecting who should receive assistance, but instead automatically checked "everyone."

Manipulation checks indicated that we created the intended conditions: Subjects in the thought condition reported that they gave more careful con-sideration to individual claimants than subjects in the no-thought condi-tion, $F (1, 128) = 13.88$, $p < .001$, with neither a main effect for political ide-ology nor an interaction between ideology and thought condition. Both liberals and conservatives gave more careful consideration to individual claimants in the thought condition than the no-thought condition.

*AZT allocations.* We asked subjects to allocate AZT to claimants who varied in locus of responsibility for their disease [internal-controllable (IC): contracted AIDS from engaging in high-risk sexual behavior even after learning how AIDS is transmitted; internal-uncontrollable (IU): modified sexual behavior after learning how AIDS is transmitted, but had been exposed to the HIV virus before AIDS was known to be a sexually transmitted disease; external-controllable (EC): contracted AIDS from a long term but unfaithful partner; external-uncontrollable (EU): blood transfusion (before the AIDS antibody test developed to screen blood)]; sexuality (homosexual, heterosexual); and treatment effectiveness (treatment would extend person's life 1 or 4 years). In other words, claimant descriptions varied in a $4 \times 2 \times 2$ design yielding 16 claimants whom subjects could give or deny resources.

Results indicated that 54% of the subjects assisted all AZT claimants, whereas 46% denied assistance to at least one claimant. Consistent with previous results, "givers" were less conservative than "deniers" (people who denied aid to at least one claimant). Analysis of the Thought (2) $\times$ Locus of Responsibility (4) $\times$ Efficiency (2) $\times$ Target Sexual Preference (2) mixed analysis of variance (ANOVA) revealed no effects for the thought manipulation, but significant main effects for political ideology, target sexuality, locus of responsibility, and efficiency, as well as two interactive effects: Ideology $\times$ Sexuality, and Ideology $\times$ Locus of Responsibility.

Of primary interest, no effects emerged for the thought manipulation. Liberals (and conservatives for that matter) were unaffected by whether they were required to think carefully about claimants before allocating AZT to AIDS patients. Regardless of the thought condition, 77% of liberals chose all claimants to receive aid. Making liberals think carefully about claimants before allocating did not change their behavior. Under scarcity, liberals are forced to think carefully about which claimants should receive resources (see Skitka & Tetlock, 1992). Allocations under no scarcity do not require liberals (or conservatives) to carefully attend to claimant characteristics. According to the mindlessness hypothesis, liberals don't even bother to learn about the individual claimants before taking the "easy road" and allocating equally. The results reported here, however, indicate that even when liberals are "forced" to notice and encode claimant characteristics, most still help all claimants, even those who are personally responsible for needing help.

In conjunction with the results of our earlier studies, the overall picture of liberal egalitarianism is coherent: Liberals dislike winnowing claimants under scarcity, and would rather avoid doing so. Liberals are not, however, mindlessly plugging in an egalitarian script, ignoring the "true" relative deservingness of claimants under no scarcity. Even when required to attend carefully to claimant characteristics, they allocate aid equally. Under scarcity, liberals perceived personally responsible claimants to be less deserving of assistance than other claimants, and liberals denied them assistance (see Skitka & Tetlock, in 1992). But despite the fact that liberals see those personally responsible for their plight as less deserving, and regardless of the extent to which they are forced to evaluate each individual claimant and cannot ignore variation in personal responsibility, liberals still typically provide assistance to all AIDS victims under no scarcity. Taken together, these results support the "thoughtful" rather than "mindless" portrait of liberal egalitarianism.

In contrast, conservatives were more likely than liberals to withhold help from personally responsible claimants under no scarcity, and regardless of thought condition (a judgment policy one could defend in the name of efficiency). Conservatives were also more likely than liberals to withhold help from homosexual claimants, regardless of how these claimants developed AIDS (a policy that is much more difficult to defend on efficiency grounds). Controlling for homosexual defensiveness (Herek, 1987) did not change this result. This finding is consistent with the portrait of conservatives as motivated by a desire to punish violators of traditional norms – be they norms of self-reliance or appropriate sexual behavior – rather than solely a desire to maximize efficiency. This interpretation is supported further by the fact that no ideological differences emerged in reaction to the efficiency manipulation. Liberals and conservatives were approximately equally sensitive to the relative efficacy of providing resources to different claimants.

As an additional measure of mindlessness, Skitka (1992a) examined reactions to the "extra" claimant who was not described in the claimant pool. If liberals are mindlessly egalitarian, we would expect that they would be more indiscriminately generous. A mindless egalitarian should check "give" for all claimants without careful thought, and therefore also give person Q assistance even though no Q was described in the claimant pool. If allocators are carefully considering each claimant before deciding whether to give or deny assistance, person Q would be noticed as a "mistake" on the selection worksheet. In further refutation of the "mindlessness" hypothesis, no differences as a function of ideology emerged in whether people selected, denied, or noticed the incorrect insertion of person Q.

*Vocational training allocations.* Do these results replicate in other allocation domains? To investigate this question, we had subjects allocate vocational training to claimants who varied in locus of responsibility for being unemployed (IC: lost previous job due to poor effort; IU: physical handicap; EC: laid off from a profitable firm that wanted to avoid unionization; EU: poor economy) as well as two operationalizations of efficiency: The claimants' aptitude for the job for which training was available (high or moderate scores on a job aptitude test), as well as current market demand for that position (50% or 75% probability of getting a job if training is provided). In other words, claimant descriptions varied in a $4 \times 2 \times 2$ design yielding 16 claimants whom subjects could choose to help. Similar to the AZT study, we varied the amount of thought subjects had to give to each claimant before making allocations.

In contrast to the AZT domain, relatively few subjects, only 22%, assisted all claimants for vocational training. As expected, however, "givers" were less conservative than "deniers." Analysis of the Political ideology (2) × Locus of responsibility (4) × Market demand (2) × Job aptitude (2) mixed ANOVA yielded significant main effects for ideology, job aptitude, and market demand, and a significant interaction of ideology and locus of responsibility ($p < .05$).

Once again, the thought manipulation had no effects. The amount of assistance provided under no scarcity did, however, vary as a function of both political ideology and locus of responsibility. Consistent with the AZT results, conservatives withheld more assistance than liberals from all claimants – an ideological difference that was most pronounced with personally responsible claimants. Even liberals, though, were unenthusiastic about helping personally responsible claimants. Only 37% of liberals assisted everyone who sought vocational training. These results differed dramatically from those in the AZT condition, in which 77% of liberals assisted all claimants.

Both market demand and claimant job aptitude also affected who received vocational training. Claimants with higher probabilities of employment were given more assistance than those with lower probabilities, and claimants with higher job aptitudes were selected more often than claimants with lower job aptitudes.

We once more included a Person Q on the selection worksheet as an additional test of the mindlessness hypothesis. Again, contrary to this hypothesis, no significant ideological differences emerged in whether this fictitious person was given or denied assistance, or was noticed as a "mistake."

*Comparing the AZT and vocational results as a function of locus of responsibility and political ideology.* Because the data from AZT and vocational training came from the same subjects, we could explore whether ideology and locus of responsibility interacted across domains. The three-way interaction of ideology, locus of responsibility, and domain was not significant, indicating that the Ideology × Locus of Responsibility interaction replicates well across domains. The Domain × Locus of Responsibility interaction was significant, $F(3, 399) = 36.51$, and the marginal effect of the Ideology × Domain interaction deserved attention, $F(1,133) = 3.04$, $p = .05$. Follow-up comparisons yielded two major results: (1) Personally responsible claimants were more likely to receive AZT treatment than vocational training; and (2) conservatives' willingness to help was stable across domains (they generally denied personally responsible claimants assistance, regardless of domain). In comparison, liberals were less likely to provide vocational training than AZT treatment (especially to personally responsible claimants), but provided more of both kinds of aid than conservatives.

Subjects in the thought experiment also rated their perceptions of the task after making their allocations. Consistent with our earlier results that liberals were motivated to avoid value trade-offs and conservatives to punish norm violators, conservatives were more likely than liberals to report that they were harsher than they thought others would have been in making allocation decisions, and liberals were more likely than conservatives to report that they would rather not make such decisions, and that they felt awkward doing so.

In summary, liberal egalitarianism in these studies is not the product of mindless generosity. Even when forced to consider carefully each claimant's relative deservingness under no scarcity, liberals tend to allocate resources equally to all claimants, whereas conservatives withhold help from those personally responsible for their need. In addition, based on the lack of any interactive effects of ideology with the efficiency of providing claimant assistance (i.e., how long AZT would extend each claimant's life in the AZT domain; extent of market demand and job aptitude in the vocational domain), we cannot argue that liberals are insensitive to efficiency concerns. Whereas the majority of liberals allocate resources equally to all claimants who need assistance in the AZT domain, this result is tempered in situations where the goal of the social system is to increase productivity (e.g., labor markets).

Although the major goal of the thought studies was to investigate flattering and unflattering portraits of liberals, we also learned more about conservatives. Conservatives withheld assistance from people responsible for their plight because of a desire to punish norm violators rather than to maximize efficiency. Conservatives not only consistently refused to help personally responsible claimants, they also discriminated against homosexual claimants for AZT – a result that was not weakened by controlling for homosexual defensiveness. Conservatives' reactions to homosexual claimants cannot therefore be explained by invoking homophobia. In light of the other results (in particular, the absence of ideology "effects" on efficiency – liberals and conservatives alike assisted claimants who could be helped and denied assistance to those who could not), the most plausible interpretation is that conservatives were indeed motivated by the desire to punish violators of sexual norms.

### Conservative withholding: Punitive or prudent?

The "thought" studies explored alternative explanations for why liberals help everyone under no scarcity. Skitka (1992b) posed the mirror-image question: Why do conservatives refuse to help everyone when there are sufficient resources to do so? In the next study, we were particularly interested in testing two possible explanations for the judgment policies of conservatives:

1. *General deterrence and creating incentives for self-reliance.* It is rational from a societal point of view to encourage people to take care of themselves by promoting a fear of falling through the safety net if they misbehave (see also Baron, this book). As John Rockefeller is reputed to have once said, "Capitalism without poverty is like Christianity without Hell." In the name of efficiency and self-reliance, conservatives feel obligated to set an example by withholding aid from people personally responsible for their plight.
   versus
2. *Punitiveness.* Conservatives feel moral outrage toward norm violators. It is very disturbing for conservatives – whose lives are so carefully structured by the self-control and hard work they believe it takes to achieve success – to see others obtain comfort without the attendant sacrifices (Altemeyer, 1988). The election imagery of the welfare cheat in his Cadillac, according to this perspective, doesn't arouse mild annoyance among conservatives: It brings them to the boiling point. They are livid that anyone should get a free ride, especially at their expense. But what are the limits on this hostile response? Are conservatives so outraged by free riders that they wish to punish them even once they have reformed?

To test the deterrence and punitiveness hypotheses, we need to examine conservative reactions to personally responsible claimants who have reformed.

The punitiveness hypothesis predicts that conservatives will withhold assistance from personally responsible claimants, even if they have reformed. According to this hypothesis, the point is not only to punish people for misbehaving, but to give vent to moral outrage and to convince oneself that one's own sacrifices have not been in vain. The deterrence hypothesis predicts that if allocators are convinced that personally responsible claimants have really reformed and learned their lesson, then they deserve to be rewarded for their change in behavior by being reintegrated into the moral community. The logic underlying this action is that other loafers will witness this reward-contingency, and will be inspired to reform their behavior as well.

*Reactions to reformed personally responsible AIDS patients.* Schwarzer and Weiner (1991) studied reactions to AIDS patients who varied in their responsibility for contracting AIDS, and in how they coped with the onset of the disease. Some were described as coping well (dramatic changes in life-style) and others were described as coping poorly (no life-style changes). Subjects blamed all personally responsible patients, regardless of the life-style–change manipulation. However, subjects reported increased pity for personally responsible claimants who had changed their life-style. Because affect mediates the relationship between attributions of responsibility and perceptions of deservingness (Skitka & Tetlock, 1992), these results hint that subjects (i.e., conservatives) may be more likely to help personally responsible claimants who reform.

In further support of this notion, reconsider the descriptions of the internal-controllable and internal-uncontrollable claimants in the AZT thought study. The internal-controllable (personally responsible) claimant contracted AIDS through unsafe sexual practices, even though aware of the risks. The internal-uncontrollable claimant modified his behavior once he became aware of the risks of AIDS (but contracted AIDS before the discovery of the sexual transmission of AIDS). Therefore the internal-uncontrollable claimant can also be seen as a personally responsible claimant who subsequently reformed.

Post hoc testing of the AZT thought data supported the deterrence hypothesis. Liberals and conservatives alike were highly likely to select reformed personally responsible AIDS patients to receive treatment, nearly to the same level as claimants not responsible for contracting the disease. Most liberals helped all claimants, regardless of the cause of need, whereas conservatives still rejected unrepentant personally responsible AIDS patients.

This post hoc analysis provides some insight into the limits of the punitiveness hypothesis. Whereas the bulk of the data hints that conservatives want to punish norm violators, this desire diminishes if norm violators reform. We can interpret this result by qualifying the moral of Aesop's fable from "dance" to "reform or dance."

However, post hoc results do not persuade the skeptic. Given that we know that ideological differences in allocation behavior are moderated by situational goals, we designed a study to examine the deterrence versus punitiveness hypothesis in the vocational domain.

*Reactions to reformed personally responsible claimants for vocational training: The alcoholic and the loafer.* To study reactions to claimants who have reformed, Skitka (1992b) collected data on reactions to unemployed claimants with alcohol or work-effort problems as a function of reform in the vocational training domain. Two changes were made in the claimant descriptions: (1) An extra internal-controllable claimant was added. In addition to the "lazy" claimant, we added an "alcoholic" ("this person lost his most recent job due to an alcohol problem"); and (2) the within-subjects' manipulation of reform was added. Half the internal-controllable claimants were described as reformed (e.g., the person who lost his job due to alcohol-related problems has now "successfully quit drinking and regularly attends Alcoholics Anonymous meetings"). These changes resulted in a pool of 28 claimants. Manipulation checks indicated that subjects were more likely to believe that the alcoholic had reformed than the loafer.

Consistent with earlier results, ideological differences were weak in the vocational setting. We did, however, find locus of responsibility and market demand effects. Subjects typically denied unreformed, personally responsible claimants vocational training. Reformed loafers were unlikely to receive assistance unless market demand was high. Reformed alcoholics usually received assistance, especially if market demand was high. Reformed alcoholics were only slightly less likely to receive assistance than claimants with other causes of unemployment.

*Summary.* These results further support the limits of conservative punitiveness. If personally responsible claimants "turn over a new leaf," conservatives assist them if the reform is credible. The results also illustrate the limits of liberal egalitarianism and generosity. Liberal egalitarians may assume that few people abuse entitlement programs – that only the deserving ask for assistance, and that "leakage" from the transfer-payment bucket is minimal (Okun, 1975). However, even the patience and generosity of liberals are tried when confronted with blatant abusers of the system (unreformed personally responsible claimants) whose claims are pitted against those who have successfully reformed.

## Conclusion

This chapter has explored ideological differences in allocation preferences for public assistance. Taken together, the results of this research program paint a coherent picture of conservative and liberal judgment policies in different allocation settings. Conservative allocations under no scarcity are remarkably consistent across situations: They typically deny help to claimants who are personally responsible for their predicament, and they do so even in life-and-death settings. Claimants with other causes of need receive some help from conservatives, but less than they would have from liberals. Conservative sympathy and helping is triggered primarily by people with external-uncontrollable causes of need (victims of circumstances clearly out of the person's control). In all the situations studied – allocations to health care programs, individual claimants for treatment (AZT, organs for transplantation), vocational training, housing, or postwar foreign aid – results consistently point to punitiveness as a key motive that drives conservatives' allocation behavior, a motive that is often independent of efficiency concerns. Although the libertarian image of conservatism would predict that conservative reluctance to expand social programs is motivated solely by a commitment to personal freedom and self-reliance, the data point more in the direction of negative affective reactions toward norm violators than efficiency concerns.

However, this research program also points to the limits of conservative hostility toward people personally responsible for their predicament. If people reform their behavior and live up to societal norms, conservatives don't hold a grudge and continue to withhold assistance. If conservatives find the personal transformation credible, they are highly likely to provide assistance.

Liberal allocations are more variable and contextually dependent than conservatives. On the one hand, like conservatives, liberals withheld assistance from personally responsible claimants under scarcity. Liberals also allocate resources more like conservatives when the allocation setting is geared toward the goals of the market place (e.g., vocational training for the unemployed) than toward the goal of reducing suffering (health care allocations). On the other hand, under no scarcity, liberals helped all claimants for AZT, organ transplants, or low-income housing.

How can we explain this pattern of findings? First, it may reflect differences in the perceived costs of making type I versus type II errors across policy domains. If a deserving person does not get AZT treatment (a type I error), the cost of this error is certain death. But if a deserving person does not get vocational training, the cost is not nearly as high; he or she loses a job opportunity. Liberals seem willing to accept a higher type II error rate in the AZT domain (i.e., accept the possibility that some "undeserving" people may receive assistance) in order to minimize type I errors. These results further indicate that liberals are motivated to avoid painful trade-offs between important values. Lives-for-money implies a much more painful trade-off than job-opportunities-for-money. Second, a somewhat related explanation is that liberal egalitarianism may be most powerfully primed in resource domains that are critical to physical survival (e.g., food, health, and shelter). Although job training increases the likelihood that claimants can satisfy these primary needs, it acts only indirectly to satisfy primary needs and may be perceived as a relative luxury given the number of job openings at the low end of the income distribution. Dignity, status, and upward mobility may be perceived as extras, not to be doled out even by liberals to people who have brought ill-fortune upon themselves. But when allocating resources linked directly to survival, such as medical treatment, liberals expand the boundaries of the moral community to include even those who have recklessly placed themselves in peril.

In closing, we caution against allowing our own political preconceptions to color our psychological portraits of liberal and conservative policies (see also Tetlock & Mitchell, this book). It is possible to use our data to argue for flattering portraits of *both* liberal and conservative allocation behavior. Conservatives allocate resources to reward self-reliance and punish irresponsibility and laziness. They set up these reward contingencies regardless of context – scarcity or no scarcity, or within normative settings that encourage either individualism or egalitarianism. Conservatives' allocation decisions are motivated by a belief in the responsibility of the individual to the collective; in order for our society to function properly, checks and balances on socially appropriate behavior need to be in place and enforced. Psychologists have long recognized the powerful force of reward contingencies of this sort; conservatives rationally apply these principles to promote the good of society. This is not to say that conservatives dispassionately enforce societal norms, but their anger toward norm violators is better characterized as righteous indignation – a reaction that diminishes if free riders reform – than moral outrage ("If you break the rules, I'll *never* forgive you").

Liberals, on the other hand, do not indiscriminately distribute public resources to help everyone who asks for assistance. Instead, liberals' decisions to help are based on careful consideration of not only the people involved, but also whether providing help will successfully ameliorate the problem (i.e., efficiency), and whether aid is used to satisfy primary versus secondary needs.

In sum, this chapter has demonstrated the utility of integrating social psychological perspectives into a unified model of allocation decision making. By applying theories of distributive justice beyond wage settings and close relationships (the most commonly examined domains in our field), we can gain a much richer understanding of competing conceptions of justice and of the political and economic forces that shape allocation decisions.

### References

Abelson, R. P. (1976). A script theory of understanding, attitude and behavior. In J. Carroll & T. Payne (Eds.), *Cognition and social behavior*, Hillsdale, NJ: Erlbaum.

Abelson, R. P., & Levi, A. (1985). Decision making and decision theory. In E. Aronson & G. Lindzey (Eds.), *Handbook of social psychology* (3rd ed., pp. 231–310). Reading, MA: Addison-Wesley.

Altemeyer, B. (1981). *Right-wing-authoritarianism*. Winnipeg: University of Manitoba Press.

(1988). *Enemies of freedom: Understanding right-wing-authoritarianism*. San Francisco: Jossey-Bass.

Berkowitz, L. (1969). Resistance to improper dependency relationships. *Journal of Experimental Social Psychology, 5*, 283–294.

Carroll, J., Perkowitz, W., Lurigio, A., & Weaver, K. (1987). Sentencing goals, causal attributions and personality. *Journal of Personality and Social Psychology, 52*, 107–118.

Chapman, D. P., Levin, I. P., & Kuhn, K. M. (1991). Information integration in AIDS treatment decisions. Paper presented at the Midwestern Psychological Association, Chicago.

Collins, B. E. (1974). Four components of the Rotter Internal-External Scale: Belief in a difficult world, a just world, a predictable world, and a politically responsive world. *Journal of Personality and Social Psychology, 29*, 381–391.

Coon, R. C., Lane, I. M. & Lichtman, R. J. (1974). Sufficiency of reward and allocation behavior. *Human Development, 17*, 301–313.

Dahl, R. (1989). *Democracy and its critics*. New Haven, CT: Yale University Press.

Darley, J. M., & Latané, B. (1968). Bystander intervention in emergencies: Diffusion of responsibility. *Journal of Personality and Social Psychology, 8*, 377–383.

Deutsch, M. (1985). *Distributive justice.* New Haven, CT: Yale University Press.

Dionne, E. J., Jr. (1991). *Why Americans hate politics.* New York: Simon & Schuster.

Einhorn, H., & Hogarth, R. M. (1981). Behavioral decision theory. *Annual Review of Psychology, 31,* 53–88.

Feather, N. (1985). Attitudes, values, and attributions: Explanations of unemployment. *Journal of Personality and Social Psychology, 48,* 876–889.

Fiske, S., & Taylor, S. (1991). *Social cognition* (2nd ed.). New York: McGraw-Hill.

George, A. L. (1980). *Presidential decision-making in foreign policy: The effective use of information and advice.* Boulder, CO: Westview Press.

Greenberg, J. (1981). The justice of distributing scarce and abundant resources. In M. J. Lerner & S. C. Lerner (Eds.), *The justice motive in social behavior,* New York: Plenum Press.

Hastie, R. (1984). Causes and effects of causal attribution. *Journal of Personality and Social Psychology, 46,* 44–56.

Hatziandreu, E., Graham, D. D., & Soto, M. A. (1988). AIDS and biomedical research funding: Comparative analysis. *Review of Infectious Diseases, 10,* 159–167.

Herek, G. M. (1987). Can functions be measured? A new perspective on the functional approach to attitudes. *Social Psychology Quarterly, 50,* 285–303.

Herek, G. M., & Glunt, E. K. (1988). An epidemic of stigma: Public reactions to AIDS. *American Psychologist, 43,* 886–891.

Janowitz, M., & Marvick, D. (1953). Authoritarianism and political behavior. *Public Opinion Quarterly, 17,* 185–201.

Jervis, R. (1976). *Perception and misperception in international politics.* Princeton, NJ: Princeton University Press.

Katz, I., & Hass, R. G. (1988). Racial ambivalence and American value conflict: Correlational and priming studies of dual cognitive structures. *Journal of Personality and Social Psychology, 55,* 893–905.

Kite, M. E., Whitley, Jr., B. E., Michael, S. T., & Simon, T. L. (1991). Response to AIDS patients: The roles of source of infection and victim sexual orientation. Paper presented at the Midwestern Psychological Association, Chicago.

Kluegel, J. R., & Smith, E. R. (1986). *Beliefs about inequality.* New York: Aldine.

Krieger, N. (1988). AIDS funding: Competing needs and the politics of priorities. *International Journal of Health Services, 18,* 521–541.

Lane, I. M., & Messé, L. A. (1972). Distribution of insufficient, sufficient, and over-sufficient rewards: A clarification of equity theory. *Journal of Personality and Social Psychology, 21,* 228–333.

Langer, E. J. (1978). Rethinking the role of thought in social interaction. In J. Harvey, W. Ickes, & R. F. Kidd (Eds.), *New directions in attribution research* (Vol. 2). Hillsdale, NJ: Erlbaum.

Lerner, M. J. (1977). The justice motive: Some hypotheses as to its origins and forms. *Journal of Personality, 45,* 1–53.

Leventhal, G. S. (1976). Fairness in social relationships. In J. W. Thibaut, J. T. Spence, & R. C. Carson (Eds.), *Contemporary topics in social psychology.* Morristown, NJ: General Learning Press.

Leventhal, G. S., Karuza, J., & Fry, W. R. (1980). Beyond fairness: A theory of allocation preferences. In G. Mikula (Ed.), *Justice and social interaction.* New York: Springer-Verlag.

Leventhal, G. S., Weiss, T., & Buttrick, R. (1973). Attribution of value, equity, and the prevention of waste in reward allocation. *Journal of Personality and Social Psychology, 27,* 276–286.

Levin, I. P., & Chapman, D. P. (1990). Risk taking, frame of reference, and characterization of victim groups in AIDS treatment decisions. *Journal of Experimental Social Psychology, 26,* 421–434.

Major, B. & Deaux, K. (1982). Individual differences in justice behavior. In J. Greenberg & R. L. Cohen (Eds.) *Equity and justice in social behavior.* New York: Academic Press.

Mallery, P. (1990). Attributions and attitudes toward AIDS. Unpublished manuscript, University of California, Los Angeles.

Mead, L. M. (1988). *Beyond entitlement.* New York: The Free Press.

Mikula, G. (1980). On the role of justice in allocation decisions. In G. Mikula (Ed.), *Justice and social interaction,* New York: Springer-Verlag.

Nilson, L. B. (1981). Reconsidering ideological lines: Beliefs about poverty in America. *The Sociological Quarterly, 22,* 531–548.

Okun, A. M. (1975). *Equality and efficiency: The big trade-off.* Washington, DC: The Brookings Institute.

Rasinski, K. A. (1987). What's fair is fair: Or is it? *Journal of Personality and Social Psychology, 53,* 201–211.

Rescher, N. (1966). *Distributive justice.* Indianapolis: Bobbs-Merrill.

Rogers, D. E. (1989). Federal spending on AIDS – How much is enough? *The New England Journal of Medicine, 320,* 1623–1624.

Ross, M., & Ellard, H. (1986). On winnowing: The impact of scarcity on allocators' evaluations of candidates for a resource. *Journal of Experimental Social Psychology, 22,* 374–388.

Rotter, J. B. (1966). Generalized expectancies for internal versus external control of reinforcement. *Psychological Monographs, 80* (1, Whole No. 609).

Rundell, J. B. (1956). *Aesop's fables.* Boston: Lothrop.

Schwarzer, R., & Weiner, B. (1991). Stigma controllability and coping as predictors of emotions and social support. *Journal of Social and Personality Relationships, 8,* 133–140.

Skitka, L. J. (1992a). Liberal egalitarianism: Ideological reflex or considered moral judgment? Paper presented at the Midwestern Psychological Association Convention, Chicago.

(1992b). Punitive or prudent? Withholding assistance from personally responsible claimants. Paper presented at the Midwestern Psychological Association Convention, Chicago.

Skitka, L. J. & Tetlock, P. E. (1991). Setting limits and living with them: Ideological reactions to scarcity and change. Paper presented at the Western Psychological Association Convention, San Francisco.

(1992). Allocating scarce resources: A contingency model of distributive justice. *Journal of Experimental Social Psychology, 28,* 491–522.

Skitka, L. J., McMurray, P. J., & Burroughs, T. E. (1991). Willingness to provide post-war aid to Iraq and Kuwait: An application of the contingency model of distributive justice. *Contemporary Social Psychology, 15*(4).

Sniderman, P., & Tetlock, P. E. (1986). The interrelationships between political ideology and public opinion. In M. Herman (Ed.), *Handbook of political psychology.* San Francisco: Jossey-Bass.

Steinbruner, J. D. (1974). *The cybernetic theory of decision.* Princeton, NJ: Princeton University Press.

Tetlock, P. E. (1986). A value pluralism model of ideological reasoning. *Journal of Personality and Social Psychology, 50,* 819–827.

Tetlock, P. E., & Boettger, R. (1992). Accountability amplifies the status quo effect when change creates victims. Unpublished manuscript, University of California, Berkeley (Psychology).

Tetlock, P. E., & Mitchell, P. G. (1992). Liberal and conservative approaches to justice: Conflicting psychopolitical portraits. In B. Mellers & J. Baron (Eds.), *Psychological Perspectives on Justice.* Cambridge: Cambridge University Press.

Tetlock, P. E., Skitka, L. J., & Boettger, R. (1989). Social and cognitive strategies for coping with accountability: Conformity, complexity, and bolstering. *Journal of Personality and Social Psychology, 57,* 632–640.

Tomkins, S. S. (1965). Affect and the psychology of knowledge. In S. S. Tomkins and C. E. Izard (Eds.), *Affect, cognition, and personality.* New York: Springer.

Triplet, R. G. (1989). Discriminatory biases in medical decision-making: The application of the availability and representativeness heuristics to the AIDS crisis. Paper presented at the Midwestern Psychological Association, Chicago.

Triplet, R. G., & Sugarman, D. B. (1987). Reactions to AIDS victims: Ambiguity breeds contempt. *Personality and Social Psychology Bulletin, 13,* 265–274.

Trodahl, V., & Powell, F. (1965). Short dogmatism scale. *Social Forces, 44,* 211–214.

Turner, C. F., Miller, H. G., & Moses, L. E. (1989). *AIDS: Sexual behavior and intravenous drug use.* Washington, DC: National Academy Press.

Walzer, M. A. (1983). *Spheres of justice.* New York: Basic Books.

Weiner, B. (1986). *An attributional theory of motivation and emotion.* New York: Springer-Verlag.

—— (1991). Metaphors in motivation and attribution. *The American Psychologist, 46,* 921–930.

—— (1992). AIDS from an attributional perspective. In J. B. Pryor and G. D. Reeder, (Eds.), *The social psychology of HIV infection.* Hillsdale, NJ: Erlbaum.

Weiner, B., Perry, R. B., & Magnusson, J. (1988). An attributional analysis of reactions to stigmas. *Journal of Personality and Social Psychology, 55,* 738–748.

Williams, S. (1984). Left–right ideological differences in blaming victims. *Political Psychology, 5,* 573–581.

Winkenwerder, W., Kessler, A. R., & Stolec, R. M. (1989). Federal spending for illness caused by the human immunodeficiency virus. *New England Journal of Medicine, 320,* 1598–1603.

### Notes

1 This result is probably due to the use of different instruments to measure locus of control. Carroll et al. (1987) used 20 items from Collins's (1974) Locus of Control scale, whereas the present study used Rotter's (1966) scale.

2 All results reported in the chapter are significant at $P < .01$ unless otherwise noted. All single degree-of-freedom comparisons were corrected for familywise error using Tukey's Honestly Significantly Different (HSD) tests. Detailed descriptions of follow-up analyses are beyond the scope of this chapter, but can be obtained from the first author. In addition, the five-way interaction of Scarcity × Locus × Control × Need × Efficiency could not be tested with the dependent variable choice, because choice varied in range depending on scarcity condition (i.e., any individual claimant could be chosen from 3 to 12 times under low scarcity, and 0 to 9 times under high scarcity across resource domains).

3 Results were generally consistent across measures of both liberalism and conservatism, although the cognitive conservatism component usually had the strongest correlations with other variables. For simplicity of presentation, we won't continuously refer to the separate measures of cognitive conservatism and liberal humanism, but will report the results for the cognitive conservative component. High cognitive conservatives will be referred to as "conservatives" and low cognitive conservatives will be referred to as "liberals."

4 The cognitive conservatism and liberal-humanism factors we identified in our first study seemed to be captured by Altemeyer's (1981, 1988) well-validated Right-Wing-Authoritarianism (RWA) scale. Because of its psychometric qualities, we felt it would be superior to our prior methods of assessing political ideology. Altemeyer (1988) indicates that the scale ranges from liberal-democrat to authoritarian. In the "thought" and "reform" studies, we included Katz and Hass's (1988) humanitarianism scale, and Rasinski's (1987) personal values (egalitarianism/proportionality) scales, in addition to the RWA scale. Principal components analysis of these scales yield two-component solutions consistent with Carroll et al.'s (1987) cognitive conservatism and liberal humanism clusters. The cognitive conservatism component usually yields the strongest correlations with perceptions of deservingness, affective reactions to claimants, and allocation decisions. High cognitive conservatism scores reflects a more authoritarian-styled conservatism and anti-egalitarianism, rather than a libertarian value orientation. However, we consistently get clearer results using multiple measures of political ideology, that include broad measures of political values, than when we use RWA alone. Finally, homosexual defensiveness was measured by Herek's (1987) Functional Attitudes Towards Gays and Lesbians scale. None of the other functional attitudes toward homosexuals (experiential-schematic, social-expressive, or value-expressive) significantly relate to the dependent variables in the Setting Limits or Thought studies.

# 11 Liberal and conservative approaches to justice: Conflicting psychological portraits

*Philip E. Tetlock and Gregory Mitchell*

Political philosophers have advocated a wide range of interpretations of justice: from the extreme libertarian to the extreme egalitarian to various compromise or value pluralism positions (e.g., Ackerman, 1980; Barry, 1989; Buchanan, 1975; Nozick, 1974; Rawls, 1971; Walzer, 1983). The prescriptive conclusions these writers reach often depend on the psychological assumptions from which they start. Rawls (1971), for example, sees the just society as one in which the maximin principle (maximize the living standards of the worst off) guides policy – as long as this egalitarian objective does not violate the essential liberty of individuals. He arrives at this conclusion by arguing that people in the hypothetical "original position" (in which they know nothing about themselves or their future life prospects) would be extremely risk averse and would agree to enter into any social contract only if they were sure that society was committed to the maximin principle. People, in this view, want to be absolutely certain that they are not assigned to the bottom rung of a social order that is indifferent or hostile toward their fate. By contrast, Nozick (1974) sees the just society as a libertarian one in which the powers of the state are limited largely to protecting individual rights and enforcing contracts. He arrives at this conclusion by positing the primacy of Lockean property rights and personal freedom – self-evident truths, to paraphrase the authors of the U.S. Constitution. People, in this view, want a social order that allows them to keep what they earn (through legitimate transfers of wealth) and to dispose of their holdings as they choose. Free individuals should be allowed to pursue their self-interest in free markets.

Psychological researchers tend to have humbler, more positivist, objectives than their philosophical colleagues. The goal has been not to lay down the ethical foundations for a just society, but rather to describe and explain

We appreciate the thoughtful comments of Barbara Mellers, Jonathan Baron, Aaron Wildavsky, Linda Skitka, and Mark Spranca on earlier versions of this chapter.

how ordinary people reason their way through problems of social justice – problems such as how to allocate wages or public resources, how to remedy past injustices, or how to design fair procedures for resolving disputes. At first glance, this division of labor looks natural enough, with the political philosophers assigned to prescriptive tasks and behavioral scientists assigned to empirical and explanatory tasks. We shall argue here, however, that this division is far from airtight. Indeed, we fear that psychological approaches to justice may turn out to be as dependent on political assumptions as political philosophical approaches are dependent on psychological ones. The empirical conclusions that research psychologists draw may reflect – in no small measure – their own normative and political preferences. From this perspective, we should not be surprised that psychologists who subscribe to Kantian moral philosophy find Kohlberg's (1984) hierarchy of moral development quite persuasive (a scale in which rights-based reasoning is cognitively and morally superior to the trade-off reasoning of British utilitarianism) whereas psychologists who subscribe to utilitarianism reject the Kohlbergian approach. We should also not be surprised that liberals (mostly egalitarians in twentieth-century America) are more easily convinced than conservatives of the merits of unflattering psychological portraits of conservatives (and vice versa). In short, behavioral research on justice runs the risk of becoming an extension of the political struggle between left and right, a struggle waged with the conceptual and methodological weapons of scientific psychology.[1]

Our chapter explores this disturbing possibility by focusing on potential sources of political bias in justice research. Our argument consists of three parts:

(1) Initial assumptions in justice research are, for an assortment of reasons, profoundly influential.

(2) Most researchers are politically liberal and have explored the empirical implications of a politically quite circumscribed set of premises about human nature and the functioning of society.

(3) Our long-term scientific credibility hinges on our ability to give fair consideration to psychological hypotheses about justice that we find morally or politically objectionable.

As a corrective to ideological tunnel vision, we propose a taxonomy that highlights the wide range of political psychological assumptions from which testable hypotheses can be derived. Productive researchers could devote their entire careers to testing hypotheses drawn from each of the eight "psychological portraits" in the taxonomy: flattering and unflattering cognitive and motivational characterizations of liberals and conservatives.

### Initial assumptions matter

Science is supposed to be self-correcting. One deduces hypotheses from a theory, designs a study to test the hypotheses, and revises the hypotheses in light of the data. This textbook account of the hypothetico-deductive method is, however, incomplete in many ways. Which hypotheses do we consider worth testing? Where do they come from? What methods do we adopt to test these hypotheses? What counts as a fair test? What alternative interpretations do we consider when unexpected data emerge? And when do we decide to reject not just a hypothesis, but the entire theoretical framework from which it was derived?

We agree with those philosophers of science who argue that initial assumptions play a key role at each of these choice points (e.g., Lakatos, 1970; Suppe, 1977). We also believe that behavioral research on justice is, if anything, especially vulnerable to the influence of initial assumptions. Most researchers come to the field with strongly held political convictions; these convictions generally favor egalitarian and social democratic causes; the professional review process has, on notable occasions, displayed a bias in favor of liberal perspectives on social controversies (for many examples, see Suedfeld & Tetlock, 1991); and finally, given the lack of standardized, widely accepted research methods and given the difficulties of replication in "soft psychology" (Meehl, 1978), there are plenty of opportunities for unintentional biasing of results at the level of the individual study. In brief, there are many reasons for expecting one's assumptions to exert an unusually strong influence on one's conclusions in this empirical domain.[2]

It is not difficult to generate concrete examples of how one's normative assumptions and preferences can influence the research process. In some cases, the influence is overt and heavy-handed. Sears and colleagues, for example, advance the theoretical argument that opposition to policies designed to increase racial equality (e.g., busing, affirmative action) is the product of hostility toward minorities that has been cloaked in the conservative rhetoric of self-reliance, law and order, and economic individualism (Kinder & Sears, 1981; Sears & Kinder, 1985). They call such opposition "symbolic racism" and typically operationalize the concept with attitude scales that assess support for government programs to assist minorities in various ways. As Sniderman and Tetlock (1986a) note, if one responds to these scales in an ideologically principled conservative or libertarian manner (i.e., opposes government programs), one is automatically labeled a symbolic racist. By operational fiat, conservatism becomes racism (we will later classify symbolic racism theory within our taxonomy as an unflattering motivational portrait of conservatism).

Initial assumptions can also influence empirical work in subtler ways. Considerable research in social cognition suggests that people, in a variety of settings, tend to exaggerate the importance of dispositional causes of behavior and to underestimate the controlling power of the situation (Jones, 1979; Ross, 1977). Drawing on this research literature, some justice researchers have suggested that one explanation for the conservative emphasis on individual responsibility for economic outcomes is the greater susceptibility of conservatives to the "fundamental attribution error". There is nothing tautological about this hypothesis; it is a testable proposition. As we shall see, however, it is not a straightforward matter to test this hypothesis in a value-neutral manner. To call a response tendency an error presumes that one knows what the true state of the world is (in this case, the relative importance of dispositional and situational determinants of poverty). To call a response tendency an error also presumes that one knows what people were trying to do when they made judgments of a particular sort. Conservatives may, for example, prefer dispositional explanations not because of cognitive shortcomings but because they fear the consequences of one type of attributional error (failing to hold people responsible for outcomes under their control) much more than the consequences of another attributional error (holding people responsible for something not under their control). This theoretical possibility has, however, been almost completely overlooked and we return to it later.

Political preconceptions can influence not only the hypotheses one considers, but also the research procedures one chooses to test those hypotheses. The judgments people make about the fairness of public policies are notoriously sensitive to how questions are posed (Tourangeau, Rasinski, Bradburn, & D'Andrade, 1989). What qualifies, however, as a neutral way of assessing people's attitudes toward taxation, income redistribution, affirmative action, or abortion? Should the question make salient the sacrifices required or the suffering attenuated? Whose sacrifices? Whose suffering? Should arguments and counterarguments be presented? If so, how should they be "calibrated"? There are obviously no right answers to these questions (Sniderman & Tetlock, 1986b). Suffice it to say that the best we can hope for is to sample in reasonably unbiased fashion from the "conceptual universe" of possible issue framings and arguments/counterarguments. What, however, does this conceptual universe look like?

### Toward a taxonomy of initial assumptions

If normative assumptions do influence justice research, and if most researchers show a preference for egalitarian and liberal assumptions, what can be done to restore theoretical balance in the field? Our proposed remedy is dialectical. We do not believe it is possible to eliminate the influence of initial assumptions, but we do believe that it is possible to balance one set of influences against another.

In this section of the chapter, we sketch eight possible sets of assumptions from which behavioral research on justice might proceed. These eight possibilities can be organized into a $2 \times 2 \times 2$ contingency table: flattering and unflattering cognitive and motivational perspectives on liberalism and conservatism. We shall show that it is possible to construct radically different psychopolitical portraits of liberals and conservatives by drawing selectively on theoretical concepts and empirical findings in the psychological and social science literatures. For instance, one could argue that the conservative emphasis on individual responsibility is due to the greater susceptibility of conservatives to the fundamental attribution error (an argument that we will classify as an unflattering cognitive portrait of conservatism). Or, one could argue that liberal concern for the poor reflects the greater capacity of this group for emotional empathy (a flattering motivational portrait of liberalism) or a greater tendency to envy the well-off (an unflattering motivational portrait).

Our goal is not, of course, to praise or stigmatize particular points of view, but rather to draw attention to the full range of psychological premises to be explored in studying justice. We also seek to highlight the moral and political implications of psychological explanations: Labeling conservatives as symbolic racists or as especially prone to the fundamental attribution error, for instance, implies the need for correction. Have we so conclusively eliminated alternative explanations that we feel comfortable equating conservatism with either a cognitive defect or social pathology? If we value our collective integrity as a science, we should be explicit about the logical and empirical justifications for attaching value-laden theoretical labels to political points of view (Suedfeld & Tetlock, 1991).

In categorizing initial assumptions, we not only distinguish sharply between liberalism and conservativism, we also treat "cold" cognitive and "hot" motivational processes as independent. Although the two categories of processes are best thought of as interdependent (Dweck & Legget, 1988; Sorrentino & Higgins, 1986; Tetlock & Levi, 1982), there is still heuristic value in distinguishing between them. It is also useful to distinguish between flattering and unflattering psychological portraits. Most of us would rather be viewed as rational and altruistic than as irrational (error prone or biased) and selfish. But even this seemingly straightforward distinction blurs on close inspection. Many policy positions that are superficially selfish or irrational can be plausibly presented in exactly the opposite light if we tamper with basic assumptions about individual motives or beliefs about the political workings of society. The same intellectual exercise can be put into reverse to challenge conventional thinking about policy positions that, on their face, are altruistic or rational. With these qualifications in mind, we present the psychopolitical portraits.[3]

### Flattering liberal portraits

Cognitive. Liberals better understand the structural limits on upward mobility and control over one's fate and thus are less prone to commit the fundamental attribution error (cf. Ross, 1977; see also Pettigrew, 1979, on the "ultimate attribution error"). Liberals are also better able to put themselves in the place of the disadvantaged (cognitive empathy) and to see the pressures to turn to crime in a social system that simultaneously limits opportunities for economic advancement and places enormous cultural value on material achievement (cf. Merton, 1968). Moreover, liberals do not rely excessively on simple heuristics such as representativeness and availability in making attributions for poverty: (1) They do not equate downtrodden or impoverished status with inherent unworthiness or inability; (2) they go beyond the most readily available attribution of individual responsibility for failure and make more complex and nuanced causal claims; (3) their judgments are less likely to be dominated by salient stimuli than those of conservatives. (See Fiske & Taylor, 1991, for detailed discussion of these cognitive mechanisms.) Finally, liberals have a deeper understanding of the long-term positive externalities of welfare measures: We all ultimately benefit when people are rescued from lives of crime, drug addiction, hopelessness, and dependency. Life need not be a zero-sum game.

Shifting from a primarily theoretical to a primarily empirical argument, there is both survey and content analytic evidence that liberals rely on more integratively complex cognitive strategies in reaching policy conclusions than do conservatives (Tetlock, 1989), suggesting liberals may be more tolerant of cognitive dissonance and willing to acknowledge that policymaking requires making painful trade-offs (e.g., crime control vs. liberty, efficiency vs. equality). There is also evidence from personality research that liberals receive higher scores on measures of tolerance of ambiguity and intellectual flexibility and lower scores on dogmatism (Stone & Schaffner, 1988).

*Motivational.* Liberals are more emotionally empathic than conservatives (Tompkins, 1962, 1963; see Stone & Schaffner, 1988). They experience the distress of the disadvantaged especially intensely and hence are especially motivated to help them. Moreover, liberals possess a greater sense of social responsibility to care for the less fortunate (see Berkowitz, 1972, on the norm of social responsibility). As a result, liberals will be primarily "altruists" or "cooperators" in interdependent settings (see Stone & Schaffner, 1988, who cite evidence that liberal ideology is "prosocial" and that the parenting styles of liberals foster prosocial behavior; see also McClintock, 1972; Messick & McClintock, 1968; for a relevant typology of social motives). Finally, liberals are more tolerant of deviant opinions and life-styles and willing to stand up for the basic democratic rights of widely disliked groups (McClosky & Brill, 1983; Sniderman, Tetlock, Gleser, Green, & Hout, 1988).

In a nutshell, liberals are less selfish and more empathic and tolerant than conservatives. Their fear of aiding the undeserving is outweighed by their fear of not helping the truly needy. And this emphasis on increasing equality and helping others is the result of humanitarian concern rather than fear of falling (risk aversion) or envious desire to bring the wealthy down (leveling). Liberals do not need to bolster their self-esteem by living in a stratified society in which they can claim superiority over this or that group; in social identity terms, liberals place all Americans – sometimes all of humanity – within their in-group and try to improve the lot of lower status group members (cf. Lane, 1959) (or alternatively, group identities are simply of little concern to liberals, and they are a conspicuous exception to the generalization that people discriminate against out-groups; cf. Brewer, 1979; Tajfel, 1982). Finally, liberals do not blame the victim (Ryan, 1972) or make defensive attributions (cf. Shaver, 1970) that would lead them to conclude that the world is a just place where people deserve what they get and get what they deserve (Rubin & Peplau, 1975). Liberals acknowledge that fate can be capricious and that bad things can happen to good people (and vice versa).

### Flattering conservative portraits

*Cognitive.* Conservatives understand not only the limits to advancement but also the possibilities of advancement. Conservatives realize the importance of incentives and that no, or little, aid is often the best help of all (i.e., welfare is a disincentive to taking responsibility for oneself; Murray, 1984; Wiseman, 1986). The conservative response to social problems avoids the simplistic first response of treating the symptom by creating a new and expensive government program. Indeed, the liberal "social welfare" cure is actually an example of the representativeness heuristic in that people with fewer resources are simply given more rather than addressing deeper causes. Conservatives appreciate that reactions to help are complex rather than uniformly positive and that help sometimes evokes resentment and feelings of incompetence (cf. Broll, Gross, & Piliavin, 1974; Depaulo & Fisher, 1980), and they do not fall prey to emotionally charged but often unrepresentative vivid information (i.e., they are less stimulus bound; see Nisbett & Ross, 1980) that would bias responses toward giving the quickest but perhaps not most effective form of aid. Furthermore, conservatives understand that although you will never be able to eradicate inequality (Hirsch, 1976), you may be able to improve the absolute standard of living for all; rather than worry about trading off equality and efficiency, you should look for ways to increase both. The best way to do this is by stimulating economic growth through market mechanisms ("a rising tide lifts all boats"), not political means that tend to decrease efficiency (conservatives understand the negative externalities of bureaucratic and political intervention on market operations) or legal means that are often slow and ineffective. Conservatives are aware that legislators often spend money carelessly and are motivated less by concern for the public good and more by concern for purchasing the goodwill of powerful special-interest constituencies who can advance their political careers (see Buchanan & Tullock, 1962; Friedman, 1962). In these senses, conservatives are more integratively complex than liberals because they understand how often well-intentioned political reforms have unintended consequences or perverse effects (see Hadari, 1989a,b; Hirschman, 1986).

Conservatives also appreciate the extraordinary resourcefulness of the individual. Ingenuity and determination can overcome enormous obstacles; entry into the marketplace by motivated workers will usually result, sooner or later, in socioeconomic progress (cf. Kluegel & Smith, 1986; Lane, 1959). Moreover, the marketplace rewards individual actions whereas the polity emphasizes group outcomes and will usually not acknowledge individual achievement (i.e., group members are equals) (see Lane, 1983, 1986). Political redistribution from an advantaged to a disadvantaged group does not ensure that the "right" people in the respective groups will be hurt or helped (i.e., the poorest of an advantaged group may lose the most and the poorest of a disadvantaged group may gain the least) (Beer, 1991).

Finally, conservatives understand how free markets work. Whereas liberals reflexively disapprove of the profit motive (a manifestation of greed), conservatives recognize that the invisible hand of free market competition leads in the long term to incentives to produce goods at levels of quality and quantity that satisfy effective demand for those goods. The alternatives of direct state control (central planning) or government regulation create perverse incentives that often simultaneously impede efficiency and exacerbate inequities (e.g., collectivized agriculture, rent control). This understanding of markets, moreover, increasingly cuts across national boundaries. Conservatives have become the principal (and principled) supporters of free trade among nations. Although one might conclude from superficial analysis that one weakens one's country by permitting "cheap imports" (arguing that it leads to unemployment, abandoned factories, and so on), conservatives can see beyond the obvious. In the long run, the concept of comparative advantage tells us that free trade reduces inflation (by allowing consumers access to lower-cost goods) and encourages the disappearance of uncompetitive domestic industries and their replacement by industries that are capable of succeeding in the global marketplace.

*Motivational.* Conservatives are willing to let the disadvantaged suffer temporarily in order to motivate them to do what is necessary to improve their lot in the long run. They are willing to think in a broad time frame when assessing the fairness of resource distributions within society. If reducing poverty is the common goal, then conservatives can delay their need for this type of gratification longer than liberals can (see Mischel, 1974, on correlates of capacity to delay need gratification). Also, conservatives are concerned that progressively greater reliance on political services will interfere with efficient market forces and seriously reduce the living standards of future generations. This reluctance to redistribute stems from a greater respect for the achievements and property rights of others ("they earned it, they should dispose of it as they see fit"). Conservatives, quite appropriately, believe in a "just world" (cf. Lerner, 1980; Rubin & Peplau, 1975): In general, people do get what they deserve in the economic realm;

to think otherwise is to place too little faith in individual control of circumstances. Conservatives relish the challenges of self-reliance.

### Unflattering liberal portraits

*Cognitive.* Liberals rely on the representativeness heuristic in their misguided search for societal solutions to individual problems. They practice, in effect, a kind of social homeopathic medicine that treats symptoms rather than underlying causes (if people need money, housing, or medical care, then cure the need by giving it to them – cf. Nisbett & Ross, 1980). Unfortunately, liberals are oblivious to fundamental facts about the workings of political and economic systems (see Lipsett & Raab, 1978). Government programs rarely solve the problems they were intended to solve and invariably create a whole new set of problems that take on a life of their own. Once one creates a bureaucracy to serve a constituency (e.g., the bureaucracies that administer farm price supports, research grants, and welfare subsidies), two consequences follow: The constituency immediately develops a strong sense of entitlement (any programmatic cuts will be perceived as losses and protested vociferously) and the bureaucracy acquires a strong interest in perpetuating and expanding the program. It follows that it will be much easier to add than to subtract government programs. Liberals, however, are too shortsighted to appreciate the long-term societal consequences of proliferating programs designed to satisfy one "need" after another. They fail to take into account the growing burden on the economy and the perverse incentives that dependency on public programs creates.

Liberals may also be susceptible to mirror images of the cognitive biases of conservatives. They may be too quick to see people as victims of circumstance (chronically exaggerating the power of the situation and setting the stage for self-fulfilling prophecies of failure). It may often be adaptive (from both an individual and societal perspective) to be optimistic about one's control over one's destiny and one's chances of success (Seligman, 1990; Taylor, 1990). Liberals may also be too slow to change their minds about the efficacy of government and prone to both theory-driven and wishful thinking when they argue that the more money one spends on public programs, the greater the collective benefits.

Liberals not only exaggerate the efficacy of government; they underestimate the creativity of the free market. Many liberals mindlessly condemn capitalism as a culture of greed and ignore the power of the market to stimulate hard work, investment, and entrepreneurship. They don't think through the systemic implications when they evaluate the fairness of market transactions. To draw on the research scenarios of Kahneman, Knetsch, and Thaler (1986), liberals fail to see the useful economic-signaling functions served by allowing the merchant to raise the prices of snow shovels after a blizzard (encourages other stores to build up inventories next season to satisfy surges in demand), by allowing an employer to cut wages in response to a labor surplus (encourages people to go into other lines of work where they are more needed), or by allowing a landlord to increase rents in response to a tenant surplus (encourages building of more rental units). Liberals can't see beyond the evidence of greed and the (temporary) suffering it produces.

*Motivational.* There is a kernel of truth in the "bleeding heart" stereotype. Many liberals base their policy recommendations on highly vivid and emotional, but not particularly representative or even informative, stimuli. Liberals' perceptions of inequity in society represent not veridical assessments of how the distribution came about but rather emotionally charged preconceptions about capitalism and meritocracy (which they consider exploitive, heartless, and so on). One should be careful, however, not to exaggerate the role that excessive emotionality and sympathy play in shaping liberal responses to social issues. Not all liberals are bleeding hearts. Many liberals are motivated less by compassion for the poor and more by a combination of self-interest and animus toward the rich. It is no coincidence in this view that liberals are overrepresented among net beneficiaries of government largesse (the poor, government employees, academics, and more) and government regulation (unions). To appreciate how shallow the liberal commitment to the poor is, we need only consider the position that many liberal elites take on free trade. As soon as imports from poverty-striken Third World nations threaten well-paying American jobs, they rally to support protectionist policies that will plunge those nations into even deeper misery. The driving motive behind many liberal positions is the desire to bring the wealthy down a notch or two, and to achieve this goal, liberals must speak of structural constraints and inequities that need to be redressed by redistribution.

Just as psychodynamic explanations for conservatism have received careful attention (Adorno, Frenkel-Brunswik, Levinson, & Sanford, 1950), so perhaps such explanations should receive equally careful attention for liberalism. For example, external attributions for failure in society may serve an ego-defensive function for liberals, protecting their self-esteem whenever they themselves experience failure (cf. Tetlock & Levi, 1982). In a similar vein, social and economic insecurity may motivate an emphasis on governmental welfare programs (Who will take care of me if I fall?). Liberalism, in this view, is a reflection of the widespread "psychology of dependency" in which government, by transference, takes on the role of the nurturant, powerful parent (Etheredge, 1989). A government that fails to take care of its people (i.e., children) has abdicated its most fundamental responsibility, and liberals react with bitter disappointment and anger.

### Unflattering conservative portraits

*Cognitive.* Here we discover a formidable list of judgmental shortcomings. First, and most important, conservatives do not understand how prevalent situational constraints on achievement are and thus commit the fundamental attribution error when they hold the poor responsible for poverty. Simplistic use of judgmental heuristics underlies this error. Even if lack of initiative and marketable skills are the proximal causes of poverty, systemic forces (e.g., high unemployment, institutional racism, poor education) have produced these conditions and so are the true distal causes of poverty. Conservatives rely on a superficial analysis of the causes of social outcomes (see Baron & Hershey, 1988 on the "outcome bias"). Second, conservatives overgeneralize: From a few cases of poor persons who exploit the system, they draw sweeping conclusions about all poor persons; in this case welfare is erroneously seen as the problem, not the solution for the majority of the poor (cf. Nisbett & Ross, 1980). Third, by placing so much faith in individual effort and ability, conservatives evince the illusion of control (cf. Langer, 1975); chance happenings play a much greater role in success or failure than conservatives realize. People often do not control their destinies. Accidents, misfortunes, and disease strike down even the most deserving. Fourth, conservatives are too prone to engage in zero-sum thinking (either I keep my money or the government takes it). They fail to appreciate the possibility of positive-sum resolutions of societal conflicts. Fifth, conservatives fall prey to the omission bias (cf. Spranca, Minsk, & Baron, 1991; Baron, personal communication) that justifies the laissez-faire "minimal-state" view that, although we have a moral obligation to refrain from hurting others, we have no obligation to help others. Conservatives cling to the comforting moral illusion that there is a sharp distinction between allowing people to suffer and making people suffer. Finally, conservatives fail to recognize that even if each transaction in a free market meets their standards of fairness (exchanges between competent adults who have not been coerced or tricked into contracts), the cumulative result could be colossally unfair. Some people will acquire enormous power over others. Our judgment of the fairness of the systemic whole should not be reduced to the individual transaction parts. Freedom for big fish is tyranny for little fish.

*Motivational.* Conservatives react with anger and contempt toward the poor whom they blame for their predicament (see Tompkins, 1962, 1963; cf. Weiner, 1980). These feelings lead conservatives to be punitive and stingy toward the disadvantaged (Skitka & Tetlock, 1992). Conservatives are selfish, competitive, and individualistic in their social motives (cf. Kuhlman & Marshello, 1975). They don't want to give up what they have and they certainly do not want their former possessions "redistributed" to people they consider to be either incompetent or lazy (free riders) or even evil. Conservatives do not identify the disadvantaged as members of their ingroup and derogate the poor as members of an out-group, thereby promoting their own self- and social identities as superior (cf. Tajfel, 1982). Conservatives fear demands for equality because of the implications of those demands for their own standing and status (Lane, 1959).

The tendency of conservatives to distance themselves psychologically from the poor occurs even in ethnically and racially homogeneous societies. The tendency is all the stronger, however, when the poor are ethnically or racially "different." As a result of early socialization (emotionally cold and repressive family environment), conservatives are much more likely to have a lot of repressed hostility that they "displace" or "project" onto low-status out-groups. The more dissimilar the out-group, the more psychodynamically attractive it becomes for status-starved "authoritarian personalities" to devalue and stigmatize them (Adorno et al., 1950; Altemeyer, 1981; Greenstein, 1975). Beyond such blatant old-fashioned prejudice, conservatism may also be deeply implicated in new, more subtle, forms of racism. Conservative values may "fuse" with resentment of minorities (to create "symbolic racism" – Kinder, 1986, or conservative values may merely mask or serve to justify hostility toward disadvantaged minorities (McConahay, 1986). Either way, conservatism and compassion are antithetical. Conservatives disparage the disadvantaged in order to justify the economic and psychodynamic status quo.

## About the taxonomy and its purposes

### To illustrate the range of explanation

We do not assume that these psychopolitical portraits are equally valid. Some portraits may capture the thoughts and feelings of only relatively few people, and then only under special conditions. The primary purpose of the taxonomy is to highlight the range of possible explanations, not to argue for any particular position. We also do not assume that most people can be easily pigeonholed into our taxonomic categories. Very few of us make judgments of fairness in a rigid syllogistic style in which we begin with a major ethical premise (maximize liberty or equality), apply that premise to a concrete situation (equality requires progressive taxation or liberty requires a flat-rate system of minimal taxation, and deduce a policy consequence (see Sniderman, Brody, & Tetlock 1991). Most of us have a plurality of intuitions about fairness that can be primed by particular attributes of the proposals and evidence confronting us (Tetlock, 1986, on value pluralism). Accordingly, our judgments are highly sensitive to the particular context in which they are studied and to how they are studied (Tourangeau et al., 1989). As situational goals and relations shift, so do distributive norms (e.g., Fiske, 1990; Hochschild, 1981; Lerner, Miller, & Holmes, 1976; Prentice & Crosby, 1987; Schwinger, 1980). Minor alterations in research design can dramatically alter the acceptability of different distributions of wealth (Mitchell, Tetlock, & Mellers, 1991; see also Harris & Joyce, 1980, on the importance of research design in distributive justice research).

Elsewhere, we (Mitchell et al., 1991, p. 23) have proposed that judgments of social justice have a cybernetic component that leads to "predictable shifts in distributive strategies as different beliefs about justice and governance are primed" (cf. March & Olsen, 1989). In this view, people know they have had enough of a particular approach to distributive justice (e.g., egalitarianism or libertarianism) only when they have had more than enough. Each approach inevitably entails excesses that trigger public backlash (cf. Schlesinger, 1986, on the long cycles of American politics). As political conditions evolve, one would expect different aspects of justice to be emphasized and different psychological processes to be activated. One would also expect that, at various times and in various contexts, each portrait of justice sketched here should capture some significant slice of reality. For instance, unflattering portraits of liberals may be especially descriptive in the final stages of an egalitarian political-economic cycle (when those on the political left spend much of their time defending increasingly inefficient state programs that benefit increasingly narrow and not especially needy constituencies). Conversely, unflattering portraits of conservatives may be especially descriptive in the final phases of a laissez-faire political-economic cycle (when those on the political right spend much of their time trying to explain away massive inequalities). This line of argument suggests a rich array of micro–macro linkage hypotheses for future testing.

Of course, to argue that judgments of justice are context sensitive is not to argue they are completely context dependent. There are limits to the malleability of judgments of justice. People strongly object, for example, to income distributions that allow the poor to fall below the "poverty line," regardless of whether those at the bottom are there for reasons within their control (Alves & Rossi, 1978; Mitchell et al., 1991; Rossi & Nock, 1982; see also Scitovsky, 1986). Consider also that procedural fairness is a consistent concern across legal (Tyler, 1984, 1990), political (Tyler & Caine, 1981; Tyler, Rasinski, & McGraw, 1985), and managerial (Alexander & Ruderman, 1987; Folger, 1987; Folger & Bies, 1989; Folger & Konovsky, 1989) contexts. Thus, we are not arguing for the radical contextualist position that, given the proper set of circumstances, any conception of justice can be made to dominate. Again, our goal is to draw attention to the range of possible hypotheses, in the process encouraging caution in positing value-laden explanations that indiscriminately mix psychological theory and political preferences.

### To illustrate the political nature of the work

In addition to highlighting the empirical complexity of justice, a further purpose of the taxonomy is to draw attention to the political nature of the study of justice. By dividing the psychological portraits along ideological and evaluative dimensions we can demonstrate that it is difficult, perhaps impossible, to avoid political and moral issues in justice research. The difficulty is especially great, in part, because of the passions evoked in the investigators and, in part, because of the causal ambiguity and complexity that shrouds key issues. For example, the questions of how best to fight poverty and to cope with the spillover effects of doing so have been topics of intense debate for centuries and do not at the moment appear close to resolution (Jencks & Peterson, 1991). As Himmelfarb (1991) notes, nine-teenth-century Victorians argued just as vehemently as twentieth-century Americans over the comparative roles of structural factors and personal conduct as contributors to a large urban underclass. When the evidence comes from badly confounded natural experiments (the interpretation of which hinges on complex counterfactual conjectures: What would have happened if we had done X or Y instead of Z?), there is great leeway for both theory-driven information processing and self-fulfilling prophecies. The control groups "exist" only in the imaginations of the investigators. Under such conditions, many justice researchers have wisely decided that their task is not to evaluate the substantive validity of various beliefs but rather to map out these beliefs and their apparent effects.

Evaluating the rationality, morality, and accuracy of political positions is profoundly problematic. It places psychologists in the presumptuous role of claiming to know the true state of the political world. What are the causes of poverty, inequality, and tyranny? What goals should we individually and collectively strive for? What weight should we place on values that (at least sometimes) conflict: social equality versus economic efficiency and personal liberty versus state control? What are the likely long-term conse-quences of pursuing egalitarian policies (alleviating suffering, reducing class and racial tensions, oppressive regulations, stagnant economy . . .) or lib-ertarian policies (squalor and deprivation for those who lack marketable skills, a surge of creativity and self-initiative that stimulates prosperity for all)? For our part, we do not believe psychologists have the answers to these questions.

Psychologists who claim to possess answers (at least implicitly by their value-laden characterizations of particular viewpoints) have in our view gone "too far." In part, they have gone too far by supposing that funda-mental puzzles concerning the causes of poverty and prosperity have been solved, and solved in favor of the diagnosis preferred by egalitarians. They suppose that people who attribute poverty to personal attributes of the poor have made a mistake and that people who oppose government aid to minorities must be motivated by racial animus, not ideological conviction.

Even, however, if largely external attributions for poverty were shown to be correct (and the evidence is decidedly mixed – Jencks & Peterson, 1991), the evaluative labels attached to conservative positions would still be premature. Such labels would be premature for the simple reason that existing research has failed to explore what people perceive to be the moral and societal consequences of making particular attributional judgments. Liberals and conservatives may differ not only in their perceptions of pov-erty, but in the values they place on the logically possible attributional "hits" and "misses." Liberals may set a high threshold for holding someone responsible (fully culpable) for their conduct because they find the Type I error of incorrectly blaming someone much more distasteful than the Type II error of incorrectly exonerating someone. Conservatives may set much lower thresholds of proof because they hold the mirror-image values. Each side may justify its choice of threshold by invoking both factual claims that could, in principle, be tested (e.g., people can be motivated to work harder if they believe a stern state has little tolerance for situational excuses) and value-based claims that are not testable (e.g., it is morally right to hold people strictly accountable). By failing to test carefully the hypothesis that the conservative attributional style is rooted in moral preference, not cognitive defect, investigators who accuse conservatives of a fundamental error have themselves erred.

A much more egregious example of how political values can contaminate psychological research on justice is, as noted earlier, the symbolic racism tradition. Here, conservatism became racism by operational definition. If one opposes higher taxes or affirmative action to help minorities, or believes that minorities should rely less on government and more on themselves, one is, ipso facto, racist. This approach is methodologically suspect. By mixing conservative and racial themes in symbolic racism scales (a virtue in Kinder's, 1986, opinion), it becomes impossible to disentangle ideological and racist determinants of policy preferences (as, for example, Sniderman, Piazza, Tetlock, and Kendrick, 1991, have done in a series of experiments embedded in representative-sample surveys). Equally important, however, this approach raises the prospect of the complete politicization of the psychological research process. If researchers can advance an unflattering motivational portrait of conservatives by labeling conservative policy preferences as symbolically racist, then by the same epistemic ground rules, researchers can advance unflattering motivational portraits of liberals by labeling liberal policy preferences (support for government regulation of the economy, opposition to military intervention against left-wing insurgencies) as symbolically Marxist. The specter of such ideological warfare is perhaps the strongest argument for making serious efforts to distinguish sharply between psychological facts and political wishes. The big loser in this war would be our collective scientific credibility.

### To facilitate research

This chapter has had a cautionary theme, emphasizing the threats of tunnel vision and political bias. The consistent refrain has been: "Be careful not to allow your normative preferences to restrict the hypotheses you consider or to influence the standards of evidence and proof you use in accepting or rejecting those hypotheses." We sketched relatively extreme psychological portraits both as a role-reversal exercise (How does it feel to see one's own political viewpoint subjected to psychological attack?) and as an illustration of how political preconceptions can color initial judgments of the reasonableness of psychological hypotheses.

Yet on a more positive note, it should be recognized that the psychopolitical taxonomy can be a useful research tool. The taxonomy offers a scheme for organizing research and generating testable hypotheses (many of which we have laid out in particular portraits). One especially promising area of research is disentangling the perceptual/cognitive and motivational/affective roots of disagreement between liberals and conservatives illustrated in the taxonomy. Some generalization of the signal detection paradigm offers a means to differentiate these psychological processes across the political groups. One may conceive of the distribution process as a dichotomous choice of giving or not giving resources to a group. Four outcomes are possible in this distributive matrix: Resources are given to those who should receive them (either because of merit, need, or however the researcher operationalizes deservingness), resources are given to those who should not receive them (a Type I error), resources are withheld from those who should receive them (a Type II error), and resources are withheld from those who should not receive them.

One's response threshold along a deservingness continuum will depend on (1) one's aversions to the different types of errors (is a Type I error worse than a Type II error?) and (2) one's perceptions of the likelihood of the different errors. By manipulating the costs of the various errors, and the base rates for different states of the world, or by measuring dispositional aversions to errors and perceptions of base rates, one can assess how these components interact to affect distributive outcomes. Moreover, one can compare the distributive strategies of liberals and conservatives on these dimensions to judge how motivational and cognitive factors contribute to their respective distributive strategies and to differences across groups in distributive outcomes. Do conservatives and liberals differ primarily in their perceptions of how likely Type I versus Type II errors (subjective base rates) are or in the values they place on avoiding one or the other category of error? Are there distinctive subgroups within each ideological camp? Are error tolerance and subjective base rates causally connected? How do error tolerance and subjective base rates shift as one moves from one issue domain to the next (criminal justice, corporate liability, affirmative action, trade, taxation, and others)? It is worth emphasizing that one can answer such questions – and model political belief systems in rigorous ways – without taking any stand on the correctness or moral soundness of liberal versus conservative points of view.

In conclusion, the taxonomy can direct and facilitate research as well as remind us of the plurality of normative perspectives on justice. The two functions, moreover, are intertwined. As a group, psychologists are disproportionately (if not overwhelmingly) liberal and appear drawn to flattering portraits of liberals and unflattering ones of conservatives. This intellectual attraction is understandable but has unfortunate consequences.

Researchers have explored the empirical implications of some psychopolitical portraits much more thoroughly than others. Such selective sampling of starting assumptions may ultimately turn out to be a relatively
harmless error. There may be little merit in the unflattering portraits of
liberals and the flattering portraits of conservatives. We, however, are
skeptical. What one finds in psychological research often hinges on what
one is looking for and how hard one looks.

### References

Ackerman, B. A. (1980). *Social justice in the liberal state.* New Haven, CT: Yale University Press.

Adorno, T. W., Frenkel-Brunswik, E., Levinson, D. J., & Sanford, R. N. (1950). *The
authoritarian personality.* New York: Harper.

Alexander, S., & Ruderman, A. (1987). The role of procedural and distributive justice in organizational behavior. *Social Justice Research, 1,* 177–198.

Altemeyer, B. (1981). *Right-wing authoritarianism.* Winnipeg: University of Manitoba
Press.

Alves, W. M., & Rossi, P. H. (1978). Who should get what? Fairness judgments of
the distribution of earnings. *American Journal of Sociology, 84,* 541–564.

Baron, J., & Hershey, J. C. (1988). Outcome bias in decision evaluation. *Journal of
Personality and Social Psychology, 54,* 569–579.

Barry, B. (1989). *Theories of justice.* Berkeley: University of California Press.

Beer, W. (1991). Affirmative action as shibboleth. In P. Suedfeld and P. E. Tetlock
(Eds.), *Psychology and social advocacy.* Washington, DC: Hemisphere Press.

Berkowitz, L. (1972). Social norms, feelings and other factors affecting helping behavior and altruism. *Advances in Experimental Social Psychology, 6,* 63–108.

Brewer, M. (1979). In-group bias in the minimal intergroup situation: A cognitive-
motivational analysis. *Psychological Bulletin, 86,* 307–324.

Broll, L., Gross, A. E., & Piliavin, I. (1974). Effects of offered and requested help
on help seeking and reactions to being helped. *Journal of Applied Social Psychology, 4,* 244–258.

Buchanan, J. M. (1975). *The limits of liberty.* Chicago: University of Chicago Press.

Buchanan, J. M., & Tullock, G. (1962). *The calculus of consent.* Ann Arbor: University
of Michigan Press.

Depaulo, B. M., & Fisher, J. D. (1980). The costs of asking for help. *Basic and Applied
Social Psychology, 1,* 23–35.

Douglas, M., & Wildavsky, A. B. (1982). *Risk and culture: An essay on the selection of
technical and environmental dangers.* Berkeley, CA: University of California Press.

Dweck, C. S., & Legget, E. S. (1988). A social-cognitive approach to motivation and
personality. *Psychological Review, 95,* 256–273.

Etheredge, L. S. (1989). On being more rational than the rationality assumption:
Public drama, economic growth, and the agenda for learning. Unpublished
manuscript, University of Toronto Department of Political Science.

Feather, N. T. (1984). Protestant ethic, conservatism, and values. *Journal of Personality and Social Psychology, 46,* 1132–1141.

Feldman, S. (1988). Structure and consistency in public opinion: The role of core
beliefs and values. *American Journal of Political Science, 32,* 416–440.

Fiske, A. P. (1990). The cultural relativity of selfish individualism: Anthropological evidence that humans are inherently sociable. In M. S. Clark (Ed.), *Review of Personality and Social Psychology* (Vol. 12). New York: Sage.

Fiske, S., & Taylor, S. (1991). *Social cognition* (2nd ed.). Reading, MA: Addison-Wesley.

Folger, R. (1987). Distributive and procedural justice in the workplace. *Social Justice Research, 1,* 143–159.

Folger, R., & Bies, R. J. (1989). Managerial responsibilities and procedural justice. *Employee Responsibilities and Rights Journal, 2,* 79–90.

Folger, R., & Konovsky, M. A. (1989). Effects of procedural and distributive justice on reactions to pay raise decisions. *Academy of Management Journal, 32,* 115–130.

Friedman, M. (1962). *Capitalism and freedom.* Chicago: University of Chicago Press.

Greenstein, F. I. (1975). Personality and politics. In F. Greenstein & N. Polsby (Eds.), *Handbook of political science.* Reading, MA: Addison-Wesley.

Hadari, S. A. (1989a). Value trade-off. *Journal of Politics, 50,* 655–676.

(1989b). Unintended consequences in periods of transition: Tocqueville's "Recollections" revisited. *American Journal of Political Science, 33,* 136–149.

Harris, R. J., & Joyce, M. A. (1980). What's fair? It depends on how you phrase the question. *Journal of Personality and Social Psychology, 38,* 165–179.

Himmelfarb, G. (1991). *Poverty and compassion: The moral imagination of the late Victorians.* New York: Knopf.

Hirsch, F. (1976). *Social limits to growth.* Cambridge, MA: Harvard University Press.

Hirschman, A. O. (1986). *Rival views of market society.* New York: Viking.

Hochschild, J. (1981). *What's fair? American beliefs about distributive justice.* Cambridge, MA: Harvard University Press.

Jencks, C., & Peterson, P. (Eds.) (1991). *The urban underclass.* Washington, DC: Brookings Institution.

Jones, E. E. (1979). The rocky road from acts to dispositions. *American Psychologist, 34,* 107–117.

Kahneman, D., Knetsch, J., & Thaler, R. (1986). Fairness and the assumptions of economics. In R. Hogarth and M. Reder (Eds.), *Fairness and the assumptions of economics.* Chicago: University of Chicago Press.

Kinder, D. R. (1986). The continuing American dilemma: White resistance to racial change 40 years after Myrdal. *Journal of Social Issues, 42,* 151–171.

Kinder, D. R., & Sears, D. O. (1981). Prejudice and politics: Symbolic racism versus racial threats to the good life. *Journal of Personality and Social Psychology, 40,* 414–431.

Kluegel, J., & Smith, E. (1986). *Beliefs about inequality: Americans' views of what is and what ought to be.* New York: Aldine de Gruyter.

Kohlberg, L. (1984). *Essays in moral development: The psychology of moral development* (Vol. 2.). New York: Harper & Row.

Kuhlman, D. M., & Marshello, A. F. J. (1975). Individual differences in game motivation as moderators of preprogrammed strategy effects in prisoner's dilemma. *Journal of Personality and Social Psychology, 32,* 922–931.

Lakatos, I. (1970). Falsification and the methodology of scientific research programmes. In I. Lakatos and A. Musgrave (Eds.), *Criticism and the growth of knowledge.* Cambridge: Cambridge University Press.

Lane, R. E. (1959). The fear of equality. *American Political Science Review, 53,* 35–51.

(1983). Market thinking, political thinking. In A. Ellis and K. Kummar (Eds.), *Dilemmas of liberal democracies*. London: Tavistock.

(1986). Market justice, political justice. *American Political Science Review, 80,* 383–402.

Langer, E. J. (1975). The illusion of control. *Journal of Personality and Social Psychology, 32,* 311–328.

Lerner, M. J. (1980). *The belief in a just world*. New York: Plenum.

Lerner, M. J., Miller, D. T., & Holmes, J. (1976). Deserving and the emergence of forms of justice. *Advances in Experimental Psychology, 9,* 133–162.

Lipsett, S., & Raab, E. (1978). *The politics of unreason*. Stanford, CA: Stanford University Press.

March, J. G., & Olsen, J. (1989). *Rediscovering institutions*. New York: Free Press.

McClintock, C. G. (1972). Social motivations – a set of propositions. *Behavioral Science, 17,* 438–454.

McClosky, H., & Brill, A. (1983). *Dimensions of tolerance*. Beverly Hills, CA: Sage.

McConahay, J. B. (1986). Modern racism, ambivalence, and the modern racism scale. In J. Dovidio and S. L. Gaertner (Eds.), *Prejudice, discrimination, and racism: Theory and research*. New York: Academic Press.

Meehl, P. E. (1978). Theoretical risks and tabular asterisks: Sir Karl, Sir Ronald, and the slow progress of soft psychology. *Journal of Consulting and Clinical Psychology, 46,* 806–834.

Merton, R. K. (1968). *Social theory and social structure*. New York: Free Press.

Messick, D. M., & McClintock, C. G. (1968). Motivational bases of choice in experimental games. *Journal of Experimental Social Psychology, 21,* 480–500.

Mischel, W. T. (1974). Delay of need gratification. *Advances in Experimental Social Psychology, 7,* 249–292.

Mitchell, G., Tetlock, P. E., & Mellers, B. A. (1991). Judgments of social justice: Compromises between equality and efficiency. Unpublished manuscript, University of California, Berkeley.

Murray, C. (1984). *Losing ground: American social policy 1950–1980*. New York: Basic Books.

Nisbett, R. E., & Ross, L. (1980). *Human inference: Strategies and shortcomings of social judgment*. Englewood Cliffs, NJ: Prentice-Hall.

Nozick, R. (1974). *Anarchy, state, and utopia*. New York: Basic Books.

Pettigrew, T. F. (1979). The ultimate attribution error: Extending Allport's cognitive analysis of prejudice. *Personality and Social Psychology Bulletin, 5,* 461–476.

Prentice, D. A., & Crosby, F. (1987). The importance of context for assessing deservingness. In J. C. Masters & W. P. Smith (Eds.), *Social comparison, social justice, and relative deprivation*. Hillsdale, NJ: Erlbaum.

Rawls, J. (1971). *A theory of justice*. Cambridge, MA: Belknap.

Rokeach, M. (1973). *The nature of human values*. New York: Free Press.

Ross, L. (1977). The intuitive psychologist and his shortcomings: Distortions in the attribution process. *Advances in Experimental Social Psychology, 10,* 174–220.

Rossi, P., & Nock, S. (1982). *Measuring social judgments: The factorial survey approach*. Beverly Hills, CA: Sage.

Rubin, Z., & Peplau, L. (1975). Who believes in a just world? *Journal of Social Issues, 31,* 65–89.

Ryan, W. (1972). *Blaming the victim.* New York: Vintage.

Schlesinger, A. M. (1986). *The cycles of American history.* Boston: Houghton Mifflin.

Schwinger, T. (1980). Just allocations of goods: Decisions among three principles. In G. Mikula (Ed.), *Justice and social interaction.* Bern: Hans Huber.

Scitovsky, T. (1986). *Human desire and economic satisfaction: Essays on the frontiers of economics.* New York: New York University Press.

Sears, D. O., & Kinder, D. R. (1985). Whites' opposition to busing: On conceptualizing and operationalizing group conflict. *Journal of Personality and Social Psychology, 48,* 1141–1147.

Seligman, M. (1990). *Learned optimism.* New York: Knopf.

Shaver, K. G. (1970). Defensive attribution: Effects of severity and relevance on the responsibility assigned for an accident. *Journal of Personality and Social Psychology, 14,* 101–113.

Skitka, L., & Tetlock, P. E. (1992). Allocating aid: The roles of scarcity, ideology, causal attributions, and distributive norms. *Journal of Experimental Social Psychology, 29,* 397–409.

Sniderman, P. M., & Tetlock, P. E. (1986a). Reflections on American racism. *Journal of Social Issues, 42,* 173–188.

(1986b). Symbolic racism: Problems of motive attribution in political analysis. *Journal of Social Issues, 42,* 129–150.

Sniderman, P. M., Brody, R., & Tetlock, P. E. (1991). *Reasoning and choice: Explorations in political psychology.* Cambridge: Cambridge University Press.

Sniderman, P. M., Piazza, T., Tetlock, P. E., & Kendrick, A. (1991). Racism and the American ethos. *American Journal of Political Science, 35,* 423–447.

Sniderman, P., Tetlock, P. E., Gleser, J., Green, D., & Hout, M. (1988). Principled tolerance and mass belief systems. *British Journal of Political Science, 18,* 343–362.

Sorrentino, R. M., & Higgins, E. T. (Eds.) (1986). *Handbook of motivation and cognition: Foundations of social behavior.* New York: Guilford.

Spranca, M., Minsk, E., & Baron, J. (1991). Omissions and commissions in judgment and choice. *Journal of Experimental and Social Psychology, 27,* 76–105.

Stone, W. F., & Schaffner, P. E. (1988). *The psychology of politics.* New York: Springer-Verlag.

Suedfeld, P., & Tetlock, P. E. (1991). Psychologists as policy advocates: The roots of controversy. In P. Suedfeld & P. E. Tetlock (Eds.) *Psychology and social advocacy.* Washington, DC: Hemisphere Press.

Suppe, F. (1977). *The structure of scientific theories.* Chicago: University of Chicago Press.

Tajfel, H. (1982). Social psychology of intergroup relations. *Annual Review of Psychology, 33,* 1–39.

Taylor, S. (1990). *Positive illusions.* New York: Basic Books.

Taylor, S., & Fiske, S. (1979). Salience, attention, and attribution: Top of the head phenomena. *Advances in Experimental Social Psychology, 11,* 249–288.

Tetlock, P. E. (1984). Cognitive style and political belief systems in the British House of Commons. *Journal of Personality and Social Psychology: Personality Processes and Individual Differences, 46,* 365–375.

(1986). A value pluralism model of ideological reasoning. *Journal of Personality and Social Psychology, 50,* 865–875.

(1989). Structure and function in political belief systems. In A. R. Pratkanis, S. J. Breckler, & A. G. Greenwald (Eds.), *Attitude, structure, and function*. Hillsdale, NJ: Erlbaum.

Tetlock, P. E., & Levi, A. (1982). Attribution bias: On the inconclusiveness of the cognition–motivation debate. *Journal of Experimental Social Psychology, 18,* 68–88.

Thompson, M., Ellis, R., & Wildavsky, A. B. (1990). *Cultural theory.* Boulder, CO: Westview Press.

Tompkins, S. (1962). *Affect, imagery, consciousness* (Vol. 1): *The positive affects.* New York: Springer.

(1963). *Affect, imagery, consciousness* (Vol. 2): *The negative affects.* New York: Springer.

Tourangeau, R., Rasinski, K. A., Bradburn, N., & D'Andrade, R. (1989). Belief accessibility and context effects in attitude measurement. *Journal of Experimental Psychology, 25,* 401–421.

Tyler, T. R. (1984). The role of perceived injustice in defendant's evaluations of their courtroom experience. *Law and Society Review, 18,* 51–74.

(1990). *Why people obey the law: Procedural justice, legitimacy, and compliance.* New Haven, CT: Yale University Press.

Tyler, T. R., & Caine, A. (1981). The role of distributional and procedural fairness in the endorsement of formal leaders. *Journal of Personality and Social Psychology, 41,* 642–655.

Tyler, T. R., Rasinski, K., & McGraw, K. (1985). The influence of perceived injustice on support for political authorities. *Journal of Applied Social Psychology, 15,* 700–725.

Walzer, M. (1983). *Spheres of justice.* New York: Basic Books.

Weiner, B. (1980). A cognitive (attribution)-emotion-action model of motivated behavior: An analysis of judgments of helpgiving. *Journal of Personality and Social Psychology, 39,* 186–200.

Wiseman, M. (1986). Obligation and welfare. *Policy Sciences, 21,* 97–107.

### Notes

1 Douglas and Wildavsky's (1982) cultural theory of political ideology leads us to expect psychological research on justice to become sharply politicized. This theory distinguishes four cultural world views that provide sharply discrepant answers to basic questions about human nature, the natural world, and the appropriate goals of social institutions. These answers, moreover, serve primarily to justify culturally prescribed ways of living: "Advocates of each way of life seek to develop views of human nature compatible with their preferred pattern of social relations" (Thompson, Ellis, & Wildavsky, 1990, p. 12). Individualists who uphold the invisible hand of free markets view people as unalterably self-centered. Only competitive markets can constructively channel this selfishness to promote the general good. Egalitarians who advocate aggressive government measures to redistribute wealth view people as fundamentally decent, but corrupted and perverted by repressive institutions, hence the need for radical transformation of those institutions. Hierarchists who favor an active societal role in perfecting human nature maintain that people are born bad (cognitively shortsighted, greedy, lustful, impulsive, lazy, etc.) but can be improved by creating institutions for monitoring and controlling social conduct (churches, courts, vanguard parties). Fatalists who are deeply skeptical of social engineering schemes of any sort view human beings as diverse and unpredictable.

If Douglas and Wildavsky (1982) are right, there will be a powerful temptation for psychologists to apply different standards of evidence and proof to findings that challenge rather than reaffirm their preferred cultural form of life. Insofar as psychologists are disproportionately egalitarian (distrustful of capitalism) and hierarchist (believe that they know how to design institutions that will "improve" how people think and act), cultural theory suggests that a biased, even self-serving, view of human nature will emerge from their research.

2 Although we emphasize how starting assumptions can guide inquiry, we do not support extreme subjectivists who view scientific inquiry as just another cultural way of knowing. Some approaches to generating knowledge are manifestly superior to others. Heart transplants would never have been possible in a voodoo medical culture; genetic engineering, never possible in Lysenkoist biology; space travel, never possible in Aristotelian physics. Our quarrel is not with the scientific method or its extraordinary accomplishments; it is with biased, sometimes self-serving, applications of the method in behavioral and social science work on justice.

3 We seriously oversimplify the complexity of possible political positions by positing a liberal–conservative dichotomy in which (1) liberalism denotes support for state regulation of the economy (to protect the environment, consumers, victims of discrimination, workers, tenants, and more) and an active government role in redistributing income (through a combination of progressive taxation and social welfare programs); (2) conservatism denotes support for the principles of free-market economics (a reluctance to support government regulation) and a willingness to accept the social inequalities that arise from the operation of those principles (a reluctance to tax and to transfer wealth from one group to another). By these definitions, liberalism is moderate egalitarianism and conservatism is moderate individualism. A more nuanced and differentiated classification system would allow (1) continuous variation between liberal and conservative approaches to distributive justice; (2) identification of internal disagreements within the liberal and conservative camps. Such classification systems do exist. We could classify political viewpoints on the two continuous, roughly orthogonal, dimensions of personal liberty (subsuming such diverse issues as economic freedom, religious freedom, and sexual freedom) and social equality (subsuming such diverse issues as taxation, welfare spending, and affirmative action). Political advocates who value both liberty and equality might be labeled liberals or social democrats (egalitarians constrained by concern for liberty); advocates who value equality but not liberty might be labeled doctrinaire socialists; advocates who value liberty but not equality might be labeled libertarian conservatives; advocates who value neither liberty nor equality might be labeled authoritarian conservatives (cf. Rokeach, 1973; Tetlock, 1984, 1986). This classification system would allow us to identify different, perhaps qualitatively different, types of liberals and conservatives (e.g., radical egalitarians who are prepared to pursue equality no matter what the cost in liberty versus moderate egalitarians who seek integratively complex compromise solutions; libertarian conservatives who oppose all restrictions on the choices of mutually consenting adults and authoritarian conservatives who oppose most restrictions on markets but support state regulation of sexual or religious practices).

For ease of exposition, we rely in this chapter on the simpler dichotomous classification scheme (the difference between an 8-cell versus a 16-cell contingency table). We do believe, however, it will prove fruitful to look for distinctive psychological markers of moderate versus extreme egalitarianism and authoritarian versus libertarian conservatism.

# Part V

# Policy perspectives

# 12 Justice and the allocation of scarce resources

*Jon Elster*

*Local justice* can be defined as the allocation by institutions of scarce goods and necessary burdens.[1] In this chapter I discuss allocative practices in three arenas: the selection of patients for transplantation, the admission to selective institutions of higher education, and the selection of workers to be laid off when a firm decides to reduce its work force. Occasionally, I shall also refer to some other issues.[2] The issue I consider in most detail is the allocation of organs, more specifically of kidneys. My concern is descriptive and explanatory, not prescriptive. The aim is not to evaluate allocative mechanisms from a particular normative point of view, but to identify the principles and procedures used to allocate scarce goods and necessary burdens, and to explain, in each case, why a certain principle is used. Normative considerations enter only to the extent that they have explanatory force. The process that results in the selection of an allocative principle involves a number of actors, within the allocative institution and outside it. Often, they appeal to normative premises when arguing for some allocative principle. Sometimes, these arguments are more or less thinly disguised rationalizations of self-interest, but often they spring from deeply held conceptions of what is a fair or equitable allocation. Although this explanatory use of normative principles will be the main focus of the essay, I shall occasionally step back and offer a few normative comments on my own account.

Different arenas use different principles for allocating scarce goods. *Need* is central in allocating organs for transplantation, *merit* in admitting students to college, and *seniority* in selecting workers for layoffs. In one sense of *local*, therefore, the word refers to the fact that different institutional sectors use different substantive principles of allocation. In another sense,

The work reported in this chapter has been supported by the Russell Sage Foundation. I am indebted to Patricia Conley, J. Michael Dennis, and Stuart Romm for invaluable research assistance and to Barbara Mellers and Jonathan Baron for their comments on a draft.

it refers to the fact that different countries use different principles to allocate the same good. In Germany, need is an important factor in deciding which workers to lay off. In Holland, admission to medical school is done by a weighted lottery, with high school grades being used as the weights (Hofstee, 1983). Finally, there is considerable variation within a given arena in a given country. In the United States, collective bargaining agreements differ widely in the relative importance they assign to seniority and ability as criteria for retaining workers in layoff situations (Romm, 1990). As I shall explain later, regional organ banks adopt different schemes for allocating kidneys to patients.

When I talk about local justice, there is an implicit contrast with global or societywide justice. Roughly speaking, globally redistributive policies are characterized by three closely related features. First, they are designed centrally, at the level of the national government. Second, they are intended to compensate people for various sorts of bad luck, resulting from the possession of "morally arbitrary properties." Third, they typically take the form of cash transfers. Principles of local justice differ on all three counts. They are designed by relatively autonomous institutions, which may be constrained by guidelines laid down by the center, but usually have some autonomy to design and implement their preferred scheme. Also, they are not compensatory, or only partially so. A scheme for allocating scarce medical resources may compensate patients for bad medical luck, but not for other kinds of bad luck. Finally, local justice concerns allocation in kind of goods (and burdens), not of money.

My interest in issues of local justice stems from three sources. First, I find the infinite variety and diversity of institutional practices intrinsically absorbing and fascinating. Second, I believe that these choices provide a privileged source of information about prevailing social norms and values, superior in many respects to surveys and interviews. Finally, I believe that some of the findings may be useful to decision makers, both by extending their repertoire of possible allocating mechanisms and by improving their understanding of their own practices.

In the remainder of this essay I consider three issues that arise in several allocative contexts, using transplantation as the main but not the only example to illustrate how they look in practice. The issues are equity versus efficiency; discrimination; and incentive effects. I conclude with some comments on explanatory matters.

### Equity versus efficiency

This issue arises in virtually all allocative contexts. I should give notice that I am not using *equity* in a very precise sense, only as a catch-all term for a number of nonefficiency-oriented considerations. In the layoff context, seniority may be seen as an embodiment of equity: The workers who have worked longer in the firm deserve to retain their jobs. Considerations of efficiency (or profit), on the other hand, suggest that the more skilled workers be retained. In collective bargaining agreements, these two criteria are combined in one of two ways. Sometimes, ability is the main criterion and seniority is used only to break ties. In other agreements, seniority is the main criterion, with a minimal ability serving as a constraint.

In the context of university admission, efficiency is usually understood in terms of expected academic performance, although other interpretations are also possible. If equity is seen as requiring a fair chance of admission for all, the Dutch system of admission of medical school represents a typical compromise. Equity can also be seen, however, as involving compensation for bad luck. At some state colleges, for instance, applicants are given extra points if they come from a low-income family or if neither parent has attended college. These points can compensate for lower grades, although it is hard to get information about the exact trade-off.[3]

In organ transplantations the equity–efficiency conflict can take a number of forms. I shall discuss two issues, one involving kidneys and the other hearts and livers.

In the United States, kidneys are currently allocated by a point system. The allocation of kidneys, i.e., the matching of an available kidney by matching with a patient on the waiting list, is made under a number of medical constraints. First, the donor and the recipient must be of compatible blood types.[4] Second, the recipient must not have cytotoxic antibody formation against the donor kidney. This constraint can be severe, as some candidates for transplants have antibody formation against most kidneys in the population at large. These patients are referred to as "sensitized." Third, the recipient should be well matched to the donor, in the sense of having as many as possible of six antigens in common. Unlike the first two constraints, this is not an absolute one, but is a determinant of the probability of success.[5] Last, donor and recipient should not be too far from the transplantation center, as organs deteriorate rapidly with time. This constraint is negligible, however, and will be ignored in the following.

Currently, the allocation of kidneys is regulated by the United Network for Organ Sharing (UNOS).[6] It is based on a scheme for allocating points to potential recipients of a donated kidney and then selecting the patient with the largest number of points. I shall describe only the parts of the scheme that are relevant for my concerns here.

First, patients receive points (from 0 to 1) for their time on the waiting list. This part of the scheme reflects the idea that all should have a chance of getting transplanted.

Second, they receive points (from 0 to 10) corresponding to the number of antigen matches (or, rather, of nonobserved mismatches). This part of the scheme embodies efficiency considerations, as the probability of graft survival varies positively with the number of antigen matches.

Third, they receive 4 points for high "panel reactive antibody formation." As explained earlier, many patients have preformed antibodies that make them strictly unsuitable as recipients for particular kidneys. By medical necessity, antibody formation retains its exclusionary function in matching individual recipients with individual kidneys. In addition, however, the point allocation just described ensures that a low chance of ever finding a suitable kidney can offset low antigen matching when a suitable kidney is finally found. By giving extra weight to the patients who have the bad luck of being incompatible with most donated kidneys, it embodies considerations of equity. The same patients also tend to accumulate points from being on the waiting list. As they usually get some points from antigen matching as well,[7] their selection is virtually ensured *if* a suitable kidney becomes available. (Note, however, that the more points they get from antibody formation, the bigger the if.)

This system, introduced in 1989, replaced one in which patients received up to 12 points for matching, up to 10 points for time on the waiting list, and up to 10 points for preformed antibody formation (depending on the percentage of kidneys in the overall population with which their antibodies make them incompatible). The import of the changes is described as follows: "The initial UNOS point system emphasized queuing whereas the proposed modifications stress good [antigen] matching ordered by queuing" (United Network for Organ Sharing, 1989, p. 31). A better summary might be to say that whereas the early system involved trade-offs between matching and waiting, the new system uses time on the waiting list as a tie-breaker.[8] Because ties are frequent, time on the list retains considerable importance.

The system – old or new – provides insurance against two forms of bad medical luck. One, just mentioned, is that of having a high panel antibody formation. This handicap is offset both by the waiting list and by explicitly awarding points for the antibodies. The other is that of having an unusual antigen pattern that makes it unlikely that one will ever achieve a good antigen match. If efficiency – that is, number of antigen matches – was all that counted, patients with such patterns would stand a low chance. Adding points for time on the waiting list partially offsets that handicap. This compensation mechanism is especially important for black patients. For cultural and genetic reasons, blacks are overrepresented in the population of patients. For cultural reasons, blacks are underrepresented in the population of donors. Also, their antigen patterns are markedly different from those of the white population. Any scheme in which number of antigen matches is the major determinant of selection would therefore work against them. I return to this question subsequently.

The allocation of kidneys is not a life-and-death issue, at least not in the United States where dialysis is universally available as a fallback solution.[9] For hearts and livers, however, there are no real substitutes. In these cases, other conflicts arise. On the one hand, efficiency dictates that the organs should be given to those whose bodies are least likely to reject the graft. On the other hand, doctors are often moved by two norms that I shall refer

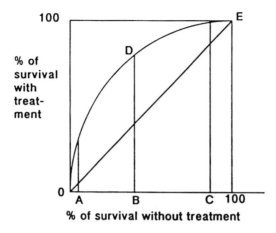

Figure 1    Allocating scarce life-saving medical resources: the dichotomous case.

to as the *norm of compassion* and the *norm of thoroughness,* and which suggest
priorities at odds with efficiency.

The norm of compassion is especially poignant in life-threatening illness. It tells doctors that when not all who need treatment can get it, they
should treat the most serious or critical cases first, leaving for later treatment patients who can be expected to survive for a while. This norm is
opposed to more instrumental considerations, which would suggest that
one give priority to the patients who can benefit most from treatment.

In other cases of this kind, these two criteria coincide. The worst off are
also those who can benefit most from the good. Poor people can benefit
more from a given sum of money than rich people, because of the decreasing marginal utility of money. In the allocation of life-saving medical resources, there seems, however, to be a systematic tension between the two
criteria, as suggested by the above diagram. This diagram presupposes
that treatment is a dichotomous variable. Later, I shall discuss the case of
treatment of variable extent and degree.

This conflict is quite important in heart and liver transplantation. Urgency of need is a major criterion in selecting patients for liver transplantation. It also has the perverse effect, however, of reducing the number of
lives that are saved. At any given time, there are some patients whose need
for a liver transplant has been diagnosed, and who could benefit optimally
from it were they to get a transplant at that time. They may eventually get
one, but not until their need has become so urgent that they are less likely
to benefit from it. In such cases, the norm of compassion – treating the
most acute cases first – tells the doctor to give priority to patients around
A in Figure 1. Instrumental concerns usually dictate that patients around B
be given priority. These are the individuals whose probability of survival
is raised most by treatment.

There is a further consideration that might shape the selection of patients along the continuum from A to C. The medical staff might tend to select patients from the area to the right of B, to avoid too many failures. It is demoralizing to see over and over again that treatment fails to keep the patient alive. To some extent, this concern may be justified. It is more problematic, however, if it leads to heavy selection of patients around C, for the sake of doctors and other staff having a quiet life. One study found evidence that in the mental health profession, "large numbers of highly trained provider groups are being well paid mostly to talk about personal matters to people with mild emotional problems" (Knesper, Pagnucco, & Wheeler, 1985, p. 1367). Although such behavior may be rational from the point of view of doctors, it is not socially desirable. I am suggesting, in other words, that professional ethics move doctors in one direction away from the most efficient selection, and their personal interest in a quiet life in the opposite direction.

We may speculate about the origins of the norm of compassion. In addition to spontaneous empathy, I believe some cognitive factors could be involved. For patients around A, there is a "clear and present danger" that has a special salience, compared to the more uncertain and conjectural risks of patients further down the continuum. Cognitive psychologists talk about a "certainty effect" that can distort judgment (Kahneman & Tversky, 1979). Also there may be some framing effects (Tversky & Kahneman, 1981). Instead of comparing the fates of different individuals if treated, doctors compare their fates if left untreated. A similar framing effect can occur in public policy, if funds are allocated to social issues as a function of how important the problems are, not of how effective the funds would be in solving them. Some educational programs for disadvantaged groups fall in this category.

Consider now the norm of thoroughness. Efficiency dictates that when allocating scarce resources, whether as inputs for production or as goods for consumption, one should equalize the marginal productivity or the marginal utility of all units. The point may be illustrated by a simple case of consumption. Even if we disregard nutritional constraints, it would be strange to spend all one's income on milk and bread, and nothing on meat and vegetables. Because consumer goods have decreasing marginal utility, the utility derived from the last unit of bread and milk will certainly be smaller than the utility derived from the first unit of bread and vegetables. A rational consumer would, therefore, spread his income more thinly over a large number of goods, rather than concentrate it on just a few.

We can apply similar reasoning to the behavior of doctors. With respect to any given patient, the doctor's time has decreasing marginal productivity, at least beyond a certain point. The functional relationship is probably S-shaped. This implies that if the doctor makes a very thorough examination of the patient, his behavior is not instrumentally efficient with respect to the objective of saving lives or improving overall health. Other patients might benefit much more from the time he spends on the last and most esoteric tests. Nevertheless doctors seem to follow a norm of thoroughness, which tells them that once a patient has been admitted, that patient should get "the full treatment." It is as if a consumer, once he has decided to make milk a part of his daily consumption, should decide to drink milk up to the point where the marginal utility of milk becomes zero.

In Norway, a recent parliamentary commission found that eye specialists tend to admit too few patients and treat each of them very thoroughly. When I confronted my own eye doctor with this claim, she refuted it by telling me about a case in which she had been able to diagnose a rare eye disease only after exhaustive examination, thereby saving her patient's sight. I did not remind her of the cases that go undetected because the patient never gets to see a doctor at all.

In transplantation, the norm of thoroughness seems to affect behavior in two kinds of situations. First, there are cases of multiple transplants. Recently, one patient in Pittsburgh received as many as five different organs, which in theory could have been used to save the lives of four other people, kidneys not being vital for survival. Second and more important, there is the issue of retransplantation. Success rates tend to be lower for retransplantations than for primary transplantations. The difference is not just due to a sampling effect, in the sense that the patients who need a second transplant had smaller chances of success in the first place. There also seems to be a genuine aftereffect, in the sense that the rejection in itself reduces the chances. Instead of being given to a patient who has already received one transplant, scarce organs could be given to others who stand a better chance of success (Matthieu, 1988, pp. 44–45).

Again we may speculate about the origins of the norm of thoroughness. In the American context, fear of litigation may be at work. But I believe that the norm is too old and too widespread for this to be the whole explanation. To some extent, I'm sure, the sunk-cost fallacy may be responsible. Here as elsewhere, it is hard to cut one's losses, even if it may be the rational thing to do. The most important factor may be that doctors get to know their patients and feel responsible for them. The nonpatients, by definition, have no face. Here as elsewhere, helping identifiable persons takes precedence over helping anonymous individuals.

In a broader perspective, however, these norms might not conflict with efficiency. Although the norms of compassion and thoroughness are not in themselves socially optimal, it is at least conceivable that they are part of a socially optimal package solution. The perfectionist norms might have good side effects that offset whatever inefficiency they might appear to have when seen in isolation. It might be impossible to sustain the dedication and motivation of doctors if they were constantly called upon to make comparisons and cost–benefit calculations. An analogy might be the side effects of the somewhat pointless perfectionism of the postal services in some countries, especially in the past. By imposing the principle of next-

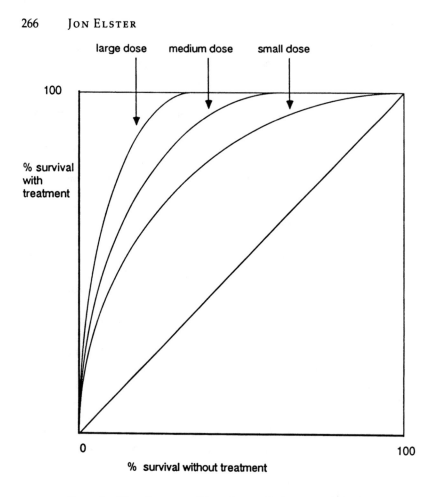

large dose     medium dose     small dose

100

% survival
with
treatment

0

100

% survival without treatment

Figure 2    Allocating scarce life-saving medical resources: the continuous case.

day delivery for all letters, no matter how remote the destination, costs were incurred that would also appear excessive if seen in isolation. Yet the unbreakable principle, together with the heroic tales spun around its strict implementation, may have contributed to an occupational pride and motivation that led to better service than any commercial system could ever offer at the same cost.

In many cases, both the norm of efficiency and the norm of thoroughness may be at work. Their interaction can then be represented in Figure 2.

If there are several patients who need a scarce, life-saving drug, and the effect on their prospects is as indicated in Figure 2, doctors are faced with two choices. They can give either large doses to a few patients or smaller doses to many. And they can give priority either to the more or to the less critically ill patients. If both the norm of compassion and the norm of thoroughness operate, only very ill patients will receive the drug and few of them will benefit. Considerations of instrumental efficiency would dictate that the drug be spread thinly over the moderately ill patients. If either the norm of compassion or the norm of thoroughness operates in the absence of the other, still different allocations would be observed.

### Discrimination

The next set of issues I want to discuss concern discrimination on the basis of gender, ethnicity, and similar grounds. I shall not discuss overt negative discrimination of the classical kind, as when Harvard in the 1920s had quotas for Jews, but focus on various forms of positive discrimination. Again I begin with some nontransplantation examples.

All firms are subject to federal legislation, notably Title VII of the Civil Rights Act of 1964, which offers protection for women and ethnic minorities and the Age Discrimination in Employment Act. Title VII explicitly says that bona fide seniority agreements are not affected by the Act, even if they happen to work against a protected group. If a bona fide seniority system (1) is used for promotion rather than for layoffs and (2) is calculated on a departmental rather than a plantwide basis, courts have nevertheless set aside seniority-based agreements. One early case involved a departmental seniority system that perpetuated the effects of a previously segregated work force by giving blacks little opportunity to be promoted out of their less desirable jobs.[10] The Fifth Circuit ruled that this constituted a violation.[11] In layoff cases, however, one has to prove disparate intent, and not simply disparate impact. Although it is difficult to prove actual intent, courts have found that a seniority system is not bona fide when the arrangement of seniority units is irrational and not in conformance with industry practice, its only possible purpose being its adverse effect on a protected group.[12] When there are two seniority progressions with blacks segregated into one and whites into the other, courts are likely to find that these systems are not bona fide.[13] When female or minority employees are not granted the same seniority benefits as white males of equal seniority, it will be found that the system is differentially applied and not bona fide.[14]

Affirmative action in the universities can take several forms. The Bakke decision states that strict quotas are unacceptable, but that "preferences" are admissible.[15] I wonder whether this is not a distinction without a difference. In one large state university system, for instance, the desire to admit more underrepresented minorities has taken a number of forms. At one of the most prominent institutions in the system, until recently, all eligible minority applicants (i.e., those who finished in a certain percentile of their high school class) were accepted. The admission office is now changing to a system using "flexible targets" for minority admissions. At another institution in the system, a different scheme is used. Here, applicants get points for minority membership, with the points being deliberately chosen so as to ensure a desired final distribution. None of these practices, as far as I can understand, is really compatible with the idea of the Bakke court that each applicant should compete with all others for a given place.

Note, however, that the targeted ethnic distribution could also be realized by increasing the number of points given for low-income and low-education background, given the high correlation between these variables and ethnicity. More generally, it is often possible to use racially neutral criteria to achieve a certain nonneutral pattern of admission. In the 1920s, Yale College did not want to fall into the Harvard trap and use quotas to reduce the number of Jews. Instead they opted for a criterion of geographical diversity, which had the effect of reducing the number of students from New York City who were admitted. These were, of course, predominantly Jews (Oren, 1985, p. 198).

There have been no proposals to establish kidney quotas for ethnic minorities or women, although these categories are underrepresented in the population of kidney transplant recipients. In the case of women, the underrepresentation is partly due to self-selection (that is, women choose not to go on the waiting list for transplantation), and partly due to higher degrees of sensitization among women. The underrepresentation of blacks is quantitatively more striking, and demands a fuller explanation in terms of the following three facts.

First, blacks are highly overrepresented in the population of patients with end-stage renal disease, partly for cultural and partly for genetic reasons. Hypertension, a main cause of renal disease, is much more frequent in the black population, a fact that may be due to "psychosocial stress caused by darker skin color" in lower socioeconomic groups (Klag et al., 1991).[16]

Second, blacks are underrepresented among organ donors.[17] The low rate of donation is mainly due to the reluctance of relatives to give their permission to recover an organ that could be used for transplantation. The reluctance has several causes, one of them being a belief that the organs are mainly going to white patients (as of course has to be the case, given that blacks form a small proportion of the population as a whole).

Third, blacks (as well as other minority groups) have antigen patterns unlike whites' patterns.[18] In an allocation system in which antigen matching plays a major role, this fact, in conjunction with the two others, is certain to ensure that blacks will get fewer transplantations. This is especially so under the new point system. Under the old system, blacks could hope that if they waited long enough, they would eventually accumulate enough points to offset their lower matching score. Under the new UNOS point system, waiting time mainly serves to break ties in matching. Because of the facts cited above, however, blacks are unlikely to achieve parity of matching.

For this reason, doctors in areas with a heavy proportion of black patients have acted as a pressure group to change the point system. Last year, for instance, one regional organ bank decided, in a 4 to 3 vote, to increase the number of points allocated for time on the waiting list, in the expectation that more blacks would be transplanted. Since the change would also benefit other groups with unusual antigen patterns, it could well be defended on neutral grounds of fairness and equity. The actual argument and intent, however, were not neutral.

The reluctance of blacks to donate a kidney because it is more likely to go to a white person violates a principle one may call ethical individualism. The principle asserts that in evaluating states of affairs with respect to justice or fairness, one has to use information about individuals. Thus one would not be justified in preferring one state over another simply on the grounds that the average incomes of men and women are more equal in the former. Similarly, the idea that a white recipient does not deserve a kidney because of the harm that whites inflict on blacks is flawed because it makes each white person responsible for the behavior of the whole group to which he or she belongs. The converse fallacy is sometimes encountered in conversation. Among some groups in the transplantation community, there is a reluctance to change the point system so as to increase the prospects of black patients. Since blacks are not willing to donate kidneys, they cannot expect special treatment as recipients. This argument, too, unfairly treats each black patient as if he or she were responsible for the behavior of the whole group. In other words, the fallacy takes the form of making each black person responsible for the fact that many members of the black community commit the same fallacy.

Although one should not make the allocation of organs to members of a group conditional on the average willingness of that group to donate organs, the objection does not apply if a link of this kind is established at the level of the individual. In the French system for allocating sperm for artificial insemination, women who bring a donor along move six months up in the queue (Herpin, 1990). Under Singapore law, "those who object to serving as posthumous kidney providers are given second-priority access to the cadaver kidney pool in the event of need; that is, only if an available kidney is not able to be used by a needy nonobjector (i.e., a presumed consenter), will it be offered to a needy objector" (Peters, 1989, pp. 177–178). In countries that do not have the principle of presumed consent, the converse scheme could be used: To prefer as recipients for organ transplantations those who have indicated their willingness to donate organs (a proposal made in Kamm, 1989).

## Incentive effects

These examples can serve as a transition to the third set of issues I want to consider, that of incentive effects. Allocative principles can induce behavior that affects the supply and the demand for the scarce good that is being allocated. In addition, they may induce behavior that affects the eligibility of individuals for the good.

The main way in which incentive effects shape the demand for scarce goods is through *moral hazard*, a phenomenon that arises when an individual's knowledge that he will receive compensation or treatment in the case of an accident or other unforeseen event influences behavior so as to make that event more likely to occur. Fire insurance, for instance, makes fires more likely because the knowledge that they will be compensated makes house owners behave more recklessly. A plausible instance in local justice contexts is seniority.[19] If layoffs are made strictly by seniority, or with only minimal qualification requirements, workers may be less diligent in acquiring skills than if they know that firms will use ability as the main criterion.[20] Furthermore, if less qualified senior employees are retained in a layoff, then the profits of the firm may be negatively affected, thus creating a need for more workers to be laid off than would otherwise have been the case. Against this we must cite the fact that the use of seniority creates an incentive for workers to stay in the firm, thus reducing turnover and increasing productivity. This is a general feature of many reward schemes: They may have good as well as bad incentive effects, with the net effect often being uncertain.

Moral hazard in the provision of medical goods is more controversial. Many argue as if the welfare state were like a circus. Acrobats fall more frequently when they have a safety net; similarly, the knowledge that medical goods and services will be available if needed may reduce the incentive for precautionary behavior. Conversely, one might try to reduce the demand for the scarce good by choosing a principle of allocation that deters people from engaging in behavior that increases the likelihood of one day coming to need it. Specifically, smokers might get low priority in the heart transplantation queue, heavy drinkers in the queue for liver transplants, and drug abusers in the queue for kidney transplantation. Some might argue for this proposal on grounds of desert, effectively telling the patients in question that having made their bed, they must lie in it. This is not the line of argument I want to pursue here. Instead, I shall concentrate on the incentive effect arguments for the proposal, to the effect that "an assignment of responsibility to the individual for self-caused illness may have a useful deterrent effect" (Wikler, 1987, p. 338).

It is an interesting and important fact that arguments from moral hazard and incentive effects are virtually never used in the health sector. Virtually no allocative principles in this area are based on the idea of deterrence. If drug abusers or alcoholics have low priority for transplantation, it is because they cannot be expected to comply with the strict posttransplantation regime. In Norway, people who have had one heart transplantation and need a second one because they cannot give up smoking are treated as low-priority patients. The reason behind the practice, however, is not deterrence, but simply the desire to avoid wasting organs on those who cannot be expected to benefit from them. I cannot exclude that there are elements of desert-based reasoning behind such decisions, but I am fairly confident that incentive-effect reasoning plays no part in them.

I'd like to offer some speculations about the absence of incentive reasoning in the health sector. Earlier, I used the analogy of a circus acrobat to suggest that security may increase the probability of an accident occurring. For some acrobats, though, the fear of falling when there is no net might be psychologically destabilizing and make them fall more easily. The strong desire not to fall causes their hands to shake and makes them more likely to fall. This is not an incentive effect, but the result of a nonintentional causal mechanism.[21] Unconditional access to free medical treatment could have a similar effect. While possibly leading people to behave more recklessly than if they knew they had to pay for self-induced illness, it also reduces worry and stress with their concomitant medical problems.

More important, the incentives may be too weak, in the sense that rational individuals would not be swayed by them. Assume that I knew that I would not be treated for cancer of the pancreas if the cause could be shown to be excessive intakes of coffee. Nevertheless, the chances of getting the illness *and* being successfully treated for it are so small, and the importance of coffee in my life so large, that I would be willing (rationally, I believe) to take the risk. Furthermore, even strong incentives may not reach individuals who are subject to myopia, weakness of will, self-deception, and other irrational propensities. An incentive system is then little more than a scheme for punishing imprudent behavior, with the punishment in some cases amounting to a death penalty for a very minor offense. In addition to being inhumane, the practice would be unjust, since the ability to be swayed by incentives is not randomly distributed among socioeconomic groups. Impulse control is a complicated matter (Ainslie, 1992). It can require great material and social resources, as well as considerable stability in the environment. Those who are deprived of these resources may not be swayed by schemes that rely on their ability to defer gratification and to believe things they don't want to believe.

I now turn now to incentive effects on the supply side. Before an organ can become available for transplantation, a number of actions must be taken. A neurosurgeon must declare that the patient is brain dead. The potential donor must have given permission to recover the organs; otherwise, a representative of the hospital must ask the relatives for permission to recover the organs. Next, the relatives must give their permission. Finally, a transplantation surgeon must perform the actual extraction of the organs. Incentive problems arise at all stages.

Many argue that the reluctance of neurosurgeons to declare brain death is the main bottleneck in the system. They have no positive incentive to issue a declaration, and several negative incentives. To keep a patient on a respirator is costly, both in terms of direct expenses and in terms of opportunity costs for other patients. Critical care physicians know that in many cases the family will refuse to give permission, in which case the provided services will not be reimbursed. The fear of litigation that is pervasive in American medicine also extends to the fear of being charged by the patient's relatives of declaring brain death prematurely. This risk is now reduced, as most states have a brain death statute that offers legal immunity to neurosurgeons.

Incentive problems also arise for the donors and their relatives. For living donors, the only motivation is altruism, since under American law the sale of organs from living donors is forbidden. Moreover, the altruism must be quite strong to overcome the negative incentives created by the pain and risk that are involved. Nor does a person have a positive incentive to authorize use of the organs in the event of an accident that results in brain death. In this case, however, there are few negative incentives. Although some people believe that if they sign a donor card the doctor will try less hard to save them, the fear is unfounded and probably uncommon. A minimal degree of altruism should ensure willingness to have one's organs used. Nevertheless few people sign donor cards, a fact that has been variously explained in terms of transaction costs, reluctance to have one's organs used by an individual of a different race, and unwillingness to face one's mortality.

Formerly, requesting permission from relatives was optional. Most states have now passed "required-request" laws that make this a mandatory action. Each system has its critics. The earlier system was criticized for involving negative incentives. When faced with grieving relatives, many hesitated to make a request for organs. The new system is criticized for routinizing the request situation, with less effort and competence on the part of the requesters.

Relatives face no incentives of any kind when asked to authorize recovery, yet many refuse to do so. The reasons may be religious, or stem from the reluctance to benefit individuals from another race. In addition, they may harbor the suspicion that brain death may be declared prematurely. Proposals have been made to create a positive incentive for relatives, for example, by offering to pay funeral expenses. So far, such proposals have not been implemented.

To overcome these problems on the side of donors, two solutions have been proposed. Some European countries have a policy of "presumed consent," so that organs can be recovered unless the person has explicitly forbidden it. In practice, doctors still feel compelled to ask for permission. In other European countries, no consent is required or presumed: Organs can be recovered without authorization or permission from anyone. Speaking for myself, this seems to be the obviously correct solution. It is surely the procedure that rational individuals would choose behind the veil of ignorance, before they knew whether they would be potential donors or potential recipients. The right of individuals to dispose of their dead bodies is routinely violated in autopsies, and it is hard to see why transplantation would pose any special problems.

Consider finally the incentives of the transplant surgeons who have to carry out the actual organ extraction.[22] Many argue that the cooperation of transplant surgeons, notably in persuading the relatives to give their permission, is vital. To encourage that cooperation, the procuring surgeon should be allowed to keep one of two kidneys for the waiting list of the transplant center with which he is affiliated. This is an argument from efficiency for allocating some kidneys locally. Another argument from efficiency says that all kidneys should be shared with other transplant centers and allocated from a common list, since this procedure will increase the probability of finding a well-matched patient. The relative importance of these two effects remains controversial.

## Explaining allocative principles

I conclude with some comments on the problem of *explaining* why a particular principle is chosen to allocate a particular scarce good. This explanatory issue can be further broken down in two questions. Where do the motivations come from? How do they interact to yield the final selection of a principle? I shall illustrate the two questions by considering how they may be answered in particular contexts.

### Preference formation

Issues of local justice may be classified along two dimensions, numerical importance and urgency. Some issues affect many, others a small minority. Some issues are of momentous importance to the individuals who are concerned, whereas others are more trivial or at least not vitally important. The issue of organ transplantation is a small-number, high-importance problem. Each year there are about 9,000 kidney transplantations in the United States, whereas heart and liver transplantations represent about 1,700 cases each. Roughly speaking twice as many could have benefited from an operation. The opposite combination is offered by a high-number, low-importance problem such as college admission. Almost all applicants to college eventually end up somewhere. Although many do not get into their first choice, this is much less of a blow than not getting a liver transplant. To convey an idea of the difference in numerical importance, the University of Texas at Austin each year has about three times as many applicants as there are people on the waiting list for transplantations. High-number, high-importance problems include selection of soldiers for military service in wartime and rationing of consumer goods in disaster situations. Closer to the opposite end of the spectrum, layoffs represent a medium-sized problem for a medium-sized number of persons.

The small-number, high-importance cases can be expected to have some distinguishing features. In particular, one might expect selection to be highly information-intensive and discretionary. Since the decisions are so important, one should try to pay great attention to details of the individual case. Since there are relatively few decisions to be made, such attention is actually affordable. By contrast, high-number, high-importance cases cannot afford discretion and finetuning, whereas low-importance cases do not need them. This is not, however, the pattern that one finds. The college admissions procedure at Stanford University is more information-intensive and much more discretionary than the selection of patients for transplantation. The allocation of kidneys, for instance, follows a highly mechanical and nondiscretionary procedure. The allocation of hearts, which ranks even higher on the urgency scale, also follows a mechanical pattern.

I have tried to speculate about some possible explanations for this paradox, if it is one. One possible account might go as follows. There is always fear that a discretionary procedure might lend itself to corruption and bribery. In small-number, high-importance cases this fear is likely to be especially strong. Since the number of available places is small, even a single instance of corruption is seen as a threat to oneself; and the high stakes makes the idea even more intolerable. Or there might be a feeling that since discretionary procedures consider the whole person and not simply a few selected traits, rejection means that one is found to be inferior as a person. Since mechanical principles always are arbitrary to some extent, they might be better for the self-respect of the losers. Once again, the feeling might be more intolerable when the stakes are high. If these speculations are valid, they might explain the formation of *applicant preferences* with regard to allocative procedures. They can be supplemented by explanations of *allocator preferences*, as in the discussion of the norms of compassion and thoroughness above.

### Preference aggregation

Once we know the preferences of all the parties involved, we must specify an aggregation mechanism: majority voting, logrolling, bargaining, or alliance formation. Here I shall use organ transplantation and layoffs to illustrate the last possibility. Doctors, hospital administrators, politicians, potential beneficiaries, losers in the allocative struggle, public opinion – all of these are animated by specific conceptions of justice that go into the shaping of allocative policies. Often, agreement is reached by the forming of an alliance around a specific policy, which the members of the coalition may espouse on very different grounds. Consider again the importance of time on the waiting list in the point system for kidney allocation. Some may emphasize waiting because they believe in the inherent fairness of queuing. Others may advocate more points for waiting to compensate people for the bad medical luck of having unusual antigen patterns. Still others may support the policy because some of the persons with bad medical luck also happen to be disadvantaged on other grounds. None of these are self-interested arguments. None of them are based on efficiency considerations. They represent different conceptions of distributive equity, which in this particular case happens to point in the same direction.

In other cases, coalitions may build with members motivated by a larger variety of concerns – equity, efficiency, and self-interest. The use of seniority in layoff contexts can be defended on many grounds. Workers, in particular, have a number of reasons for preferring seniority. First, a majority of organized workers want seniority out of self-interest. As long as workers feel confident that the firm will never lay off more than half the work force, the senior 51% of the workers will always prefer seniority over any other layoff principle. Second, seniority, like queuing, reflects the ethics of desert. Workers feel they ought to be rewarded for having devoted the best years of their lives to the firm.[23] Third, the jobs become more valuable to them the longer they have worked in the firm, because of job-specific skills and the like. Fourth, seniority, being a mechanical principle, protects workers from arbitrary managerial decision making. Historically, this was probably the main reason for the introduction of the seniority system (Gersuny, 1982). Finally, seniority can be seen as protecting older and more vulnerable workers, and thus being to some extent a proxy for need.

Managers, too, have multiple reasons for preferring seniority. By encouraging workers to stay in the firm, the seniority principle reduces turnover costs. Also, because workers like seniority, using another system could be bad for morale and productivity. In particular, arbitrary foreman behavior is costly for the firm if it causes work stoppages and discontent among the workers (Goldberg, 1980). Moreover, as seniority rights ensure that the workers have more to lose from being fired, they also enhance the efficacy of the firing threat as a worker discipline device (Golden, 1990). In a crisis, of course, managers would always like to be free to retain the most productive workers. Although the ensuing problem of credibility can be solved by having unions to enforce the seniority principle, this solution obviously has other costs that, in the eyes of managers, may well offset the benefits. American studies indicate, in fact, that unionized firms are more productive and less profitable than nonunionized ones. Given the presence of a union, however, managers and workers form a strong coalition for the seniority principle. If Congress, say, should become so worried about youth unemployment that it would prefer the *least* senior workers to be retained in layoffs, the coalition would prevent any such proposal from even being made.

I do not believe we shall ever be able to formulate anything like a *theory* of the selection of allocative principles. Nor do I think we have to limit ourselves to mere *description*. There is an intermediate level of analysis – the study of *mechanisms:* a relatively small number of or frequently recurring causal patterns.[24] Although the "relatively small" number of mechanisms may be quite large, it will be orders of magnitude smaller than the number of cases they are used to illuminate. In that sense, the study of local justice will be guided by the goals of parsimony and generality that characterize science in general.

### References

Aaron, H. J., & Schwartz, W. B. (1984). *The painful prescription*. Washington, DC: Brookings Instutution.

Ainslie, G. (1992). *Picoeconomics*. Cambridge: Cambridge University Press.

Calabresi, G., & Bobbit, P. (1968). *Tragic choices*. New York: Norton.

Davidson, D. (1980). *Essays on actions and events*. Oxford University Press.

Dennis, J. M. (1990). Reflections on the unintended consequences of planning local justice: The case of organ transplantation in the U.S. Working Paper No. 11, Local Justice Project, Department of Political Science, University of Chicago.

Elster, Jon. (1989a). *The cement of society*. Cambridge: Cambridge University Press.

    (1989b). *Nuts and bolts in the social sciences*. Cambridge: Cambridge University Press.

    (1992). *Local justice*. New York: Russell Sage Foundation.

Gersuny, C. (1982). Origins of seniority provisions in collective bargaining. *Labor Law Journal, 33*, 518–524.

Goldberg, V. (1980). Bridges over contested terrain: Exploring the radical account of the employment relationship. *Journal of Economic Behavior and Organization, 1*, 249–274.

Golden, M. (1990). A comparative inquiry into systems for allocating job loss. Unpublished manuscript, Department of Political Science, University of California, Los Angeles.

Herpin, N. (1990). "Le don de sperme." *Archives Européennes de Sociologie, 31*, 141–173.

Hofstee, W. (1983). The case for compromise in educational selection and grading. In S. B. Anderson & J. S. Helmick (Eds.), *On educational testing* (pp. 109–127). San Francisco: Jossey-Bass.

Kahneman, D., & Tversky, A. (1979). Prospect theory. *Econometrica, 47*, 263–291.

Kamm, F. M. (1989). The report of the U.S. Task Force on Organ Transplantation: Criticisms and alternatives. *The Mount Sinai Journal of Medicine, 56*, 207–220.

Klag, M. J., Whelton, P. K., Coresh, J., Grim, C. E., & Kuller, L. H. (1991). The association of skin color with blood pressure in US blacks with low socioeconomic status. *Journal of the American Medical Association, 265*, 599–602.

Knesper, D. J., Pagnucco, D. J., & Wheeler, J. R. C. (1985). Similarities and differences across mental health services providers and practice settings in the United States. *American Psychologist, 40*, 1352–1369.

Matthieu, D. (1988). Introduction to Part 2. In D. Matthieu (Ed.), *Organ substitution technology* (pp. 33–51). Boulder, CO: Westview Press.

Milford, E. L., Ratner, L., & Yunis, E. (1987). Will transplant immunogenetics lead to better graft survival in blacks? *Transplantation Proceedings, 19*.

Opelz, G. (1988). Allocation of cadaver kidneys for transplantation. *Transplantation Proceedings, 20*, 1028–1032.

Oren, D. A. (1985). *Joining the club: A history of Jews and Yale.* New Haven, CT: Yale University Press.

Perez, L. M., Matas, A. J., & Tellis, V. A. (1988). Organ donation in three major U.S. cities by race/ethnicity. *Transplantation Proceedings, 20*, 815.

Peters, D. (1989). A unified approach to organ donor recruitment, organ procurement, and distribution. *Journal of Law and Health, 3*, 157–187.

Romm, S. (1990). Local justice and layoffs. Working Paper No. 3. Local Justice Project, Department of Political Science, University of Chicago.

Shapiro, C., & Stiglitz, J. (1984). Equilibrium unemployment as a worker discipline device. *American Economic Review, 74*, 433–444.

Starzl, T. et al. (1987). A multifactorial system for equitable selection of cadaver kidney recipients. *Journal of the American Medical Association, 257*, 3073–3075.

Tversky, A., & Kahneman, D. (1981). The framing of decisions and the psychology of choice. *Science, 211*, 453–458.

United Network for Organ Sharing. (1989, April 7). UNOS policy regarding utilization of the point system for cadaveric kidney allocation. Richmond, VA: UNOS.

Walzer, M. (1983) *Spheres of justice: A defense of pluralism and equality.* New York: Basic Books.

Wikler, D. (1987). Personal responsibility for illness. In D. VanDeVeer & T. Regan (Eds.), *Health care ethics* (pp. 326–358). Philadelphia: Temple University Press.

### Notes

1  For a fuller exposition, see my *Local Justice* (1992). Earlier discussions include Calabresi and Bobbit's *Tragic Choices* (1968) and Walzer's *Spheres of Justice* (1983).

2  Other allocative issues addressed in *Local Justice* (Elster, 1992) include military service in wartime, demobilization from the army, allocation of sperm for artificial insemination, selection of adoptive parents, award of child custody, admission to kindergarten, division of household work, allocation of prison space, selection among applicants for immigration, and rationing in wartime.

3  In theory, awarding points for economic and educational disadvantage could also be justified on the grounds that high school grades underpredict performance in college for students from disadvantaged backgrounds.

4  In practice, this is interpreted as a requirement that they have the same blood type. Kidneys from blood type O donors can be used for recipients with any blood type, but blood type O recipients can use only kidneys from blood type O donors. Earlier, this led to blood type O patients receiving fewer kidneys. Recently, however, UNOS has lain down that kidneys from blood type O donors should go only to blood type O patients. This policy is based on equity considerations, not on medical reasons.

5  Although the medical literature is divided, this statement appears to remain true even after the introduction of cyclosporin. See notably Opelz (1988).

6  For a fuller description, see United Network for Organ Sharing (1989).

7  Antibody formation and antigen matching do not vary independently of each other. "Widely reacting cytotoxic antibodies often have specificity against the class 1 antigens of the A and B histocompatibility loci; because of this, the demonstration of a negative cytotoxic cross match for a highly sensitized patient should predict a good antigen match. Thus, the antibody and antigen credits tend to be reinforcing." (Starzl et al., 1987, p. 3075.)

8  Strictly speaking, however, the system is not lexicographic. Time on the waiting list can make a tie as well as break one. In practice, this happens infrequently.

9  In Great Britain, dialysis remains scarce; see Aaron and Schwartz (1984).

10  *Local 189 United Papermakers and Paperworkers v. United States*, decided by the Fifth Circuit in 1969 (416 F. 2d 980).

11  In today's more conservative legal climate the argument that a system perpetuates legal discrimination will not be effective; see, for example, the Fifth Circuit's 1984 decision in *Salinas v. Roadway Express* (35 FEP Cases 533), or the Eleventh Circuit's 1983 decision in *Freeman v. Motor Convoy* (31 FEP Cases 517).

12  See, for example, the Tenth Circuit's 1981 decision in *Sears v. Atchinson*, 645 F. 2d 1365.

13  See, for example, the 1981 decision of a Georgia District Court in *Miller v. Continental Can Co.*, 544 F. Supp 210.

14  See, for example, the 1981 decision of a Wisconsin District Court in *Wattleton v. Ladish Co.*, 520 F. Supp 1329.

15  98 S. Ct. 2733 (1978).

16  The authors mention, however, that another interpretation is also possible: The hypertension might be due to an interaction between some environmental factor (stress or diet) caused by socioeconomic disadvantage (shared by blacks and low-income whites) and a gene that has higher prevalence among blacks with darker skin color. On both hypotheses, being a *disadvantaged black* explains the hypertension, but only on the first is the explanation in terms of stress caused by this double disadvantage.

17  In the only systematic study of minority organ donation: Perez, Matas, and Tellis (1988) found in their 40-month survey that black and Hispanic family refusal rates were 45 and 43 percent, respectively, while for the white population it was 17 percent in New York, Los Angeles, and Miami between January 1984 and April 1987.

18  See Milford, Ratner, and Yunis (1987), p. 37, for a table comparing antigen frequencies by race. A second table demonstrates that blacks are more likely to have "blanks," that is, antigens yet to be designated by tissue-typing experts. Under the new UNOS system, the latter fact no longer works to the disadvantage of blacks, as it did under the old. The new system gives points for the absence of observed mismatches, whereas the old was based on the number of observed matches.

19  The following is indebted to Romm (1990) and to Golden (1990).

20  This is a variation on the theme that firms may benefit if workers run some risk of unemployment (see Shapiro & Stiglitz, 1984).

21  For such "non-standard causal chains" in the analysis of action, see Davidson (1980, p. 79).

22  The following draws on Dennis (1990).

23  In my opinion, this is a spurious argument. To devote one's life to a task is meritorious only when it involves forgoing other activities that would have been more satisfying personally. But most workers do not have any such alternatives. A fortiori this spuriousness applies to the argument that the elderly deserve to take priority because of what they have contributed to those who are now in the work force. (Parents may deserve reward for what they do for their children, but that is another matter.) Whether spurious or not, the argument is effective.

24  For a general argument for the mechanism approach, see my *Nuts and bolts in the social sciences* (1989b). For an application to problems of bargaining and collective action, see my *The cement of society* (1989a).

# 13 Models of equity in public risk

*Rakesh K. Sarin*

## Introduction

In a recent program on television, it was reported that the infant mortality rate in the United States declined in the year 1990. Much of the discussion, however, centered on the fact that, despite the decline for the population as a whole, the gap between infant mortality rates for blacks and whites is still large. The commentators on that program agreed that steps (e.g., increasing the availability of prenatal care) must be taken to reduce relatively high infant mortality rates among blacks. Similarly, a *Los Angeles Times* front-page headline November 15, 1991 read: "Black Infant Death Rate 2½ Times That of Whites," with a subhead, "Health: State committee calls for increased spending and reallocation of resources to help close the gap."

Now consider the case of a small town in the Northwest. An industrial plant that provided employment to a significant proportion of the population was also suspected of contributing to the higher cancer rate. The people in the town faced a choice between closing the plant and thus losing the jobs or allowing its continued operation and thus suffering higher incidences of cancer among their population. The town was clearly burdened with a higher risk, but it also received benefits in terms of employment and associated economic activity. In this case both risks and benefits must simultaneously be considered in evaluating alternative policy options with regard to the industrial plant.

In this chapter I discuss models that may be useful in evaluating distributional aspects of risk in a public policy evaluation. As shown in Figure 1, the first class of models will deal with risk distribution alone. In this class of models it is assumed that the distribution of benefits is approximately the same among groups or individuals. In the second class of models

The support for this research by the Decision, Risk, and Management Science branch of the National Science Foundation is gratefully acknowledged.

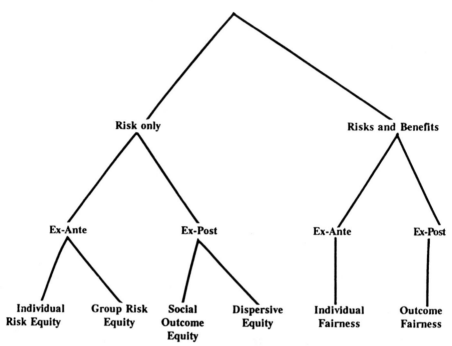

Figure 1   A summary of models.

both risks and benefits are considered simultaneously in defining the concept of equity or fairness. For expositional simplicity, references are not provided except where a direct quote is used.

### Basic concepts

Consider two individuals, 1 and 2, who are exposed to risks of injury or dying due to a specified cause in a specified time period. At the end of the time period, one of four basic consequences will be observed: $(1, 1)$ = both individuals die; $(0, 0)$ = both individuals live; $(1, 0)$ = 1 dies and 2 lives; $(0, 1)$ = 1 lives and 2 dies. At the beginning of the time period, we will assume that the probability distribution over the four consequences has been specified. From this probability distribution, we can easily derive the marginal probability, denoted $m_i$, that individual $i$ will be a fatality.

Consider the following probability distributions over the basic consequences (hereafter called lotteries).

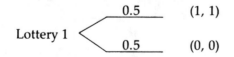

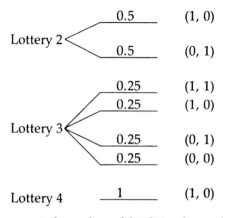

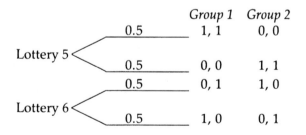

The expected number of fatalities for each of the four lotteries is one. If there is a concern for equity, however, there may be several possible evaluations of these consequences, even for a risk-neutral decision maker. Notice that in lotteries 1, 2, and 3, each individual has a 0.5 chance of dying, so that these three lotteries are equitable ex ante and either of these is superior to lottery 4 on this account. We will say that lotteries 1–3 have the identical *individual risk equity*. At the end of the time period, lottery 1 produces identical outcomes and lottery 2 produces nonidentical outcomes. Thus, ex post lottery 1 will be deemed more equitable by the society than lottery 2. We will call a measure that evaluates the relative distribution of outcomes at the end of the time period, when the actual outcomes become known, *social outcome equity*.

Now consider two groups, each with two people with the following probability distributions over the basic consequences.

Lotteries 5 and 6 have identical individual risk equity (each person has a 0.5 chance of dying in either lottery), as well as identical social outcome equity (for both lotteries 2 die and 2 live at the end of the time period). It is clear, however, that in lottery 5 only one of the groups suffers, whereas in lottery 6 both groups suffer equally (lose 1 person each). We will call a measure of equity between groups *dispersive equity*. For the purpose of defining dispersive equity, we will assume that appropriate groups (e.g., male/female, blacks/whites, rich/poor) have been specified exogenously. Since dispersive equity deals with the distribution of fatalities among groups at the end of the time period or ex post, it ignores ex ante distribution of risk among groups. For example, the dispersive equity for lottery 5 and for lottery 7, below, is identical.

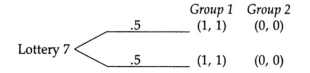

|  | Group 1 | Group 2 |
|--|--|--|
| .5 | (1, 1) | (0, 0) |
| .5 | (1, 1) | (0, 0) |

Lottery 7

It seems that lottery 5 is fairer than lottery 7, since in lottery 7 only group 1 suffers regardless of which of the two events occurs. We therefore define *group risk equity* as that which is determined by the marginal probability distribution over fatalities for each group. In lottery 5, each group has a 0.5 chance of 2 and a 0.5 chance of 0 fatalities. In lottery 7, group 1 has a 1.0 chance of 2 fatalities, whereas group 2 has a 1.0 chance of 0 fatality.

In summary, marginal probabilities that individual $i$ will die determine individual risk equity, and marginal probability distribution for the number of people in group $j$ who will die determines group risk equity. In contrast, joint probability distribution for the number of people in each group who will die determines dispersive equity, and probability distribution for the number of people in the population who will die determines social outcome equity. These four measures of equity are *independent* in the sense that if two alternatives or lotteries are identical on a given measure, then it does not always follow that these must be identical on one of the other three measures. I will now discuss some specific mathematical models for each of these four types of equity concepts.

### Individual risk equity

The relevant information for defining individual risk equity is the marginal probability of death or mortality, $m_i$, to each individual $i$. The relative distribution of $(m_1, m_2, \ldots, m_N)$, where $N$ is the number of people in the population, determines individual risk equity. The two possible measures are

$$-\sum_{i:=1}^{N} |(m_i - \bar{m})|, \quad \text{and} \tag{1}$$

$$-\sum_{i=1}^{N} (m_i - \bar{m})^2, \tag{2}$$

where $\bar{m}$ is the average probability of death. In either measure (1) or (2), the perfect individual risk equity is achieved when each $m_i$ is equal.

### Social outcome equity

At the end of the time period, one of $2^N$ basic consequence will be realized. The social outcome equity deals with the relative equity of these basic consequences.

We define a concept of the total number of inferior pairwise comparisons for a basic consequence that is obtained by counting, for each individual, the number of people whose outcomes are inferior to his and then simply summing all the numbers of inferior comparisons over all individuals. Thus (1, 0, 0, 0) and (1, 1, 1, 0) will each have three inferior pairwise comparisons and (1, 1, 0, 0) will have four inferior pairwise comparisons. A consequence with a smaller number of inferior pairwise comparisons is assumed to be more equitable. Notice that in equally equitable consequences the variance of the outcomes will be the same, as will the maximum number (or percentage) of people with identical outcomes. We now have a complete ranking in terms of social outcome equity for all possible $2^N$ basic consequences. For $N = 4$, the most equitable outcomes are (1, 1, 1, 1) and (0, 0, 0, 0) and the least equitable outcomes are (1, 1, 0, 0) and its rearrangements, for example (0, 1, 1, 0).

Social outcome equity depends on fatalities $y$. Let $p(y)$ be the probability of $y$ fatalities in a lottery $p$. In our example in section 2, if $p$ is lottery 3 then $p(2) = 0.25$, $p(1) = 0.5$, and $p(0) = 0.25$. Social outcome equity for a lottery $p$ is given by

$$\sum_{y=0}^{N} \alpha y(N-y)p(y), \tag{3}$$

where $\alpha > 0$ is associated with catastrophe avoidance and $\alpha < 0$ with common-fate preference. Thus, in the Basic Concepts section, lottery 2 has higher social outcome equity than lottery 1 if $\alpha > 0$ and the reverse order holds for $\alpha < 0$.

### Group risk equity

Suppose the population $N$ is divided into mutually exclusive but collectively exhaustive $n$ groups. The population in group $j$ is denoted $N_j$; thus, $\Sigma N_j = N$. If the groups are of approximately equal size, the expected fatalities in each group could be used to determine group risk equity. A greater group risk equity is achieved if the expected numbers of fatalities in each group are evenly balanced; conversely, if some groups suffer a large number of expected deaths and others a small number of expected deaths, then the group risk equity is low.

When population sizes in each group differ significantly, we will use fatality rates (expected fatalities/group population) to determine group risk equity. For example, health experts note that the fatality rate for black women with breast cancer is significantly higher than that for white women with breast cancer. Even though aggregate fatalities for white women with breast cancer are higher than those for black women, it is considered undesirable that, on a per capita basis, black women with breast cancer have a higher fatality rate. This group risk inequity has led many to advocate special health programs directed primarily toward black women.

Suppose $r_j$ is the fatality rate for group $j$, then a possible group risk equity measure is

$$-\sum_{j=1}^{n}(r_j-\bar{r})^2, \tag{4}$$

where $\bar{r}$ is the expected fatality rate. Since $r_j$ is computed by normalizing expected fatalities in group $j$ by its population, the group risk equity measure given by (4) assumes risk neutrality. The group risk equity measure for lottery 5 is 0, whereas for lottery 7 it is $-0.5$. Thus, on this measure lottery 5 is more equitable than lottery 7.

### Dispersive equity

Lotteries 5 and 6 have identical group risk equity since expected fatality rates for both groups are the same in both lotteries. At the end of the time period, however, lottery 5 leads to inequitable outcomes, whereas lottery 6 leads to equitable outcomes.

Suppose $(y_1, y_2, \ldots, y_n)$ represents a fatality vector, where $y_j =$ number of fatalities in group $j$. Denote $x_j = y^j/N_j$; then $x_j$ measures the proportion of people who die in group $j$. We will define dispersive equity on the vector $(x_1, x_2, \ldots, x_n)$. In many applications, use of the proportional fatality vector to capture dispersive equity seems reasonable.

One measure of dispersive equity is simply the variance:

$$-\sum_{j=1}^{n}(x_j-\bar{x})^2, \quad \text{where } \bar{x} = \sum_{j=1}^{n}x_j|n$$

Another measure for dispersive equity could be an elementary form of Gini index. We rename the groups so that $x_1 \le x_2 \le \ldots \le x_n$. Now, the shaded area in Figure 2 provides a measure of dispersive inequity. Notice that when $x_1 = x_2 = \ldots = x_n$, the shaded area under the diagonal will be zero (perfect dispersive equity), and when $x_1 = x_2 = \ldots = x_{n-1} = 0$, and $x_n > 0$, the shaded area will be largest.

The preceding two measures provide dispersive equity for a proportional fatality vector $(x_1, x_2, \ldots, x_n)$. To compute the dispersive equity for a lottery, where $p(x_1, \ldots, x_n)$ is the joint probability of obtaining $(x_1, \ldots, x_n)$, we simply take the expected value of the dispersive equity index defined over $(x_1, \ldots, x_n)$.

In defining dispersive equity, we assumed that the partition of the pop-

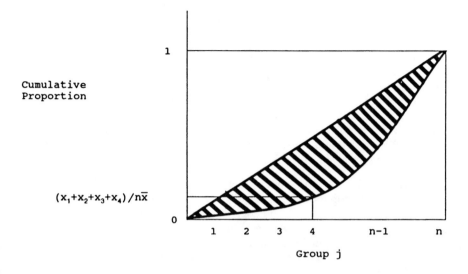

Figure 2   A measure of dispersive equity. (Dispersive equity is defined by the shaded area in the figure.)

ulation into groups is uniquely identified. There could, however, be more than one way to partition a population into groups; for example, blacks and whites could be one partitioning and men and women could be another. In the lottery below, a perfect dispersive equity is achieved with respect to race, but if sex is used as a basis to define groups then it represents a perfect dispersive inequity.

|        | Black Man | Black Woman | White Man | White Woman |
|--------|-----------|-------------|-----------|-------------|
| 0.5    | 1         | 0           | 1         | 0           |
| 0.5    | 0         | 1           | 0         | 1           |

The following lottery represents a policy that is equitable with respect to either (based on race or based on sex) definition of groups.

|        | Black Man | Black Woman | White Man | White Woman |
|--------|-----------|-------------|-----------|-------------|
| 0.5    | 1         | 0           | 1         | 0           |
| 0.5    | 0         | 1           | 0         | 1           |

**Benefit–risk trade-offs**

The models presented in the preceding sections assume that equality of risk among individuals or groups implies equity. If, however, a group receives higher benefits than the other, then it may not be equitable to distribute the risks equally among the members of the two groups. A hypothetical scenario given in Keller and Sarin (1988) illustrates this issue.

Scenario. On an island in your jurisdiction, there are two communities. Each community has an equal population size. Community 1 has an industrial plant which brings in many jobs and much income to the residents of this community. The residents of Community 2 do not receive any of the benefits of this plant. However, the plant also is producing toxic waste. The problem is to determine where the waste should be stored. There are two waste storage facilities on the island. One is in Community 1 and one is in Community 2. Where should the waste be stored? There are two proposals for storing this waste:

> A. Store all the waste in Community 1. In this case, it is expected that 10 additional people from Community 1 will die within 1 year due to exposure to this toxic waste. No people from Community 2 will die due to this waste, since they will not be exposed to it.
> B. Store half the waste in Community 1 and half the waste in Community 2. In this case, it is expected that 5 additional people from Community 1 will die within 1 year due to exposure to this toxic waste. Likewise, it is expected that 5 additional people from Community 2 will die within 1 year due to exposure to this toxic waste.

A majority of the subjects (87%) in the empirical study considered it fairer to allocate the risks to Community 1, presumably since they received all the benefits of the plant.

The concept of equity when both a benefit $B$ and a risk $R$ are to be allocated among $m$ communities can be operationalized by envy-free allocations. Let $b_i$ be the fraction of the total benefits $B$ received by community $i$ and $r_i$ be the fraction of the total risk $R$ borne by community $i$. An allocation $(b_1, r_1; ...; b_m, r_m)$ with $\Sigma b_i = \Sigma r_i = 1$ is envy-free if no community is willing to exchange its allocated benefits-risk package for a package allocated to some other community. Thus, in an envy-free allocation,

$$u_i(b_i, r_i) \geq u_i(b_j, r_j), \quad \text{for } i, j = 1 \text{ to } m.$$

Clearly, an equal division $b_i = r_i = 1/m$ for $i = 1$ to $m$ is envy-free. However, it may be possible that all communities can be better off by some other allocation that is envy-free but not an equal division. The simplest example is with $m = 2$ and $u_1(b_1, r_1) = 2b_1 - r_1$ and $u_2(b_2, r_2) = b_2 - 2r_2$. An allocation $(b_1 = 1, r_1 = 1)$ and $(b_2 = 0, r_2 = 0)$ is superior to equal division. In this example community 1 prefers to assume all the risk to reap all the benefits and community 2 prefers to assume no risk and receive no benefits.

As shown in Figure 3, any allocation in the shaded area is envy-free. If initial allocation is at point $E$ (equal division), both communities can improve their position by choosing an allocation on the frontier $2^*_F - D^* - 1^*_F$. Which point is chosen on this frontier will depend on the process of decision making. For example, if there is a supradecision maker then she can account for $u_1$ and $u_2$ and maximize her utility function over $u_1$ and $u_2$.

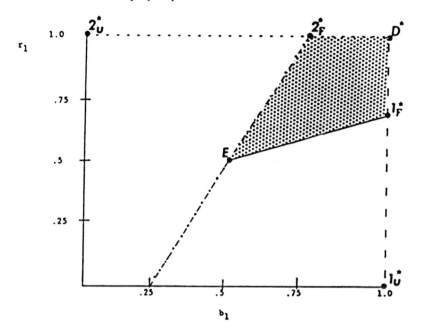

Figure 3  Feasible envy-free allocations (shaded area). Dashed line: Pareto frontier.
(From Keller and Sarin, 1988.)

Alternatively, the two communities may engage in negotiation or bargaining to arrive at an acceptable allocation.

A possible difficulty with envy-free allocation is that the initial position
of the communities may be quite different. For example, if community 1 is
poor then they may accept all of the risks to receive the benefits. Yet another difficulty is encountered when one considers efforts in addition to
risks and benefits in a fair allocation. A community through special efforts
such as recycling may reduce risks or increase benefits. Is it unfair if such
a community reaps higher benefits and lower risks even though the allocation may not be envy-free with respect to the risk-benefit package alone?
Finally, in many public policy situations risks and benefits are indivisible.
Because of the indivisibility, there may not be any envy-free allocation.
What process should one use in such cases?

These unanswered questions suggest areas for further research.

### Fairness in benefit-risk lotteries

We now consider the case where benefits accrued to an individual are
uncertain. Each individual $i$ therefore faces a lottery $A_i$ which represents a marginal benefit-risk distribution. An example of $A_1$ is given
below:

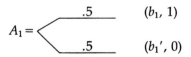

$$A_1 = \begin{cases} \underline{\quad .5 \quad} & (b_1, 1) \\ \underline{\quad .5 \quad} & (b_1', 0) \end{cases}$$

Thus in $A_1$ the individual 1 faces a 0.5 chance of receiving benefits $b_1$ and becoming a fatality and a 0.5 chance of receiving benefits $b_1'$ and surviving. Notice that we could use 1 to denote sick or injured and 0 to denote well or uninjured. We are using the ghastly consequence of death for consistency with respect to the previous literature. Similarly, instead of using large probabilities of an adverse consequence such as 0.5, we could use more realistic numbers (e.g., $5 \times 10^{-6}$).

We will illustrate our fairness measures for a two-person society. Generalizing to the $n$-person case is straightforward.

*Individual fairness* is defined by comparing the utility of individual 1 for his lottery $A_1$ to his utility for lottery $A_2$ that individual 2 receives. Thus, a policy that results in lottery $A_1$ to individual 1 and lottery $A_2$ to individual 2 is individually fair if

$$u_1(A_1) \geq u_1(A_2), \text{ and}$$
$$u_2(A_2) \geq u_2(A_1),$$

where $u_1$ and $u_2$ are individuals 1 and 2's utility functions respectively. If we denote the two-attribute consequence to individual $i$ as $x_i$, then

$$u_i(A_j) = E_{Aj} [u_i(x_j)], \ i,j = 1, 2.$$

Note that $u_i(A_j)$ is the expected utility of individual $i$ for the lottery received by individual $j$. Essentially, individual fairness ensures that each person is at least as happy with his own lottery as he would be if he were to receive the other person's lottery.

Using the criterion of individual fairness, the following lottery will be deemed fair:

|  | Individual 1 | | Individual 2 | |
|---|---|---|---|---|
|  | Benefit | Risk | Benefit | Risk |
| 0.5 | 0 | 1 | 1 | 0 |
| 0.5 | 1 | 0 | 0 | 1 |

At the end of the time period, however, in the upper branch individual 1 will envy individual 2's allocation and in the lower branch individual 2 will envy individual 1's allocation. We need therefore a concept of *outcome fairness*. For consequences $x_1$ and $x_2$ that are eventually received by individuals 1 and 2, the vector of outcomes $(x_1, x_2)$ satisfies outcome fairness if

$$u_1(x_1) \geq u_1(x_2), \quad \text{and}$$
$$u_2(x_2) \geq u_2(x_1).$$

With this stringent definition, a policy will be called outcome unfair even if there is only a one in a million chance that a joint outcome $(x_1, x_2)$ does not satisfy the above criterion. An ordinal measure for outcome fairness is simply the probability of $(x_1, x_2)$ that meets the fairness criterion. In the example below the outcome fairness measure is 0.25:

|  | Individual 1 | Individual 2 |
|---|---|---|
| .5 | (1, 0) | (0, 1) |
| .25 | (.5, .5) | (.5, .5) |
| .25 | (0, 1) | (1, 0) |

Notice that this lottery satisfies individual fairness since each individual faces the same lottery ex ante. At the end of the time period, however, only in the middle branch $(x_1, x_2)$ will no individual envy the other. In the upper branch individual 1 gets the better outcome and in the lower branch individual 2 gets the better outcome.

A useful area for further research will be to develop an integrative model that considers fatalities, benefits, and various equity or fairness measures in the evaluation of a public policy. One approach may be to maximize a group utility function subject to fairness constraints. In another approach, fairness and efficiency trade-offs may be explicitly quantified.

### References

Atkinson, A. B. (1970). On the measurement of inequality. *Journal of Economic Theory, 2,* 244–263.

Bodily, S. (1980). Analysis of risks to life and limb. *Operations Research, 28*(1), 156–175.

Broome, J. (1982). Equity in risk bearing. *Operations Research, 30,* 412–414.

Calabresi, G., & Bobbitt, P. (1978). *Tragic choices.* New York: Norton.

Dalton, H. (1920). The measurement of the inequality of incomes. *Economic Journal, 30,* 348–361.

Diamond, P. A. (1976). Cardinal welfare, individualistic ethics, and interpersonal comparison of utility: Comment. *Journal of Political Economy, 75,* 765–766.

Fischhoff, B., Lichtenstein, S., Slovic, P., Derby, S. L., & Keeney, R. L. (1981). *Acceptable risk,* Cambridge: Cambridge University Press.

Fishburn, P. C. (1984). Equity axioms for public risks. *Operations Research, 32,* 901–908.

Fishburn, P. C., & Sarin, R. K. (1991). Dispersive equity and social risk. *Management Science, 37, 7,* 751–769.

Fishburn, P. C., & Straffin, P. D. (1989). Equity considerations in public risks evaluation. *Operations Research, 37,* 229–239.

Foley, D. (1967). Resource allocation and the public sector. *Yale Economic Essays, 7,* 45–98.

Hammerton, M., Jones-Lee, M. W., & Abbott, V. (1982). Equity and public risk: Some empirical results. *Operations Research, 30*(1), 203–207.

Harrison, D. Jr. (1981). Distributional objectives in health and safety regulation. In A. Ferguson & E. P. LeVeen (Eds.), *The benefits of health and safety regulation* (pp. 177–201). Cambridge, MA: Ballinger.

Harvey, C. M. (1985a). Decision analysis models for social attitudes toward inequity. *Management Science, 31,* 1199–1212.

(1985b). Preference functions for catastrophe and risk inequity. *Large Scale Systems, 8,* 131–146.

Hoffman, E., & Spitzer, M. (1985). Entitlement, rights, and fairness: An experimental examination of subjects' concepts of distributive justice. *Journal of Legal Studies 14*(2), 259–297.

Kahneman, D., Knetsch, J., & Thaler, R. (1986). Fairness and the assumptions of economics. *Journal of Business, 59*(4), part 2, S285–S300.

(1986). Fairness as a constraint on profit-seeking: Entitlements in the market. *American Economic Review, 76*(4), 728–741.

Keeney, R. L. (1980a). Equity and public risk. *Operations Research, 28,* 527–534.

(1980b). Utility functions for equity and public risk. *Management Science, 26,* 345–353.

(1980c). Evaluating alternatives involving potential fatalities. *Operations Research, 28,* 188–205.

Keeney, R. L., & Raiffa, H. (1976). *Decisions with multiple objectives.* New York: Wiley.

Keeney, R. L., & Winkler, R. L. (1985). Evaluating decision strategies for equity of public risks. *Operations Research, 33,* 955–970.

Keller, R. L., & Sarin, R. K. (1988). Equity in social risk: Some empirical observations. *Risk Analysis, 8,* 135–146.

Kirkwood, C. (1979). Pareto optimality and equity in social decision analysis. *IEEE Transactions on Systems, Man, and Cybernetics, 9,* 89–91.

Kleindorfer P. R., & Kunreuther, H. (1981). Descriptive and prescriptive aspects of health and safety regulation. In A. Ferguson & E. P. LeVeen (Eds.), *The benefits of health and safety regulation* (pp. 25–42). Cambridge, MA: Ballinger.

Lichtenstein, S., Wagenaar, W. A., & Keren, G. B. (1985, May). Islanders and hostages: Deep and surface structures of story problems. Decision Research Report 85-7, Eugene, OR.

Lichtenstein, S., Wagenaar, W. A., Keren, G. B., & van der Schaaf, T. W. (1984). Risk propensity, action readiness and the roles of societal and individual decision makers. Institute for Perception Report No. IZF 1987-27, National Defense Research Organization, Soesterberg, The Netherlands.

Loomes, G. (1982). Choices involving a risk of death: An empirical study. *Scottish Journal of Political Economy, 29,* 272–282.

Lorenz, M. O. (1907). *Publications of the American Statistical Association, 9,* 209 ff.

Margolis, H. (1982). *Selfishness, altruism, and rationality.* Cambridge: Cambridge University Press.

Mellers, B. (1986). Fair allocations of salaries and taxes. *Journal of Experimental Psychology: Human Perception and Performance, 12,* 80–91.

Rawls, J. (1971). *A theory of justice.* Cambridge, MA: Belknap.

Sarin, R. K. (1985). Measuring equity in public risk. *Operations Research, 33,* 210–217.

Sen, A. K. (1973). *On economic inequality.* Oxford: Oxford University Press.

Suppes, P. (1978). The distributive justice of income inequality. In H. W. Gottinger & W. Leinfellner (Eds.), *Decision theory and social ethics: Issues in social choice* (pp. 303–320). Dordrecht, Holland: D. Reidel.

Thaler, R. (1982). Precommitment and the value of a life. In M. Jones-Lee (Ed.), *The value of life and safety* (pp. 171–183). Amsterdam: North-Holland.

Ulph, A. (1982). The role of ex ante and ex post decisions in the valuation of life. *Journal of Public Economics, 18*, 265–276.

Vaupel, J. (1981). On the benefits of health and safety regulation. In A. Ferguson & E. P. LeVeen (Eds.), *The benefits of health and safety regulation* (pp. 1–22). Cambridge, MA: Ballinger.

Zajac, E. E. (1978). *Fairness or efficiency: An introduction to public utility pricing* Cambridge, MA: Ballinger.

  (1985). Perceived economic justice: The example of public utility regulation. In H. Peyton Young (Ed.), *Cost allocation: Methods; principles applications* (Ch. 7). Amsterdam: Elsevier, North-Holland.

# 14 Fairness of distribution of risks with applications to Antarctica

*Ivy E. Broder and L. Robin Keller*

In this chapter we consider distributional fairness issues in decision making regarding health, safety, and environmental risks in Antarctica. Alternative safety improvements or operating procedures can result in different risk distributions among different groups of individuals at risk in Antarctica. We describe some of the risk trade-offs involved in balancing safety and environmental concerns. The focus of the chapter is on the insights for modeling fairness gained by examining the potential application of models incorporating fairness to Antarctic policymaking. Illustrative examples of alternative Antarctic policies are used to motivate the discussion of the implications for fairness modeling.

Decision analysts have recently been investigating ways to incorporate equity considerations into preference functions for guiding decision making about policy issues involving substantial risks to humans or the environment. Most of this work has been at the foundational level, with a focus on the mathematical models that can incorporate preferences for equity (see, e.g., Fishburn, 1984; Fishburn & Sarin, 1991; Fishburn & Straffin, 1989; Harvey, 1985a,b; Keller & Sarin, 1988; Keeney, 1980a,b,c; Keeney & Winkler, 1985; and Sarin, 1985 and in this book). This stream of work uses the

Work on this chapter was done while both authors were serving as program directors at the National Science Foundation; Keller was with the Decision, Risk, and Management Science Program and Broder was with the Economics Program. As part of our National Science Foundation service, we participated on an NSF task force on health and safety in Antarctica. We thank Deh-I Hsiung and Gary Staffo of the NSF's U.S. Antarctica Program for their help in supplying background information on Antarctica. We also appreciate helpful comments on an earlier version of the manuscript by volume editor Barbara Mellers, Colin Camerer, and Richard Harris. Broder also thanks American University for providing sabbatical support. Keller's work on equity has been partly supported (prior to joining NSF) under NSF grant SES-8721423 to Duke University from the Decision, Risk, and Management Science Program. The views expressed in this chapter are entirely the authors' and do not necessarily reflect the views of the National Science Foundation.

term *equity* to refer in general to the *fairness* of the distribution of risks, with or without added information on the distribution of benefits, effort, and so on. Related work by psychologists uses the terms "equality" when outcomes are equally balanced and "equity" when deserved outcomes are balanced with inputs such as effort. (See Harris 1976, 1980, and in this book; Walster, Walster, & Berscheid, 1978.) We hope that this chapter and Sarin (this book) will stimulate fruitful merging of the decision analytic and psychological streams of research on equity. A key purpose of decision analytic equity modeling is to develop models that can be operationalized to aid in choosing between alternative policy options.

A number of features of health, safety, and environmental risks in Antarctica make it interesting as an application arena for examining the equity models that have been proposed. Historically, the primary focus of the U.S. Antarctica Program (USAP) was on the substantial scientific benefits of Antarctica as an international location for important research and exploration. Recently, however, the issues of health, safety, and environmental risks have been receiving increasing attention. In 1988, a detailed report, *Safety in Antarctica*, was prepared by a blue-ribbon panel of experts following a year-long review of the United States' facilities in Antarctica, which are managed by the National Science Foundation (NSF). The report made many procedural and policy recommendations. The U.S. Congress, which directs the funding of the USAP through NSF, has been particularly concerned about the process of managing the safety and environmental risks in Antarctica, mirroring the concerns of the public or at least the concerns of certain interest groups. Attitudes toward catastrophic risks and perceived fairness of risk distributions may play a role in the public concern about Antarctica.

In USAP operations, there are many affected groups with overlapping memberships: military personnel, civilian contractors, scientists, NSF personnel, workers from different countries, tourists, environmental activists, and others. Under alternative regulatory and management policies, different distributions of risks could result among the different groups.

The harsh and remote physical environment in Antarctica, along with limited financial resources, places tight constraints on operations. Severe weather, communication difficulties, and limited availability of medical and other health and safety personnel and resources combine to make Antarctic operations relatively high in health and safety risks. Thus, trade-offs must be made between short-term health and safety risks and long-term environmental risks in Antarctic operations, because NSF must allocate financial and other resources between these short-term and long-term management issues. This chapter is a first attempt to apply methods of decision analysis to risk trade-offs in Antarctica. Although environmental concerns are an important component of the public policy debate, this application of equity models will focus on health and safety risks.

### Background on Antarctica

The continent of Antarctica contains 10% of the world's land mass (approximately the size of the United States and Mexico combined) and 70% of its fresh water. In addition to the scientific stations of 24 countries, Antarctica is home to 33 million seals, 75 million penguins, 80 million seabirds, 700 million tons of krill, and half a million whales. The USAP runs three year-round stations as well as remote field operations and refueling facilities during the austral summer (late October through late January). McMurdo is the largest of the three stations in both the number of personnel (about 1,150 during the November peak) and the number of structures (about 100). Projects are also carried out or supported from ships (*Research Vehicle* (*R/V*) *Polar Duke* or icebreakers). The South Pole Station is at an elevation of 9,500 feet and is built on ice and snow. The peak personnel load is about 100 people, with only about 15 to 20 who stay the entire winter. There are only about a dozen buildings at the site, which is supplied by ski-equipped aircraft during the austral summer. Palmer Station is the smallest of the three permanent stations, with a peak of about 40 people during the summer and a correspondingly small number of structures. It is accessible by ship year-round.

### Health and safety risks

The cruel and distant environment of Antarctica poses some obvious risks to the people who work in and visit the area. Between 1946 and 1987, there were 29 incidents involving fatalities of U.S. Antarctic personnel, resulting in 52 deaths. There have also been more than 300 fatalities among tourists in the area during the past dozen years.

*Air safety.* Air operations pose the single most significant risk to workers and tourists alike in Antarctica. Since 1946, there have been 10 fatal airplane accidents involving USAP personnel, which led to 32 deaths. The largest single accident was in 1966, when 6 people died after an aircraft crashed during a landing approach. More recently, this risk appears to have been reduced, there having been only one fatal crash since 1969. It occurred in late 1987, when two people on a salvage mission died after a crash during a landing approach. However, a far greater number of tourists have died as a result of airplane crashes – in fact, all of the tourist fatalities mentioned were the result of airplane crashes. Quite recently, another catastrophic incident occurred when a tourist expedition bound for Antarctica crashed in Chile on February 14, 1991, with a loss of 19 lives (*Washington Post*, 1991).

Several factors have been identified as leading to a possible reduction in the risk of airline travel: more modern radar equipment, landing on "blue ice" areas, increased training requirements, additional airline operation resources, increased air refueling capability and modernization of the aircraft fleet. Increased air operations are necessary to reduce the risks in other arenas of Antarctica's operations. Therefore, the risk of air operations plays a central role in the overall risk levels in Antarctica, as well as the distribution of those risks among different groups of people.

*Health and medical care.* The difficult environmental conditions in Antarctica pose physical and mental health risks to personnel. Suggestions of ways to reduce health risks among U.S. personnel include increasing the number and training of medical staff, regular inspections and upgrading of medical facilities, blood storage, expanded survival training, improved materials for clothing, better preassignment psychological screening, substance abuse instruction, and increased recreational facilities. A more physically and mentally fit community would make fewer mistakes, lowering the risks of field operations.

*Communications.* When remote scientific field parties are in operation, they are completely reliant on high-frequency radio for communication with their home stations. Sometimes, these parties travel as far as a thousand miles away. All distant operations are required to check in on a daily basis, and search and rescue operations will automatically begin if a communication is missed. However, atmospheric disruptions occur and there are frequent equipment breakdowns. Better equipment maintenance and equipment modernization could lead to improved communications networks with remote field parties. This would reduce the risks to such operations, as rescue teams could be deployed more quickly.

### Environmental risks

Human activity produces many by-products that must be disposed of. The very existence of a scientific mission necessarily has an effect on the environment of Antarctica. Any venture produces solid waste, such as scrap metal, chemicals, batteries, combustibles (including paper and wood products, oils, experimental animal carcasses, plastics, and rubber products) and liquid waste (such as human waste, garbage and laundry effluents, and photographic liquids), and other debris. Given the frigid temperatures, almost nothing is degradable and the accumulation of debris is thought to be unsightly. Waste will remain if it is not hauled away to the United States (retrograded). Sewage and other liquid waste is discharged into McMurdo Sound after treatment, and some combustible materials are burned, which discharges pollutants into the air. Antarctica's land and water areas are enormous, with a corresponding absorptive capacity. So, it is unknown what the risks to the environment might be and the corresponding impact on USAP personnel or the natural habitat of wildlife, although a simple modeling exercise done by NSF suggests that the air quality meets or far exceeds U.S. National Ambient Air Quality Standards (see draft *Supplemental Environmental Impact Statement*, 1990, sec. 5.2.1.2.).

### Balancing environmental and health and safety risks

It should be clear from the discussion so far in this section that there is a trade-off between reducing the health and safety risks to the people who live and visit Antarctica and reducing the risks to the environment of Antarctica. The solution to reducing many of the health and safety risks cited involves increasing the personnel at the NSF stations, increasing the safety of aircraft operations, building more facilities, and so on. But with the additional activity would come additional waste products. On the other side of the coin, Congress has reacted to increased pressure from environmentalists to attend to the problems in Antarctica.

One option for decreasing environmental impacts is to streamline personnel, which could lead to increased health and safety risks for workers and tourists alike. Having fewer medical personnel would increase the risk of fatality in medical emergencies (such as the onset of a heart attack, stroke, or other life-threatening illness among workers and visitors). Having fewer flights into and out of the region would result in a smaller total risk of death from an airline crash and lower environmental impacts, but would lead to a greater risk to health and safety from more limited supplies. Having fewer search and rescue team personnel, safety, recreation, or communication specialists could also jeopardize the safety of workers and tourists, as described earlier. Assuming that the scientific mission requires a minimum number of individuals to support the experimentation and observations that are conducted in Antarctica, the reduction in personnel would necessarily come from support staff.

Trade-offs also occur when a resource allocation decision is made about risks in Antarctica. In this case, Congress actually made such a decision when it made its fiscal year 1990 appropriation: Of an estimated $8.21 million for Antarctica's health and environmental programs, $5 million was specifically allocated to the environment. The majority of the funds spent on the environment were targeted to wastewater and solid waste management, clean-up of old research sites, and the purchase of additional fuel tanks and hoses to lower the risk of fuel spills.

### Tourists

In 1989 approximately 3,000 tourists visited Antarctica, generating about $1.3 billion for the travel industry, with projections of further annual increases in those numbers. Arrival to the area is by air (military and commercial) and by sea. Costs for these visits range from $1,500 for three days to $70,000 for a seven-week cross country ski trip to the South Pole (Bly,

1989; Slater & Basch, 1991). This price range suggests that the typical tourist to Antarctica is from a high-income household and certainly adventurous. Chile was the first country (and at this point still the only one) to open a hotel on the continent, at its Teniente Marsh Station.

Most tourists expect to be able to visit the scientific station of their country. There is great variation in the degree of "welcome" received at the installations of different countries, with the United States being among the less receptive. Although a traveler's code suggesting appropriate behavior toward wildlife and the environment has been developed and distributed to tour companies, there is anxiety among NSF officials as well as environmentalists about a potential explosion in tourism in the area: NSF is concerned about its role in any potential emergency rescue operation and environmentalists worry about the disruption to wildlife and the environment.

### Equity in safety trade-offs

#### Worker safety versus environmental impacts

Congress has authorized that the NSF direct a Safety, Environment, and Health (SEH) Initiative with a $150 million budget over a five-year period (*Antarctica Journal of the United States*, 1989; Booth, 1990). In this time of severe fiscal constraints, these expenditures loom large and clearly compete with other domestic programs that address the health and environmental needs in the United States. Despite a potentially large budgetary appropriation, dollar estimates are not available for many of the major or marginal changes considered for the SEH Initiative in Antarctica. Because much of the money allocated so far under the initiative has been spent on studies and surveys, it is not feasible in this chapter for us to quantitatively identify any actual management decisions and analyze potential trade-offs. However, four alternatives were considered in the December 1990 draft *Supplemental Environmental Impact Statement for the USAP* (pp. 3–17). The alternative recommended by the agency involves completing the five-year SEH initiative begun in fiscal year 1990, applying U.S. environmental laws and regulations to the U.S. presence in Antarctica, and consolidating USAP activities leading to a reduction in support personnel in Antarctica. The report suggests that there might be a 20% to 24% support staff reduction at McMurdo Station. Although streamlining of redundant personnel could lead to improved safety and health by allowing other support staff to service a smaller number of people, the current Antarctic health and safety system's reliability may have been enhanced by retaining usually redundant staff for occasional emergency periods. Also, the additional science and support operations during the winter could pose additional safety and health risks: riskier flight operations, more difficult search and rescue operations, more difficult emergency medical evacuations, and so on. Also, a forgone option would be increasing the support staff to lower medical risks, provide more effective rescue operations, better mental health through expanded recreation facilities, and so on.

The obvious equity challenge here involves increased safety and health risks (an increased risk of death) to clearly identified individuals who are operating in a dangerous and harsh environment to provide benefits to society (from scientific research) weighed against the reduced risks of degradation to the environment with unknown (and probably low) benefits that would accrue to a small proportion of the wildlife in Antarctica.

A major oil spill in 1989 provides an example of a catastrophic event in Antarctica. On January 28, 1989, the *Bahia Paraiso*, an Argentine tourist and resupply ship, ran aground and broke up, spilling more than 150,000 gallons of fuel. The ship was leaving Arthur Harbor near Palmer Station after a sightseeing visit on shore for the 81 tourists aboard. Wildlife fatalities and breeding failures followed the spill, and several scientific studies were imperiled by the change in the baseline data that occurred because of it. The costs of the spill included a $2 million cleanup, with financial and labor resources diverted from other missions, and a scientific mission with a team of 15 scientists assigned to continue with studies to determine the environmental impact of the spill (Noblet, 1989).

This background provides a focus for a qualitative discussion of equity and risk trade-offs between the environment and human health and safety. It is possible to lower the risks of a fuel spill in Antarctica by (1) building more safeguards into the storage tanks, and (2) decreasing the fuel supply by having lower reserves or by having fewer people at the stations (and therefore having lower fuel requirements). Any of these alternatives might increase the risk to worker safety and therefore pose an equity issue that would require weighing worker against environmental concerns: Different types of storage tanks would be costly (diverting resources from other programs) and would need to be transported to Antarctica; having lower reserves would jeopardize operations if there were a major catastrophe and a portion of the lower reserves were lost (operations might have to close down completely); and having fewer people at the stations would pose the risks described above.

### Tourists versus workers

Consider the following two views on Antarctic tourism:

1. The USAP is supported by the taxpayers of the United States. Most of the tourists visiting Antarctica are U.S. taxpayers. Therefore, tourists have a right to visit Antarctica and the U.S. research stations located there.
2. Science has a very short season in Antarctica. The cost of doing science is very high because of the support, materials, and person-

nel necessary to conduct research in the remote and harsh environment. Diverting time and resources away from scientific research to mollify tourists could be crippling to the research efforts and detrimental to the fragile environment of Antarctica.

These two views reflect the extreme positions regarding tourism and the USAP. Concerns expressed by influential Americans about their poor treatment at USAP stations have prompted a great deal of discussion of the trade-offs involved in allowing tourists in the area. One of these trade-offs involves the equity issue of potential risk exposures in a voluntary setting. There have been four catastrophic events involving tourists in the past dozen years: the crash of an Air New Zealand plane in 1979, killing 279 people; a 1986 tourist plane crash killing 10; the 1991 crash killing 19 tourists; and the *Bahia Paraiso* oil spill in 1989. Therefore, a potential emergency involving tourists is not just a theoretical possibility, and the risks have been increasing as the number of tourists has been increasing. Although tourists presumably understand that travel to Antarctica entails risks to personal safety and those risks are undertaken voluntarily, potential spillover risks are not internalized by the tourists or tour operators. If a tourist expedition is caught in an emergency, the USAP is typically called upon for assistance. This has the effect of not only diverting resources from the scientific program, but also putting at additional risk any personnel who may be involved in a search and rescue operation. Of course, emergencies are likely to occur during extreme weather, when other failures at the USAP stations are also likely to happen.

The *Bahia Paraiso* breakup, which occurred after a tourist visit, is a good example of the enormous resources that may have to be devoted to a tourist emergency. Another incident involving U.S. emergency teams brings out the vulnerability of U.S. support personnel during multiple emergencies. In January 1990 two members of the Indian expedition to Antarctica, in separate incidents, suffered medical emergencies at the same time: The first experienced a severe heart attack and a second suffered a duodenal ulcer and needed immediate evacuation. A request for help was immediately issued to the USAP, despite the fact that the Indian station is located 2,000 miles away from that of the United States. This situation points out the high likelihood of multiple emergencies, especially given the large number of tourists visiting the area (*Hindustan Times*, 1990).

### Distributional equity

This section presents models that can represent the fairness of the distributions of risks across groups of people in Antarctica. Such models can take into account the possibility and impact of multiple emergencies at once, using joint probability distributions over mortality or morbidity outcomes. We use the models to compare the fairness of two hypothetical scenarios for Antarctic operations. Such models might be used to help clarify a societal decision maker's thinking about alternatives. The selection of relevant groupings of people would be made by the decision maker, given the decision context and input from members of affected groups.

Fishburn and Sarin (1991) classify distributional equity concepts by the level of specificity in data required to measure each equity notion. See also Sarin (this book) for an overview of equity concepts. For simplicity, assume each person can either live or die, with known probabilities. *Individual risk equity* is modeled using each person's probability of death. Since these are probabilities before an accident or exposure event occurs, this is also called ex ante equity (see, e.g., Keller & Sarin, 1988). Experimental subjects queried by Keller and Sarin preferred an equal distribution of a 1% ex ante chance of death for each of 10 rescuers (attempting to save trapped miners) resulting from each being stationed in a possible cave-in location for 1 hour over an option in which 1 miner would be stationed in the cave-in location for an entire 10-hour shift, with a resulting 10% chance of death. In light of such preferences, Antarctic operating procedures for searches and rescues could be examined for options for spreading risks among workers.

The remaining equity categories require the classification of individuals into mutually exclusive groups. *Group risk equity* is modeled using the probability that an outcome will occur in which a *specific* number of group members die. Because the focus is now on the outcome of an accident or exposure, this is also called ex post equity. Sometimes, there is concern for the distribution of deaths within an outcome. For example, if there is a possible outcome with 100 deaths at an Antarctica Station, they could be distributed as 100 scientists or 100 support staff or some combination dying. In this outcome, there may be concern for the ex post equity of the distribution between the groups.

Sarin (1985), Keeney and Winkler (1985), and Keller and Sarin (1988) offer examples of related models to incorporate measures of individual risk equity and group risk equity into a preference model for guiding decision making on policies involving societal risks. These multiple-attribute preference models are defined over three attributes: ex ante (individual risk) equity, ex post (group risk) equity, and the total number of fatalities. In these models, a utility function is defined over the number of fatalities in the population, to represent preferences. Such preferences might include some equity concerns, such as avoidance of a catastrophe for the entire society. Fishburn and Sarin (1991) note that the probability distribution over the number of fatalities can be used as a datum to directly model *social outcome equity*. They also introduce a modeling approach for *dispersive equity*, which requires information on the joint probability of outcomes with specific numbers of people dying in each group.

In Antarctica, tourists, rescue workers, and other Antarctic workers are three groups who may have different patterns of exposures to risks. If an air crash of a tourist flight occurs, Antarctic safety personnel will attempt a

Table 1 *Scenarios 1 and 2*

| *Scenario 1: Status quo* | | | | |
| | | | Groups | |
| Mutually exclusive states | Prob. | Tourists $N_1 = 3,000$ | Rescuers $N_2 = 50$ | Others $N_3 = 950$ |
| --- | --- | --- | --- | --- |
| *Fatal crash of tourist plane* | | | | |
| Rescuer dies. | .050 | 100 | 1 | 0 |
| No rescuers die. | .100 | 100 | 0 | 0 |
| *Fatal emergency occurs in Antarctic operations* | | | | |
| Rescuers and others die. | .110 | 0 | 2 | 5 |
| No rescuers die. | .165 | 0 | 0 | 11 |
| *No deaths* | .575 | 0 | 0 | 0 |

| *Scenario 2: Streamlining option* | | | | |
| | | | Groups | |
| Mutually exclusive states | Prob. | Tourists $N_1 = 3,000$ | Rescuers $N_2 = 50$ | Others $N_3 = 900$ |
| --- | --- | --- | --- | --- |
| *Fatal crash of tourist plane* | | | | |
| Rescuer dies. | .050 | 100 | 1 | 0 |
| No rescuers die. | .100 | 100 | 0 | 0 |
| *Fatal emergency occurs in Antarctic operations* | | | | |
| Rescuers and others die. | .150 | 0 | 2 | 5 |
| No rescuers die. | .200 | 0 | 0 | 10 |
| *No deaths* | .500 | 0 | 0 | 0 |

*Note:* Entries in table are number of deaths in each group in each state.

rescue, but with some risks to themselves. Also, given current resource levels, diversion of personnel efforts for health and safety maintenance are quite costly to the ongoing scientific operations.

To illustrate the application of the various equity measures, we developed the two stylized scenarios in Table 1, with a quantification of risks that bears some resemblance to the risks and exposures in Antarctica: Scenarios 1 and 2, respectively, show the status quo and the changes that could result under the streamlining plan proposed in the draft *Supplemental Environmental Impact Statement* of the USAP. Under Scenario 2, the number of Antarctic (nonrescue) workers is decreased, so fewer people are exposed to risks in Antarctica, but there will be fewer people available to aid safety and maintenance operations. So, risks may increase for the fewer people who are there. For example, the risk of workers dying from a fire or other

effects of poor maintenance may be increased, if there is a decline in maintenance on the aging USAP dormitories. Such a disaster occurred at the
Indian station, where four people died in the men's dormitory of suspected
carbon monoxide poisoning from a diesel generator (*Hindustan Times*, 1990).[1]

We constructed Scenario 1 to have ex ante probabilities of death over a
one-year period for tourists, rescue workers, and other workers to be of
the same magnitude as the actual risks. A tourist's risk is estimated by
noting that there have been 3 crashes in about 600 round-trip flights (over
20 years), which is a $3/600 = .005$ probability that the tourist's round-trip
flight will crash and (nearly) all on board will die. So if each tourist takes
only one trip, the individual probability of death due to a crash would be
about .005. Other workers' risk is estimated from the information that there
have been about 50 deaths since 1946, with roughly 20,000 worker-expo-
sures (on a seasonal rather than annual basis), giving an ex ante probability
of death of .0025. We assume rescue workers face a little more than double
the risk faced by other workers, modeled in this example with a .0054 probability of death. We used these ex ante probabilities for the simple five-
state example in Table 1 to construct compatible probabilities for the five
states. In Scenario 1, representing the status quo, the expected number of
fatalities is 17.635 in one year, which is close to the actual average number
of tourist and worker fatalities over the years. The streamlining option in
Scenario 2 reflects higher ex ante risks to workers and rescuers, but the risk
to tourists remains the same. The expected number of fatalities in Scenario
2 is 18.100, representing almost one expected death more per each two-
year period. In the following subsections, various equity measures are calculated and compared for both scenarios.

### Individual risk (ex ante) inequity

Fishburn and Sarin (1991) outline desired properties of equity models and
give suggestions of functional forms satisfying certain properties. They
suggest the following measure of individual risk inequity, where subscript
$I$ represents individual inequity, which neutralizes the effect of differences
in expected numbers of fatalities:

$$d_I(m_1, m_2, \ldots, m_N) = \sum_{i=1}^{N} (m_i/\bar{m} - 1)^2.$$

If each individual $i$ had probability of death $m_i = 0$, the formula would
require division by zero, so in this special case $d_I(0, 0, \ldots, 0)$ is defined to
be 0, with no disutility or inequity. Higher numbers indicate more inequity.

For this example, $d_I(\text{Scenario 1}) = 236.5$. For Scenario 2, in comparison
with Scenario 1, the ex ante probability of death (a) remains at .005 for each
of the 3,000 tourists, (b) increases from .0054 to .0070 for each of the 50

rescuers, and (c) increases from .0025 to .0031 for the 900 other workers (which is 50 fewer workers than in Scenario 1). These changes result in Scenario 2 being more individually risk equitable, with $d_I$(Scenario 2) = 138.8, which is roughly 60% of the $d_I$ value for Scenario 1. This decrease is primarily due to the smaller difference in the ex ante probabilities of the two heavily weighted large groups in Scenario 2 (a range from .0031 for other workers to .0050 for tourists) compared with Scenario 1 (a wider range from .0025 to .0050).

### Group risk (ex post) inequity

Two components of group risk inequity have been distinguished by Fishburn and Sarin (1991), intergroup and within-group inequity. They suggest modeling *nonuniformity of expected fatality rates across groups* by

$$d_G^1(\text{Scenario}) = \sum_{j=1}^{n}(r_j - \bar{r})^2,$$

where

$r_j$ = expected fatality rate for group $j$,

$\bar{r}$ = mean group fatality rate = $\sum_{j=1}^{n=3} r_j/n$, and

the subscript $G$ represents group risk inequity.

This measure is calculated for Scenario 1 with the following information:

|  | $N_j$ | Expected fatalities | $r_j$ |
|---|---|---|---|
| Tourists | 3,000 | .05(100) + .1(100) = 15.00 | 15/3,000 = .0050 |
| Rescue workers | 50 | .05(1) + .11(2) = .27 | .27/50 = .0054 |
| Other workers | 950 | .11(7) + .165(11) = 2.59 | 2.59/950 = .0025 |
|  |  | Mean group fatality rate $\bar{r}$ = .0043 |  |

So $d_G^1$ is $4.98 \times 10^{-6}$ for Scenario 1 and $7.78 \times 10^{-6}$ for Scenario 2. Thus, Scenario 2 is less group risk equitable in the sense of having less uniformity of expected fatality rates across groups, with $r_j$ values ranging from .0031 to .0070 rather than the narrower range from .0025 to .0054 for Scenario 1.

   Note that in this simple example, the ex ante probability of death is the same for each person in a group, so the expected fatality rate $r_j$ for a group is the same as the ex ante probability of death for one group member. Scenario 2 is more inequitable with respect to the individual risk inequity measure (which uses each person's ex ante probability, weighing each person equally and thus larger groups more heavily) but Scenario 1 is more inequitable with respect to the measure of the nonuniformity of expected fatality rates across groups, which weighs each group equally.

Groups' sizes will usually vary, requiring a choice between using the *number* of fatalities in a group or the *proportion* of a group's population dying. The fatality rate is used in this $d_G{}^1$ measure of intergroup risk inequity. So, if 15 of 3,000 tourists die, this is represented not as the absolute number who die, but as a rate of $15/3000 = .005$ dying in the group. But when judging the fairness or acceptability of risk distributions, the public may sometimes focus more on the absolute number dying (weighing groups equally) rather than focusing on the fraction of the group dying. Then, equalization of the numbers dying across groups may be seen as most fair.

Fishburn and Sarin (1991) suggest that *within-group risk inequity* can be modeled as follows, assuming preference for common fates. In this formula, it is seen as fairer for people in a group to have identical outcomes:

$$d_G{}^2(\text{Scenario}) = + \sum_{j=1}^{n} \sum_{k=0}^{N} p_j(k)k(N_j - k)/(N_j{}^2),$$

where $p_j(k) = $ probability of $k$ deaths in group $j$; $N_j = $ population size of group $j$, assumed to be all even numbers; and $n = $ number of groups. Higher numbers are more inequitable. The positive sign in front of the double summation is for the common-fate form of the measure; a negative sign would be for the catastrophe-avoiding version. Note that in the catastrophe-avoiding form, a common fate of 0 deaths in a group of 10 contributes $-k(N_j - k)/(N_j{}^2) = -0(10 - 0)/100 = 0$ to the calculation, which is less equitable than 1 death, which contributes $-9/100 = -.09$ to the calculation.

For Scenario 1, $d_G{}^2 = .0125$ and for Scenario 2, $d_G{}^2 = .0146$. So, streamlining (Scenario 2) is more inequitable in the common-fate preference form of within group inequity, due to a combination of factors. Each component of the calculation, corresponding to one group and one state, is $k(N_j - k)/N_j{}^2$, which is weighted by the probability. So, increasing the probability of the outcome that 2 rescuers and 5 other workers die from .11 to .15, and increasing the probability of the outcome when only other workers die from .165 to .200 (despite one less worker dying in that outcome), makes Scenario 2 more inequitable. Also, streamlining the number of other workers from the status quo of 950 to 900 in Scenario 2, and keeping the same numbers of deaths (0, 5, or 11), makes the components corresponding to the other worker group bigger and thus less equitable: 5 deaths out of 950 people is more equitable $[5(950 - 5)/950^2 = .005235]$ than 5 deaths out of 900 people $[5(900 - 5)/900^2 = .005525]$.

Note that, in the catastrophe-avoidance form of the model, a catastrophe is the loss of nearly all of a group's population. The impact of a catastrophe is represented by the product of the number of fatalities times the number of survivors in the entire group. When this product is small, as in when almost all die, this model yields high inequity, since the sign is negative and higher numbers represent more inequity. The model yields minimum inequity when exactly half the population dies, since the product of number of deaths times number of survivors is maximized.

However, in the case of airplane crashes, all travelers in one plane may die, but the entire population of travelers won't die. The layperson still tends to call such an outcome a catastrophe and react to the event as a horrible, upsetting disaster. So, a modification of the measure might be made to account for the modal size of a catastrophic event. For this example, such a modification might treat any number of deaths from the modal amount $M_j$ to the total population size as equally onerous, by replacing $k(N_j - k)$ with $M_j(N_j - M_j)$ for all $k > M_j$, and using the common fate preference version (with the positive sign). Then the maximum product, indicating *maximum* inequity, would occur at any number of deaths $k$ equal to the catastrophic modal amount of deaths $M_j$ or larger.

Finally, a possible measure of *total group risk inequity* could combine the intergroup and within group inequity measures. One possible combined measure would calculate the weighted average,

$$d_G(\text{Scenario 1}) = c_1 d_G{}^1(\text{Sc. 1}) + c_2 d_G{}^2(\text{Sc. 1}),$$

where $c_1$ and $c_2$ are positive scaling constants.

### Social outcome inequity

Social outcome inequity can be modeled, assuming common-fate preference, by

$$d_s(\text{Scenario}) = + \sum_{y=0}^{N} y(N-y)p(y),$$

where $p(y) =$ probability of $y$ fatalities in the total population of size $N$ (see Fishburn & Sarin, 1991). Opposite orderings would be obtained with the catastrophe-avoiding form, with a negative sign before the summation. For Scenario 1, $d_s = 69004.6$, and Scenario 2 has greater inequity from the social outcome measure with $d_s = 69957.6$. Scenario 2's worse performance is due to the increase from .11 to .15 in the probability of 7 rescue and other workers dying, and to the increase from .165 to .200 in the probability of only nonrescue workers dying, despite the decrease from 11 to 10 worker deaths.

A summary comparison of the various equity measures for both scenarios shows that changing group size and changing risks affected the relative inequities between scenarios. Note that these equity measures can be modified by dividing by a constant to avoid numbers being close to zero. Since the purpose is to compare across scenarios, the relative numerical values are of more importance than the absolute numbers. As shown in Table 2, Scenario 2's streamlining option is less individually risk inequitable than Scenario 1 (the status quo), but more intergroup risk inequitable, more within-group inequitable, more social outcome inequitable, and more dis-

Table 2 *Summary of equity measures for scenarios*

|  | Scenario 1 | Scenario 2 |
|---|---|---|
| Expected number of fatalities | 17.635 | 18.100 |
| *Inequity measures* | | |
| Individual risk inequity $d_I$ | 236.5[a] | 138.8 |
| Group risk inequity | | |
|   Intergroup $d_G^1$ | .00000498 | .00000778[a] |
|   Within-group $d_G^2$ | .0125 | .0146[a] |
| Social outcome inequity $d_S$ | 69004.6 | 69957.6[a] |
| Dispersive inequity $d_D$ | .00022 | .00026[a] |

[a] Larger numbers are more inequitable and are indicated by asterisks.

persive inequitable. (Dispersive equity modeling is discussed in the next section.) So, although streamlining results in a more equal distribution of individuals' ex ante probabilities of death, from the view of different groups, it is less fair than the status quo. In addition, streamlining results in a higher expected number of fatalities. The U.S. Antarctica Program is considering streamlining of personnel numbers to decrease risks to the environment. But an unintended outcome of streamlining may be to worsen the distribution of risks among groups of individuals at risk in Antarctica, so careful consideration of the trade-offs between risks to the environment and risks to humans must occur.

Equity measures are one component in decision making about risks in Antarctica. They can aid in selecting among alternative policy options. Hypothetical scenarios similar to the ones here can be used to help create new policies with more fair distributions of risks, by identifying variables that affect fairness.

## Overlapping memberships

Although the equity models discussed in the preceding section assume mutually exclusive groups, meaningful classifications of people are not always mutually exclusive. For example, people may be described by their membership in non–mutually exclusive classifications defined by gender and by role. We can define four mutually exclusive groups from the two classifications of males versus females and Antarctica workers versus tourists. Equity models generally treat the mutually exclusive groups equally, perhaps adjusting for size of the group, but not considering varying interactions among different sets of groups.

The best way to model dispersive equity for classifications meaningful to people that span multiple mutually exclusive groups is an open research question. Sarin (this book) provides a motivating example, shown

Table 3 *Dispersive equity with interrelated groups*

| Scenario A: | 50% chance of outcome 1 | 50% chance of outcome 2 | Prob. of death |
|---|---|---|---|
| Government scientist | Dies (1) | Lives (0) | .5 |
| Nongovernment scientist | Lives (0) | Dies (1) | .5 |
| Government support staff | Dies (1) | Lives (0) | .5 |
| Nongovernment support staff | Lives (0) | Dies (1) | .5 |
| *Summary* | | | *Expected dispersive inequity* |
| Over all 4 groups | $d^1_{\text{outcome 1}} = 1$ | $d^1_{\text{outcome 2}} = 1$ | Inequitable $d_D = 1$ |
| By government/nongovernment | Both gov't die $d^1_g = 1/2$ | Both nongov't die $d^1_g = 1/2$ | Inequitable $d_{Dg} = 1/2$ |
| By role | 1 of each dies $d^1_r = 0$ | 1 of each dies $d^1_r = 0$ | Equitable $d_{Dr} = 0$ |

| Scenario B: | 50% chance of outcome 1 | 50% chance of outcome 2 | Prob. of death |
|---|---|---|---|
| Government scientist | Dies (1) | Lives (0) | .5 |
| Nongovernment scientist | Lives (0) | Dies (1) | .5 |
| Government support staff | Lives (0) | Dies (1) | .5 |
| Nongovernment support staff | Dies (1) | Lives (0) | .5 |
| *Summary* | | | *Expected dispersive inequity* |
| Over all 4 groups | $d^1_{\text{outcome 1}} = 1$ | $d^1_{\text{outcome 2}} = 1$ | Inequitable $d_D = 1$ |
| By government/nongovernment | 1 of each dies $d^1_g = 0$ | 1 of each dies $d^1_g = 0$ | Equitable $d_{Dg} = 0$ |
| By role | 1 of each dies $d^1_r = 0$ | 1 of each dies $d^1_r = 0$ | Equitable $d_{Dr} = 0$ |

in Table 3, adapted here for the Antarctica context. This simple example has just four people, one in each of the four groups of government-employed scientists, nongovernment scientists, government-employed support staff, and nongovernment support staff. In both Scenarios A and B, each person has an equal 50% chance of death, so the scenarios are equitable with respect to individual risk equity. However, Scenario A leads to an inequitable distribution of risks by government-employment classification, but an equitable distribution by role. Scenario B leads to an equitable distribution of risks by both government classification and role. Over all four groups, both scenarios lead to the same level of dispersive inequity.

Fishburn and Sarin (1991) suggest a possible measure for *dispersive inequity*,

$$d^1(y)\sum_{j=1}^{n}(x_j-\bar{x})^2.$$

The fatality vector $y=(y_1, \ldots, y_j, \ldots, y_n)$ lists the number of fatalities in each of the $n$ groups that would result with one specific outcome. The proportional fatality vector $x=(x_1, \ldots, x_n)=(y_1/N_1, \ldots, y_n/N_n)$ adjusts the number of fatalities $y_j$ in each group $j$ by the group size $N_j$. So, this measure of dispersive inequity, $d^1(y)$, sums the squared differences between the fatality rate $x_j$ in each group and the mean fatality rate,

$$\bar{x}=\sum_{j=1}^{n}(y_j/N_j)/n=\left(\sum_{j=1}^{n}x_j\right)/n.$$

For outcome 1 in Scenario A, the fatality vector $y$ is (1, 0, 1, 0). The proportional fatality vector $x$ is $(1/1, 0/1, 1/1, 0/1)=(1, 0, 1, 0)$, since each group $j$ has size $N_j=1$. The mean group fatality rate is $\bar{x}=(1+0+1+0)/4=1/2$. So, the dispersive inequity of outcome 1 over all four groups can be measured by $d^1_{\text{outcome 1}}(1,0,1,0)=1$. Higher numbers indicate greater inequity.

The dispersive inequity with respect to government-employment classification is

$$d_g^1{}_{\text{outcome 1}}(2/2 \text{ gov't workers die, } 0/2 \text{ nongov't die})=1/2.$$

The dispersive inequity with respect to role is

$$d_r^1{}_{\text{outcome 1}}(1/2 \text{ scientists die, } 1/2 \text{ support workers die})=0.$$

So outcome 1 is dispersive equitable with respect to role, but not government classification. Then, the expected dispersive inequity for a scenario can be calculated by weighting the dispersive inequity for each outcome by the probability of the outcome. For example, over all four groups, the expected dispersive inequity for Scenario A is

$$d_D(\text{Scenario A})=.5d^1_{\text{outcome 1}}+.5d^1_{\text{outcome 2}}=1.$$

The challenge now is to develop a measure of dispersive inequity that takes into account the overlapping membership structure. One possibility is to sum the three measures of dispersive inequity, $d^1+d_g^1+d_r^1$. For scenario A this would result in $1+.5+0=1.5$ for each of the two outcomes. In contrast, the fairer scenario B would have $d^1+d_g^1+d_r^1=1$ for both outcomes. A refinement of this would be to weight the dispersive inequity measures by a parameter reflecting their relative importance,

Overall dispersive inequity:   $od^1=d^1+w_g d_g^1+w_r d_r^1.$

The judgment of the magnitude of the weights, $w_g$ for government-employment classification inequity and $w_g$ for role inequity, would be made by the decision maker. More research is needed on the advantages and disadvantages of this type of model of dispersive inequity for overlapping memberships.

Sometimes, mutually exclusive groups cannot be formed, such as the following classifications: Antarctic staff working versus Antarctic staff on off-hours recreation, scientists using military airplanes versus scientists using civilian airplanes. At different times, a person, say Smith, can be in each of the four groups. One possibility for future research is to make a person into a vector of entities, such as Smith–civilian worker, Smith–off-hours recreation user, Smith–scientist, and Smith–expeditionary adventurer. Then, these entities are not overlapping and can be placed in mutually exclusive groups to which the existing equity models could be applied.

### Conclusions and future research

We have identified a number of implications for incorporation of fairness concerns into preference models for societal risk, motivated by the application arena of Antarctica. The Antarctic risk examples used in this chapter are only meant to be suggestive. Before any thorough scientific analysis can proceed, a quantification of the risks, costs, and benefits of the status quo and alternative programs must be undertaken. Because of the implications for scientific research and therefore the greater societal benefits, it is important that estimates of the risk/cost/benefit distributions be made and used in cost/benefit and equity modeling. This step is critical if the methodologies suggested in this chapter are to be used to clarify risk and equity trade-offs in Antarctica. Nevertheless, it may always be difficult to get the detailed probability distribution information needed for the equity measures as they currently exist. One possibility is to modify the measures to include components that could be estimated by expert judgment. For example, when modeling overlapping memberships (say voluntary and work activities), the correlation could be estimated between the probabilities of death for each person due to volunteer versus work activities.

More attention should be placed on extending the equity modeling work to multiple, rather than just binary, outcome levels (see Harvey, 1985b). In many cases, hazards can lead to multiple morbidity and mortality outcome levels across the population.

Also, the equity models discussed above focus only on the fairness of the distribution of the risks, disregarding jointly received benefits. But Keller and Sarin (1988) found that subjects tended to prefer a distribution of risks that matched the distribution of benefits (in a facility siting scenario) over a more equal distribution of risks. In Antarctic operations, there are sizable scientific benefits plus the benefits to tourists and expeditions. Sometimes a scientist with preexisting health risk factors will be given a medical waiver allowing travel to Antarctica to carry out research. In such a case, the medical risks must be weighed against the criticality of the person to the scientific mission. Most people voluntarily choose to go to Antarctica, and thus the personal benefits are probably relatively clear, but the corresponding health and safety risks may not be accurately perceived. Furthermore, even if Antarctic workers and tourists are willing to accept accurately perceived risks, the risks may not be acceptable to Congress or the public. The public's reaction to the Challenger disaster may give insight into the greater risk aversion of the public compared to that revealed by the voluntary choices of the astronauts.

Future equity modeling efforts should include both risk and benefit information. In some situations, such as siting noxious facilities, an envy-free allocation of benefits and risks may be achieved by adjusting the benefit and risk distributions so each participant prefers his or her own allocation over any one else's, thus creating a state of equilibrium (see Sarin, this book, and Keller & Sarin, 1988). However, in the Antarctic case of voluntary risk exposures, the members of different groups already accept the risks (so the status quo is in equilibrium), but policymakers may feel the current risk and benefit allocations are unacceptable.

The contexts of the risk exposures faced by different groups in Antarctica vary by factors that have been shown to affect perceived riskiness and that may affect perceived fairness of distributions of risks (see, e.g., Slovic, Fischhoff, & Lichtenstein, 1979; and Gould et al., 1988). These factors, which frame the risk in alternative contexts, include:

1. voluntary versus involuntary exposures to hazards or toxics;
2. exposures during work, off-hour recreation, expeditionary adventures, or as a tourist on a cruise ship or airline charter flight;
3. the degree of actual and perceived control over risks or exposures.

Thus, it is important to examine how such factors affect the perceived fairness of distributions of risk. In one experiment, Keller and Sarin (1988) observed that framing risks in alternative contexts affected perceived fairness. Further experimental and modeling work is needed on this topic.

Finally, one way of incorporating the risk exposure context into models is to represent the risks faced by one individual by a vector of probabilities of fatality due to different risk contexts. So, if the distinction between work and recreational exposure is important in a specific problem, a person could be identified by the probability of death due to work activities and the probability of death due to recreational (nonwork) activities. Then, preference models and equity measures would keep track of the risk exposure context, perhaps by having different weights on different contexts. Instead of modifying the measures, the group definition could be modified. For example, we could split the group of personnel into volunteers and non-volunteers. But one person may be exposed to the same risk sometimes in a voluntary status and sometimes in an involuntary status, so the problem of overlapping memberships will be faced. Further, there may be too many alternative frames or contexts to distinguish each of them in the model.

### References

*Antarctica Journal of the United States.* (1989, June). NSF, 24 (2).

Bly, L. (1989, September 10). Antarctica tourism worries authorities. *Milwaukee Journal.*

Booth, W. (1990, September 28). Face-off forming on Antarctic ice: Watchdog group threatens to sue NSF over researchers' waste. *Washington Post.*

Fishburn, P. C. (1984). Equity axioms for public risks. *Operations Research, 32,* 901–908.

Fishburn, P. C., & Sarin, R. K. (1991, July). Dispersive equity and social risk. *Management Science, 37,* 751–769.

Fishburn, P. C., & Straffin, P. D. (1989). Equity considerations in public risks evaluation. *Operations Research, 37,* 229–239.

Gould, L. C., Gardner, G. T., DeLuca, D. R., Tiemann, A. R., Doob, Leonard W., and Stolwijk, J. A. J., (1988). *Perceptions of technological risks and benefits.* New York: Russell Sage Foundation.

Harris, R. J. (1976). Handling negative inputs: On the plausible equity formulae. *Journal of Experimental Social Psychology, 12,* 194–209.

    (1980). Equity judgments in hypothetical four-person partnerships. *Journal of Experimental Social Psychology, 16,* 95–115.

Harvey, C. M. (1985a). Decision analysis models for social attitudes toward inequity. *Management Science, 31,* 1199–1212.

    (1985b). Preference functions for catastrophe and risk inequity. *Large Scale Systems, 8,* 131–146.

*Hindustan Times.* (1990, January 21). US aid for Indian Antarctic team.

Jasanoff, S. (1986). *Risk management and political culture.* New York: Russell Sage Foundation.

Kanamine, L. (1990, November 19). Summit held on Antarctic future. *USA Today,* p. 11A [summit on mineral exploration].

Keeney, R. L. (1980a). Equity and public risk. *Operations Research, 28* 527–534.

    (1980b). Utility functions for equity and public risk. *Management Science, 26,* 345–353.

    (1980c). Evaluating alternatives involving potential fatalities. *Operations Research, 28,* 188–205.

Keeney, R. L., & Winkler, R. L. (1985). Evaluating decision strategies for equity of public risks. *Operations Research, 33,* 955–970.

Keller, L. R. & Sarin, R. K. (1988). Equity in social risk: Some empirical observations. *Risk Analysis, 8* (1), 135–146.

Levitt, A. (1990, October 13). Mutually inclusive. *Washington Post,* p. A19.

Noblet, K. (1989, October 15). Antarctica: End of the innocence. *The Sun Sentinel,* Fort Lauderdale, FL.

*Safety in Antarctica,* (1988). Report to the National Science Foundation.

Sarin, R. K. (1985). Measuring equity in public risk. *Operations Research, 33,* 210–217.

Slater, S., & Basch, H. (1991, August 4). Antarctic tourism issues surfacing. *Los Angeles Times*, p. L18.

Slovic, P., Fischhoff, Baruch, & Lichtenstein, S. (1979). Rating the Risks. *Environment, 21*, 14–20, 36–39.

*Supplemental Environmental Impact Statement* for the United States Antarctic Program. (1990, December) draft.

Walster, E., Walster, G. W., & Berscheid, E. (1978). *Equity: Theory and research.* Boston: Allyn & Bacon.

*Washington Post.* (1991, February 19). 19 US tourists killed in Beagle Channel Crash: Chilean plane was on leg of Antarctica trip. p. A14, Associated Press.

### Note

1 Although the people who would lose their jobs in Antarctica due to streamlining would face risks in their new jobs, those risks are excluded from the model of Scenario 2, since they won't be in Antarctica. In that sense, this is analogous to a partial equilibrium model.

# Part VI

# Conclusion

# Postscript

*Jonathan Baron*

Inequity and injustice are not trivial. Some couples spend more money on a single meal in a restaurant than hundreds of millions of families earn in an entire year. People are jailed and tortured in one country for saying what, in another country, might get them elected to office. We are disturbed by inequity, but our disturbance is uneven. We are sometimes more upset by small violations, especially when they are close at hand, than by apparently much greater ones farther away.

Our collective judgments of equity and inequity will play a large role in determining what is done and not done, which inequities are remedied and which are not. Past psychology has demonstrated that judgments of equity do affect our actions, whether these judgments concern two people together in the laboratory or mass political movements. In the future, such judgments will be no less important, as the world grapples with problems of how to distribute the costs of global warming, environmental destruction, and population growth.

The essays in this book represent a new approach to the study of equity judgments. The authors are committed – to varying degrees, to be sure – to an approach that can loosely be called *behavioral decision theory*. One prominent feature of this approach is a concern with normative models, idealized standards of judgment or decision making. Researchers in this tradition take various positions on the role of such models, as I shall discuss shortly, but we all have something to say about them.

An advantage of this approach is that it is not frivolous. It has implications for application. Specifically, to the extent to which we are justified in claiming that people are making errors by departing from normative models, we are justified in trying to persuade people of their errors. If we are less confident, we can at least raise questions and other points of view. We (scholars, that is) do this through writing articles and textbooks (which are read by students), designing educational interventions, and doing research on "debiasing," which can help in the development of such interventions.

The study of equity represents an interesting extension of the behavioral-decision-theory approach for two related reasons. First, equity judgments are moral judgments. For the first time, the approach is being applied to something other than self-interested judgments. (Although many problems used by researchers have concerned problems of policy, these problems were not chosen because they raised issues different from those raised by gambles involving money.) Second, as Mellers notes in her introduction, normative models for equity judgments are not well established, so more attention than usual should be given to development of the normative models themselves. These two features create special problems and opportunities for the extension of the behavioral-decision theory approach to judgments of justice and equity. This field is, as it develops, likely to inspire heat as well as light. People are committed more deeply to their moral beliefs than to their intuitions about proper decision making. But, at the same time, if the field can succeed in understanding why intuitions differ, it can play a role in resolving human conflict about the nature of justice and in increasing the level of justice around the world.

In this chapter, I shall discuss the preceding chapters with respect to three issues: their assumptions about normative models, the descriptive theory of how judgments of fairness are made and where they come from, and the prescriptive question of what recommendations might follow from such findings. I shall conclude with some suggestions about future research.

### Normative approaches

Normative models are idealized standards by which a judgment or decision may be evaluated. They are distinguished from prescriptive models for making judgments or decisions: Normative models need not be applicable in practice in everyday decision making; prescriptive models are intended exactly for such application. Prescriptive models should be designed so that decisions are evaluated as highly as possible according to a normative standard, taking into account the descriptive psychology of how decisions are made in the absence of prescriptive advice. Normative models are important because they provide the ultimate justification of any effort to improve decision making, whether through advice, education, or formal techniques.

A wide variety of normative approaches is represented in these chapters. One issue is the "metanormative" question of how normative theory should be discussed. Bar-Hillel and Yaari point out that most philosophical discussions of the theory of justice depend on intuitions about justice. "Intuitionist" philosophers make arguments directly from their own judgments about cases. To varying degrees, they compare their intuitions about different cases and try to discover general principles that account for them, in the manner of linguists. Rawls (1971) argues that the ultimate achievement of this method is a state of "reflective equilibrium," in which we account for our intuitions with a small number of principles, which may lead to modification of intuitions that conflict with the principles. Bar-Hillel and Yaari ask their subjects for intuitions, but they do not force their subjects to reflect at all. Still, they argue, their data are relevant to normative theory, because these intuitions are at least the starting point for normative inquiry.

At the other extreme, I have suggested (following Hare, 1981) that intuitions about justice need to be examined critically and that, in order to do this, we need to derive normative principles of justice from something other than our intuitions about justice itself. I suggest that we derive them from reflection on the ultimate purposes of the principles. Although such reflection could involve intuitions about purposes, these are not the same as intuitions about justice. For one thing, they lead to a contingent theory of the form, "If you want to achieve this purpose then here is what you must do." Hare (1981) suggests that we derive normative principles from (intuitions about) the logic of moral terms. This leads to a system that is contingent in another way, "If you want to know what is good, then first figure out what good means; you will then be able to discover what is good in this sense."

The literature on decision making in other contexts suggests strongly that intuitions about decision making are systematically biased in various ways. These biases might even be stronger in moral domains, where the chance to learn from feedback is reduced (because we are less likely to be aware of the consequences of our choices for others than for ourselves). Another argument against reliance on intuitions is that it is the intuitions that are at issue. Bar-Hillel and Yaari's approach makes it difficult to criticize anyone's intuitions – but not impossible, since people could still be found to have inconsistent intuitions.

The essays differ in the substance of their normative claims about justice, as well as in their favored methods of normative inquiry. The simplest and least controversial claim is that of Camerer and Loewenstein, who take Pareto "efficiency" as their normative standard. In this sense of the term, an efficient outcome is one in which it is impossible to make one person better off without hurting someone else. Failure to attain such outcomes when they are available is clearly undesirable; such a failure implies that someone can be helped without hurting anyone else. A breakdown in bargaining yields such a failure, when a bargain could have been struck that would benefit both parties. It is rare that we can say anything interesting about how to avoid such failure, but Camerer and Loewenstein manage to do so by showing some impediments to successful bargaining.

The more difficult normative problem is to choose among various Pareto efficient outcomes. My chapter presents a utilitarian solution, which assumes that utility – specifically, expected goal achievement – is interpersonally comparable so that the ideal is to maximize it, if necessary by increasing utility for some at the expense of a smaller decrease in utility for others. Any other approach would reduce the total amount of goal achievement compared to this one and would therefore be difficult to justify to the losers. This view serves as a kind of normative null hypothesis. It is, in a way, not a theory of justice at all; it makes justice subsidiary to the pursuit of total good.

In some cases, it seems that utility maximization conflicts with our intuitions, as when it seems to justify great harm to one person in return for small benefit to each of many people. Sometimes, such conflicts are only apparent when a full utility analysis is done (which considers precedents, emotional effects, and the possibility of error). In other cases, our intuition might simply be wrong. As Hare (1981) argues, our intuitions developed for typical cases, and it is in principle possible to construct cases in which intuitions yield the wrong answer.

Other normative approaches derive historically from various complaints about utilitarianism. Doubts about the feasibility of interpersonal comparison (e.g., Robbins, 1938) led to the modern concept of economic efficiency (Hicks, 1939; Kaldor, 1939). This concept extends the criterion of Pareto efficiency (by which one distribution is better than another only if it makes at least one person better off and nobody worse off). Such Pareto improvements are difficult to find, so the idea was to extend it to include *potential* Pareto improvements: If the winners could compensate the losers so that they were still better off and the losers were at least no worse off, then a policy change could be considered as a Pareto improvement even if the compensation were not paid. Given that compensation is paid in wealth, then any change that increased total wealth should be brought about.

Modern economists have recognized that this concept of efficiency as wealth maximization can justify horrendous inequality, since it makes a dollar just as valuable to a corporation president as to a beggar. This ideal of efficiency allows us to reduce taxes on the rich and reduce programs for the poor that these taxes pay for, so long as the poor would prefer the unpaid taxes (divided up among them) to the programs, even though they get neither the taxes nor the programs and can therefore be left in dire straits. So economists have tried to temper the ideal of efficiency with considerations of equity. Having rejected utilitarianism once, they are unwilling to return to it, so they resort to various formulas by which equity considerations can be put into an analysis along with efficiency. Thus, Broder and Keller, and Sarin, devise measures of equity in the distribution of risks, which can be weighed against the total risk itself.

Another inspiration for these alternative models is what might be called the assumption of nonpaternalism. In a democracy, by this view, policy should reflect the wishes of the people. If people are not utilitarians, then we can capture their intuitions by modeling them and including the models in the formulation of policy.

The utilitarian might reply that the models are arbitrary, hence potentially inconsistent. For example, taking into account ex post equity among groups assumes a particular classification into groups. Elster discusses this sort of difficulty.

A final justification of nonutilitarian models is that utilitarian models require assessment of psychological states that are difficult to assess. For example, one utilitarian rationale for equalizing distributions is the reduction of envy. Applied utilitarianism cannot be done adequately on the basis of "objective" outcomes, such as allocations of money or risk. Alternative models therefore can be seen as approximations to the utilitarian ideal that can be based on objective measures alone. As such they are prescriptive rather than normative, but they could still be useful. (A disadvantage is that by ignoring psychological states, these models implicitly assume that the states themselves are beyond the control of policymakers, which might not always be the case.)

Other normative models include various concepts of proportionality of outcomes to inputs (Mellers, 1982) or to need. In most cases, these kinds of models amount to formalizations of certain intuitions, without any deeper justification. They often approximate utilitarian outcomes. An entirely different normative tradition is that of Rawls (1971) and Sen (1970), which takes as its basic principle of distribution the idea of maximizing the outcome for the least advantaged group. In this tradition, what is maximized is not utility but some index of primary goods or (what Sen, 1985, called) "capabilities." The debate among such views, and between them and utilitarianism, is a lively one. Naturally, I think that utilitarianism will subsume these other views (as prescriptive approximations), but time will tell.

As Tetlock and Mitchell remind us, discussion of normative theory is politically loaded. For example, one of the issues underlying debates about affirmative action is whether equity considerations apply to groups, as opposed to individuals. (Elster argues that such considerations should not apply to groups.) An investigator who favors affirmative action on the ground that justice does apply to groups might develop a questionnaire about group equity and then label as racist those responses that oppose group equity.

It is important that we recognize this sort of danger, for it is inherent in the whole enterprise. But our response to it need not be to give up and return to "pure science" with no obvious applications. (Tetlock and Mitchell do not suggest this response either.) Rather, it should be to maintain the high standards of scholarship, that is, to subject our normative models to the same level of critical scrutiny that we apply to data analyses. This is difficult to do, because we often start by wanting certain conclusions to be true, and we are all subject to wishful thinking. But it is not a special difficulty for philosophical analysis of normative models. The same wishful thinking occurs when we analyze our data.

### Descriptive issues

A second task of the chapters here has been to describe judgments of jus-tice as they are. As in the rest of the study of judgments and decisions, two approaches to description are in apparent tension: formal mathemati-cal models and informal heuristic rules. The tension is mostly apparent, though. Harris points out that much of the value of formal modeling is in finding out what people do and do not pay attention to. The language of mathematical models is usually translatable into the language of heuristic rules, and (for bilinguals) vice versa. Without prejudice, then, I shall em-ploy the language of heuristics in this discussion.

The term *heuristic* is somewhat misleading. As originally used by Polya (1945), it was a useful device to help solve a problem, a rule of thumb to try when you are at a loss. The term has more recently taken on a new use, which refers to the overgeneralization of heuristics to situations in which they are no longer useful. But the use of the term here requires another change in meaning. Many of the rules that people follow with respect to equity judgments are moral commitments, not mere rules of thumb. Rules of thumb are thought of by their users as time-saving approximations to more accurate methods, but commitments will not be given up even when the stakes are high (although they may still be overgeneralizations). In-deed, Skitka and Tetlock find that encouraging subjects to think about their judgments has no discernible effect on their judgments. Subjects are un-likely to be using the rules that they use in order to avoid thinking.

Hare (1981) argues that individually held moral rules, which he calls "intuitions," tend to claim this kind of commitment. Gibbard (1990) sug-gests that the commitment to moral rules is a consequence of the evolu-tionary origin of morality in our social natures. (However, other heuristics that are not obviously moral also seem to involve a similar kind of emo-tional commitment, e.g., the ambiguity effect: See Frisch & Baron, 1988.) We must be aware that, in some cases, the rules our subjects use might be casual devices to deal with the experimental tasks but, in other cases, they might be deep commitments that cannot be shaken even by good argu-ments against them.

### A classification of heuristic rules

Bar-Hillel and Yaari provide a useful classification of rules of justice that can be applied across the studies in this book. They classify rules in terms of the distributional units and the distributional ideal. The distributional units are either the given units to be distributed, e.g., dollars or grape-fruits, or the underlying goal of the distribution or output, such as units of need satisfaction, pleasure, or belief about what is received. (Bar-Hillel and Yaari also suggest that different kinds of "input" units are relevant to some distributional rules.) The distributional ideal concerns the method of distribution, e.g., equally or proportionally. Messick provides a similar classification using different terms, but he adds another useful dimension, the domain of the rule, that is, the set of individuals to which the rule applies: "A parent might believe that her son's allowance should be the same as their neighbor's son of the same age, while the son may argue for the same allowance as his older sister." For most of the rules that people use, different domains yield different results. These three dimensions – units, ideal, and domain – provide a useful classification of distributional rules.

### Types of distributional rules

The distributional ideal, which I shall focus on here, refers to the rule for generating the distribution. One common rule is equality of whatever is distributed. If the distributional units are easily measured, such as dollars or grapefruits, then this rule has the advantage of clarity. It is a "bright line." No disagreement is possible about how it is to be interpreted, so long as its domain is also clear.

When the domain is unclear, however, the results of an equality rule depend on the domain. Equality of educational opportunity, for example, means different things within a city, a state, a nation, or the world. Elster points to a "norm of thoroughness," a kind of equality rule among those who are selected: Patients who are examined by eye specialists are all given the same thorough treatment, neglecting the needs of those not seen at all.

In some cases, the equality heuristic seems to be used as a rule of thumb to minimize effort, and people can shift to other rules. Harris, for example, reports that subjects will apply the equality rule to net outcomes of a joint venture if they are told to distribute outcomes, but they will also apply the rule to expenses if they are told to distribute expenses. These two applications of the rule are inconsistent in the cases that Harris and his colleagues devised. Repeated judgments in cases in which the inconsistency is apparent, however, seem to reduce both inconsistency and the use of an equality rule for either outcomes or expenditures.

It seems likely, though, that in other cases the equality rule is not so easily given up. For example, I doubt that anyone would want to give up the idea of "one person, one vote" (except, of course, in a stockholders' meeting, where the rule is "one share, one vote"). Even when clear reason is found to give some people more votes, as in academic departments with members of various ranks and statuses (e.g., half-time), alternative solutions are found, such as excluding junior members from some votes or informally giving senior members more time to speak. An interesting research question here is when intuitions are easily changed and when they are not.

Another rule is proportionality, which says that outputs should be in proportion to some input measure, such as contribution. (When the input measure is "persons," this rule is the same as the equality rule.) This rule can also have the advantage of clarity, although variants of the proportionality rule are not so clear. (Harris discusses a generalized form of this rule that is not so easy to apply.) This rule is also used in allocating costs: Harris reports that when a group loses money, those who made the greatest *positive* contribution are sometimes asked to bear the greatest burden of the loss. Proportionality rules can be applied to a great variety of distributional units, e.g., time worked, marginal contribution to production, pieces produced, need, merit, seniority. (Elster discusses some of these.) One form of the proportionality rule is that based on need, which sometimes takes the form of what Elster refers to as a norm of compassion. In some cases, as when scarce medical resources are wasted on a patient about to die anyway, the use of this rule can result in violations of Pareto efficiency.

Ordóñez and Mellers consider other rules in the spirit of the proportionality rule. They asked their subjects to evaluate entire social distributions presented as scatterplots relating salary to an index of work. Fairness judgments were predicted best by the magnitude of the correlation between work and salary. Subjects seemed to be using a rule in which salary depends monotonically on work but is not necessarily proportional to work. This rule seems to consist of: (1), a constant term representing the "safety net," which provides some income even to those who contribute nothing; (2), an "equal pay for equal work" rule, which specifies that people who work the same should be paid the same (a limited equality rule); and, (3), a rough proportionality rule, which specifies that salary should increase with work.

A third type of distributional rule is maximization. Maximization can be applied to utility and to other quantities, such as wealth or other goods such as vitamins extracted, as in Bar-Hillel and Yaari's cases. People may resist direct attempts to maximize anything because of uncertainty about whether the maximization criterion has been achieved. Maximization typically works indirectly, e.g., through different utility functions, incentive effects, or different rates of vitamin extraction. In real life, then, maximization typically depends on uncertain predictions or guesses about these indirect effects. Attempts to maximize can lead to disagreement, whether the units being maximized are utility or dollars. (Disagreements about tax policy concern its effects on both utility and wealth.) In contrast to maximization rules, rules of proportionality or equality can be applied without error, so they are often preferred to maximization.

On the other hand, if rules of proportionality or equality are ultimately justified in terms of maximization principles – as utilitarianism or economic theory might claim – then they are in fact approximations to the normative standard rather than exact realizations of it. In terms of the normative standard, errors are being made anyway. So long as people do not ask how such a rule is justified – in which case the answer might be that it is an error-prone approximation to maximizing – they can convince themselves that no error is involved.

A rule similar to maximization is a maximin rule, which tries to maximize the situation of those worse off. Ordóñez and Mellers found a "poverty line" in their scatterplots of salary versus work. Some subjects made their judgments of distributions by minimizing the number of people below that line. Although Ordóñez and Mellers cite Rawls's (1971) difference principle (maximin, roughly), the same kind of rule could be an approximation to maximum utility, since the utility of money is (typically) marginally declining.

I consider cases in which the units to be allocated are changes, which can be positive or negative. One rule applied in such cases is "do no harm," that is, do not hurt one person in order to help another. This is in essence a combination of the ideal of Pareto efficiency with a bias toward inaction. Pareto efficiency by itself could not decide between the new state and the old one when some must be hurt for the benefit of others, so a bias toward inaction is used to break the tie. Application of this heuristic can lead to rejection of changes that are improvements according to any other normative standard.

## Rule contingency and conflict

The use of various heuristic rules seems to be contingent on the situation. For example, as Messick points out, when differential opportunities, such as the first chance to draw from a resource pool, are perceived to be determined by luck, subjects tend not to take advantage of the special opportunity. But when the opportunity is perceived to be the result of skill or some other culturally approved sign of deservingness, the opportunity is used.

Equity rules often conflict because there are different equity rules and they can be applied to different distributional units or domains. For example, when two individuals extract different amounts of vitamin from a grapefruit, most subjects will make an effort to compensate for reduced extraction ability in order to equalize the amount extracted, up to a point, by giving more grapefruit to the poor extractor. When, however, the ability to extract the vitamin is sufficiently low, subjects find the sacrifice made by the better extractor to be too much to ask, and they will sacrifice the poor extractor in order to maximize the total vitamin extracted. In this case, the equality rule (applied to need-satisfaction as output) has given way to a maximization rule. The maximization rule, in the extreme, leads to a kind of "triage" heuristic, in which we give what we can to those who will benefit the most, and nothing to those who can make do on their own or who have no hope.

Skitka and Tetlock present a model for the resolution of conflicts of rules within the individual. They examine four determinants of allocation decisions: need of the individual for the good in question; efficiency, the benefit derived from a given allocation; controllability of the outcome that creates the need; and internality, the extent to which needy individuals are

"responsible" for the existence of their need. When the good to be allocated is relatively plentiful, liberals tend to allocate it to everyone while
conservatives tend to allocate it only to those who did not bring about their
own need. Under conditions of high scarcity, liberals become more like
conservatives. But, in general people go through the various factors in order, considering each one only if it is needed in order to eliminate potential
recipients of a scarce good. This model is consistent with Bar-Hillel and
Yaari's finding of a triage heuristic, as noted. In this way each heuristic is
invoked as a way of fine tuning the results of previous heuristics, as needed.
The general question of how people resolve conflicts is a topic worthy of
further study, including tests of this model against alternatives.

Conflict among equity rules can lead to disagreement among people,
especially (but not only) when people choose rules in a self-serving way.
Van Avermaet's experiment, described by Messick, shows that self-serving
interpretation is facilitated by the availability of a variety of rules, some of
which are in fact self-serving.

A symptom of such disagreement is breakdown of bargaining (Elster,
1989), which yields Pareto-inefficient outcomes. Camerer and Loewenstein
show that such a breakdown can be exacerbated by providing information
to the parties. When the buyer of a piece of land knows the seller's minimum price and the seller knows the buyer's maximum price, negotiation
can break down when each thinks that a particular compromise is unfair.
Ignorance prevents these fairness heuristics from being used. In a second
study based on an out-of-court settlement of a lawsuit, Camerer and Loewenstein found that providing arguments for the justice of each side's case
led to polarization (like the findings of Lord, Ross, & Lepper, 1979), with
each side tending to accept the arguments that favored its side and to reject
the arguments on the other side. As a result, the two sides moved farther
apart in what they thought was fair, and they were less likely to agree.
Information has this effect, however, only when conflicting rules are available. In an ultimatum game, the dominant rule is equal division, and information about the size of the payment to be divided allows this rule to
be used, generating increased agreement.

In real social decisions, in which a government or an institution must
agree on a procedure for dispensing justice, complex compromises among
various equity rules are often adopted, as Elster explains. For example, in
allocating kidneys, the rules typically strike a compromise between maximization of effectiveness and need (as measured by length of time on the
waiting list). Some of the rules that Elster discusses involve true trade-offs
among different criteria rather than the sequential use of criteria to break
ties after other criteria have been applied.

### The emergence of rules

Descriptive questions do not end with the discovery of rules that are used
and how disagreements are resolved. Ultimately, we must ask how rules

emerge and how they are maintained. The papers here say little about this. Baron suggests that many rules are overgeneralizations of rules that can be understood as promoting good consequences but says little about how such rules arise. Tyler and Dawes say more. Their concern is with the motivation to follow rules of justice: without such motivation a rule cannot be maintained as a social norm. They suggest that rules of justice are supported in part because of identification with the group to which they apply. They make an analogy with the literature on social dilemmas, in which cooperation is also found to increase with group identification. They contrast this view with an alternative view in which rules are supported out of self-interest. For example, supporting rules of justice might maximize self-interest in the long run even if it does not do so in the short run. Similarly, cooperation might also have long-term benefits, as suggested by Gauthier (1986) and others.

Tyler and Dawes present evidence that cooperation and support for rules of justice can exist even when the individual is disadvantaged and when no opportunity for further interaction seems to exist. They attribute such behavior to moral motives, and this is indeed a possibility. An alternative possibility, though, is that some of what passes for moral motivation is just another kind of overgeneralization. People might develop heuristics of cooperating or supporting rules of justice out of long-term self-interest, but they then might generalize these heuristics to cases in which the original motivation is absent. On the other hand, such overgeneralization might be one of the sources of *true* moral motivation. If so, we should not disparage it.

The study of child development could, in principle, also contribute to an understanding of what possible heuristics can be maintained as social norms, both in the individual and in society. Moore, Hembree, and Enright point out in their chapter that many developmental theorists have postulated strict sequences for the acquisition of equity concepts. Their chapter, however, reports results that cast serious doubt on these sequential stage theories. Although the interpretation of this conflict is unclear, it remains possible that at least the simpler heuristics used by adults – those that point to equality, need, or contribution as a criterion of reward, for example – are quite easy for young children to understand, so that the major determinants of development are cultural rather than cognitive. If so, what remains to be understood is the difficulty of learning the more complex justifications behind these heuristics, such as those I discuss in my chapter. For example, are young children incapable of understanding the deterrent rationale of punishment or the idea of declining marginal utility (suitably expressed)?

### The prescriptive question

Normative standards specify the ideal, but they are not typically intended as practical advice. The attempt to follow normative standards can be self-defeating. For example, we might approximate utility maximization more closely by applying equality and proportionality rules than by trying to assess the relevant utilities and maximize their sum. When we try to maximize utility directly, we must tolerate either the errors that result from hasty estimates of utility or the disutility of the effort required to make more exact assessments. Whatever our normative standard, the practical advice that we give is not necessarily to try to follow this standard. The attempt to follow the standard could be self-defeating. The prescriptive question is, then, what to do. Since prescription is a matter of giving advice, the answer to this question may depend on who is advising whom.

### Better and worse heuristics

Most of the rules discussed are heuristics in the sense that they are useful approximations to some ideal that cannot be easily achieved. As Messick points out, the term *heuristic* originally had a positive meaning, a useful device. Later, he suggests, the meaning became negative when it was found that heuristics led to systematic deviations from ideal normative models. Yet, in evaluating these equity heuristics, we must ask, useful in doing what, *compared to what?* Often it is impossible to do any better than an equity heuristic does, as Messick suggests. At least it is impossible to be confident that one has done better. (An omniscient observer might do better.)

In other cases, as Baron argued, equity heuristics can be truly harmful in the sense that people might be able to learn to use better heuristics than they use, without excessive cost. For example, the "Do no harm" heuristic prevents the realization of social gains that would greatly benefit many people at the expense of a relatively small cost to a few. Most such "negative" heuristics are *not* used by all subjects, sometimes not even a majority. Those who use heuristics that better approach the normative ideal do not seem to suffer for it (Larrick, Nisbett, & Morgan, 1990). I argued that this kind of improvement would come from understanding the purposes of heuristics. With this kind of knowledge, people would be better able to use heuristics when they serve their purposes and not otherwise. Overgeneralization would be reduced.

Although my argument is based on questionnaire studies, Elster provides cases of real social rules that appear to impugn the purposes that the rules are meant to serve. As noted, the norm of compassion can do harm in the long run when it applies to hopeless cases, and the norm of thoroughness can lead to unfairness by any account when considered in terms of a broader domain.

In a sense, even the view that heuristics can be harmful is optimistic and positive in two ways. First, it gives us a way to improve our judgments and decisions and therefore to improve the human condition, a way that would be blocked if we used the best of all possible heuristics at all times.

Second, it presents a charitable view of the causes of human social problems – such as overpopulation, poverty, and environmental destruction – compared to the view that these problems result from selfishness or thoughtlessness. According to the erroneous-heuristics view, people are trying to do what is right. All the research described in this volume is consistent with this view. (And for additional research, see Dawes & Thaler, 1988; Kahneman, Knetsch, & Thaler, 1986; Thaler, 1988.) We err not in our intentions but in our thinking. We are not neglectful of our fellow people; we are just foolish, sometimes, in how we attend to them.

## Judgments and politics

Judgments of justice are related to political controversies, which often hinge on conflicts between exactly these judgments. Tetlock and Mitchell point out that liberal (egalitarian) and conservative (libertarian) political views can be characterized in terms of the heuristics used by each and the motivations thought to underlie the use of the heuristics. Moreover, each heuristic can be presented as either positive (flattering) or negative (unflattering). (In their chapter, some of the "positive" characteristics consist of the absence of negative ones, and vice versa, but the point still holds.)

An important contribution Tetlock and Mitchell make in the chapter is the suggestion that the use of rules or heuristics may be motivated. One major source of motivation is the subjective costs assigned to different kinds of errors, such as helping people who do not deserve it versus failing to help those who do. Equality heuristics would be more likely to make the first error, while distribution in proportion to contribution would be more likely to make the second. Indeed, as they suggest, it would be of interest to determine whether individual differences in such motives affect individual differences in the use of rules.

Tetlock and Mitchell argue against the implicit value assumptions made by many psychologists. They cite some clearly egregious examples in which reasonable conservatives might be labeled as racists. (Another possible example is the contamination of a measure of moral sophistication by a liberal bias, as shown by Emler, Renwick, & Malone, 1983.) They argue for a more modest research strategy, which seeks to understand rather than evaluate.

An alternative strategy is not to evaluate entire positions but, rather, to evaluate particular arguments used by one side or the other. For example, if conservatives oppose redistribution of income because they are unwilling to "hurt one person in order to help another," this argument is, on its face, an example of the omission bias I discussed in my chapter. Of course, further empirical analysis may be needed to make sure what it is, and further philosophical argument may be needed in order to establish that (or when) omission is a bias. Conversely, if liberals argue that mortgage loan officers should not take into account the neighborhood a person lives in because it is not relevant once the person's income is known, this argument, on its face, appears to be an example of neglect of base rates.

Is it out of place for psychologists to point out to *each* side the fact that certain arguments they make are examples of well-known errors of thinking? If psychologists and other social scientists cannot do this, then what *can* we do to raise the level of discussion or improve the outcome? What good is "understanding," if not to allow criticism? If we can point to such fallacious arguments, we can raise the level of discussion and put aside the arguments that are not so easily criticized. To do this well might require as deep a commitment to clear thinking about social issues as to clear thinking about research methodology. Social scientists who do this kind of research must be willing to question their own previous views and to see both sides charitably. Here, I think that Tetlock and Mitchell would agree.

A possible alternative answer to the one I just suggested is provided implicitly in the chapters of Sarin and of Keller and Broder. The task of social science is to study intuitions about justice, systematize them into formal rules, and instruct policymakers in the use of these derived rules, without necessarily endorsing the rules. Such an approach seems to imply that we are incompetent to discuss prescriptive questions. Perhaps, but incompetence can be a matter of degree.

### Future research

Current work on psychological conceptions of justice leaves many questions unanswered. Let me list some of them, recognizing fully that my own perspective will lead me to omit others that are at least as worthwhile as those I include.

First, more can undoubtedly be learned about the rules people use for judging distributions and when they use them. For this purpose, as Elster notes, we cannot rely solely on the psychology laboratory. The real world is a rich source of data about rules of justice. Moreover, it would be sensible to examine cultural differences in rules of justice. Cultures appear to differ in their reliance on different distributional rules, and these differences, in turn, may be related to different forms of social organization (Fiske, 1991).

Second, we need to study the modifiability of people's conceptions of justice – the extent to which they can be changed through education or argument – for two reasons. First, people disagree. These disagreements are not mere matters of taste, since rules of justice are moral questions, and a moral claim implies that other people should agree with it (Hare, 1952). If people are to agree, then someone is going to have to change, perhaps everyone. Second, some rules of justice may be better than others in terms of the consequences they produce. By trying to teach people the rules that lead to the best consequences, we, collectively, can improve the consequences for ourselves. For example, I have suggested that all citizens should at least understand the consequentialist rationale of rules of punishment and distribution, even if they go on to reject these rules. As a first step in this sort of enterprise, we might carry out educational experiments of the sort done by Larrick, Morgan, and Nisbett (1990). Further study of the development of thinking about justice in children will inform the educational endeavor.

Third, we must recognize that the adoption of rules of justice involves emotions and desires as much as intellectual reasons. Violation of rules of justice is an occasion for anger, perhaps the major occasion for anger (Sabini & Silver, 1981). On the other side, emotions connected with group solidarity can lead to willing support for rules of equity. (Such emotions can also be dangerous when they oppose the application of rules of justice to outsiders.) To some extent, these emotions and the motives that underlie them could be a product of normative beliefs, so that they would change as belief changes (Baron, 1992). In other cases, however, the emotions might be more difficult to modify. They would have to be taken as limiting factors on possible social arrangements. So in the context of all the other kinds of research described here, we must consider the emotions and desires that lead to support for various justice rules, as Tyler and Dawes do in their chapter.

In all this, we must also remember that the study of rules of justice is not a dry intellectual pursuit. It is, rather an attempt to bring the light of scholarship onto some of the most heated questions in politics, in the broadest sense. As Tetlock and Mitchell point out, most of us are immersed in these questions personally, and, indeed, our personal concern is often the source of our academic interest. So we must guard against the partiality that can occur so easily. I think, though, that the issues are too important for us to be held back from stating our best considered views by the fear that we might be biased despite all our efforts not to be. We might do well to remind ourselves that theories of justice and its psychological basis already exist as part of folk psychology and (what we might call) folk philosophy. To withhold our best considered views amounts to an endorsement (by omission) of these alternatives.

### References

Baron, J. (1992). The effect of normative beliefs on anticipated emotions. *Journal of Personality and Social Psychology, 63,* 320–330.
Dawes, R. M., & Thaler, R. H. (1988). Anomalies: Cooperation. *Journal of Economic Perspectives, 2,* 187–197.
Elster, J. (1989). *The cement of society.* Cambridge: Cambridge University Press.
Emler, N., Renwick, S., & Malone, B. (1983). The relationship between moral reasoning and political orientation. *Journal of Personality and Social Psychology, 45,* 1073–1080.

Fiske, A. P. (1991). *Structures of social life: The four elementary forms of social relations.* New York: Free Press.

Frisch, D., & Baron, J. (1988). Ambiguity and rationality. *Journal of Behavioral Decision Making, 1,* 149–157.

Gauthier, D. (1986). *Morals by agreement.* Oxford: Oxford University Press.

Gibbard, A. (1990). *Wise choices, apt feelings.* Cambridge, MA: Harvard University Press.

Hare, R. M. (1952). *The language of morals.* Oxford: Oxford University Press (Clarendon Press).

(1981). *Moral thinking: Its levels, method and point.* Oxford: Oxford University Press (Clarendon Press).

Hicks, J. R. (1939). The foundations of welfare economics. *Economic Journal, 49,* 696–712.

Kahneman, D., Knetsch, J. L., & Thaler, R. H. (1986). Fairness and the assumptions of economics. *Journal of Business, 59,* S285–S300.

Kaldor, N. (1939). Welfare propositions of economics and interpersonal comparisons of utility. *Economic Journal, 49,* 549–552.

Larrick, R. P., Morgan, J. N., & Nisbett, R. E. (1990). Teaching the use of cost-benefit reasoning in everyday life. *Psychological Science, 1,* 362–370.

Larrick, R. P., Nisbett, R. E., & Morgan, J. N. (1990). Who uses the cost-benefit rules of choice? Implications for the normative status of economic theory. Unpublished manuscript, Institute for Survey Research, University of Michigan.

Lord, C. G., Ross, L., & Lepper, M. R. (1979). Biased assimilation and attitude polarization: The effects of prior theories on subsequently considered evidence. *Journal of Personality and Social Psychology, 37,* 2098–2109.

Mellers, B. A. (1982). Equity judgments: A revision of Aristotelian views. *Journal of Experimental Psychology: General, 111,* 242–270.

Polya, G. (1945). *How to solve it: A new aspect of mathematical method.* Princeton, NJ: Princeton University Press.

Rawls, J. (1971). *A theory of justice.* Cambridge, MA: Harvard University Press.

Robbins, L. (1938). Interpersonal comparison of utility: A comment. *Economic Journal, 48,* 635–641.

Sabini, J., & Silver, M. (1981). *Moralities of everyday life.* Oxford: Oxford University Press.

Sen, A. (1970). *Collective choice and social welfare.* San Francisco: Holden Day.

(1985). *Commodities and capabilities.* Amsterdam: North-Holland.

Thaler, R. H. (1988). Anomalies: The ultimatum game. *Journal of Economic Perspectives, 2,* 195–206.

# Name index

# Subject index